Confronting Child Abuse

The Free Press
A Division of Simon & Schuster Inc.
1230 Avenue of the Americas
New York, N.Y. 10020

Printed in the United States of America

printing number
10 9 8 7 6 5 4 3 2 1

Library of Congress Cataloging-in-Publication Data

Daro, Deborah.
    Confronting child abuse.

    Bibliography: p.
    1. Child abuse—United States.   2. Child abuse—United States—Prevention.   3. Abused children—Services for—United States.   4. Child abuse—Law and legislation—United States.   I. Title.
HV741.D36   1987   362.7'044   87-27169
ISBN 0-02-906931-9

Confronting Child Abuse
Research for Effective Program Design

DEBORAH DARO

THE FREE PRESS

NEW YORK   LONDON   TORONTO   SYDNEY   TOKYO   SINGAPORE

Contents

Acknowledgments

In an individualistic society, a great deal of emphasis is placed upon one's personal initiative to do good and to accomplish great things. The reality of life, however, is that without the support of family, friends, and professional colleagues, one accomplishes very little and rarely generates any new knowledge. Over the past several years, I have received tremendous support from a vast number of people, many of whom I would like to publicly acknowledge.

The original research reported in this book was funded by the Federal Government's National Center on Child Abuse and Neglect (NCCAN) through a contract with Berkeley Planning Associates. Aeolian Jackson from NCCAN was a thoughtful project monitor and initiated my concern to generate a document which placed this particular study in the broader context of other child maltreatment research. Among the staff at BPA who worked with me on this project, Susan Shea, Beverly DeGraaf, Lea Stublarec, Shirley Langlois, and Richard Dodson offered critical contributions in shaping the study's research priorities, developing the data collection instruments, and interpreting the initial findings. As always, Fred Collignon, BPA President, was a careful critic who consistently challenged me to improve the product and sharpen my conclusions.

Further analysis of the data and the drafting of the manuscript has been facilitated by my good fortune to work in two dynamic settings. First, my colleagues at the University of California, Berkeley, School of Social Welfare, provided scholarly leadership to me as I refined the document to better capture the field's growing body of evaluative research. Neil Gilbert kindly offered his sage advice and the benefit of many books in keeping me on task during the most grueling of times. Others at the school to whom I am indebted include Dean Harry Specht, Richard Barth, Nike LeProhn, Richard Sullivan, and Jill Duerr.

Second, the staff at the National Committee for Prevention of Child Abuse gave me a keen appreciation for the important role research can play in the battle to prevent child abuse. Anne Cohn, with whom I originally worked at Berkeley Planning Associates, introduced me to the field of child abuse and has been an important and influential colleague and friend throughout my career. Others at the committee who graciously gave me the benefit of their collective knowledge regarding the state of programs and policies in this field include Cynthia Schellenbach, Leslie Mitchel, Sam Clark, Chris Holmes, January Scott, and Nancy Peterson. Tom Birch, coordinator of the National Child Abuse Coalition, was never too busy to clarify current federal policy.

Production of the manuscript, in its many and varied forms, would never have occurred without the patience and good nature of Louise Kreifels, word processor par excellence.

I also want to thank the staff of The Free Press, particularly Laura Wolff. Her thoughtful critique of the initial manuscript and those of the initial reviewers she secured were extremely helpful in sharpening the book, particularly with respect to practice issues.

As the literature suggests, one learns to parent from one's parents. I was blessed with two wonderful parents who gave me and my siblings, Barbara and Timothy, the full benefits of family life. The past support of my late parents and the current support of family and friends have been and continue to be an essential ingredient in my personal development. Finally, I want to express a special thanks to my husband, Coleman Tuggle, who demonstrated great courage in marrying someone with an "almost completed" manuscript. His generous nature and good humor brings joy to all I do.

Introduction

The crisis of abused children is one which touches the lives of everyone in a society. While research indicates that poor children may be particularly vulnerable to maltreatment by both their parents and the social institutions theoretically designed to help them, the potential for maltreatment exists within all social strata and within most families at some point in their development. To the extent children represent the building blocks of our future, the physical and emotional trauma they experience robs the society and all of its members of their full economic and cultural contributions. Not all childhood trauma can be avoided. However, minimizing the willful mistreatment of children or mistreatment due to ignorance is an important social policy objective.

Child maltreatment most likely has been around since the first parent-child dyad. Concern for the welfare of children, particularly those who were orphaned or abandoned, also has been longstanding among public and private social service agencies and professionals. In the late 1800's, Protestant and Catholic relief agencies such as the Society of St. Vincent de Paul, the Children's Aid Society, and the Society for the Prevention of Cruelty to Children supported programs that placed not only those children who had no families but also those children whose families were unable to care for them. These placement settings included orphanages, industrial schools, and "out" placements with families viewed by these agency officials as offering a more "Christian" and stable home life than that of the child's birth parents (Brace, 1872; Coughlin, 1965). The Progressive Era saw less tolerance for such wide-scale relocation of poor and immigrant children and placed a growing emphasis on strengthening families through informed public policy and the establishment of community ser-

1

vice agencies. Reforms in labor practices, welfare programs, and educational and health care systems offered much needed protection to families unable to cope with a new country and its highly industrial and impersonal urban areas. Settlement houses, such as Hull House in Chicago and Henry Street in New York, worked with families in their own communities to assess their needs "scientifically" and to develop the programs necessary to ensure the healthy growth of children (Folks, 1902; Addams, 1930; Leiby, 1978). All of these efforts and those that have followed assumed three principles: that the care of children rested primarily with their parents; that society had an obligation and a responsibility to support parents in this function as well as to intervene if children remained "at risk" of mistreatment or poor care; and that this public responsibility was to be realized through a system of local service agencies.

It is this tradition—public and private responsibility for the care of children at the community level—that has shaped the nation's response to child welfare in general and to child abuse in particular. As might be expected, legislation which defined child abuse and determined the appropriate balance between parental rights and child welfare rested with the individual states for almost 200 years. In 1974, however, the federal government finally took legislative action in this area in response to widespread concern among child advocacy organizations such as the American Humane Association, physicians, and social workers that this fragmented service system was not adequately protecting children. One of the key catalysts in this federal movement was a 1962 article by Dr. Henry Kempe in the *Journal of the American Medical Association.* Citing studies of hospital emergency room X-rays, he and his colleagues painted a brutal picture of the American family. Children, he said, were being beaten and sometimes dying at the hands of the very individuals whom society had entrusted with their care and well-being. Over Kempe's one-year study period, some 300 cases were reported to 71 different hospitals across the country, with 11% of these cases resulting in death and over 28% resulting in permanent brain damage (Kempe et al., 1962).

The impact of Kempe's findings on modern child maltreatment policy and practice was threefold. First, it provided empirical data for what, up until that time, had been an issue subject to one-time news stories or brief campaigns in local communities following the exposure of a single, particularly gruesome incident. Second, it offered a number of symptoms or indicators which physicians and other concerned professionals could look for in suspected cases. Finally, it suggested a beginning step for policy makers, namely the adoption of laws requiring the official reporting of these cases to local law enforcement or child protective service agencies.

The scholarly and popular literature on child maltreatment written since 1962 is, to say the least, abundant. Topics range from descriptive studies of the perpetrators and victims, to program evaluations, to longitudinal studies of intergenerational maltreatment, to legal analyses of existing and pending legislation. In addition to the written word, movies, television specials, and the nightly news are also filled with the more dramatic stories of child abuse and with the seemingly endless ways in which society mistreats the future generation. Unlike the situation facing policy makers in 1974, today practitioners and policy makers at all levels of government now have a rich base of empirical research from which to draw in designing their laws and interventions.

Unfortunately, the results of these research efforts have not been as accessible or as useful to the decision-making process as their authors had hoped. Barriers to effective utilization have included methodological problems such as small, nonrepresentative samples, an uncertainty over which variables to explore and monitor, a very narrow range of intervention strategies to assess, and the absence of control groups. Communication problems also exist. Specific research findings are frequently not connected to planning or programmatic concerns and the various disciplines involved in child maltreatment research often fail to transmit their findings to each other in a meaningful manner.

The effective use of research findings also has been hampered by a tendency on the part of practitioners to lump together all variants of maltreatment in searching for the most salient causal explanation, treatment strategy, or prevention effort. Although definitions of maltreatment have routinely identified specific clusters of behaviors as comprising distinct subpopulations, program and policy development rarely has been based upon an explicit recognition that families involved in different types of maltreatment require different types of intervention. In many respects, establishing effective programs and policies with respect to child maltreatment has been plagued by the overgeneralization of certain findings based upon a caseload of one type of maltreatment or the disregarding of an intervention because it failed to be effective with families involved in all types of maltreatment.

By drawing together a wide range of research findings from a number of different disciplines and highlighting these findings in terms of their relative success in remediating or preventing the four major types of maltreatment—physical abuse, physical neglect, sexual abuse, and emotional maltreatment—this book reconceptualizes the nature of the program and research questions surrounding child maltreatment. Rather than seeking a singular solution to child abuse, a subpopulation framework clarifies why certain so-called innovations in the field can simultaneously hold great promise for reform yet generate even further controversy. The appropriate role of the criminal courts in cases of child abuse, the appropriate scope of child abuse reporting laws and investigatory procedures, the appropriate use of foster care placement, and the appropriate allocation of resources among various treatment and prevention strategies will differ depending upon the maltreatment involved. Similarly, different aspects of the maltreatment problem will require a different balance between support and therapeutic services at the individual client level and a different balance between individual services and system reform at the policy level. By placing individual practice within the broader context of the personal and social causes of maltreatment and the nature of the social service environment, the framework assists practitioners in understanding the limits of their individual efforts with abusive and neglectful families and the differential outcomes often produced by similar service strategies.

Addressing the unique needs of the four major child maltreatment subpopulations, this book highlights the major service and policy implications of more than 100 research studies and program evaluations conducted over the past 20 years. In addition, original analyses have been conducted on client-level data generated by the author's evaluation of 19 clinical demonstration programs funded throughout the country between 1978 and 1982 by the federal National Center on Child Abuse and Neglect. These projects, each of which focused on a specific maltreatment subpopulation, served over 1,000 families, including 1,200 adults, 900 adolescents, and 1,000 infants and children. A full discussion of the research design and analytic techniques utilized in the National Clinical Evaluation Study is included in Appendix A.

The book begins with a brief overview of the scope of the child abuse problem and the federal and state statutes that influence how the problem and the current response system have been defined. Chapter 2 expands upon this definitional framework, highlighting the specific behaviors and individual demographic characteristics that differentiate families involved in the four major types of maltreatment. Individual and social factors associated with the increased likelihood of maltreatment are reviewed in Chapter 3 in terms of their relative merits with respect to different maltreatment patterns. Drawing upon numerous program evaluations of different therapeutic and nontherapeutic services, Chapter 4 highlights the most effective of these strategies with respect to various client populations. This chapter draws heavily upon the results of the National Clinical Evaluation Study which offered a unique opportunity to explore the differential impacts of similar services on families involved in different types of maltreatment. Chapter 5 reviews the evaluations of prevention programs in light of the potential impact of the two most common strategies—parenting enhancement services and child assault prevention instruction—on preventing different types of maltreatment.

The final section of the book, Future Strategies, considers the fiscal, program, and policy implications of weaving this growing knowledge base into the way in which society defines and responds to different types of maltreatment. Again drawing on the results of the federal program evaluations cited in Chapter 4, Chapter 6 identifies the actual costs associated with different treatment and prevention services and the immediate and long-term social costs of maltreatment. Chapter 7 summarizes the utility of applying the collective results of program evaluations and basic research to future planning in three major areas—the better integration of research principles and program planning, the utility of the subpopulation framework in shaping child welfare reform, and the specific services and organizational components necessary for the creation of an effective child abuse and neglect prevention network.

Part I

Overview: Problem Scope and Cause

Chapter 1

The Scope of the Problem

Children are dependent members in any society and rely on their parents to provide for their physical and emotional well-being. Since the dawn of civilization, however, certain parents have failed in these responsibilities, often with society's permission and blessing. No one intervened in ancient Greece and Rome when parents abandoned deformed infants to face almost certain death. No one intervened in the Middle Ages or in Colonial America when children were flogged by their parents for minor infractions. And no one saw the need before the 1920's to intervene when parents sent their young children to work 14-hour days in the mines or textile mills of an expanding industrial America.

Today, public policy and clinical practice reflect more concern for the welfare of children. Child labor laws, compulsory education laws, and a wide range of child protection laws are central tenets in our modern judicial system. While virtually no tolerance exists for the most obvious cases of child physical abuse, neglect, or sexual abuse, public intervention in the area of child maltreatment is still tempered by the belief that parents, not the state, have the primary responsibility for child-rearing. Intervention is warranted only if children have suffered or may suffer imminent physical or emotional harm at the hands of their parents. Most, if not all, support the abstract value of child protection. The difficulty lies in defining the extent to which society is willing to risk danger to the child before intervening.

Public intervention into families experiencing child maltreatment is justified on several grounds. First, child abuse causes immediate and often permanent physical and emotional trauma. Over and above the physical wounds battered children experience, recurring medical problems such as poor nutrition, anemia, hearing deficits, and possible congenital anomalies are found in higher proportion among maltreated children (Kempe, 1962; Caffey, 1972; Martin et al., 1974; Schmitt and Kempe, 1974; Schmitt, 1978). These children are at greater risk of intellectual deficits, learning disabilities, delays in language, and poor motor functioning. They are also at greater risk of suffering depression, poor self-image, poor peer relationships, aggression, apathy, and hyperactivity (Gregg and Elmer, 1969; Koel, 1969; Morse et al., 1970; Martin, 1972; Warner, 1977). In one sample of abused children with a mean age of 8.5 years, over 8% had attempted suicide and 10% had self-mutilative behavior (Green, 1978a). A five-year follow-up study of 58 abused children identified 5% as having abnormally small heads, 30% with heights or weights below the third percentile, and 31% with moderate or severe neurologic abnormalities (Martin et al., 1974).

Second, deviant or problematic behavior is often found among adolescent and adult populations who were abused in childhood. In addition to claims that the abused child grows into the abusive parent, a growing body of literature suggests that serious adjustment problems for the abused child begin in adolescence. While no clear cause-effect relationship between maltreatment and subsequent delinquency has been established, overall, abused children have higher delinquency rates than the general population (Carr, 1977; Alfaro, 1981; Mouzakitas, 1981; Kratcoski, 1982). A relationship between abuse and delinquent violence is also supported by findings that delinquents who were abused or neglected are more often involved in violent offenses than are nonmaltreated delinquents (Bolton et al., 1977; Lewis et al., 1979; Alfaro, 1981; Gutierres and Reich, 1981). The fact that maltreatment may result in or require youths to commit status offenses, such as running away, places them at higher risk of committing more serious offenses such as prostitution or theft in order to support themselves (URSA, 1984).

Third, given these impacts, public intervention in cases of child abuse is warranted to avoid the sizable social costs associated with an unproductive or destructive citizen. Emergency medical and foster care, hospitalization and rehabilitation services, special education services, and extended counseling to remediate the emotional trauma of abuse may be the most easily documented costs. Less easily documented but far more substantial are the costs associated with adjudicating and incarcerating juvenile delinquents and adult criminals, maintaining long-term out-of-home placements, and the loss of earnings due to permanent disability or poor social adjustment. As discussed in subsequent chapters, these costs far exceed the present or projected costs of a coordinated system of child abuse prevention and early intervention services.

Finally, society intervenes in social problems such as child abuse because the existence of these problems are contrary to broader social values. Commenting on this unique aspect of social problem-solving, one researcher has noted:

Essentially, services are not provided because they benefit the recipient but rather because they benefit the providers (the society). That is, social problems worthy of social investment are defined as such partly because they are sufficiently disturbing to the society that it must try to do something about them (Giovannoni, 1982:29).

Child abuse is a problem "sufficiently disturbing" to warrant public intervention. Children who have been beaten, infants who show little sign of life or an ability to respond to human touch, adolescents who have disclosed years of sexual abuse at the hands of their fathers are pictures which motivate individuals to act on their own and in concert with their colleagues and neighbors. Fueled by expanded public awareness campaigns and popular media attention to the issue, public outcrys have resulted in an expanded service system for victims and their families. More recently, this concern has translated into legislative initiatives aimed at generating funds for a growing and diversified number of prevention programs.

Recognizing that a problem has painful individual, social, and moral consequences is often not sufficient to initiate public action. Placing and sustaining an issue on the political agenda requires the coalescence of several pragmatic factors. Program managers and practitioners need some sense of the problem's scope and magnitude and an appreciation for the legal and practical limits on their capacity to intervene. Once this type of baseline is established, a more detailed description of the problem and an understanding of its predictors and antecedents need to be developed before specific interventions can be designed and implemented. The ongoing evaluation of these interventions and a careful assessment of their differential impacts on families and their communities provide the final component for ensuring that administrators and practitioners have useful and defensible strategies to promote through national and community-based initiatives.

Over two decades of child maltreatment intervention and research have produced the knowledge necessary for more effectively confronting the crisis of child abuse. While that knowledge is far from complete, basic and applied research efforts have established reasonable parameters regarding the essential questions of incidence, content, cause, treatment, and prevention. No one factor triggers maltreatment in all families and, once triggered, the abuse or neglect may take many forms. Similarly, no one intervention will successfully remediate the consequences of all types of maltreatment nor will it prevent reincidence or initial maltreatment in all families. Selecting the appropriate intervention is largely in the hands of practitioners and those allocating scarce public and private resources to specific community-based programs. The principal function of this book is to outline the continuum of choices available to these decision makers in a way which makes best use of what we have learned.

While there are myriad ways to organize the wealth of child abuse research, the emphasis here has been placed on articulating specific maltreatment subpopulations and using this framework to dismantle some of the apparent contradictions that currently plague the field. Efforts to use research findings in establishing practice standards and child welfare policy have suffered both from an overgeneralization of certain findings based upon a caseload of one type of maltreatment to the characteristics and service needs for all types of maltreatment, as well as from an inappropriate pooling of data on clients experiencing all forms of maltreatment to arrive at the characteristics of the "average" maltreating family. By defining specific subpopulations and then assessing what has been learned from past basic and applied research in light of these subpopulations, the book strives to identify the specific causal factors, treatment needs, and prevention inroads that are most salient for different types of abuse and neglect. Such clarity is essential if practitioners are to make best use of the field's current knowledge base in improving practice. Before initiating this review, however, it is useful to look at the scope of child abuse in this country as defined by national incidence studies, official reports of maltreatment, and federal and state statutes.

Incidence of Child Abuse and Neglect

The exact scope of child maltreatment in this country is subject to wide debate. Interviews with a random sample of households or individuals consistently project higher incidence and prevalence rates than indicated by formal reporting data. One of the earliest and most rigorous studies on the annual incidence of maltreatment estimated that in 1968 between 2.5 and 4 million families either failed to act or used physical force with the intent of hurting, injuring, or destroying their children (Gil, 1971). A 1975 study on the level of physical violence in families estimated that between 3.1 and 4 million children in America are kicked, bitten, or punched by their parents at some point in their childhood (Straus et al., 1980). Perhaps more alarming was the level of serious violence against children noted in that study. One in every 25 children 3–17 years of age living in a dual-parent household were seriously beaten by a parent or threatened with a gun or knife. The authors projected that over 46,000 children were actually shot or stabbed by their parents, and over 1,000 died as a result of these attacks.

A replication of the 1975 study, completed in 1985, noted a 47% reduction in the level of the most serious forms of physical violence towards children but relatively consistent levels in incidents of pushing and slapping, the predominant forms of physical violence toward children (Straus and Gelles, 1986). Even with the decline in beatings of children, however, the authors estimated that a minimum of a million children ages 3–17 residing in two-parent families were subjected to serious physical child abuse in 1985.[1]

These numbers, while dramatic in their own right, are even more disturbing when one considers that these researchers focused on only a portion of all maltreatment. They provide few, if any, insights into the number of children who experience chronic emotional maltreatment or fall victim to sexual abuse. In the initial Straus study, child neglect was excluded from the operational definition of maltreatment, and the sample included only two-parent families. By including even a conservative estimate of sexual abuse and serious emotional maltreatment and assuming potentially higher rates of abuse among single-parent families, the suggestion that millions of children fall victim to maltreatment annually becomes believable.

Recent random and nonrandom surveys to determine the prevalence of sexual abuse further support these estimates. A 1978 survey of 930 randomly-selected women in San Francisco revealed that 28% of the respondents had experienced unwanted sexual touching and other forms of abuse before the age of 14 and that the percentage of victims increased to 38% if one included all episodes occurring before the women turned 18 (Russell, 1984). In 12% of these cases the perpetrators were relatives. Others have projected more conservative but no less dramatic incidence levels. A mail survey of 1,054 randomly-selected Texas driver's license holders found that 3% of all males and 12% of all females experience some form of sexual abuse during their lifetimes (Kercher, 1980). Finkelhor (1984) reported that 6% of all males and 15% of all females in his random sample of 521 Boston parents had experienced sexual abuse before age 16 by a person at least five years older. Thirty two percent of these cases involved relatives. In an earlier nonrandom study conducted by this same author, 9% of the males and 19% of the females experienced at least one unwanted sexual encounter before the age of 16, including intercourse, oral-genital contact, fondling, and encounters with an exhibitionist.

These and similar studies have been used by child advocates to define the broad parameters of the maltreatment problem. Federal and local public officials, however, must rely upon more formal estimates of the problem, estimates which suggest that the problem is by no means trivial. For example, the American Association for Protecting Children (AAPC) notes that 1,726,649 children were reported as maltreated in 1984, an increase of 158% since 1976, the first year the agency began collecting and analyzing these data. Unlike the studies that focus primarily on one aspect of maltreatment, all kinds of child abuse and neglect, as defined by law, are reported to local protective service agencies. Approximately one-quarter of all substantiated cases in 1984 involved major or minor injury to the child due to physical abuse; 55% of the cases involved deprivation of necessities (e.g., physical neglect); 11% of the cases involved emotional maltreatment; and 13% of the cases involved sexual abuse (AAPC, 1986).[2] The number of maltreatment cases reported nationwide has steadily increased since 1976, although the size of this increase has fluctuated. For example, between 1976 and 1977, the number of reported cases increased by 25%, while between 1979 and 1980 the rate of increase was only 17%. Between 1980 and 1981, the rate of increase again dropped, climbing less than 6%, and between 1981 and 1982 the increase was only 3%. The number of reported cases jumped 17% between 1982 and 1983 and increased another 17% between 1983 and 1984 (AAPC, 1985). Estimates on 1985 and 1986 figures suggest a return to slower increases, with annual rates of increase of 10% and 6% respectively for these two years (AAPC, 1986; Daro and Mitchel, 1987a).

Although the rate of increase has varied over the past decade, the absolute number of reported cases continues to climb, even though the number of children in this country is declining. In addition, the percentage of reported cases requiring protective service intervention increased from 30% in 1979 to 36% in 1980 to 49% in 1983. Although the rate of substantiation has experienced a moderate decline in recent years, the *absolute* number of cases receiving child protection services has steadily increased. By 1983, the projected number of substantiated cases had risen to over 493,000, and in 1984, over 727,000 children were considered substantiated victims of maltreatment. In other words, the rate at which families are being identified and placed into the protective service system appears to be growing at a significant pace, particularly in the last two years for which national data are available. The number of children "officially" categorized as having suffered physical abuse, physical neglect, emotional maltreatment, or sexual abuse rose 145% between 1977 and 1983.

The variance between "official" cases of maltreatment and the actual incidence of abuse and neglect was specifically highlighted when a federally-funded National Incidence Study revealed that only 33% of the cases identified by a representative sample of professionals across the country were formally reported (Westat, 1981). Drawing upon formal reports of maltreatment as well as those cases identified by school teachers, medical personnel, and others who work with children in a representative sample of counties across the country, the National Incidence Study projected an annual incidence rate of 652,000 cases, of which only 212,400 were known to local protective service workers. The National Incidence Study revealed approximately equal percentages of abuse and neglect, a contradictory finding to the maltreatment pattern found among reported cases. Overall, some 54% of the cases identified by the National Incidence Study team involved abuse, with 31% of these cases involving physical abuse, 7% involving sexual abuse, and 22% involving emotional abuse. Of the 50% of the cases involving neglect, 17% involved physical neglect, 28% involved educational neglect, and 9% involved emotional neglect.[3] The relatively few neglect cases identified through the National Incidence Study has been explained by the study's inclusion of only those cases that resulted in substantiated physical or emotional harm and the fact that neglect, more so than physical abuse, is subject to wide interpretation and influenced by community standards as well as personal standards of good parenting and adequate care.[4] Despite questions regarding the adequacy of its methodology, the National Incidence Study's identification of three times the number of substantiated maltreatment cases as had been uncovered through formal reporting systems that year has prompted policy makers to be more cautious in relying upon "formal" (i.e., reported) maltreatment statistics in defining the scope of the problem.

Critics argue that relying solely upon official reports of maltreatment or the National Incidence Study for accurate assessments of the level of child maltreatment is faulty because the actual incidence levels most likely exceed either of these projections. Despite this criticism, both of these estimates offer at least a base upon which to begin discussing the scope of the problem and the relative frequency of different types of maltreatment. While neither is able to provide a definitive ceiling for the problem, few will deny that these estimates are fairly accurate projections of the minimum scope of the problem. Taken as a minimum level, these numbers make a powerful case for public intervention.

Current Legislation: Federal Efforts

State statutes dealing with child abuse and neglect have been in existence since New York State first passed legislation in 1874, under the headings of the Protective Services Act and the Cruelty to Children's Act (Katz et al., 1977). It took 100 years, however, before the rights of children to be free from willful physical or emotional trauma at the hands of their parents or caretakers were granted in federal legislation. As discussed in Chapter 3, the appropriate scope of this legislation was widely debated and hinged on the perception of child abuse either as a limited problem rooted in the dysfunctioning of individual parents or as a symptom of broader social dysfunctioning. The passage of the Child Abuse Prevention and Treatment Act (PL 93–247) in 1974 marked a clear victory for those who advocated a broader interpretation of the problem and served as a significant catalyst for the expansion of federal and state efforts in this area. Specifically, the legislative intent of the Act was to provide for:

a broad and uniform definition of child abuse and neglect;

nationwide coordination of efforts to identify, treat, and prevent child abuse and neglect;

research leading to new knowledge and demonstration of effective ways to identify, treat, and prevent child abuse and neglect;

compilation of existing knowledge and dissemination of information about successful methods and programs;

training of professionals, paraprofessionals, and volunteers;

encouragement of states, as well as private agencies and organizations, to improve their services for identifying, treating, and preventing child abuse and neglect a complete and full study of the national incidence of child abuse and neglect (U.S. DHEW, 1975)

To implement these objectives, the Act established the National Center on Child Abuse and Neglect (NCCAN), which has, over time, become the lead agency in monitoring both federal and state activities in this area. Although initially only three of the 50 states and U.S. territories were awarded direct grants, at present virtually all states receive federal funding for the treatment of child abuse and neglect (U.S. Comptroller General, 1980). Originally authorized through fiscal year 1977, NCCAN and the Act itself have received continuous support from Congress, even in the face of the most recent fiscal battles and calls for a balanced budget. Since passage, authorization levels have expanded from an initial funding level of $15 million in 1974 to almost $31 million in the latest budget approved by Congress for fiscal year 1987. Certainly these levels are insufficient to address effectively the rising demand for service dollars generated by increasing caseloads and declines in other federal social service appropriations. However, given that the Reagan administration took office with the intent of eliminating NCCAN, and has succeeded in reducing federal appropriations for child protective services, day care and the federal social service block grants program (Title XX), NCCAN's continued existence and even modest growth is notable.

In addition to supporting ongoing research and the development of innovative strategies at the national and state levels, NCCAN also has provided the field with "model" standards for operating child abuse and neglect prevention and treatment systems and a uniform definition of maltreatment. Articulating the minimum requirements for an efficient and effective response to child abuse at the local level, the NCCAN model statutory and program package includes:

a reporting system that ensures the swift and efficient handling of all reported incidents;

adequate legal representation for all of the parties involved in the maltreatment episode, including the child;

the establishment and funding of a comprehensive and coordinated service system, including 24-hour hot line emergency services and ongoing counseling and support;

a mechanism to ensure the prompt and effective interagency coordination among public and private service providers;

establishment of a multidisciplinary team for the review of all suspected cases of maltreatment;

training of all legal, medical, and mental health professionals and school personnel in the identification of abuse and neglect and the procedures for reporting such cases; and the establishment of community coordination councils, including representatives of both the professional and lay communities (U.S. Comptroller General, 1980).

As discussed in subsequent chapters, the timely investigation of reports, the simultaneous development and use of therapeutic and support services, the encouragement of interagency and interdisciplinary task forces in assessing cases and developing specific treatment plans, and the expansion of professional training opportunities have consistency been linked to enhancing client outcomes. While the content and scope of these practices vary greatly across the 50 states and have had different impacts with respect to the four major types of maltreatment, these policies have come to represent core goals for both local child protective service agencies as well as child welfare advocates.

Although practitioners are governed by state statutes in determining what constitutes a reportable act of child abuse, the federal definition of maltreatment established in the 1974 legislation represented one pragmatic solution to the question of the appropriate balance between parental rights and child protection. Justifying legal intervention into private parent-child relationships has been interpreted by some as requiring the documentation of actual maltreatment and the negative impacts on victims. Intervention, in these cases, is needed to protect children from the worst. For others, intervention can be justified if the causes of maltreatment can be isolated such that specific high-risk groups can be identified. Consequently, only those likely to be guilty of maltreatment in the future are subjected to the intrusiveness of intervention. Intervention, in these cases, is needed to shore up deviant families or those families least able to protect themselves against the stresses of modern life. Finally, others justify intervention by focusing on the positive gains for all parents and children which can be realized through early intervention and primary prevention. In these cases, intervention is needed to achieve the best for all families.

In establishing federal standards for child abuse, a rather broad interpretation of the problem was adopted both in terms of what constituted abusive behavior and in terms of justifying intervention in the absence of actual harm to the child. Specifically, under the NCCAN model, child abuse and neglect was defined as

> the physical and mental injury, sexual abuse, negligent treatment or maltreatment of a child under the age of 18 by a person who is responsible for the child's welfare under circumstances which indicate that the child's health and welfare is harmed or threatened thereby, as determined in accordance with regulations prescribed by the Secretary [of HEW]. (PL 92–247)

This definition moved beyond a specific focus on physical abuse and extreme neglect and into the more controversial and less easily defined problems of emotional maltreatment and sexual abuse. Also, the definition incorporated acts which, while not resulting in immediate harm to the child, posed a potential for eventual harm.

Wide discrepancies exist in the extent to which the federal definition has been adopted by the individual states. On balance, the most common trend in legislative initiatives and reporting laws has been to expand the definition of maltreatment, often exceeding federal guidelines. Commenting on this expansion, a prominent child abuse researcher recently told a U.S. Senate subcommittee that "the debate between the service idealists who would open wider the portals of entry into the service system, and the civil libertarians, who were concerned with the prospect of more incompetent and damaging intrusion into family life appears to have been resolved in favor of the idealists" (Newberger, 1983:3). Although others continue to interpret current definitions as too narrow, noting, for example, that most focus solely on the *effect* of parental action rather than on parental *intent*, such criticism fails to come to grips with the very real limit on the power of the law to intervene into family life. Focusing on the observable consequences of maltreatment as opposed to making judgments regarding parental intent offers the courts the firmest possible case for public intervention.

The actual or potential consequences of specific acts are easier to document than the consequences of possible actions or intentions. However, even this line of reasoning becomes questionable as one moves away from the most obvious cases of physical battering and serious neglect and begins articulating the psychological trauma of maltreatment. The legal system, more so than the social service system, must begin from the perspective that care by birth parents is preferred unless certain conditions emerge to suggest that this care is or will be harmful. To the extent the definition of maltreatment constitutes the basis for justifying legal action, the language in these definitions needs to be precise and equitable. As discussed below, the definition of maltreatment and the application of this definition in specific cases has fueled a growing controversy over the appropriate scope of the problem, from a legal perspective, and the ability of the current child welfare system to address all types of maltreatment.

Current Legislation: State Efforts

Between 1963 and 1967, all states and the District of Columbia passed child abuse reporting laws, a trend which represented one of the most rapid diffusions of a legislative innovation to occur in this century (Nelson, 1984). The seemingly uncontroversial nature of the legislation (i.e., no legislator wanted to go on record opposing mandatory reporting of such a heinous crime as child abuse) and the belief during this period that government could legislate away social problems contributed to the swift passage of these laws. In addition to the federal model statute, two other model statutes were being promulgated by 1965, one by the American Medical Association (Physical Abuse of Children—Suggested Legislation) and one by the Council of State Governments (Program for Suggested State Legislation) (Nelson, 1984). Collectively, these three documents offered state policy makers a number of ideas concerning the appropriate definition of reportable conditions, who should be required to report, the actual procedures for reporting, and the consequences for failing to report.

Although NCCAN's actions established a set of uniform operating standards, individual state statutes, investigative procedures, and service options initially demonstrated wide variation and have continued to vary in content and impact. The problem is that there is no single child maltreatment law for the United States as a whole; instead there are 50 different laws, each of which has its own definition of maltreatment, its own standards for reporting known cases of maltreatment, and its own sanctions against those found guilty of such offenses (Green, 1975; Katz et al., 1977).

All of the states, however, face a common set of legal problems in developing and operationalizing their statutes. These include:

> the classification of abuse or neglect as criminal or civil wrongdoing;
>
> the definition of abuse and neglect in as objective a manner as possible;
>
> the variation in these definitions among individual jurisdictions (e.g., counties) within a state;
>
> the added complexity of dealing with inter- and intrastate jurisdictions;
>
> the exclusion of certain minority groups, such as the American Indian, from local statutory regulations;
>
> the problem of balancing children's rights and parental rights; and
>
> the efficacy of applying the legal system to the solution of intricate human problems (Katz et al., 1977:152–153).

Despite these difficulties, all states currently have some type of reporting statutes and they frequently revise and expand these statutes. For example, California has revised its reporting statute 15 times since 1963, to expand the list of mandated reporters, to remove discretionary language so that all designated reporters must report known or suspected cases, and to add to the behaviors considered to be abusive or neglectful (Commission on the Enforcement of Child Abuse Laws, 1985)

The statutes governing child maltreatment offer social welfare professionals their only avenue for coercive intervention into the family setting. While the trend has been toward more comprehensive statutes, the utility of this tool in facilitating intervention into the private family continues to vary greatly by state. Notable differences exist in such key legal components as the definition of maltreatment, the age of the covered population, the reporting procedures, and the penalty for failure to report. For example, while over 50% of the states and territories include all young people under the age of 18 in their definition of "victims," three states place the maximum age at 16 and nine states cite no specific age limitation. Although an actual definition of maltreatment is part of 49 state statutes, the level of specificity varies greatly across states. Finally, while all states include mandatory reporting of suspected cases, only about half of the states include penalties for not reporting these cases and even fewer have the capacity to enforce these penalties (Smith, 1986).

Although the *actual definitions* of maltreatment have been viewed by some as too narrow, the *conditions for reporting* have led others to suggest that existing maltreatment laws are perhaps affording professionals and private citizens too much leeway. For example, virtually all of the statutes require that the reporting individual have only "reason to believe" or "reasonable cause to suspect" that a child is suffering harm as a result of maltreatment. Potential liability issues with such a system are enormous. Social workers and other mandated reporters can theoretically be sued for failing to report or adequately protect a child suspected of being maltreated as well as for reporting a case which is eventually deemed not to have involved abuse or neglect. While significant concern exists among professionals that reporting a suspected case of maltreatment may result in a lawsuit if the case is determined to be unfounded, in reality few such suits have been filed and even fewer successfully litigated. Overall only 1% or 2% of all active social workers have ever been sued (Green, 1975; Besharov, 1981; Besharov, 1985a).

All states specifically grant immunity from civil and criminal liability to persons who report situations which they believe place a child at risk of injury. These provisions, while not eliminating lawsuits, make it almost impossible for such suits to succeed if the reporter acted "in good faith." The potential downside of these statutes, however, is that they may encourage the reporting of situations that represent questionable parental practices rather than actual or potential maltreatment, as defined by law. Certainly the fact that less than half of all reported cases are substantiated lends support to the argument that current laws may be encouraging professionals to report even the most remote risk situations in order to avoid potential lawsuits. Concern with the impacts of such defensive decision making on child welfare caseloads and practices has led six states to limit civil liability to "knowing" or "willful" failures to report (Besharov, 1985a).

Limitations and Problems
with Current Statutes and Response

The legal and programmatic responses to child maltreatment have been extensive over the past two decades. The federal initiative and increasingly comprehensive state statutes and programs have produced reporting and investigatory systems to which professionals as well as private citizens are able to direct their concerns regarding "at risk" children. While the debate over the appropriate scope and dimension of these laws and systems continues, few deny the basic need for their existence. Yet, despite the increase in public awareness of the problem since 1974 and the improvement on the part of states in identifying and addressing the problem of child abuse and neglect, the capabilities of state and local agencies effectively to identify, treat, and prevent child abuse and neglect remain inadequate. For practitioners, two issues are of paramount importance in improving the manner in which cases of child maltreatment are handled. The first of these issues pertains to the most effective way of responding to the needs of clients within the context of mandatory reporting. The second relates to selecting the most appropriate and useful interventions given a family's specific maltreatment pattern.

Dissatisfaction with the existing legal and legislative system governing public intervention in cases of maltreatment has recently focused on the reporting system itself. The cornerstone of the initial child abuse movement of the 1960's has become, in the eyes of many, one of the most controversial policy implementation problems of the 1980's. While consensus still exists regarding the need for mandatory reporting, the actual implementation of this system (i.e., determining who would report what activities and under what conditions) is far more controversial. Mandatory reporting laws are now viewed both as too intrusive and as failing to capture only a fraction of known cases. Reasons for these failings vary from problems with the content of the reporting laws themselves, to problems with the service system to which reports are made, to problems with the professional judgments involved in the identification and reporting of known or suspected maltreatment.

In defense of professionals not reporting all known cases, many practitioners feel they can better protect the child by not reporting known or suspected cases. These workers cite the inflexibility in certain child protective service (CPS) procedures and the poor follow-through during the investigative and treatment planning process as resulting in increased client frustration, anger at the system, and a sense of personal betrayal by the community-based agency or professionals from whom they had originally sought assistance (Alfaro, 1984). In the battle between their legal obligation to report known or suspected maltreatment and their professional judgment as to how best to help their clients, many professionals appear to be resolving the problem in favor of bypassing the reporting system.

In recognition of this practice, an "information only" reporting category was included in the 1977 federal model statute as a means of allowing professionals to use their discretion in determining the level of CPS involvement. When using this category, the professional or service agency making the report would continue to work with the family in resolving those conditions or behaviors contributing to maltreatment. Protective service agencies would become involved in these cases only if the family discontinued services against the advice of the reporting professional or if the situation escalated to the point at which the child was in imminent risk of serious maltreatment. This strategy has the advantage of providing professionals with a way of complying with reporting laws while protecting their ongoing relationship with their clients.

While understandable practice, selective reporting is problematic for at least two reasons. First, it violates the legal notion of equal protection and places individual practitioners in the role of judge. Child maltreatment is a crime. Although relatively few cases of physical child abuse and neglect are prosecuted through the criminal courts, those guilty of reportable acts should be equally liable for prosecution. Second, serious concern has been raised that whether parents are reported for maltreatment has less to do with the severity of the abuse or neglect or the circumstances surrounding the maltreatment and more to do with socioeconomic status. Minority families, single-parent families, and poor families are subject to greater scrutiny by a variety of public welfare and health professionals, and therefore have a greater likelihood of being reported. The overrepresentation of these groups among those reported for child abuse may be a function of this increased surveillance rather than a function of a hgher incidence rate of maltreatment among these populations (Jason et al., 1982). In addition, it has been argued that practitioners may be less inclined to report white middle-class families than they are poor, single mothers (Newberger, 1983).[5] To the extent that more economically stable families are systematically excluded from the current reporting system by professionals because they fear public intervention would be unnecessary and a misuse of scarce resources, the adoption of an "information only" category may provide the field with a more accurate picture of the scope and prevalence of maltreatment across all socioeconomic groups. The drawback to this approach, however, is that it retains a great deal of discretion in the hands of the professionals making these reports and continues to run the risk of fueling a two-tiered child welfare system, one in which poor children are systematically treated differently than more affluent children.

Over and above the potential bias in who is reported for maltreatment, any system that correctly identifies less than 50% of its cases is most certainly vulnerable to criticism. In interpreting this statistic, however, great caution is warranted. The substantiation rate does not always equal the percentage of reports that received CPS services. Frequently a family reported for suspected maltreatment may not present a convincing enough case to be legally defined as involved in abuse or neglect but does present a set of disorders serious enough to warrant social services. Such families may be accepted onto CPS caseloads as "high risk" families or may be referred to local community agencies for support or therapeutic services. Further, cases may be classified as unsubstantiated as a means of securing the family's cooperation in voluntarily entering a treatment program or to avoid the complex and often destructive aspects of adjudicating a case.

These interpretation difficulties aside, it is rather surprising that the current campaign by professionals and citizens alike to limit who can report and the basis for making a report did not surface sooner. Since uniform adoption by all states, the reporting system has never had much higher than a 50% confirmation rate. A number of factors, however, may be contributing to the present wave of concern. First, the sheer increase in the number of reported cases has put thousands more families in direct contact with the system. Failure to substantiate these reports may be less common, but the absolute number of unsubstantiated cases is over three times higher today than in 1979, for example. Second, the stigma associated with being reported for maltreatment is more pronounced. Public awareness campaigns have sensitized society not only to the existence of maltreatment, but also to its short-term and long-term consequences on children and families. Finally, a number of reports involve charges of sexual abuse, by far the most repelling form of maltreatment. If social stigma is associated with being a child abuser, being labeled as a potential molester is even more damning and can result in a loss of social status and, in some instances, one's job. While a significantly higher percentage of cases reported for sexual abuse are substantiated than are reports of general neglect or emotional maltreatment, extended investigations and the filing of formal criminal charges constitute very invasive practices which most certainly are resented if the charges are eventually dropped or identified as unfounded.

Those who propose a massive restructing of the current reporting system suggest that definitions of maltreatment need to be sharpened; mandated reporters need better training on what and how to report; emergency response units need specific guidelines for screening the growing number of calls they receive; and federal guidelines need to be altered to support states in casting smaller reporting nets (Besharov, 1985b). Any of these suggestions, implemented in moderation, would certainly not undermine, and might well enhance, the legitimate functions of child abuse reporting laws. Taken to an extreme, however, they could result in a less efficient system and place children at considerable risk. As discussed in Chapter 4, the setting of stricter standards regarding the definition of child neglect has been a reform proposed by some on the basis that neglect is less "life threatening" than physical abuse. While certainly a large number of neglect cases are not life threatening, chronic neglect has been associated with severe developmental delays in children and account for approximately half of all child abuse fatalities (AAPC, 1986).

Evidence suggesting that professionals are not reporting a sizable number of the cases known to them supports the need for more extensive and comprehensive training (Westat, 1981; Alfaro, 1984). These findings also support the need to develop an information system which provides reporters with specific feedback as to the results of their actions. Individual states and counties are responding on both of these fronts. In California, for example, clinical social workers are required as a condition of their license renewal process to attend regular training seminars which summarize the current reporting statutes and the latest clinical research on the characteristics children exhibit as a result of abuse or neglect. Such training is particularly critical with regard to the identification of emotional maltreatment and sexual abuse where physical evidence may not always be present and the empirical findings with respect to possible behavioral symptoms are most controversial. More important than actual training in improving the use of the reporting system has been the emergence in several states of a feedback system to inform reporters of the status of their report and of any actions that have been taken or that are pending. Such systems not only provide a tangible response for the professional, but also serve a field training function. Specific feedback as to why a case was or was not substantiated may help the reporter in the future attend to other types of information or change the manner in which he or she forwards that information to the protective service agency.

While training and consistent feedback may improve the rate with which professionals report cases, they may have only limited impacts on the system's overall substantiation rate or overall functioning. Today, professionals are responsible for only 50% of all reports, with friends, relatives, neighbors, self-reports, and anonymous reports accounting for the other 50%. In general, reports coming from professionals, particularly medical staff and police, already have the highest rate of substantiation, leaving less room for improvement than overall substantiation rates would suggest. In fact, many of the reports that generate the most controversy involve custody battles between estranged parents. While a certain percentage of these charges are valid complaints, many more are not, and those accused, most often the fathers, are swelling the ranks of such organizations as VOCAL (Victims of Child Abuse Legislation). Because these charges are often motivated by a sense of anger toward the former spouse, rather than a misunderstanding of the child abuse reporting laws, educational efforts regarding the purpose and correct application of reporting laws are unlikely to alter this possible misuse of the system.

Regardless of the overall reforms made in the reporting system and its implementation, the system is but one component of a complex and increasingly diversified network of child and family services. In many respects, as the reporting system becomes better known and more effectively used, more, not less, maltreatment will be identified, at least in the short run. The identification of maltreatment is not the same as its treatment or prevention. Without adequate service alternatives, even a well-functioning reporting system will only highlight its targeted problem; it cannot resolve it. As increased reports of maltreatment pressure already overburdened protective service workers, the selection of the most appropriate and useful interventions with maltreating families and the case management of these families will rest with individual practitioners. Selecting among the growing array of treatment and prevention strategies will require a clear grasp of the underlying differences in causal factors, individual characteristics, and service needs inherent in different forms of maltreatment. Twenty years of field research on parents who have been or are "at risk" of abusing their children and on the victims of maltreatment offer practitioners a solid knowledge base upon which to draw in improving practice. Information pertaining to the various subpopulations of maltreatment and to the specific treatment and prevention strategies that demonstrate the most promise in confronting these different subpopulations offers administrators and individual practitioners specific guidelines for shaping reforms both at the individual service delivery level and at the broader legislative level.

Chapter 2

Unraveling the Problem:
The Notion of Subpopulations

Child maltreatment, as a summative term, incorporates a wide range of behaviors. Parents who beat their children, the father who sexually molests his daughter, and the single parent who fails to ensure that her children attend school or receive adequate medical care are guilty, in the eyes of the law, of the same infraction—child maltreatment. From a public policy perspective, child maltreatment is the generic problem comprising a variety of different, but theoretically similar, behaviors. Mistreatment of children or the failure to care for children is the central legal and policy issue; precisely *how* parents or caretakers choose to mistreat their children is of secondary concern. For purposes of clinical practice, however, quite the reverse is true.

As more is known about the diversity within the maltreatment population, unique subpopulations are being singled out for specific program or legislative attention. This process is useful for at least two reasons. First, the development of distinct subpopulations mitigates the definitional problems surrounding maltreatment. Attempts to arrive at a global, all-encompassing definition of maltreatment are hampered by a number of factors particularly if one attempts to apply the same criteria employed in defining a disease. As discussed in the following chapter, no single, universal virus causes maltreatment. Families cannot be innoculated against abuse or neglect, nor is the form of progression of maltreatment the same in all families. Some children appear, on the surface, to cope effectively with a wide range of maltreatment while others suffer overt long-term physical and emotional trauma. Similarly, certain services are effective in curbing maltreatment and remediating its negative consequences in some families but have no notable impact on others. Finally, the ability to predict future maltreatment based upon the presence of certain individual characteristics or social factors is questionable at best, making it extremely difficult to define clear, unambiguous "at risk" families. Faced with these contradictions and uncertainties, local child protective service statutes are based on definitions of child maltreatment which bear only limited resemblance to the definitions employed in the adjacent county or state. "Cholera may be cholera in Bombay or San Diego," wrote one researcher, "but child abuse may not be child abuse in San Diego and Los Angeles Counties" (Giovannoni, 1982:25).

Parenting practices such as supportive praise, attention to health care needs, consistent application of rules and expectations clearly promote a child's healthy growth and development. Other practices such as severe physical beatings, inattention to a child's basic needs for food, clothing, and health care, and constant belittling and humiliating clearly restrict a child's ability to achieve his or her full human potential. Identifying the precise point at which parenting becomes abusive is an issue of degrees and professional judgment. Calling for public intervention when behaviors have immediate and observable harm on the child is relatively straightforward. Such determinations, however, are far more complex when parental behavior is more ambiguous and when the potential negative consequences are theoretical as opposed to actual. Since most parenting and most maltreatment involves the latter types of behaviors, the need for judgment calls is inescapable. While the identification of maltreatment subpopulations does not fully resolve these concerns, assessing families in terms of different types of abuse or neglect at least narrows the behavioral territory one needs to cover in setting practice guidelines and developing programs.

Second, the initial limited success of child abuse and neglect treatment programs lent support to the subpopulation approach and to the hopes that programs targeted to specific subpopulations might achieve greater clinical success than those targeted to the general maltreatment population. The growing number of substantiated cases and the emergence of multiple causal explanations for maltreatment suggest that focusing on a more limited segment of the problem is necessary if practitioners are to make progress in identifying the reasons for initial and repeated maltreatment. If the identification of subpopulations produces more homogeneous clusters of families in terms of their demographic characteristics, social stresses, and functional abilities, treatment and prevention strategies could be better targeted to those types of families most likely to benefit.

As indicated in Figure 2.1, four major types of maltreatment are consistently cited in the literature—physical abuse, physical neglect, emotional maltreatment, and sexual abuse. While most agree with this gross categorization, several researchers have developed a number of additional subdivisions within each of these broad categories. In most cases, those who have advocated these more refined typologies argue that significant variation

Figure 2.1

Child Maltreatment Typologies

Physical Abuse/Assault Classifications

    Physical abuse

    Major physical injury

    Minor physical injury

    Physical injury, severity unknown

    "Flashpoint"

    "Spare the rod"

    "You asked for it"

    "Who needs it"

    Uncontrolled battering

    Controlled abuse

Physical Neglect Classifications

    Physical neglect

    Deprivation of necessities

    Educational neglect/deprivation

    Medical care neglect

    Intentional drugging

    Abandonment/lack of supervision

    Failure to provide

    Fostering delinquency

Emotional Maltreatment Classifications

    Emotional maltreatment

    Emotional/psychological abuse

    Emotional/psychological neglect

    Emotional assault

    Acts of rejection

    Acts of coldness

    Acts of inappropriate control

    Acts of extreme inconsistency

Sexual Maltreatment Classifications

    Sexual abuse/maltreatment

    Sexual exploitation

    Sexual abuse without consent

    Sexual abuse with consent

    Incidental sexual contact

    Ideological sexual contact

    Psychotic intrusion

    Rustic environment

    True endogamous incest

Figure 2.1 continued

Misogynous incest

Pedophilic incest

Child rape

Perverse or pornographic incest

Other Classifications Cited

Parental sexual mores/drug or alcohol abuse

High risk

Potential abuse

Potential neglect

SOURCES: Boisvert, 1972; Bedger et al., 1976; BPA, 1977; Summit and Kryso, 1978; Dean, 1979; Giovannoni and Becerra, 1979; Abt Associates, 1981; Westat, 1981; Miller, 1982; Kent et al., 1983; BPA, 1983; AAPC, 1986; Garbarino and Garbarino, 1986.

remains within each of the gross categories, variation which, if left unaddressed, leads to faulty conclusions regarding causal factors and treatment strategies.

This chapter describes these four major subpopulations and summarizes the factors that have been articulated in defining the behaviors represented by each type. The chapter concludes with a discussion of the extent to which these various subpopulations warrant different applications of existing statutes and development of unique treatment strategies.

Physical Abuse: The Most Visible Form of Maltreatment

In many respects, physical abuse can be termed the "classic" form of maltreatment. Beginning with Kempe's 1962 article and continuing through today, the popular image of the abused child is one who has suffered physical battering at the hands of his or her parents. Physical abuse is generally accepted as a clear form of child maltreatment and, in extreme forms, to justify quick and extensive public intervention into the private family (Giovannoni and Becerra, 1979; Magura and Moses, 1986). Given this universal image of physical abuse, it is not surprising to find that few researchers delineate additional subcategories under the physical abuse heading. Those studies which do suggest a more complex scheme, however, differentiate the population along a number of interesting dimensions. First, the American Association for Protecting Children includes three forms of physical abuse in its summary of statewide reporting data, differentiating cases in terms of their severity. This type of distinction is most commonly made not only by professionals but also by the general public. Very different levels of concern emerge in cases involving broken bones or permanent brain damage versus cases involving minor bruises. In addition, bruises that result from what some may term "normal" corporal punishment are less likely to draw public scrutiny than bruises resulting from an intentional unprovoked attack on a child (Giovannoni and Becerra, 1979; Gil, 1981).

In contrast to this simple division, others have developed more complex models. Boisvert constructed a physical abuse typology differentiating families along three dimensions—the characteristics of the perpetrators, the age of the child and the nature of the injury, and the casework strategy as determined by the legal action and the services advocated. In general, Boisvert identified two major types of physical abusers. The first type, "uncontrollable battering," includes such variations as the psychotic personality, the inadequate personality, the passive-aggressive personality, and the sadistic personality. For all of these cases, placement, at least temporarily, is warranted to avoid continued, and progressively more severe, maltreatment. In contrast, "controlled abuse" families are viewed as being far more amenable to therapeutic intervention and can even be treated, in certain cases, without the use of any out-of-home placement options.

Boisvert's concern that physical abuse might be too broad a term has been supported by the recent work of Dr. James Kent.[1] Kent and his colleagues found that the physical abuse cases they examined clustered into four specific groups which he termed "flashpoint," "spare the rod," "you asked for it," and "who needs it" (Kent et al., 1983). Basing these categories upon the characteristics of the child, the characteristics of the parents, and the circumstances immediately preceding the maltreatment, he argues that a physical abuse case may be treated in a number of ways and is far from the unidimensional concept depicted in Kempe's "battered child" syndrome. Like Boisvert, Kent outlines specific interventions for each of his four types:

> *flashpoint*—implies the need for psychotherapy to address the individual's psychopathology and/or interpersonal conflict:
>
> *spare the rod*—implies the need for help in learning to use and to trust alternative modes of discipline and socialization to address the parents' overemphasis on teaching "right from wrong" and on ensuring their children grow into "good citizens"
>
> *you asked for it*—implies a similar need for help in managing the behavior of more assertive and active children without physically abusive methods to address the parents' lack of economic security and self-confidence; and
>
> *who needs it*—implies a need for therapeutic intervention coupled with the use of a "lay therapist" or "parent aide" to help bridge the gap between the parents' expectations and the kind of help formal therapy can actually provide (Kent et al., 1983:15–26).

Some 25% of all cases reported to protective services in 1984 involved physical abuse, either as the sole type of maltreatment or in combination with other forms of abuse or neglect. On balance the victims of severe physical abuse are younger than those children experiencing minor or unspecified physical abuse or other forms of maltreatment (AAPC, 1986). A larger percentage of physical abuse victims are hospitalized and physical abuse accounts for over 56% of all fatalities due to child abuse; physical abuse is the major cause of abuse-related deaths among young children. A study comparing victims of physical abuse and sexual abuse noted that the physical abuse victims were five times more likely to die as a result of injuries (Jason et al., 1982). Compared to nonmaltreated children and children who have experienced neglect or emotional maltreatment, the victims of physical abuse were noted in one 42-month follow-up study to be the most distractible and least persistent or enthusiastic in preschool settings (Egeland et al., 1983). When compared to parents involved in other forms of maltreatment, most notably neglectful parents, the physically abusive parent appears more volatile and presents more intraphychic and interpersonal difficulties (Bedger et al., 1976; Giovannoni and Billingsley, 1970; Giovannoni, 1971).

Identification of physical abuse generally results from observations of the potential victims by medical personnel, day care providers, schoolteachers, or concerned neighbors or family friends. Occasionally, older children will report themselves victims of physical abuse, although it is more common for these victims to leave the abusive situation (i.e., running away, moving in with relatives, etc.).[2]

While a variety of factors may trigger reports of physical abuse, the most common "warning signs" include broken bones, bruises, unusual scars or burns, or repeated accidental injuries. Injuries to infants generally receive greater scrutiny than do bruises found on older children. Children who have shown repeated signs of physical injury are more suspect than children who demonstrate an occasional cut or bruise. Finally, the ability of parents or caretakers to explain the source of the injury is often the most critical factor in the substantiation of the report, although it will often not be a factor in whether or not an initial report is made.

Though tempered somewhat by societal approval of corporal punishment, public intervention in cases of physical abuse enjoys widespread support. Identification is primarily made through observation of the victim and reports can be, and often are, made on the sole basis of the child's condition. The nature of the injuries is often such that only one plausible explanation can exist for them. While removal of the child from the home in the most serious of these cases is the most frequent intervention, a wide range of family-based interventions are also employed. The most common service options offered families involved in physical abuse are parenting education regarding alternative forms of discipline, parent aid services to provide a support for parents unable to cope with daily stress, and therapeutic services for the victims to remediate the consequences of the abuse and, in some instances, to improve the child's behavior so that the parent can better manage him or her.

Physical Neglect: The Most Forgotten
Form of Maltreatment

As with physical abuse, researchers have been generally content to consider physical neglect a homogeneous concept. Characteristics that have been more closely associated with child neglect than with other forms of maltreatment include low income; larger, multiproblem families; nonwhite families; AFDC recipients; poor housing and living conditions; and low educational and employment levels (Boehm, 1964; Lewis, 1969; Polansky et al., 1974; BPA, 1982a). Social isolation is also found to be particularly common among neglectful families. For example, over 20% of all the neglect families included in one sample were totally isolated from all forms of informal supports. In contrast, over 85% of the control group, who had been matched on such critical variables as income and race, were identified as being well-supported by extended family members and friends (Polansky et al., 1979a). The universal picture of a neglect case, therefore, is that of a poor, socially isolated, and chaotic family where the need to care for children is lost among the more immediate demands of basic survival.

In looking at the specific subpopulations identified in Figure 2.1 under the general heading of neglect, therefore, it is not surprising to find very few of these categories representing different family characteristics, causal factors, or any other of the dimensions captured in the refined physical abuse typologies. Instead, these typologies focus on differences in the neglectful act itself. For example, Miller's distinction of subpopulations (e.g., educational neglect, medical neglect, intentional drugging, and abandonment) was based less upon the development of more homogeneous subgroups of maltreators and more upon isolating unique symptoms which could be used by physicians to document neglect. Similarly, the subclassifications cited by Giovannoni and Becerra (e.g., educational neglect, abandonment, failure to provide, and fostering delinquency) reflect different behaviors and do not suggest that different types of families are involved in these different behaviors.

In defining neglect, significant attention is often paid to the notion of community standards of care. Similar to the variation allowed for differing standards and approval of corporal punishment in different communities, definitions of neglect are often tempered by what a given community or culture considers to be adequate supervision, household cleanliness, child cleanliness, and medical care. Again, the consistent omission of care is considered neglectful in all communities; less than consistent care warrants more careful applications of the reporting standards. Critics of the more

comprehensive statutes claim that broad definitions of
often based on middle-class standards of care establis
when the majority of women remained home with th
standards, those critics argue, are inappropriate and un
in which 49% of mothers with children one year or younger are in
labor force, or in a society comprised of multiple cultures and parenting
values. While certain of these criticisms are warranted,[3] more than passing
agreement exists on the factors that constitute neglect and the relative
severity of these behaviors. Professionals and the general public generate
similar ranking of various neglectful behaviors in terms of their potential
severity and need for public intervention. Fostering delinquency and the
lack of adequate supervision are concepts generally viewed as more serious
forms of child neglect than failing to bathe a child regularly, change a
child's clothing, or ensure a child attends school (Giovannoni and Becerra,
1979; Magura and Moses, 1986).

Research has also documented similarities across socioeconomic groups
regarding the types of parenting behaviors or living conditions considered
child neglect. Addressing the argument that current child neglect laws reflect a middle-class bias toward child-rearing, Polansky and Williams (1978)
constructed a test to discover whether Polansky's Childhood Level of Living Scale contained middle-class value biases or was inappropriately applied to working-class mothers. The authors collected opinions on the scale
from a sample of working-class mothers who resembled the parents in their
case study sample and from a contrasting group of middle-class women.
The most impressive finding of this study was the similarity among average
judgments in both groups. When significant differences did emerge, these
differences were always matters of degrees and showed no conflict in the
direction of the average evaluation.

While middle-class and working-class mothers may share common values regarding appropriate levels of parenting and child care, the ability of
working-class and lower-class mothers to achieve these standards is often
more limited. Lack of adequate financial resources not only prohibits these
mothers from securing amenities seen as desirable for their children, but
also contributes to the stress of child-rearing in general. Such increased
stress, in turn, may increase the likelihood of other forms of maltreatment,
most notably, physical abuse or emotional maltreatment.

Data on the characteristics of families reported for physical neglect suggest a strong correlation between income and this particular form of maltreatment. Over 51% of the children reported for neglect reside in single-
parent families, and over 43% of the primary caretakers are unemployed
(AAPC, 1986). Neglect is far more likely than other forms of maltreatment
to be the sole form of maltreatment documented in the family. While a
certain percentage of neglectful families also experience other forms of
maltreatment, especially emotional maltreatment or physical abuse, multiple forms of maltreatment among this population are relatively rare (BPA,

/82a; AAPC, 1986). This dominance of a single form of maltreatment may partially explain the homogeneous nature of the population and the fact that a typical family profile is more easily developed for child neglect than for any other form of maltreatment.

Similar to the most severe forms of physical abuse, identification of chronic neglect is most often made by medical personnel or others who have direct, ongoing contact with the child such as a day care provider or school nurse. Common warning signs may include consistent lack of clean clothing, skin and scalp conditions that result from a lack of regular bathing, a chronic or unattended medical problem, and dramatic under- and overweight. In older children, those who are consistently tardy or absent from school or lethargic in the classroom are considered potential victims of neglect. Other common sources of neglect reports include neighbors, extended family members, and welfare case workers. In making an assessment of the validity of these reports, protective service workers will consider not only the condition of the child but also the condition of the housing unit and parents' recognition of the harm being caused their child due to the lack of adequate care. The severity of harm to the child and the ability to the parent to improve the quality of the child's care are factors that determine the level of social service involvement. Children are generally removed from the home only when their housing situation is unsafe (e.g., faulty wiring, lack of running water, lack of heat) or when a judgment is made that the caretaker is unable or unwilling to provide for the child's basic material needs or supervision. Left unaddressed, however, the impact of even moderate forms of neglect on a child's functioning can be quite severe. Of all the children studied by Egeland and his colleagues over a 42-month period, the neglected children received the lowest ratings in self-esteem as well as in confidence and assertiveness in approaching learning tasks. "This is an unhappy group," noted the researchers, "presenting the least positive and the most negative affect of all groups" (Egeland et al., 1983:469). Unfortunately, as discussed in subsequent chapters, families involved in neglect are among the most resistant to intervention. Although it is the most common and one of the most damaging forms of maltreatment, child neglect remains the most resistant to current treatment and prevention strategies.

Emotional Maltreatment: The Most Ambiguous Form of Maltreatment

Until recently, emotional maltreatment received little specific attention. The reasons for its omission from most policy and research agendas involved the very difficult practical problems of defining the term, predicting the impact on its victims, and developing effective treatment alternatives (Frost, 1982). Unlike the more visible and immediate consequences resulting from physical abuse and neglect, the consequences of emotional mal-

treatment are often far more elusive. As a result, most maltreatment typologies tend to use this type of maltreatment as a residual category, covering
all behaviors that are not captured under the physical abuse, physical neglect, and sexual abuse headings. A few stratification systems for emotional
maltreatment have been developed. For example, Dean (1979) defined
three principal types of emotional maltreatment: emotional neglect, including acts of omission; emotional assault, including verbal attacks by parents or other adults or siblings on a one-time or continuing basis; and emotional abuse, including chronic attitudes or acts by parents or caretakers
that are detrimental to or prevent the development of a positive self-image
for the child. Others have segmented emotional maltreatment into four
basic behaviors: rejection, coldness, inappropriate control, and extreme in-
consistency (Garbarino and Garbarino, 1986). Although emotional maltreatment is difficult to define, public concern regarding the potential impacts of at least one aspect of it is significant. A recent Louis Harris public
opinion poll conducted for the National Committee for the Prevention of
Child Abuse found that almost three-quarters of the respondents thought
that "repeated yelling and swearing" at a child very often or often results
in long-term emotional problems for the child. In contrast, only 42% perceived a similar level of harm resulting from the use of corporal punishment (Daro and Mitchel, 1987b).

More recently, the medical profession has identified a form of emotional
maltreatment in which parents insist their children have physical illnesses
despite all medical evidence to the contrary. Referred to as the "munchausen syndrome," the symptoms of this form of maltreatment include
poor school attendance due to supposed illness; parents exhibiting para-
noid thinking and conviction that the child is seriously ill; and "doctor
shopping" or numerous visits to multiple physicians within a relatively
brief period of time (Woollcott et al., 1982). At least one researcher also
suggests that a parent may actually substitute his or her own specimens
for that of the child in an effort to confirm a given illness (Meadow, 1979).
Victims of this type of maltreatment will frequently become lethargic and
assume the frail and dependent status their parents foster upon them.

Despite its damaging consequences for children, emotional maltreatment is not always covered under state reporting statutes. While all states
consider the failure of parents to send their children to school a form of
neglect, not all states allow for public intervention in cases where the parents refuse to send the child to school because they believe the child to
be ill. Harsh words or constant ridicule rarely leave visible scars on their
victims and consequently offer professionals little basis for justifying public
intervention into the private family. Finally, since all parents criticize their
children, say things they wish they had not, or fail to provide emotional
support and encouragement when needed, it is difficult to determine
when such acts or omissions cross the threshhold dividing understandable
and acceptable parental mistakes from emotional maltreatment.

The amorphous nature of emotional maltreatment is reflected in the fact that a very limited number of families are reported to local protective service agencies for this particular form of maltreatment alone. Unlike physical neglect, and to a lesser extent physical abuse, most families involved in emotional maltreatment also present one or two other types of maltreatment. While it is less likely to exist in pure form, it is the type of maltreatment most commonly noted among families involved in therapeutic treatment programs for abuse or neglect. In the National Clinical Evaluation Study, for example, emotional maltreatment was noted for over 60% of the cases, although only 5% of the families were involved in only this form of maltreatment (BPA, 1983). On balance, children reported for emotional maltreatment average 8.5 years of age compared to an average of 5.3 for victims of physical abuse and 6.4 for victims of child neglect. While approximately two-thirds of all reports involve white children, almost three-quarters of the emotional maltreatment reports involve whites (AAPC, 1986). While preschoolers who have experienced repeated verbal assault tend to be more aggressive and angry in their interactions with family and peers, the victims of emotional neglect have been found to be highly dependent on their preschool teachers for help, support, and nurturance (Egeland et al., 1983).

The pervasiveness of emotional maltreatment largely accounts for the inability of researchers to develop a typical profile of the emotional maltreating parent. Characteristics common to physically abusive parents, such as poor parenting skills, lack of alternative discipline methods, and an inability to manage anger and stress, are also found among parents who emotionally maltreat their children. Low self-esteem, inappropriate expectations for their children, and social isolation are also frequent traits of parents who consistently belittle their children. This type of maltreatment does not appear to be limited to families with low incomes or limited education. In several respects, parents who are aware of the dangers of physical abuse and consequently do not hit their children often have little understanding of the damage that can result from withdrawing affection for an extended period of time as a means of discipline or control. Because emotional maltreatment can only occur to the degree that a child is dependent upon the adult, parents who have the strongest bonds with their children may actually be capable of inflicting the most harm (Garbarino and Garbarino, 1986).

Unlike physical abuse or neglect, emotional maltreatment is more likely to be reported by school counselors, private therapists, or other professionals having ongoing contact with the family or child. The lack of visible scars or immediate behavioral changes as a result of a single incident contributes to the unique identification and treatment problems of this particular form of maltreatment. Professionals or private citizens who have only occasional contact with the child or family would lack the information necessary for a valid report. One cannot point to a specific scar, bruise, or other physical ailment as the result of emotional maltreatment. Depression, poor school performance, and low self-esteem, all frequent outcomes of emotional maltreatment, can also result from a host of other family or peer-related difficulties. Consequently, identification of emotional maltreatment is contingent upon the victim revealing a history of emotional abuse or neglect to a trusted adult or someone observing the parent-child interaction and, if warranted, reporting the family. Because families are generally brought into the system for a combination of emotional maltreatment and other, more demonstrative forms of abuse or neglect, interventions generally focus on resolving the family's more immediate and pressing problems. Similar to the failure of professionals correctly to identify cases of sexual abuse five years ago, careful assessments for present or potential emotional maltreatment are often not conducted.

Sexual Abuse: The Most Explosive Form of Maltreatment

Despite growing concern over sexual abuse in this country, the problem remains a taboo subject among many. Certainly, the field has made great strides over the past several years in raising public and professional awareness of child sexual abuse as evidenced by the sharp increase in reports of sexual abuse and the growing number of treatment and prevention services targeted specifically to this form of maltreatment. Between 1983 and 1984, sexual abuse reports increased 35% and now constitute almost 14% of all protective service cases (AAPC, 1986). In their study of the attitudes of professionals toward different types of maltreatment, Giovannoni and Becerra found greatest agreement among both professional and lay respondents regarding the "extreme seriousness" of sexual abuse (Giovannoni and Becerra, 1979: 242). Magura and Moses noted a similar high level of concern regarding the severity of sexual abuse in their survey of child protective service workers (Magura and Moses, 1986). Reasonable debate can take place over "acceptable" levels of corporal punishment or the degree of supervision necessary for a child at different developmental levels; there is much less room for valid disagreement regarding the issue of child sexual abuse.

Unlike child neglect, which is seen as a function of poverty, sexual abuse cuts across the full socioeconomic spectrum. The victims of sexual abuse are the children of professionals and white-collar and blue-collar workers alike. They are reared in single-parent and two-parent families. They have parents who lack high school diplomas and parents who have advanced degrees from prestigious universities. Similar to the diversity found among families involved in emotional maltreatment, the problem of sexual abuse exists in all communities and is being identified with increased frequency.

Initial comparisons between families reported for sexual abuse and those reported for other forms of maltreatment suggest that, as a group, these families generally have higher median incomes, fewer external family pressures, and more internal family functioning problems. These families are more likely to have two parents present in the household and to have at least one employed full-time. Compared to the victims of other forms of maltreatment, children reported for sexual abuse are predominantly female (i.e., 75% of all reported cases), generally older (i.e., average age is 8.1), and have been victimized by someone other than their parents (BPA, 1983; AAPC, 1986). Taken at face value, the profiles of sexually abusive families and victims derived from these and similar statistics may be misleading. Certainly the notion that families involved in sexual abuse have higher average income than families involved in child neglect, for example, appears reasonable. To the extent that the majority of reported cases involve two-parent households with an employed male, one would assume greater financial resources than would be present in a single-parent, female-headed household. Other aspects of this profile, however, are far less obvious. A growing number of clinical studies, while often based on more limited samples, suggest that the onset of sexual abuse may occur when victims are much younger than implied in the reporting statistics and that many victims are young boys. One major sexual abuse treatment center has reported that over 25% of their victims are five years of age or younger (Summit, 1983). Extensive interviews with men incarcerated for child sexual abuse reveal a surprisingly high childhood victimization pattern involving males, as do interviews with random and nonrandom samples of adult males (Gebhard et al., 1965; Finkelhor, 1979; Groth, 1983; Abel et al., 1984; Finkelhor, 1984). Finally, while the reporting statistics indicate that only slightly more than 50% of the cases of sexual abuse involve the child's natural or stepparent, most of the remaining 50% of offenders are known to their victims. This fact is supported through clinical interviews conducted not only with the victims of sexual abuse but also with the perpetrators (Summit, 1983; Abel et al., 1984; Finkelhor, 1984).

Rather than focusing on specific family characteristics as a means of grouping sexual abuse cases, research on this particular subpopulation has examined the nature of the abuse itself, the duration of the abuse, the age differential between the victim and perpetrator, the degree of force used to obtain compliance, and the extent to which the perpetrator victimizes children other than his or her own. Most of these categorization attempts are quite recent and represent only the initial attempts to unravel the complex profiles found among sexual abuse caseloads. For example, Jones (1982) has suggested that families involved in sexual abuse fall into one of three distinct categories. The first type consists of families that are generally not known to the public service system and, although isolated, will appear normal to most observers. The abuse in these families is generally nonviolent, with the father obtaining compliance through assertion of his parental authority or by playing on the daughter's need for acceptance and love. In contrast, the second type of family manifests several problems and has a long history of public agency involvement. These families tend to display the violent and chaotic characteristics noted among physically abusive families. Finally, the third type of family reported for sexual abuse is the "single-event family," where abuse has occurred when the perpetrator was drunk or on drugs. Further research is necessary to determine whether this typology would characterize larger numbers of sexual abuse cases and whether it has direct implications for the development of differential treatment plans.

The frequent absence of visible scars, the tendency of victims to accept responsibility for the abuse and to keep the abuse secret, and the strong emotional bond between the victim and perpetrator generally found in these cases make disclosure of sexual abuse uniquely problematic. In contrast, indifference to the potential harm associated with emotional maltreatment cases makes perpetrators less concerned with secrecy. Similarly, the telltale bruises and physical ailments associated with physical abuse or neglect make secrecy more difficult to sustain. Such verbal disclosures and physical symptoms are not available in the majority of sexual abuse cases. More than any of the other forms of maltreatment, identification of sexual abuse is largely contingent upon the actions of the victim or his or her family members. While professionals can be trained to be aware of certain physical and behavioral symptoms and to interview potential victims in a supportive manner, early identification and substantiation depend upon the victim's ability to describe the abuse and stand firm on the accusation often in the face of family and professional denial (Summit, 1983). Greater public awareness and openness in discussing sexual abuse most likely has contributed to the increase in its reporting and substantiation. The provision of child assault prevention instruction in the schools to children of all ages reinforces the importance for children to say no, to leave a potentially abusive situation, and to tell someone they trust. Whether this type of instruction and reliance on children to protect themselves from assault is effective in obtaining earlier disclosures or in preventing initial victimization is one of the most provocative research and treatment questions facing the field today.

The Use of Subpopulations in Improving Practice

Recognition of the existence of, and the differences among, the various forms of maltreatment is critical to effective intervention. While the quest for improved intervention methods in cases of physical abuse focuses on the characteristics of the abuser and victim, the homogeneous nature of the neglect subpopulation suggests an emphasis on broad-scale community-based interventions and social reforms may be necessary. In contrast, effective treatment and prevention of emotional maltreatment requires that parents and professionals working with children first accept the concept of emotional maltreatment as a viable component of the child abuse problem. Without such acceptance, this particular variant of maltreatment will continue to be overlooked in the development of new treatment and prevention strategies. Despite the rapid proliferation of treatment and prevention services targeted to child sexual abuse, the identification and disclosure process remains problematic in these cases. Improving our ability to address sexual abuse is heavily dependent upon creating environments in which victims feel comfortable enough to disclose current or past abuse.

Focusing on the range of maltreatment is useful for helping practitioners identify the breadth of prevention and treatment services needed to develop a comprehensive approach to confronting the child abuse crisis. An equally important aspect of this system, however, may be recognizing the unique issues and tensions, as well as strengths, presented in families at different life cycle stages.[4] Just as the service needs of a family involved in child neglect may differ from the service needs of one involved in sexual abuse, the needs of families with adolescents differ from those of families with infants and toddlers. Cutting across a wide range of abusive behaviors, adolescent maltreatment is often viewed as a subpopulation unto itself. The uniqueness of the adolescent period and the general assumption that teenagers often "deserve" the treatment they receive contribute to the tendency on the part of professionals to overlook signs of maltreatment which they might report if observed in a younger child (Lourie and Cohan 1976; Boleck and Kilpatrick, 1982). Parents of adolescents may be facing a mid-life crisis of their own, seeking greater authority over their children at the very time their children are pulling away from them in an attempt to establish their own identities.

Similarly, certain behaviors on the part of the parent or child such as drug or alcohol abuse may be so central to the family's general functioning that they become the dominant issue of concern. An alcoholic physical abuser and an alcoholic sexual abuser may have more in common from an initial treatment perspective than either would have with nonalcoholic physical or sexual abusers. The significance of these and other behaviors in determining an individual's potential for good parenting have led some to consider such behaviors, in and of themselves, forms of maltreatment. Defining maltreatment in terms of behaviors outside the parent-child dyad adds a new and extremely controversial aspect to the debate. If behaviors such as drug or alcohol abuse and sexual promiscuity are included in the definition of maltreatment, who will set the standards for what is abusive or morally damaging to the child? Yet, despite the concern over the subjective nature of these value judgments, professionals and the general public routinely and appropriately question the ability of a chronic drug abuser or alcoholic to care adequately for children. In addition, the National Clinical Evaluation Study found that maltreating parents involved in substance abuse were significantly less likely to make progress in treatment either in terms of improving their own functioning or improving their parenting skills (BPA, 1983). While many may argue that notions of the private family and individual liberties mitigate against viewing such parental behaviors as grounds for public intervention, others suggest that because a parent's personal behavior significantly affects the child's living environment, it cannot be totally excluded from the definition of child maltreatment. "The concept of parental rights does not or should not include the rights of parents to destroy themselves and their children" (Giovannoni and Becerra, 1979:254).

A second limitation is that attempts to compare the characteristics of various subpopulations have been hampered by small sample size. For example, Bedger and his colleagues found when reviewing court records that only four of their original ten subpopulations were recorded for more than 5% of all cases.[5] Even if sample size can be sufficiently increased so that valid profiles can be developed, one might still question whether the fine tuning of a given typology actually increases one's understanding of maltreatment. While certain families may manifest different forms of child neglect, identifying these particular differences may not be necessary in order to develop a responsive service plan. On the contrary, focusing on such differences may result in such a fragmented intervention strategy that the major treatment focus becomes lost in a host of interesting, but less service-relevant, differences. Winnowing down the number of categories in any given typology to those that truly distinguish among different service groups within the broader population should be the primary goal of these efforts. In addition to distinguishing among service needs, categories within a child maltreatment typology should delineate a specific range of behaviors for which practitioners can develop concrete service plans. It must be borne in mind, however, that typologies which are so fine-tuned that they require extensive diagnostic procedures in order to classify families are not useful to practitioners seeking tools for the rapid identification of high risk families and the channeling of these families to appropriate services.

Finally, typologies that have focused on differentiating families based upon the type of maltreatment or in terms of the age of the victim fail to address directly the problem of multiple patterns of maltreatment. As noted in both the AAPC data bases and the National Incidence Study, families are frequently involved in multiple types of maltreatment (Westat, 1981; AAPC, 1986). Unique differences between families involved in multiple types of maltreatment versus a single form of maltreatment were noted in the National Clinical Evaluation Study. As summarized in Table 2.1, multiple forms of maltreatment were documented in almost 60% of the sample's 986 families, 1,250 adults, 701 adolescents, and 983 infants and children. In addition to documenting the dominance of multiple forms of maltreatment, Table 2.1 also highlights the differences in abuse patterns noted for young children versus adolescents. For example, over 20% of the

Table 2.1

Pattern of Maltreatment Identified for Client Impact Samples

	Percent of Family Sample	Percent of Adult Sample	Percent of Adoles- cent Sample	Percent of Child Sample
High Risk (no maltreatment documented)	7.0	7.4	11.7	20.8
Single Type of Maltreatment				
Emotional Maltreatment	4.5	3.8	8.4	5.4
Neglect	10.3	11.0	5.6	22.3
Physical Abuse	6.1	6.1	5.4	3.1
Sexual Abuse	13.0	14.6	14.1	6.0
Two Types of Maltreatment				
Physical and Sexual Abuse	2.4	2.9	1.4	.9
Neglect and Sexual Abuse	1.3	1.5	.9	.7
Neglect and Physical Abuse	1.5	1.0	1.4	1.3
Emotional Maltreatment and Sexual Abuse	6.3	6.2	7.0	2.0
Emotional Maltreatment and Physical Abuse	9.7	10.0	13.6	4.6
Emotional Maltreatment and Neglect	15.9	15.1	8.4	21.2
Three Types of Maltreatment				
Neglect, Physical and Sexual Abuse	.2	.2	.1	.1
Emotional Maltreatment, Physical and Sexual Abuse	4.1	4.1	5.4	.7
Emotional Maltreatment, Neglect and Sexual Abuse	2.1	1.8	2.0	.9
Emotional Maltreatment, Ne- glect, and Physical Abuse	11.0	10.2	9.7	9.5
All Four Types of Maltreatment	4.6	4.1	4.9	.6
n =	986	1,250	701	983

infants and children under 12 included in the sample were identified as "high risk" cases, while only 11% of the adolescents were so classified. Of the cases experiencing a single form of maltreatment, a higher percentage of adolescents were victims of sexual abuse, while a higher percentage of young children were found in the neglect category. Similarly, the combination of emotional maltreatment and physical abuse was more common among adolescents, with emotional maltreatment and neglect occurring more frequently among young children.

In addition to noting differences in the pattern of maltreatment for adolescents and young children, this evaluation also found that families involved in multiple forms of maltreatment were significantly more likely than families involved in a single form of maltreatment to experience a greater number of functioning problems and stresses, as summarized in Table 2.2. In virtually every area, a direct relationship was noted between the frequency with which a problem was observed and the range of maltreatment existing within a family. The children in multiple maltreating families were generally identified as suffering more severe harm and the adults were among the projects' least successful clients. Both the likelihood for reincidence during treatment and the propensity for future maltreatment were judged by clinicians to be significantly higher for those families involved in multiple types of maltreatment (BPA, 1983). Collectively, these findings suggest that family functioning and severity of harm may vary not only in terms of the *type* of abuse or neglect present, but also in the *range* of maltreatment present. In considering the most appropriate treatment strategies for families, therefore, it is important to differentiate not only in terms of the four major types of maltreatment, but also by the number of these types present in a given family.

Having recognized the limitations posed by child maltreatment typologies, a subpopulation scheme focusing on the major types of maltreatment does allow one to begin dividing the maltreatment problem into more homogeneous and, it is hoped, more understandable components. As discussed in subsequent chapters, the results of the National Clinical Evaluation Study found not only that different subpopulations responded to different interventions but that service programs that limited their caseloads to only one type of maltreating family realized greater success than those drawing their caseloads from a broader range of abusive and neglectful parents.

These four types of maltreatment are not the only means of subdividing the broader maltreatment population. However, this classification scheme does produce clusters of families unique enough to warrant individual consideration in reviewing the perceived causes of maltreatment as well as in assessing service effectiveness. While each subpopulation retains a sizable degree of internal variance, the dimensions along which the four groups differ most sharply—namely in their underlying causal patterns, the current response of the child welfare system to their victims, the differential impacts of specific treatment efforts, and the development of various prevention strategies—offer practitioners and program planners guideposts for making more informed choices on how best to improve their performance.

Table 2.2

Frequency of Various Family Problems Among Families
Experiencing Different Numbers of Maltreatment Types

Function Problem	Percentage of Families Experiencing Problem Who Are Involved In:			
	Single Type of Maltreatment	Two Types of Maltreatment	Three Types of Maltreatment	Four Types of Maltreatment
Financial Difficulties	75.7% (n=305)	81.0% (n=343)	81.6% (n=163)	83.8% (n= 43)
Physical Violence Between Adult Spouses/Partners	29.3 (n=215)	46.0 (n=239)	55.9 (n=118)	65.7 (n= 32)
Disruptive Conflict Between Adult Spouses/Partners	63.2 (n=231)	77.1 (n=271)	80.7 (n=135)	85.7 (n= 35)
Detachment Between Adult Spouses	51.6 (n=211)	57.6 (n=252)	62.8 (n=129)	61.3 (n= 31)
Enmeshment Between Adult Spouses	37.0 (n=197)	49.6 (n=236)	61.8 (n=123)	67.9 (n= 28)
Sexual Performance Problems	54.9 (n=113)	57.6 (n= 99)	58.2 (n= 55)	68.2 (n= 22)
Physical Violence Between Siblings	14.8 (n=250)	28.3 (n=268)	42.6 (n=141)	79.3 (n= 37)
Disruptive Conflict Between Siblings	37.2 (n=261)	47.5 (n=274)	60.3 (n=146)	83.7 (n= 37)
Disruptive Conflict Among Other Extended Family Members	45.9 (n=265)	74.0 (n=296)	76.3 (n=139)	94.1 (n= 34)
Social Isolation	57.0 (n=286)	64.5 (n=324)	73.0 (n=152)	75.0 (n= 40)
Substance Abuse	52.9 (n=242)	56.1 (n=282)	63.2 (n=136)	71.1 (n= 38)
Disrupting Mental Illness	22.7 (n=242)	32.7 (n=276)	37.1 (n=124)	55.2 (n= 29)
Role Reversal	45.0 (n=274)	43.0 (n=302)	63.7 (n=154)	85.4 (N= 41)
Parents Powerless over Children	44.3 (n=289)	43.7 (n=307)	63.6 (n=154)	85.0 (n= 40)
Detachment Among Family Members	41.3 (n=275)	60.7 (n=310)	61.3 (n=142)	75.0 (n= 36)
Enmeshment Among Family Members	44.2 (n=260)	54.5 (n=297)	64.5 (n=141)	81.5 (n= 38)

Chapter 3

Understanding the Causes
of Maltreatment:
Individual Versus Social Factors

Resolving a social problem requires a minimal understanding of the personal and social conditions that either cause it or nurture its development. Over the past two decades, researchers have attempted to isolate those family-level and societal-level variables which individually or collectively predict child maltreatment. Such a finite list of causal factors provides clinicians and policy makers with a way to identify subsets of families and individuals "at risk" of maltreatment and a means of targeting intervention strategies to those aspects of family and social functioning which precipitate and maintain the cycle of maltreatment. The first of these objectives is critical for ensuring that public intervention into family life is focused primarily on those families least likely to provide adequately for the health and well-being of their children and for ensuring that public resources are targeted to those most in need. The second of these objectives seeks to ensure that resources are concentrated on the most effective interventions.

The efficient and effective use of public monies to combat child maltreatment are indeed worthwhile goals. Research studies that identify the correlates of maltreatment can offer practitioners clear guidance in better selecting specific prevention and treatment strategies. However, such research efforts cannot predict with any degree of certainty who will abuse or neglect their children. While a "theoretical" at-risk population has been identified, no existing methodology can correctly classify all individuals or families into a maltreating or nonmaltreating group. Cases of severe maltreatment continue to surface among so-called normal families and supportive and nurturing parenting is found among families with minimal emotional and financial resources. Despite the limitations of these causal models, they are a necessary step in designing effective practice for as diverse a problem as child maltreatment.

Theories of Maltreatment with Respect to Subpopulations

Parents mistreat their children for a variety of reasons and with a variety of outcomes. While the specific events leading up to and immediately preceding an abusive episode are unique in each case, broad causal theories have been used to explain the general relationship between specific individual or environmental conditions and the abuse or neglect of children. The theories most commonly found in the literature range from interpersonal functioning theories, such as psychodynamic and learning theories, to systemic and social explanations for maltreatment, as suggested by theories of stress and poverty (Newberger and Newberger, 1982). For purposes of developing more appropriate treatment and prevention strategies, most of these theories can be classified into three groups:

> *psychodynamic theories*—suggest that parents would be less abusive if they better understood themselves and their role as parents;
>
> *learning theories*—suggest that parents would be less abusive if they knew, more specifically, how best to care for their children; and
>
> *environmental theories*—suggest that parents would be less abusive if they had greater resources available to them in terms of material support or social support for a given set of actions.

Individually, each of these theoretical assumptions is intuitively appealing in its capacity both to explain why maltreatment occurs and to suggest specific interventions. Table 3.1 summarizes the attributes frequently cited under each of these causal models as being associated with a higher likelihood for maltreatment and their service implications. As this table indicates, each area presents a unique slant on maltreatment and suggests very different methods for addressing the problem.

Psychodynamic theories place a heavy emphasis on the parent's level of functioning in explaining abusive or neglectful behavior. Individuals with diminished capacity due to developmental disabilities or substance dependency or abuse are less able, all things being equal, to adequately care for their children than individuals without these functional limitations. It is logical to assume that individuals who have difficulty managing their personal choices and emotions would find it difficult, if not impossible, to manage and care for children, particularly if the children were unusually demanding or needy. While these individuals may have an adequate understanding of appropriate parenting skills, they lack the personal capacity to implement these skills in a consistent and effective manner. Similarly, individuals suffering from severe or even relatively moderate psychological

Table 3.1

Theories of Maltreatment:

Characteristics and Intervention Implications

Theories	Common Attributes Associated with Maltreatment	Intervention Implications
Psychodynamic	Psychopathology Alcoholism Drug abuse Mental retardation Poor attachment Low self-esteem Sadistic psychosis/violent personality	Therapeutic services: individual family group Placement of children Hospitalization
Learning/Behavioral	Lack of knowledge regarding discipline alternatives Lack of knowledge regarding child development Poor child care skills (e.g., supervision, nutrition, medical care) Lack of understanding of appropriate displays of affection Poor stress management skills	Parenting education classes Lay home visitor program Support groups Respite care
Environmental	Poverty Social isolation Racism Sexism Pornography Social tolerance of corporal punishment Unemployment	Public awareness Community action programs Systemic reform (health, education, welfare systems) Employment programs

disorders may be less able to cope with the unpredictable nature of children or the routine demands of child care. Of all the theoretical assumptions outlined in Table 3.1, the psychodynamic model has the broadest application across the four major types of maltreatment. In certain circumstances, a parent's psychopathology may be sufficient to produce severe physical abuse, sexual abuse, or emotional maltreatment. Other factors such as depression or low self-esteem may contribute to a chronic neglectful or abusive parenting pattern. Finally, certain conditions, particularly substance abuse, may reduce the natural inhibitions people may have which would stop them from severely mistreating or sexually abusing a child. If one accepts the relationship between interpersonal functioning problems and maltreatment, therapeutic services—either individual, family, or group—would be the most likely treatment modality adopted. While the focus of this therapy would differ depending upon the type and severity of the maltreatment, the primary treatment implication of this theory is consistent for all types of maltreatment: repair the damaged adult so that appropriate parenting can be realized.

In contrast, while still focusing on the parent's functioning, learning theory emphasizes the lack of skills and knowledge rather than poor psychological functioning. Under this model, abuse or neglect occurs because parents simply do not know how to care for their children or have a limited repertoire of discipline or child care techniques that are either harmful for or ineffective with their particular children. These adults may have a history of maltreatment as children or they may be too young or too inexperienced to comprehend what is expected of them as parents. The intuitive appeal of this model is that if parents can be trained or taught how to parent, the cycle of maltreatment could be broken through consistent intervention with all first-time parents. This set of assumptions is particularly appealing in cases of physical abuse and physical neglect where the definition of the problem has advanced to the identification of very specific inappropriate behaviors toward children. A lack of knowledge regarding alternatives to corporal punishment is associated with a higher likelihood of physical abuse, while a lack of basic knowledge regarding child development is associated with an increased risk of child neglect. Correct these and similar information gaps and these types of maltreatment can be eliminated or, at a minimum, significantly reduced. Providing parents with the information and skills necessary for effective and nonabusive parenting can occur in a variety of ways. Among the most common are parenting education classes, lay home visitor programs, and parent support groups. While the content of these services might vary depending upon the specific abusive or neglectful behavior being addressed, the treatment modality suggested by this theory is again consistent and remains one of providing or strengthening skills.

The final theoretical approach outlined in Table 3.1 moves the discussion away from a focus on individual characteristics and into the broader structural and cultural environments. Rather than viewing the reason for maltreatment as resting in a lack of motivation or skill on the part of the parent, this causal analysis focuses on the potentially dominant role of certain societal conditions and values. Poverty with its corresponding limits on personal choice and societal values that condone violence, racism, and sexism are forces that often overwhelm the limited resistance of families who find themselves trapped in a cycle of distress. Depending upon the type of abuse in question, the social features that contribute to the problem differ but the direction and intensity of the impacts remain. While poverty and a lack of material resources and service options are frequently associated with an increased likelihood of child neglect, a positive attitude toward corporal punishment is more likely a precondition of physical abuse. Although this is currently the subject of professional debate, at least some public officials and researchers identify a strong correlation, if not a causal relationship, between pornography and sexual violence toward women and children. As one might expect, the intervention model emerging from this theory seeks changes within communities and value systems rather than within individuals. Attacking the underlying causes of maltreatment under this theoretical assumption requires changes in social attitudes and practices. In addition to broad-scale public awareness campaigns to clarify the relationship between certain societal norms and potential maltreatment, proponents of this approach support policy changes to reduce the level of poverty or at a minimum remediate its negative consequences. Improvements in housing, health care systems, and educational services, as well as increased access to job training and employment opportunities are among the strategies frequently promoted within the context of an environmental explanation for maltreatment.

None of these three theoretical approaches is incorrect in its explanation of maltreatment; none, however, can adequately explain on its own the entire riddle of maltreatment. Even the division of the problem into distinct subpopulations has not eliminated the need to consider social as well as individual causal arguments. Historically, practitioners and researchers alike have recognized the need to look across disciplines and theoretical assumptions to understand the causal factors of maltreatment. Helfer (1973) identified a three-part etiology of child abuse, citing three necessary conditions for abuse: potential for abuse in the parents, a special kind of child, and a crisis or series of crises. Refining this concept, Green and colleagues (1974) developed specific indicators under each of these three broad categories, noting that any combination of risk factors could be potentially explosive depending upon the strength of the parents and the severity of the environmental stress that they face. This three-part etiology scheme developed by these early researchers was a clear indication that understanding maltreatment would require looking beyond the immediate and functional characteristics of individual family members.

Integrating the interpersonal characteristics of a family with the social realities surrounding it is a key concept of the ecological perspective advocated by Garbarino, among others. These theorists focus not merely on the functioning of individuals and the functioning of society, but rather on the interaction of the two spheres and the impact of these interactions on children (Garbarino, 1977; Germain, 1978; Bronfenbrenner, 1979). In an attempt to bring a hierarchical order to the different causes of maltreatment, it may be important to distinguish between sufficient causes and necessary causes, although such a distinction may be difficult to determine with any degree of uniformity. For example Garbarino (1977) suggests that the necessary or enabling conditions for maltreatment are a cultural justification for the use of force and isolation from potent family or community support systems. Within this context, parents facing a particularly stressful situation (e.g., loss of employment) may abuse their children not so much because of the frustration associated with unemployment, but rather because of a lack of social and personal supports to buffer the impact of this loss on their relationship with their children. While the sufficient and necessary causal model is useful for identifying the interplay between social and personal strengths and weaknesses in explaining eventual abuse or neglect, the model offers little guidance in setting treatment priorities. Given the above example, would the emphasis be on teaching parents better stress management techniques, reducing their level of social isolation, or changing public opinion regarding corporal punishment? Even successful remediation of the so-called necessary conditions may not reduce the actual level of physical abuse in the family if the parent's stress management skills are extremely limited.

The roots of maltreatment most assuredly lie both within the character of parents and in the character of the community and socity in which they live. The research challenge has been to identify those specific factors that individually or in concert with each other significantly increase a family's likelihood for maltreatment. Only when personal and social factors are jointly assessed can effective intervention be achieved. Until recently, greatest attention has been given to identifying the characteristics of parents that make them particularly likely to behave abusively. As outlined below, prior abuse as a child, low self-esteem, social isolation, rigidity, drug or alcohol dependency, and mental deficiencies are considered among the primary contributors to maltreatment. While not blaming the victim for the maltreatment, such research generally supports our initial two hypotheses: parents with these or similar characteristics are less able to respond to problematic children or to problematic living situations or events in a nonabusive or nonneglectful manner. This research tends to minimize the unique contribution of environmental and stress factors, suggesting that these variables are significant only in combination with interpersonal problems.

In contrast, a growing body of literature is emerging which stresses the unique and perhaps overriding influence of poverty and culturally approved forms of maltreatment such as corporal punishment. These authors suggest that poverty itself and the lack of material resources and sense of powerlessness it brings are the true culprits in understanding the so-called character disorders in parents and children which precipitate maltreatment. Instead of targeting treatment and prevention services to particular character disorders, these authors suggest that the more fruitful and logical point of intervention is poverty itself and the cultural norms that support societal violence and abusive behaviors.

The remainder of this chapter summarizes both sets of literature, highlighting the specific causal factors underlying maltreatment suggested by these two perspectives. Regardless of one's viewpoint on the potential universality of maltreatment or on its ability to be isolated for the most part to a limited number of socioeconomic groups, both sides of the debate raise a number of dilemmas central to efficient and effective service planning.

Client-Level Characteristics—Targeting the Individual

The parental characteristics identified as contributing to a higher likelihood for maltreatment range from severe psychological disorders, to an inability to manage stress properly, to poor parenting skills. For children, the high-risk characteristics often cited include premature birth, physical or developmental disabilities, and hyperactivity. In addition, households headed by single parents, families with limited financial resources, and families facing significant stress due to tenuous employment, loss of housing, chronic health problems or marital difficulties face a higher-than-average risk for maltreatment. The vast range and number of parents, children, and families represented by these groups suggests a very broad target population, identifying a significant proportion of the population at risk of abuse or neglect.

While the potential for maltreatment may indeed rest in all of us, the reality is that not all parents with these characteristics, or even a majority of them, maltreat their children. Faced with this reality, researchers have sought to identify the combination of variables that will trigger abusive behavior on the part of potentially able parents. Conclusions regarding these causal correlates of maltreatment are generally based upon studies with relatively limited samples drawn from the caseloads of local protective service agencies. When comparison groups are used, they are generally drawn from AFDC caseloads or from hospital emergency room records. As such, it is unclear whether the characteristics cited in these findings are indicators of high-risk populations or indicators of families likely to be on public assistance or to utilize emergency medical care for their children. Despite these potential methodological problems, the findings from such studies are useful for defining at-risk populations and identifying specific variables correlated with reported cases of child abuse and neglect.

Severely disturbed and psychotic individuals are found on the rolls of protective service caseloads and cut across all types of maltreatment. Although such individuals generally constitute no more than 10% of all cases (Green, 1976; Kempe and Kempe, 1978), the outlook for their families is rather dim; their children are usually permanently removed from the home and parental rights are terminated.[1] "For the severely disturbed parents who were themselves abused with little or no parenting during their first years of life," noted one researcher, "there is little hope of helping them improve their parenting capacity" (Burland et al., 1973:590).

Although not psychotic, the majority of maltreating families experience a wide range of personal disorders and a high degree of internal conflict. Reporting on the most dominant characteristics of a sample of 48 sexually abusive families served by Baltimore's Department of Social Services, for example, Sever and colleagues (1982) noted a high degree of internal conflict. Among the problems presented by these families were alcohol abuse (71%), multiple victims in the families (61%), physical child abuse (56%), spousal abuse (42%), previous criminal behavior (33%), parental history of sexual abuse (33%), drug abuse (31%), prior use of the foster care system on either a voluntary or court-ordered basis (23%), and incidences of sexual assault by multiple perpetrators (23%). Focusing on the psychological profiles of physically abusive parents, Olson (1976) found similar characteristics including an unusually high percentage of rigid or authoritarian personalities, individuals with drug or alcohol dependency, and individuals suffering from neurosis, mental deficiency, and/or emotional immaturity. When individuals with these types of characteristics have premature infants, infants with low birth weights, or infants who exhibit certain behavioral problems such as poor eating or sleeping habits, the risk for maltreatment becomes even higher (Klein and Stern, 1971; Baldwin and Oliver, 1975; Herrenkohl and Herrenkohl, 1979).

In addition to viewing the emotional and material resources of families as critical to effective parenting, intellectual capacity has also been targeted for research. Mentally retarded individuals have been cited as a uniformly high-risk group for maltreatment. Reviewing 14 studies on this population, Schilling and colleagues (1982) noted that all but one of these efforts found mentally retarded parents either unsatisfactory parents or overrepresented in child abuse and neglect samples. Although critical of these studies for their limited samples, lack of control groups, and inadequate measurement of the critical variables of IQ, parenting skills, and child maltreatment, the authors concluded that on some intuitive basis one would have to admit that mentally retarded individuals will bring fewer resources to the parenting process. While mentally retarded individuals may begin with fewer resources in these areas, it is not necessarily true that their children always will receive less attention or good parenting than the children of nonretarded parents. In a certain respect, one might argue that mild to moderate mentally retarded parents may be an easier population to target for services in that their needs, at least some of them, are clearly defined and amenable to intervention. Such is not always the case with the parent who has "normal" intellectual capacities.

Divorce and remarriage also have been studied as a potential risk factor for maltreatment, particularly sexual abuse. Several researchers have noted that children in stepparent families, particularly stepfather families, showed a higher incidence of sexual victimization as well as other forms of maltreatment (Burgess et al., 1981; Russell, 1984). Others have noted more complex results with respect to the role of stepparents. For example, Finkelhor (1979) noted that children living with a stepparent were twice as likely to have been identified by their parents as victims of sexual assault as children not living with stepparents (17% versus 8%). However, only one of the victimized children had been victimized by any kind of parent, suggesting that the increased risk of maltreatment rests not with the stepparent per se, but with the condition of changing households and family membership. Further, in her assessments of a small clinical sample of sexual abuse perpetrators and victims, Phelan (1986) noted that those cases which involved stepfathers were significantly less likely to involve full intercourse than those cases involving the victim's biological father. Overall, 54% of the biological fathers had had intercourse with their daughters, a feature in only 27% of the stepparent cases. Considering all potential victims in the family (i.e., all daughters living in the household), Phelan found that the biological fathers has assaulted 82% of all available daughters and the stepfathers had assaulted 70%.

Finally, of all the causal factors of maltreatment identified in the literature, the childhood abuse of the parent is perhaps the factor most consistently cited. Beginning with Kempe's initial work and continuing through more recent studies, researchers have found that sizable numbers of abusive parents were themselves victims of child abuse and neglect (Delsordo, 1963; Fontana, 1968; Silver et al., 1969; Gil, 1970; Steel and Pollack, 1971; Burland et al. 1973; Helfer, 1975). Similar to these studies, retrospective studies have also been conducted on violent adult and juvenile offenders. In the vast majority of these cases, males convicted of serious violent crimes have a history of being the victims of or observing parental violence (Coleman, 1980; Rosenbaum and O'Leary, 1981; Kratcoski, 1982). Commenting on the theory of intergenerational abuse, Kadushin (1980) has noted that the idea has achieved the status of an axiom. "The idea of intergenerational abuse is theoretically attractive," he writes, "not only because it is consistent with learning, modeling and socialization concepts, but because it permits the social worker to approach the parent with a greater feeling of acceptance" (Kadushin, 1980:179).

A potential intergenerational transfer of violence can occur not only from children being actual victims of abuse, but also as a result of observing violence either in their own homes or on television. Child development specialists have warned that children model the behavior they see around

them, particularly if they identify with the perpetrator. For example, physically abusive behavior by one's father, siblings, or a television character
with whom the child identifies is more likely to lead to a replication of this
behavior than if the offender is not someone with whom the child can
readily identify (Eron et al., 1983). Further, children in families where
spouse abuse is present suffer a variety of psychological problems not unlike those noted among physically and emotionally abused children. These
include delayed learning, language and gross motor skills, as well as increased agressive behavior (Moore et al., 1981; Westra and Martin, 1981).

Despite the theoretical and clinical utility of these concepts, the validity
and the strength of a "cycle of maltreatment" or a "cycle of violence" is
under question. The evidence upon which this theory is based lacks adequate control samples and runs a significant risk of error. No evidence
exists to suggest that a larger proportion of maltreated children versus non-
maltreated children grow up to become abusive parents. At least one 40-
year longitudinal study involving 232 males found that subjects who were
abused, neglected, or rejected as children had higher rates of juvenile and
adult criminal behavior and mental health problems than those individuals
identified as coming from "loving" families. The study found no significant differences among the groups, however, in terms of the use of physical punishment with their children (McCord, 1983). Similar findings have
been noted by others who have conducted both prospective and retrospective studies on abusive populations (Hunter and Kilstrom, 1979; Miller and
Challas, 1981). Until more longitudinal studies are conducted on the current generation of maltreated children or until sufficient samples of abused
children who did not become abusive parents are identified and studied,
the field will make less progress than is needed to truly unravel the trans-
ferability of abusive behavior across generations and the ability of current
treatment efforts to break this cycle (Cicchetti and Rizley, 1981).

Client Characteristics by Subpopulation

As might be anticipated, individual risk factors have different predictive
strength across the various maltreatment subpopulations. The National
Clinical Evaluation Study provided a unique opportunity to compare the
patterns of presenting problems exhibited by families involved in various
forms of maltreatment. Table 3.2 summarizes the extent to which each of
the presenting problems assessed in that national data collection system
were noted among the adult clients who exhibited different primary types
of maltreatment. As this table indicates, certain of the presenting problems
were consistent across all subpopulations. For example, roughly equal percentages of cases involved in the four major primary types of maltreatment
and who were classified as "at risk" of abusive or neglectful behaviors demonstrated a lack of knowledge regarding child development, an inaccurate

Table 3.2

Percentage of Adult Clients with Various

Presenting Problems by Primary Type of Abuse

Presenting Problem	Emotional Maltreat- ment	Neglect	Physical Abuse	Sexual Abuse	High Risk
Lack of Knowledge Regarding Child Development	80.3	92.1	87.0	90.0	92.2
Inaccurate Sense of Child's Needs	97.4	93.2	93.0	94.3	92.1
Excessive Need for Child to Obey	78.3	53.5	84.9	72.0	56.9
Role Reversal	67.7	43.2	52.5	76.7	41.3
Inability to Manage Household	69.2	80.5	73.8	58.9	79.0
Inability to Manage Anger	89.1	68.3	93.7	82.6	73.8
Sexual Performance Problem[a]	60.0	40.8	37.5	76.7	52.6
Low Self-esteem	89.4	84.4	80.0	94.5	86.7
Disruptive Mental Illness	26.4	24.7	24.4	8.4	36.2
n =	241	292	135	156	426

[a]Clinicians made an assessment with regard to this particular functioning problem in only 25% of all cases, suggesting caution in interpreting these percentages.

sense of the child's needs, and low self-esteem. In contrast, excessive need on the part of the adult to have the child obey all commands and an inability of the adult to manage anger properly were more frequently found among adults whose primary form of maltreatment was physical abuse. Similarly, those adults primarily involved in child neglect were more likely to demonstrate an inability to manage household and child-rearing tasks, but were less likely to demonstrate an excessive need for the child to obey commands or to be involved in instances of role reversal. Finally, adults involved primarily in sexual abuse were more likely than those involved in other forms of maltreatment to place inappropriate caretaking roles on their children and to have sexual performance problems. In contrast to the neglect families, fewer adults in these families had difficulty managing their households. Those adults who were identified as high-risk cases were as likely as the adults involved in actual maltreatment to demonstrate a number of the presenting problems assessed at intake. Only the excessive need for the child to obey commands and role reversal were noted with less frequency for this subpopulation.

In addition to the individual differences across the key maltreatment subpopulations identified in this national study, group differences were also noted in family functioning. As indicated in Table 3.3, families whose primary type of maltreatment was emotional maltreatment were more likely than other families within the sample to exhibit sibling violence and disruptive conflict and to have parents who felt powerless over their children. These families were also among the most isolated and the most enmeshed. In contrast to the other families on the caseload, those involved primarily in emotional maltreatment showed a higher rate of substance abuse and disruptive mental illness. Families involved in sexual abuse also demonstrated a high reported rate of internal, family functioning problems including disruptive conflict and detachment between spouses, sexual performance problems, and family situations in which children were pressured to take care of the parents' emotional needs and overall household management. As might be expected, virtually all of the families primarily involved in child neglect had financial difficulties and families primarily involved in physical abuse showed the highest rates of physical violence between adults and disruptive conflict among extended family members. These patterns tend to support the thesis underlying the development of specialized treatment programs. Families engaged in different patterns of maltreatment do have unique family dynamics and responses to external stresses and pressures.

Again, similarities across all groups were also noted. One of the dominant presenting problems cutting across all forms of maltreatment was social isolation, long considered one of the significant problems associated with maltreatment. As indicated in Table 3.3, over 60% of families in each of the identified subpopulations exhibited some degree of social isolation at intake. Further analysis of these data found that social isolation was documented among families in all income categories, attesting to the consistent presence of this problem. Whether this issue can be considered a cause of maltreatment or merely a personality characteristic of the types of families who, in addition to being isolated, also abuse or neglect their children is a question of interest to many in the field. Reviewing empirical studies on the relationship between social supports and child maltreatment, Seagull found little compelling evidence that social isolation caused or contributed to an increased risk of maltreatment. While she noted somewhat stronger evidence for a direct relationship between a lack of informal social support networks and child neglect than with cases of physical abuse, she questioned the utility of focusing too heavily on the development of a family's supportive network of family, friends, and service agencies in confronting child abuse (Seagull, 1987). As noted in Chapter 4, expanding social supports is most successful when coupled with additional

Table 3.3

Frequency of Various Family Problems

by Primary Type of Maltreatment

Problem	Emotional Maltreat- ment	Neglect	Physical Abuse	Sexual Abuse	High Risk
Financial Difficulties	75.0% (n=144)	96.1% (n=224)	77.4% (n=96)	70.5% (n=165)	76.2% (n=32)
Physical Violence Between Adult Spouses/Partners	39.5 (n=51)	47.5 (n=76	47.4 (n=45)	37.1 (n=69)	42.9 (n=12)
Disruptive Conflict Between Adult Spouses/Partners	75.0 (n=105)	66.7 (n=118)	75.3 (n=73)	77.8 (n=158)	71.0 (n=22)
Detachment Between Adult Spouses	55.0 (n=71)	49.1 (n=78)	34.5 (n=54)	65.1 (n=125)	54.8 (n=17)
Enmeshment Between Adult Spouses	58.4 (n=73)	39.1 (n=59)	59.6 (n=53)	60.2 (n=109)	37.5 (n=12)
Sexual Performance Problems	54.4 (n=31)	34.5 (n=20)	50.0 9n=19)	66.0 (n=62)	42.9 (n=6)
Physical Violence Between Siblings	43.5 (n=67)	23.5 (n=43)	31.7 (n=32)	19.9 (n=40)	14.3 (n=3)
Disruptive Conflict Between Siblings	59.5 (n=94)	30.3 (n=54)	54.9 (n=56)	50.5 (n=104)	23.8 (n=5)
Disruptive Conflict Among Other Extended Family Members	74.3 (n=124)	65.0 (n=130)	78.9 (n=86)	63.1 (n=128)	78.4 (n=29)
Social Isolation	72.8 (n=131)	61.6 (n=141)	68.5 (n=76)	63.3 (n=140)	65.1 (n=28)
Substance Abuse	60.8 (n=96)	53.2 (n=108)	57.6 (n=53)	49.5 (n=94)	38.9 (n=14)
Disrupting Mental Illness	42.6 (n=63)	31.8 (n=64)	34.1 (n=30)	13.5 (n=26)	50.0 (n=17)
Role Reversal	58.0 (n=101)	36.6 (n=75)	44.1 (n=49)	62.9 (n=141)	28.2 (n=11)
Parents Powerless over Children	71.6 (n=131)	44.2 (n=95)	55.8 (n=67)	55.1 (n=125)	33.3 (n=14)
Detachment Among Family Members	61.9 (n=109)	48.5 (n=100)	69.6 (n=78)	59.0 (n=124)	65.7 (n=23)
Enmeshment Among Family Members	66.7 (n=110)	40.1 (n=83)	54.6 (n=59)	58.2 (n=117)	39.4 (n=13)

services which address the specific knowledge gaps and functioning problems exhibited by maltreating families.

In addition to highlighting the different functioning problems which existed among families with different primary types of maltreatment, the data presented in Table 3.2 and 3.3 also noted a surprisingly high frequency of presenting problems among so-called "high-risk" families or adults. While these cases were slightly less likely to exhibit such functioning problems as enmeshment between spouses, substance abuse, role reversal, and a powerlessness over their children, they were just as likely as the maltreating families to have financial difficulties, to exhibit physical violence and disruptive conflict between spouses and extended family members, to have problems with social isolation, and to include family members with disruptive mental illnesses. These similarities suggest that child abuse and neglect prevention programs which target their services to "high-risk" populations may be serving as troubled and difficult a population as those programs targeted toward actual maltreators. By the time families have moved into a "high-risk" classification, they may have already established behavior patterns and developed functioning difficulties which may make efforts to prevent maltreatment extremely difficult.

Predicting Maltreatment Based on Client Characteristics

The factors contributing to maltreatment cited above have been identified by observing and analyzing maltreating populations. In order to determine if any of these factors can be considered as *causal explanations* of abuse or neglect, it is important to compare the profiles of abusive parents to the profiles of nonabusive parents and to assess the extent to which these models accurately predict future maltreatment. Efforts in this area have generally drawn their comparison samples from AFDC caseloads or other populations which control for certain socioeconomic variables and, to a certain degree, the stressful aspects of rearing children with limited financial resources. Studies that have been conducted in such a manner have concluded that abusive or neglectful parents do indeed have, on average, lower self-esteem, less confidence in their child-rearing abilities, and fewer realistic life goals than poor, nonabusive parents.[2]

While the majority of research in this area has focused solely on the psychological differences between abusive and nonabusive parents, some comparison studies have expanded the analyses to include both the family's characteristics and service history. In assessing the relative importance of social disorganization and the range of social services available to the family in distinguishing among abusive and nonabusive welfare clients in a rural North Carolina county, Ory and Earp (1980) found social disorganization to have strong predictive capabilities. Their specific social disorganization scale, which included both personal characteristics (e.g., mental health problems, mental retardation, and drug or alcohol dependency) and familial-social characteristics (e.g., stability of the family unit, membership in local community organizations, incidence of family violence, and social isolation), explained almost one-third of the variance between maltreating and nonmaltreating populations. Receipt of services prior to the maltreating incident or within one year of the study period and the mother's educational level collectively explained another quarter of the variance. The mother's age and family structure (i.e., single- or two-parent families), while included in the model, had virtually no independent explanatory power.[3]

One of the best researched and most widely implemented child abuse assessment tools is the Child Abuse Potential (CAP) Inventory developed by Joel Milner (1980). Drawing on those behavioral and situational predictors most frequently cited in the literature, the author's initial inventory consisted of 334 items. A preliminary evaluation of the inventory with a small and relatively homogeneous sample (i.e., rural North Carolina social service clients) found that the inventory correctly classified all respondents and that 25 of the 334 items accounted for 99% of the variance in the average scores recorded by the 19 identified abusers and the 19 matched nonabusers (Milner and Wimberly, 1979). Overall, the authors combined these items into four strong discriminant factors:

loneliness (feelings of being alone, unloved, or neglected, etc.);

rigidity (fears of failure, compulsive housekeeping, etc.);

problems with self-image, family, and friends (sexual satisfaction, physical ailments, lack of friends, etc.); and

lack of social skills and self-control.

Of these four factors, rigidity and problems with self-image were the strongest indicators of potential maltreatment.

Based on the findings generated by this research as well as subsequent assessments of the measurement scale, the inventory was reduced to 160 items and tested again for validity on a sample of 130 parents, 65 of whom were identified abusers and 65 of whom were matched nonabusing subjects. Again, the inventory proved to have strong discriminant ability, correctly classifying 96% of all respondents. Overall, 77 of the items in the revised scale were found to have significant discriminant power and to represent seven underlying constructs: distress, rigidity, having a problem or difficult child, having difficulties with other family members, general unhappiness, loneliness, and having negative concepts of the child or oneself (Milner, 1980).

Repeated testing of the CAP Inventory has produced similar results with respect to its discriminatory powers and suggests that the inventory is particularly useful as a preliminary screening tool in situations where the individuals have been identified as at risk based upon other criteria such as clinical interviews, direct observations, and the application of other standardized tests. The author has consistently cautioned professionals who use the instrument, however, not to base clinical decisions, such as the labeling of a family as abusive or taking a child into protective custody, solely upon an individual's inventory score, noting that insufficient data exist as to the instrument's predictive strength (Milner, 1980).

While these studies were successful in using descriptive and functional variables in differentiating between maltreators and nonmaltreators, most attempts at this type of distinction have produced more mixed results. Gaines (1978) explored the relationship of three areas of functioning including the personality characteristics of the parents, children "at risk" due to preexisting health-related problems, and environmental stress. Using standard scales in all areas,[4] he attempted to explain the variance among 80 mothers, representing equal numbers of abusive mothers, neglectful mothers, and nonabusive mothers. Collectively, these measures left 88% of the variance *unexplained* and allowed for the correct classification of only 15% more of the sample than might have been achieved through chance alone. Of the three factors included in the analysis, environmental stress contributed the most explanatory power, with the child's characteristics offering *no* independent explanatory power.

In a predictive study, Altemeier and his colleagues (1982) interviewed 1,400 low-income mothers receiving services from a prenatal clinic to obtain baseline data on the circumstances surrounding the pregnancy, on the mother's childhood and social support system, and on the mother's functional and emotional status. This information was then used to identify those women considered to be potential maltreators. The specific areas used to identify those at greatest risk for maltreatment were knowledge of child development, childhood nurturing, self-image, level of support available from others, parenting skills, attitudes about the pregnancy, health-related stress, and family life stress. Of all the women interviewed, 23 (1.7%) were reported for child abuse or neglect within two years of the baseline period. During the first nine months of the study, the research team had correctly predicted abuse in six of the seven reported cases, for a prediction rate of 86%. However, the research team's predictive abilities steadily declined over the remainder of the two-year period, with the team correctly classifying only nine of the additional 16 cases reported between the tenth and twenty-fourth month.

While the maltreating mothers were not significantly different from the nonmaltreating sample on such factors as age, race, educational background, social isolation, substance abuse history, or expectations regarding child development, a number of significant differences were noted. These differences included an increased incidence of having lost another child to the foster care system, having been in foster care themselves as a child, having demonstrated aggressive behavior, having had negative feelings regarding the pregnancy, and having had more children closer together. The utility of this study is hampered by the fact that the researchers relied upon reported cases of maltreatment for confirming their predictive abilities. The quality of parenting within those families not reported for maltreatment was assumed to be adequate, an assumption which may not have been valid. However, the steady drop in the researchers' ability to predict abuse with the types of variables they were utilizing suggests that even if more careful observations of expectant mothers were adopted by physicians and other health care providers, only a fraction of potential abusive or neglectful mothers could be identified. Variables such as the mother's attitudes toward her pregnancy or her expectations of motherhood become less useful over time. As the child matures, abuse may be determined more by the quality of the interactions between the parent and child than by any preconceived notions of parenting held by the mother before birth (Cameron, 1977, 1978).

Although they did not include data on the child's behavior or psychological profiles of the parents, Straus and his colleagues (1980) conducted a discriminant analysis to identify those items most highly associated with child physical abuse in their random sample of 2,143 American families. These factors, many of which have been cited by other researchers as contributing to an increased likelihood for maltreatment, included:

> verbal aggression toward the child;
>
> above average conflict between spouses;
>
> the husband being physically violent and/or verbally aggressive toward his wife;
>
> the husband's employment as a manual worker;
>
> the husband's dissatisfaction with the family's standard of living;
>
> the wife's employment as a manual worker;
>
> the wife being 30 years of age or younger;
>
> the wife having experienced physical punishment by her father after she turned 13;
>
> two or more children in the family;
>
> the wife's status as a full-time homemaker;
>
> the couple being married for less than ten years;
>
> the family residing at its current residence for less than ten years;
>
> the father lacking any memberships in social or work-related organizations;
>
> the husband having been physically punished by his mother after age 13; and
>
> the husband growing up in a family where the mother was physically abused by her spouse.

In Straus's sample, the families were assigned one point for each of the above characteristics they demonstrated. They scored an average of 5.54 points, with two families scoring 0 and the highest score being 14. While this scale showed good predictive power in identifying spousal abuse among the sample families, only 30% of the parents scoring ten or more points on this scale physically abused their children. In other words, over two-thirds of the families with ten or more of the characteristics cited above had not physically abused their children during the study period.

Reflecting on their findings, the authors drew two conclusions. First, they saw the poor correlation between these so-called causal correlates and actual abuse as indicating that the field "has a long way to go in pinpointing the causes of child abuse" (Straus et al., 1980:219). While the authors noted that additional information on the characteristics of the child and the nature of the parent-child interactions within the family would certainly have improved the scale's predictive power, they suspect that even with these improvements wide variation between theoretical abusers and actual abusers would still exist. Second, the authors cautioned case workers against using such a checklist to target interventions to so-called "high-risk families." "Tempting as the possibility may be," they wrote, "any potential gains in preventing child abuse have to be weighed against the costs and potential dangers. An attempt to use these checklists to locate high-risk parents could create an intrusive system of family surveillance" (Straus et al, 1980:219). In a society such as the United States, which places a high value on the privacy of family life and the individual pursuit of well-being, explicit surveillance systems are not an option many policy makers would openly support even if the intent of the system had such a laudable goal as protecting children.[5]

Societal Characteristics—Targeting the System

From the first public hearings to define the nature and scope of child abuse and neglect legislation, child maltreatment has been viewed as classless, with its potential existing in a broad array of American families. Child abuse was not viewed as a function of poverty nor as a disorder limited to a particular social class or culture. The questioning of David Gil by then-Senator Walter Mondale at the 1973 Senate hearings on the Child Abuse Prevention and Treatment Act was most revealing of this preference. Invoking the public scrutiny argument, Mondale pressed hard to establish that child abuse "is not a poverty problem." "It seemed," noted one author, "that the Senator wished to avoid treating child abuse as another manifestation of poverty out of a concern that the poverty issue had lost its political appeal" (Patti, 1976, as quoted in Pelton, 1981:32). Political realities aside, the preference for viewing child maltreatment as universal was rooted in existing empirical evidence generated by the field's earliest studies. The potential of maltreatment was classless or universal because the majority of the interpersonal features and certain environmental stresses believed to cause or trigger abuse or neglect could occur in any family at any time.

More recently, however, some are questioning the strength of this causal argument and suggest that perpetuating the notion that flaws in the individual parent, child, or household result in maltreatment absolves society from accepting collective responsibility for the well-being of all its children. Rather than focusing solely on the functioning of the family, it has been suggested that the quest for causal explanations of maltreatment be broadened to include abusive societal conditions. The continued focus on the family as the only arena in which maltreatment occurs creates a distorted sense of priorities and a "convenient smoke screen" which disguises the nature, scope, and dynamics of child abuse (Gil, 1981:294).

When this "smoke screen" is attacked directly, a number of issues have been identified as suggesting a unique causal relationship between poverty and maltreatment (Pelton, 1981). While possible bias in the current reporting system may account for some overrepresentation of the poor among cases of maltreatment, other evidence is less easily dismissed. For example, among the poor families reported for abuse or neglect, the confirmed incidence rate is highest among the very poor. Also, the vast majority of fatalities (over 80% in one study cited) occur among the very poor. Finally, violent crimes have historically been more predominant among lower socioeconomic groups, suggesting that child abuse may well follow a similar pattern. Commenting on the predominance of the myth that child abuse is "classless," Pelton, among others, has argued that the myth "supports the prestigious and fascinating psychodynamic medical model approach and by disassociating the problem from poverty, accords distinct and separate status to child abuse and neglect specialists" (Pelton, 1981:32). He goes on to note that, while the "universal potential for maltreatment" argument has the effect of generating more resources for the problem, in that politicians are more likely to fund programs to aid a broad array of families rather than solely welfare mothers, the myth has resulted in the development of treatment strategies and causal models that stress psychological factors rather than systemic defects or stress.

The Poverty Argument in Terms of Subpopulations

Empirical evidence of the unique role of poverty as a causal factor of both maltreatment and the developmental delays experienced by its victims is growing. For example, Wolock and Horowitz (1979) compared demographic and social characteristics of 380 abusive and neglectful families to 143 nonabusing AFDC recipients. Using discriminant analysis to distinguish the maltreators from the control group, the authors found that the number of children in the family, the social and material quality of the parent's childhood, the family's current material circumstances, and the family's degree of isolation were the strongest predictors in classifying the two groups. While these factors had only moderate predictive strength in differentiating between the maltreating poor and the nonmaltreating poor, they do suggest that the poorest of the poor are more likely to maltreat their children. This pattern was strongest for the families involved in child neglect or a combination of neglect and physical abuse. In contrast, the families who exhibited physical abuse (only 7% of the total maltreating sample) consistently showed greater similarity to the study's control group. These findings led the authors to conclude that neglect, the most common form of maltreatment reported in the United States, is not a classless issue but rather very much associated with poverty. Calling for a "fundamental realignment" of public priorities aimed at attacking the social, political, and economic bases of maintaining a large proportion of families at subsistence level, the authors suggested the most fruitful avenues to pursue in treating and preventing child neglect were "guaranteed employment, guaranteed income and a nationwide system of universal health care" (Wolock and Horowitz, 1979:191).

Elmer approached the correlation between poverty and maltreatment from a slightly different angle. Following up on her earlier study of 17 pairs of abused children and accident children matched with nonhospitalized controls on age, race, sex, and low socioeconomic status, she concluded that lower class status may be as potent a factor as abuse for retarding a child's development (Elmer, 1977). At the time of the follow-up interview, the abused children were no worse off than those children who had been hospitalized for accidental injury or than those children in the control group. All three groups of poor children showed poor language skills, with 58% of the children demonstrating some emotional disturbances. In addition, the examiners in Elmer's study, all of whom had no knowledge of the specific group to which each child they interviewed belonged, kept independent tallies of whether they thought a child had been abused, had suffered an accidental injury, or was a control group participant. In no case were these judgments more accurate than if the reviewers had randomly assigned the children to one of the three groups. In short, neither individual clinicians nor group assessment could differentiate, over time, the victims of maltreatment and poverty from the victims of poverty alone.

Despite the intuitive strength of the poverty argument, the fact remains that abusive and neglectful behaviors do not occur in all poor families. The very existence of low-income, nonmaltreating controls in the studies cited above attests to this fact. Exploring this further, Giovannoni and Billingsley (1970) looked at 186 poor families, representing three ethnic groups (i.e., blacks, whites, and Spanish-speaking) and three parenting conditions within each ethnic group (i.e., adequate, potentially neglectful, and neglectful). This two-tiered sampling strategy was used to determine the extent to which such variables as family structure, childbearing patterns, kinship patterns, knowledge of community services, and support systems explained the parenting level of mothers within or across different ethnic groups. While the neglectful mothers in all three ethnic groups were identified as among the poorest of the families in the sample, these poor mothers also shared other features not related to income. These included a higher number of children, higher incidence of marital disruptions, greater social isolation from either relatives and friends or existing community support systems, and a higher number of single mothers. In addition, the significant or discriminating characteristics of the maltreating mothers differed within each of the three ethnic groups studied.[6] One conclusion to be drawn from this study is that, while povery may well be fertile ground for abuse or neglect tendencies to mature, a great deal of variability exists within the poverty population. Ignoring these demographic, ethnic, and functional variations may well lead to faulty conclusions regarding the underlying causes of maltreatment and the most effective interventions.

In addition to ignoring key variations among those living below the poverty line, an overemphasis on poverty in explaining the abuse or neglect of children is problematic for a number of other reasons. First, Pelton's perception of maltreatment focuses on physical violence and the deprivation of necessities, behaviors which may well be more predominant among the lower classes. However, child maltreatment, as discussed above, encompasses a far broader range of behaviors, many of which are not overrepresented within lower socioeconomic classes. While physical neglect and, to a lesser extent, physical abuse may be more frequently noted among poor families, emotional maltreatment and sexual abuse have been documented across all income groups (Kempe and Kempe, 1978; Gullotta and Donohue, 1981; Bartolome, 1983; BPA, 1983). Second, notions that maltreatment is primarily a function of poverty allow policy makers the option of isolating treatment and prevention efforts as well as surveillance systems to poor children. One can imagine a two-tiered child abuse treatment and prevention system in which the wealthy pay for private care while the poor have their children placed in foster care or are provided limited services by an already overburdened and underfunded child welfare system. Given the punitive nature of the current reporting system and the use of the legal system to enforce these laws, such differential treatment based solely on ability to pay violates legal notions of equal protection.

Finally, limiting maltreatment to those behaviors unique to poverty families discourages the reporting of middle-class maltreatment by physicians, teachers, and other service providers for the well-to-do. As discussed above, the tendency to overlook or at least not formally report maltreatment found within white, middle-class families already exists. It is, at this juncture, virtually impossible to predict fully the extent of this bias or to know the cases of maltreatment which would be reported if protective service workers and public health officials had routine access to middle-class famiilies much the same way they currently have access to low-income families. Limiting child abuse treatment and prevention efforts to low-income families may well be as stifling to the development of new, more useful and productive intervention strategies as was the initial focus on physical abuse and neglect. Just as an overemphasis on medical and therapeutic interventions followed from Kempe's relatively narrow definition of maltreatment, an equally narrow range of interventions could surface from an overemphasis on poverty. To be sure, poverty is not healthy for children and policy makers must be aware of the importance of addressing poverty in any comprehensive child abuse prevention plan. Neither, however, does it seem useful to focus solely on poverty to the exclusion of other environmental or intrapersonal causal factors.

Summary and Practice Implications

Research regarding the underlying causes of maltreatment covers a broad range of individual as well as societal-level variables. Figure 3.1 summarizes the specific characteristics of parents, children, and households that place a *given* family at risk of maltreatment and lists those aspects of the society that place *entire classes* or *all* families at risk. While the field is long on "candidate" variables that correlate with maltreatment, little empirical evidence exists that consistently ties any one of these variables or any combination of factors directly to the generic problem of maltreatment or to any of the four major types of maltreatment. In explaining the relationship of any particular risk factor to actual maltreatment, most agree that each is but one dimension of the total picture and that it is the combination of factors at a given point in time that can provide the only true predictor of incidence.[7] While the key to prediction may indeed be in understanding the interplay among individual skills, stressful events, and social structure, determining a family's given status on these factors over time would require a level of personal surveillance intolerable in a free society.

The inability to predict accurately who will abuse or neglect their children based upon any single list of factors, however, does not preclude the utility of such a candidate list in designing effective intervention strategies. Both treatment and prevention planning can benefit from the knowledge generated by research on the causal factors of maltreatment. For example, the variables listed in Figure 3.1, and others highlighted in the previous discussion, provide intake workers with specific characteristics to look for in interviewing families and they provide clinicians with certain behaviors or attitudes they may want to see their clients modify or alter.[8] Support services and other outreach efforts can be made available to certain "high risk" families such as those experiencing temporary stress due to a personal or family tragedy and those experiencing the ongoing stress of trying to provide children with basic necessities in the absence of sufficient income.

Figure 3.1

Contributors to Maltreatment

Characteristics of Parents

Mental illness

Difficulty dealing with aggressive impulses

Tendency to be rigid and domineering

Lack of social skills

Low self-esteem

Depression

Substance abuse

Poor self-understanding

History of abuse as a child

Observation of physical violence as a child

Lack of attachment to the child

Adolescent parenthood

Social isolation

Inadequate household and child management skills

Lack of parenting skills

Inconsistent use of discipline

Lack of knowledge regarding child development

Sole responsibility for all parenting tasks

Inability to control anger

Characteristics of Children

Behavioral problems/hyperactivity

Unwanted during pregnancy

Premature birth

Physical illness

Physical/developmental disabilities

Mismatched to parent's personality

Similarity of child to an adult disliked by parent

Household Characteristics

Poverty/low income

Blended/reconstituted family

Single parenthood

Large number of children

Children less than one year apart

Chaotic family

Overcrowded or inadequate housing

Figure 3.1 continued

Stress Factors

   Birth of a new baby

   Loss of job

   Divorce/separation

   Death of a close friend/family member

   Sudden illness/chronic health problem

   Loss of housing

   Sudden financial burden

Social/Cultural Factors

   Culture of poverty

   Tolerance for physical punishment

   Sexual stereotypes in child-rearing

   Community isolation (i.e., lack of quality local community services
      and limited access to other neighborhoods' service systems)

   Violence in the media

   Extreme notions of individual rights and family privacy

Finally, the nature of this list and the fact that most parents exhibit any number of these characteristics at some point in their lifetime raise awareness of the potential for maltreatment in any parent. The list makes it more difficult to "scapegoat" the problem onto a specific group of parents or to oppose public support for child abuse and neglect services.

While the majority of the variables listed on Figure 3.1 can assist in better targeting existing interventions to families most in need, the issue of poverty makes a unique and compelling contribution to understanding the limits of existing intervention strategies and to broadening our notions of child abuse prevention. On some basic level, one can argue that poverty, regardless of its impact on individual parenting behavior, has negative consequences for children and, as such, should be seen as maltreating behavior on the part of the society. As Elmer's (1977) longitudinal study illustrates, over time the victims of poverty and maltreatment begin to look much like the victims of poverty alone. In much the same way that the society intervenes when parents mistreat their children, the society, proponents of this theory argue, should correct those aspects of its system which interfere with the healthy development of its children. Among the interventions suggested by this logic are adequate incomes, guaranteed employment, national health care, and improved primary and secondary educational systems (Keniston, 1977). Viewing the correlation between poverty and maltreatment at this "macro" level has the distinct advantage of removing the cloud of suspicion and surveillance from all poor families.

Responsibility for the well-being of the child is no longer solely that of the parent, but rather the joint task of the parent and the society.

The full implementation of broad, systemic changes is not likely to take place in the near future. However, recognition of the impact various social systems have on the well-being of children helps set realistic limits on the gains that can be realized through client-focused intervention efforts. Even if parenting skills are improved, more positive parent-child interactions realized, and initial developmental delays remediated, a low-income family will leave a treatment program and often return to its prior economic and household conditions. Continued poverty, inadequate health care and nutrition, and problem-riddled schools, in all likelihood, will minimize the gains that can be achieved with parents and children in the context of child abuse and neglect treatment programs. As such, those concerned with enhancing existing child abuse and neglect treatment and prevention efforts would be wise not only to focus on the improved targeting of services to families at risk but also on the broader social systems with which these families interact. The ecological perspective previously discussed has, perhaps, its clearest application in the context of defining child abuse treatment and prevention. Just as causal factors are found at both the client level and the societal level of analysis, so too are successful intervention strategies.

Part II

Current Best Practice and Policy

Chapter 4

Improving Practice:
Treatment Strategies

Modern child abuse program and policy planning has been dominated by three intervention models. The first of these, the Psychiatric model, stresses the provision of therapeutic services to maltreating adults for purposes of changing parental personalities or behaviors (Steele and Pollack, 1971; Helfer, 1975). Although originally developed for the physical abuser, the use of individual and group therapy has been incorporated over time into treatment programs serving adults demonstrating a wide range of abusive behaviors. As discussed below, this model has been particularly successful with the perpetrators and victims of child sexual abuse. Strict reliance on the Psychiatric model, however, has been generally abandoned in favor of other forms of treatment. The press of increasing numbers of reports and the diverse demands of growing caseloads have made in-depth psychotherapy more difficult to provide within the constraints of limited budgets and limited personnel. Also, psychotherapy is not always an effective treatment strategy in working with physically abusive or neglectful families because these families are often too dysfunctional and chaotic to benefit from formal therapy (Kempe and Kempe, 1978).

The practical limitations of the Psychiatric model, as well as a growing body of literature relating child abuse to socioeconomic factors, gave rise to a second intervention model, the Sociological model, which stresses the need for society to correct those aspects of its system that either add to the stress of child-rearing (e.g., unemployment, insufficient welfare beneifts) or fail to mitigate the negative consequences of a postindustrial society (e.g., failure to provide adequate day care alternatives) (Gil, 1975; Bronfenbrenner, 1979). This model presupposes that achieving sustained changes in parenting attitudes or behaviors is possible only if the system changes to reinforce nonabusive or nonneglectful parenting, and it supports such macro-level policy changes as higher basic welfare payments, nationalized health insurance, legalization of abortion, guaranteed employment, and federal funding for day care. The realization of such changes is usually associated with achieving a reduction in the incidence of child neglect.

While advocates of this position have realized some gains (e.g., changes in abortion policies), the inability to achieve broad-scale reforms and the continued identification of client-level correlates of maltreatment suggest that more immediate gains can be realized through comprehensive direct interventions with maltreating families. The third common intervention strategy, the Psychosocial model, combines elements of both the previous models. It is built upon the premise that the most efficient treatment and prevention efforts are those that simultaneously attack the problem from both the client perspective and the system perspective, offering therapeutic as well as supportive services (Gelles, 1973; Alvy, 1975). This theory currently dominates service planning and has the most consistent appeal across the four major maltreatment subpopulations.

Recognition of the difficulty in achieving client change within the context of existing economic and political realities has increased efforts to develop systematic responses to child maltreatment. Today, model child abuse intervention systems are composed of multiple programs, providing a broad target population—including actual abusers, high-risk families, and the general population—with a full continuum of service options, ranging from therapeutic interventions, to educational efforts, to the provision of concrete services. In addition, these systems call for improved coordination among all key subsystems (e.g., protective service systems, legal systems, medical systems, and the nonprofit service sector) for purposes of enhancing the community's service system as well as advocating for key legislative and systemic reforms. Under this model, responsibility for confronting child abuse rests not only with the public child welfare system, but also with private service providers and the public at large.

Service planning for maltreating families occurs at two levels. At the broadest level, the definition and degree of public involvement with a family accused of abuse or neglect rest with the local child protective service system. The formal investigation of charges of abuse and neglect, the possible removal of a child from the home, and the actual use or threat of court action to assure that families receive those services deemed acceptable are decisions governed by legal statutes as well as professional judgments regarding best practice. Beyond these official interventions, professionals in private practice and those in public or private social service agencies have responsibility for assessing a family's overall service needs, developing a specific service plan, and insuring that the plan is appropriately implemented. Research studies assessing the impact of both types of decisions on family functioning and child welfare suggest that the nature of these decisions will differ depending upon the primary type of maltreatment involved.

The initial section of this chapter outlines the central role child protective service (CPS) agencies play in the identification and treatment of abuse and neglect. A review of the overall structure of the nation's child welfare system lies beyond the scope of this book; readers are referred to studies that have specifically addressed this topic (Kadushin, 1980; Stein, 1981; McGowan and Meezen, 1983; Laird and Hartman, 1985). The focus here is on the unique challenges faced by CPS workers in their initial investigation of families involved in various types of maltreatment, their recommendations regarding specific service alternatives, including placement, and their compliance with the decision time frames mandated by the Adoption Assistance and Child Welfare Act of 1980 (PL 96–272).

To guide the reader in the development of specific service plans, the second section of this chapter reviews the outcome evaluations of a number of child abuse and neglect treatment programs. Unfortunately, the majority of these evaluations have not given explicit consideration to the differences among the four major types of maltreatment in determining service impacts, making conclusions as to their specific utility with different types of maltreatment necessarily tentative. The National Clinical Evaluation Study, however, did assess outcomes in terms of the client's primary type of maltreatment and therefore offers a unique empirical base for determining the different service needs of families involved in child neglect versus sexual abuse versus emotional maltreatment. Following the presentation of these findings with respect to those services found most effective with adults and children, the chapter summarizes those treatment issues of primary importance in working with families involved with different types of maltreatment.

Enhancing Investigation and Placement Decisions

In 1986, an estimated two million reports of child abuse were filed with local protective service agencies. All these reports required at least an initial investigation and over half involved maltreatment serious enough to require formal child protective services. Although the number of children placed in foster care steadily declined between 1977 and 1983, more recently the growing number of child abuse reports has been reflected in an increase in foster care placements. At the beginning of 1985, 276,000 children were in foster homes or group care settings primarily as a result of child abuse, physical neglect, parental incompetency, or abandonment (Sudia, 1986). Monitoring these cases, as well as the thousands of cases in which the child continues to reside with his or her parents while receiving either voluntary or court-ordered services, places an overwhelming burden on CPS workers.

Concern over the ability of the system to provide adequate protection for those children reported for maltreatment has been raised both inside and outside child welfare agencies. In addition to individual state reviews of local child abuse reporting, investigatory, and service systems, several national organizations, including the American Humane Association, the National Association of Public Child Welfare Administrators, and the Child Welfare League of America, are developing model practice standards for CPS workers. Court actions are also being taken to improve the conditions in which child welfare workers operate. For example, class action suits to reduce CPS caseloads have been filed or successfully litigated in Massachusetts, Missouri, and Maryland (Fritsche, 1986).

While preserving the family and avoiding unnecessary foster care placements always have been child welfare service goals, the Adoption Assistance and Child Welfare Act of 1980 (PL 96–272) placed primary attention on reducing the number of children in foster care. Child welfare supervisors and case managers were to adopt more concerted efforts to avoid initial placement, to reunify as soon as possible those children actually placed in foster care, and, if reunification attempts failed, to move more rapidly toward the termination of parental rights and the identification of long-term placement alternatives. Regular administrative and judicial reviews have been used to ensure that progress on these goals is steady and that children do not fall victim to "foster care" drift.

Although CPS agencies are not the sole determiners of the quality or depth of a community's response to child abuse, they are a critical component of any local service system. It is important for child welfare workers to consider the differential needs of the four primary child maltreatment subpopulations at three major decision points in the case planning process: at the time the initial report of suspected maltreatment is investigated, at the time the use of foster care placement is determined, and at the time service is terminated. The implications of these decisions in light of current caseload size and permanency planning regulations are outlined below.

Investigating Maltreatment Reports

Although protective service workers are required to respond in a timely and efficient manner to all reports of child maltreatment, local CPS emergency response workers often find it difficult to do so. A recent survey conducted by the Child Welfare League of America found that approximately one-third of the state administrators it contacted routinely do not investigate reports within the 24 or 48 hours mandated by their state's child welfare legislation (CWLA, 1986). Similarly, a review of New York City's response system found that after 40 days a home visit had not been made in 11% of the cases, the reported children had not been seen in 22%

of the cases, and the alleged perpetrators had not been interviewed in 17% of the cases (Besharov, 1986). In 1986 alone, San Francisco's Emergency Response Unit's staff of 20 professionals handled reports involving over 13,000 children, an average of one call received every three hours. This mismatch between the number of families needing assistance and the staff available to respond most certainly compromises the potential effectiveness of local CPS agencies.

Perhaps more alarming than the delay in responding to reports is the number of jurisdictions reporting increased child deaths due to maltreatment. A 50-state survey conducted by the National Committee for the Prevention of Child Abuse (NCPCA) in 1986 noted that from 1985 to 1986, reported deaths due to maltreatment rose 23% in the 34 states able to provide these data to NCPCA (Daro and Mitchel, 1987a). While no national statistics exist, investgations undertaken in individual counties or states suggest that the percentage of these fatalities previously known to local child welfare agencies ranges from 25% to 50%.[1] Studies investigating the most common immediate causes for these deaths find that approximately half of the children die as a result of battering. In some instances, death is the cumulative result of repeated beatings; in other cases death results from a single violent episode. The other half of the victims die as a result of neglect when parents fail to provide for a child's basic needs such as necessary medical care or adequate supervision (AAPC, 1986).

Even when agencies follow best practice, the unpredictability of human behavior makes some deaths unavoidable. Child protective services are only one component of a broader community service system, including other public agencies, private social service providers, and informal support networks, which share responsibility for protecting children and improving the environment in which they live. In the eyes of many, however, the death of a child due to abuse or neglect, particularly if that child is an active or prior client of local protective service agencies, is viewed as a failure of the child welfare system. Thus many believe that improving the ability of emergency response units to investigate cases in a more timely and comprehensive manner is an important step in better protecting children from serious or fatal harm.

The most common proposals to accomplish this task involve either the development of a systematic method for prioritizing cases or a reduction in the number of reports through changes in the reporting laws (Johnson and L'Esperance, 1984; Besharov, 1985a). The first of these strategies assumes that risk can be accurately predicted; the second assumes that some categories of maltreatment are less severe than others and, therefore, can be excluded from the reporting statutes or given a lower priority for response. The empirical evidence on the underlying causes of maltreatment, the development of accurate prediction models, and the differential response of children to similar forms of maltreatment suggest that, in the short run, neither of these approaches will substantially improve CPS performance. At the extreme end of the maltreatment continuum, the need for public intervention is clear. In the absence of observable harm to the child or gross forms of maltreatment, greater care must be taken in investigating child maltreatment reports, with the level and extent of intervention being largely determined by caseworker assessment. Prioritization systems that rank reports in terms of such factors as the source of the report, the age of the mother, prior history of maltreatment, family income, substance abuse by the caretaker, and observable harm to the child can offer some guidance to overburdened caseworkers in identifying those cases that are most likely to be substantiated or to represent particularly volatile situations. However, gathering sufficient data to assess adequately a child's risk or a report's validity might well take as much time as many current investigations. Further, these systems, no matter how sophisticated, will never fully eliminate the need for human judgment and the application of multidisciplinary reviews. For example, the comprehensive child outcome study conducted by the Child Welfare League of America found that workers were able to successfully rank the relative severity of different types of maltreatment by rating the family's or child's position on 43 separate dimensions, covering parenting role performance, familial capacities, child role performance and child capacities (Magura and Moses, 1986). While severity ratings on distinct maltreatment behaviors were highly correlated with a recommendation for placement, the association was far from perfect. In determining whether to recommend placement, workers generally consider not only the relative severity of the case but also the extent to which individual factors pertaining to specific abusive or neglectful behaviors interact with each other and with the family's overall support system. Consequently, cases representing similar types of abuse will not always result in emergency or long-term placement. In keeping with the intent of current child welfare reform policies, workers can be rather cautious in recommending placement in cases where risk is less obvious, opting instead to provide family-based services.

Those who would narrow the types of reports deemed acceptable for investigation face similar problems. For example, limiting the CPS response system to those cases in which a child or his or her siblings have already experienced physical harm as a result of mistreatment overlooks the fact that the progression of child abuse and neglect often follows a pattern similar to many diseases. The initial symptoms or consequences may appear quite superficial or result in only mild discomfort. If untreated, however, these symptoms can eventually mushroom into permanently disabling or fatal conditions. Intervening after a child has suffered is simply too late for the child, for the family, and for a credible child protective service system.

An alternative method for improving response time and better targeting resources would be to develop specialized response units for at least the three most common maltreatment subpopulations. While several CPS units have already adopted this practice with respect to sexual abuse, the strategy would be equally useful in better addressing the service needs of physically abusive or neglectful subpopulations. Each unit would be staffed by personnel well versed in the unique indicators of maltreatment, presenting problems, and service needs that research suggests are dominant among each particular maltreatment subpopulation. As reports were received, they could be channeled to the appropriate unit based upon the primary type of maltreatment identified. Although a majority of cases involve multiple forms of maltreatment, initial reports are fairly explicit: the child has bruises or burns, the mother has left a young infant alone, or a child has disclosed sexual abuse. If the staff who are most familiar with the reported type of maltreatment conduct the initial investigations, these assessments would be better focused and might be completed in a more timely manner.

Figure 4.1 summarizes the issues workers should be versed in with respect to three of the most common maltreatment subpopulations and to the types of issues that should be raised in reviewing reports in a useful and efficient manner. For example, staff responding to reports of child neglect should be knowledgeable about the range of child-rearing standards and practices found within the local community and about the array of support services available to families to deal with the extrafamilial stresses often associated with child neglect, such as poor housing, poverty, inadequate medical care, limited child care options, and few employment opportunities. In contrast, those workers investigating cases of physical abuse should be able to recognize the physical signs of abuse and be familiar with the best methods for assessing the ability of parents to manage anger, stress, and the discipline of their children. Finally, those working in the area of sexual abuse would be trained in the types of interviewing and assessment techniques most appropriate in these cases. Not only must the initial assessment determine if abuse did or did not occur, it must also be of sufficient quality to withstand legal scrutiny without further traumatizing the child. The skills required to conduct such interviews include a unique blend of psychodynamic insights and a familiarity with legal terminology and standards of evidence. Because so much depends on the quality of these interviews, it is imperative that potential victims be channeled to workers who have the skills and experience necessary to address these issues (Thomas, 1980; Sgroi, 1982; Summit, 1983).

Determining the Use of Placement

Variance between the services provided by child protective agencies and the services families desire or will accept voluntarily results in situations where children who continue to reside with their parents do so at high risk of further maltreatment. Faced with these situations, caseworkers use

Figure 4.1

Client and Service Issues Most Relevant
for Various Types of Maltreatment

PHYSICAL NEGLECT

Indicators of
Maltreatment:
Physical signs of neglect (chronic health
problems, poor school attendance, poor hygiene)
Parents' inability/unwillingness to care for child
Parents' lack of knowledge with respect to child's
basic needs

Areas of
Expertise:
Realistic understanding of the community's
standards of parenting and child care
Familiarity with cultural differences within the
community
Ability to assess family's access to support
services
Knowledge of medical terminology
Knowledge of substance abuse identification

Service
Familiarity:
Local community organizations and neighborhood
associations
Welfare and emergency relief services
Parent aid and home visitor programs
Family support services
Substance abuse treatment programs

PHYSICAL ABUSE

Indicators of
Maltreatment:
Physical signs of abuse (bruises, lacerations,
burns, etc.)
Parent's inability to manage anger/stress
Parent's limited knowledge with respect to appro-
priate discipline and child development stages

Areas of
Expertise:
Familiarity with cultural differences with respect
to physical punishment
Knowledge of medical terminology
Ability to assess parent functioning with respect
to impulse control, attitudes toward corporal
punishment

Service
Familiarity:
Respite care facilities
Family/adult support groups
Parenting education services

SEXUAL ABUSE

Indicators of
Maltreatment:
Physical signs of abuse (medical evidence of
sexual contact, bruised or swollen genitals, etc.)
Behavioral signs of abuse (unusual fear of
adults, withdrawal, depression, sexually acting
out, etc.)
Inappropriate sexual expressions of affection
between parent and child

Areas of
Expertise:
Knowledge of the legal system and evidential
standards
Knowledge of medical terminology
Interviewing victims of sexual abuse
Experience and training in assessing family
interactional patterns

Service
Familiarity:
Victim and offender therapy and support groups

emergency or temporary foster care placements to ensure the child's safety until services are able to alter parental behavior or environmental conditions so that the child can return home without further risk of abuse. When changes cannot be realized, however, the child remains in foster care on a permanent basis until he or she reaches the age of majority or parental rights are terminated and the child is adopted.

Debate over the appropriateness of foster care placement and its potential misuse by caseworkers is longstanding. Writing in 1962, Kempe noted that until successful intervention models could be developed and the field gained a better understanding of the mechanisms involved in the control and release of aggressive impulses, the only safe remedy in cases of abuse was "the separation of battered children from their insufficiently protective parents" (Kempe et al., 1962:20). The return of children to their homes, in the absence of proper therapeutic precautions, was thought to run a 50% chance the child would be further abused and a 10% chance of death (Green and Haggerty, 1968). Given these odds, it is not surprising that caseworkers frequently utilize placement for at least a short period of time during investigations or following confirmation. Resistance to taking a child away from his or her parents, however, remains high. All things being equal, it is considered far preferable for a child to remain with the parents than to be cared for by strangers.

For maltreated children, however, all things are not equal and placement is often unavoidable. While some argue that the social and emotional damage created by the foster care system may outweigh the potential harm a child faces by remaining with his or her birth parents (Besharov, 1981), empirical evidence suggests that quite the contrary is true. In a retrospective study of abused children who were placed out of the home, Kent (1976) found that these children improved on nearly all of their problem behaviors, especially incidence of emotional withdrawal. The neglected children, who had substantially more delayed development at intake, improved markedly at follow-up, although as a group they still had a higher incidence of developmental delays than the physically abused group. The abused children, who had demonstrated more aggression, more disobedience, and more problems in peer relationships at intake, improved more with respect to management of aggression, resembling the neglect group at follow-up. These findings, coupled with the sustained poor development of maltreated children returning to or remaining with their parents (Martin et al., 1974; Elmer, 1977) and a 30% reincidence rate among terminated cases (Herrenkohl et al., 1979; Laughlin and Weiss, 1981), highlight the point that in many cases placement, not reunification, may be the preferred intervention.

Still, reducing the number of children requiring placement and minimizing the length of stay for those who are placed continue to be prime objectives of the child welfare system. Efforts to accomplish these goals include crisis intervention to prevent imminent placement in cases where the child is believed to be at risk of serious maltreatment, as well as intensive services to high-risk families as a means of averting the types of crisis situations that precipitate placement. In assessing the effectiveness of these efforts, the Child Welfare League of America questioned the efficiency of attempting to prevent an event as seemingly unpredictable as placement. "Devoting disproportionate amounts of time and effort to the uncertain prevention of some placements may inevitably short-change the majority of children referred to protective services who lack adequate nurturing and could benefit from additional casework." (Magura, 1981:208). The straining of already scarce resources in order to prevent placement becomes even more questionable if the results of placement are not negative for children and indeed may be beneficial for them.

While Magura's survey suggests a rather disappointing performance level for placement prevention services, independent evaluations of several family-based service models document more promising outcomes. Kinney et al. (1977) reported that the Homebuilders program in Tacoma, Washington, through a combination of professional and lay services, prevented placement for 90% of the 134 abused children or status offenders served during the program's initial 16 months. Follow-up studies indicated that 97% of those initially avoiding placement continued to do so over time. Replication of this model in Florida has shown similar results. A review of the over 4,000 abusive and troubled families served by the state's Intensive Crisis Counseling Program since 1981 noted that over 95% of these families had avoided any placement episodes or had been reunited by the time services terminated. Eighty-four percent of these families continued to avoid placement for at least the initial post-program year. Since initiation of the program in 1981, Florida's rate of foster care placement per 1,000 children under the age of 18 has dropped from 3.3 to 1.4 (Paschal and Schwahn, 1986). An assessment of 14 child placement prevention projects in Wisconsin also produced promising results. Of the 826 children served by these projects, 93% of all abused or neglected children who were living with a parent at project intake were prevented from entering foster or institutional care and 45% of the children who were living in substitute care at project intake because of maltreatment were reunited with their families (Landsman, 1985). Although it monitored a relatively small number of families, an evaluation of Nebraska's Intensive Services Project found only four of the 28 dysfunctional families receiving intensive, family-based services required any use of foster care placement on either a temporary or permanent basis (Leeds, 1984).

These types of program evaluations have focused on the avoidance of placement rather than on the absolute elimination of continued maltreatment. It is not known, based upon these and similar evaluations, what specific quality the parent-child relationship had or if the gains initially exhibited by the parents are sustained over time such that a child's safety can be assured. What the evaluations do indicate is that a significant percentage of families involved in serious physical abuse and neglect can benefit from family-based services such that the removal of their children can be totally avoided or significantly reduced. Certainly, as long as a child remains in what has been a volitile situation, some degree of risk will be unavoidable. The degree of risk remaining in those families receiving family-based services, however, appears to be significantly reduced at the time intensive services are terminated and to remain sufficiently low, as neither the child welfare worker following the case nor other professionals or individuals involved with the family have reason to report the family for abuse or to recommend removal of the child.

The most common features of all of these interventions include an emphasis on treating the family unit as opposed to individual family members, the provision of services in the family's home, and an intensive concentration of services over a relatively short period of time, generally six to nine months. It is the intensity of this service model that is most frequently attacked as unrealistic, given the fiscal constraints CPS agencies face. In response to these critics, proponents of the family-based service models emphasize the potential long-term savings these services would generate if consistently employed. To be sure, foster care placement is one of the most costly children's services offered by the public sector. The level of federal and state expenditures for child protective programs, including foster care placements, now exceeds $3.5 billion annually.

Cost-benefit analyses which have contrasted the costs of providing the types of family-based services outlined above with the use of foster care placement, however, have found the former intervention to be far less costly. For example, a comparison of the two interventions within the context of the Maryland Department of Human Resources projected significant system savings if a family received intensive therapeutic and support services at the time of initial referral. The primary reasons for these savings are the shorter duration of the service and the elimination of an average $2,323 annual foster care payment per child (Haugaard and Hokanson, 1983). If a child is not placed in foster care as a result of successful family-based services, the total projected state savings in foster care placement and administrative costs is estimated to be $27,000.[2] Based on their actual performance rate, the Homebuilders program staff projected that in their initial 16 months they had saved the State of Washington over $278,300 in foster care costs (Kinney et al., 1977). Assuming only a 60% success rate, Hutchinson (1982) projected a potential state savings of over $8 million over three years if an emphasis was placed today on early, intensive intervention with all families identified as being at risk of losing their children to the foster care system. Although further empirical testing is needed, the underlying assumption in all three of these models is that relatively short-term intervention can completely eliminate the need for foster care placement in a sizable percentage of cases. The initial positive results of these programs and the magnitude of the projected cost savings are significant enough to warrant further attention by all child welfare administrators.

Even if family-based prevention efforts are not successful in stopping placement, however, their intensive work with families may facilitate the child's transition to a new living arrangement and more positive social adjustment. Harling and Haines (1980) reported on the efforts of the Family Reunification Bureau in Sacramento which operated two intensive foster care homes, each with a capacity of four children between the ages of two and seven. The treatment team consisted of a psychiatric consultant, a psychologist, a homemaker, a volunteer student, the project social worker, and specially trained foster parents who worked with both the children and their birth parents for a three-month period. Of the 43 children served by the project during the study year, all showed marked improvement in emotional and physical development, in general behavior, and in peer relationships. While fewer than 50% of the children could be returned home to their birth parents, of those transferred to permanent foster care, all remained in their initial placement. This finding led the authors to conclude that involvement in the project had either prepared the children better for foster care or had generated better data on the child such that the initial placement was more appropriate.

The diversity of maltreatment cases, even within specific subpopulations, and the number of public and private agencies often involved with a given family necessitate that expertise from a variety of disciplines be considered in the case management and service planning process. Collaboration among those disciplines routinely involved in child abuse cases has been consistently documented as both an efficient use of public resources and an effective way to enhance outcomes.[3] While responsibility for a given case should be retained by one worker, input from all relevant sources should be sought in the assessment and service planning process. This type of collaboration not only widens the worker's understanding of the case, but also acts as a safeguard against individual human error. The specific case management practices that can improve outcomes include:

> providing CPS line workers with periodic updates on practice and policy changes in other local agencies routinely involved in cases of child abuse, such as the district attorney's office, the public defender's office, the juvenile court, the public health department, and the welfare department;
>
> establishing and regularly updating interagency agreements to exchange information on jointly staffed cases;
>
> establishing a management information system that provides all workers involved in a given case with the most current information on the child's status and that of his or her parents regardless of which agency secured the information;

> including time for team meetings and telephone consultation regarding a given case in determining individual caseloads and unit staff allocations; and

> having personnel experienced in the major type of maltreatment presented by the family play a central role in all major case decisions including temporary or permanent placement, reunification, goal setting, service planning, and termination.

The success documented by a variety of family-based interventions in avoiding the use of placement is significant enough to warrant further expansion of such programs. The provision of intensive services directed at the family's overall needs is intuitively attractive given what we know about the causal factors associated with various forms of maltreatment. Instead of working with the parents individually while the child remains in foster care, the family-based service model directly addresses the parent-child interaction in the context of the family's home. While some evaluators of this service have found it less successful with chronic neglect cases, its potential seems high in cases of physical abuse, sexual abuse, and emotional maltreatment. In any event, the parallel development of these services alongside the more traditional foster care system offers CPS workers expanded options in achieving the dual goals of protecting the child and strengthening the family.

The emphasis on family-based services and the avoidance of placement needs to be kept in perspective, however. The group homes described above, as well as specialized foster homes, can be used not only as a safe refuge for children but also as a treatment opportunity. Under this conceptualization of placement, protective service workers can explore ways to improve the assessment process when a child first enters placement and develop a specific intervention package for remediating, during placement, the most common developmental and social delays noted among abused and neglected children. The outcomes cited by Kent and others attest to the fact that progress with victims of maltreatment can be achieved independent of their parents. While the possibility for family reunification may indeed depend upon the parents' capacity to change, eliminating the negative consequences of maltreatment for children is a valid treatment objective in its own right. A placement system targeted to change rather than merely maintenance not only mitigates the most immediate consequences of maltreatment but also enhances the child's long-term prognosis. This may be particularly critical in cases of child neglect where the outlook for reunification remains rather dim. An early, comprehensive assessment of the child's functioning will provide caseworkers with a greater understanding of the child's ongoing service needs and will identify those problems which, if left unaddressed, might result in future disruptions or reincidence. Once available to caseworkers, this information can be included in the long-term planning for the child's family if the child is to return home, or in identifying other, more appropriate long-term placement options. It was this recognition of the therapeutic importance of the placement process that led Missouri to establish a mandatory training program for all foster care parents and the maintenance of a "life book" for all children presently in that state's foster care system outlining the child's history prior to and during placement (Fritsche, 1986).

Terminating CPS Involvement

The Adoption Assistance and Child Welfare Act of 1980, with its rapid, almost formulaic, approach to problem solving raises serious questions for achieving successful intervention with certain types of maltreating families. Two basic issues need to be considered in light of the present child welfare reforms: (1) will these reforms increasingly result in the public child welfare system limiting its resources to the most severe cases of maltreatment? and (2) how will the legislation's 18-month (or in exceptional cases, two-year) time limit on child welfare services affect the reunification rate for maltreating families? Although empirical evidence regarding the impacts of PL 96-272 on the types of maltreating families receiving child welfare services or on the outcomes of these interventions is not yet available, anecdotal evidence and speculation based upon our current knowledge of abusive and neglectful families suggest some disturbing scenarios.

First, the new system's focus on family reunification and early intervention to avoid placement is compatible with what we know is effective intervention with a broad range of maltreatment. As discussed in the following section, treatment strategies that involve direct services to all family members and consider the overall needs of the family unit in addition to the needs of individual family members hold out greater hope for achieving family stability and a safe living environment for the child than do strategies lacking these elements. To the extent that CPS workers approach all families with the intent of avoiding placement or reunifying the child with his or her parents as soon as possible, more comprehensive assessments generating more comprehensive treatment packages will result. CPS agencies' abilities to provide this broad array of services to the families on their caseloads, however, has been limited in the past and is unlikely to improve in the absence of increased resources. For example, in their review of the effects of California's permanency planning legislation (SB 14), the state's Legislative Analyst's Office noted that families reported for maltreatment were generally placed into two categories—those for whom the reports were unfounded and those where the maltreatment was so severe that the child needed to be removed. This was especially true in counties with large caseloads where, despite the policy intent of SB 14 to retain children at home, very few resources were being devoted to families either "at risk" of initial maltreatment or involved in milder forms of maltreatment (*Child Welfare Services,* 1985).

While current child welfare reforms support prevention, it is important to bear in mind that this focus represents a concern for preventing placement, not child maltreatment. As Magura (1981) noted, this focus, though seen as early intervention from the point of view of foster care placement, is a far cry from early intervention from the point of view of child maltreatment. A family that is considered appropriate for such an "early intervention" program will have to demonstrate that it is on the verge of losing the child, a situation that can result only from past or imminent serious maltreatment. In this sense, permanency planning reforms have placed the point of public child welfare intervention at the opposite end of the severity continuum from that which past child maltreatment research has suggested would be the most beneficial.

Limiting public child welfare dollars to the most dysfunctional families or, at a minimum, to those families who have already seriously mistreated their children has been further supported by changes in the voluntary placement system. In the past, families experiencing short-term crisis, due either to illness or death of the primary caretaker or to a sudden loss of income or housing, were able voluntarily to place their children in foster care for a limited period. Perceived abuses of this system resulted in a tightening of restrictions on its use under PL 96-272. At present, voluntary placement is available for a maximum of six months, during which time the parents and CPS caseworker must establish and implement a plan for permanent reunification. If, after six months, reunification is not possible, the child becomes an involuntary placement and the regular system of administrative and judicial reviews commences, leading to reunification in 18 months or to the termination of parental rights. The automatic shift from voluntary to involuntary placement makes the use of this system for high-risk families a far more dangerous venture. While these changes might, indeed, have been needed to prevent families from routinely using the foster care system as a temporary baby sitter, they have also had the effect of removing this option from parents who would use voluntary placement as a productive child abuse prevention strategy. At present, families who have not yet abused or neglected their children have less access to the child welfare system's resources than they had in the past. Whether this shift in resource allocation proves appropriate will be determined in the long run by the extent to which placement can indeed be avoided by targeting services to families who have already demonstrated abusive tendencies and the extent to which primary and secondary prevention efforts emerge to fill the gap resulting in a withdrawal of public resources from this population.

Second, the underlying causal factors and prognosis for treatment success documented for various types of maltreatment suggest that certain types may be more compatible with the current structure of the child welfare system than others. Cases of physical abuse, particularly those resulting in serious harm to the child, and, increasingly, cases of child sexual abuse, will most likely command swift attention from both CPS investigatory and casework units. As data from a study by the American Humane Association demonstrates, these types of maltreatment are the ones most frequently resulting in investigation and inclusion on CPS caseloads (AHA, 1981; AAPC, 1986). In those instances where parents exhibit serious psychological dysfunctioning or a gross inability to protect their children from future harm, termination of parental rights or reunification with the non-maltreating parent, in the case of child sexual abuse, will be the continued course of action. The major impact of child welfare reforms for these cases, therefore, will be facilitating the placement process. Hopefully, mandated six-month reviews and decision time lines will secure new permanent homes for these children more rapidly than did a less regulated system.

In maltreating cases in which the harm to the child is less evident and the inability of parents to parent less clear, the impact of the new child welfare system may be quite different. Under permanency planning regulations, the burden of proof rests with the caseworker who is required to demonstrate to the court that a parent is inadequate. While this system is consistent with the broader legal tenet of "innocent until proven guilty," it represents a change from the pre-reform period where the burden of proof rested with the parents to justify they "deserved" to have their children returned. Caseworkers, knowing they will need to resolve a family's situation in 18 months and also present evidence of their findings to a court, may be understandably reluctant to take cases that are unclear. This will be particularly true in cases of neglect and emotional maltreatment where confusion is found over what behaviors constitute maltreatment and the present and long-term consequences of this behavior for the child.

The extent to which changes in certain types of maltreating behaviors can be expected in an 18-month period is also subject to wide debate. Altering abusive and neglectful parenting patterns means not only convincing the parent that such behaviors are inappropriate and harmful to their children, but also replacing these behaviors and attitudes with more positive parenting skills. Terminating parental rights can be a traumatic event for both the child and the parents. While it is important that caseworkers recognize when continued service provision becomes an exercise in futility, it is equally important that all children who can safely be reunited with their parents be allowed to do so, even if this requires interventions with their families beyond an arbitrary 18-month or two-year time period.

Proponents of early termination point out that it is not at all clear that longer interventions are a priori better for families or that they result in higher reunification rates. While there is some evidence of a high correlation between length of time in treatment and low reincidence (Silver et al., 1971), the interpretation of this relationship is not clear-cut. Prior to permanency planning, child welfare cases tended to remain open for at least two years, with the specific treatment being a function of the number and severity of problems in the family, the client's motivation or willingness to remain in treatment, and the structure and content of the given service package. Questioning the maxim that "longer is better," at least one author has noted the importance of client preference and openness to treatment in determining a family's length of stay. Although there is little evidence that great progress can be achieved with families engaged in service for less than six months, there is no evidence that all families reported for maltreatment require multiple years of assistance. "There may be a tendency to think of all child welfare cases as requiring prolonged service, since some certainly do, and the most difficult and intractible cases capture the greatest attention" (Jones et al., 1981:71). At least one study conducted in an urban protective service agency suggests that the families who remain on CPS cascloads the longest represent those parents most willing to cooperate with the caseworker, not those whose profiles suggest they would be most at risk of reabusing their children (Johnson and L'Esperance, 1984). Another interpretation of this specific study, however, is that reabuse did not occur because the family continued to be an active CPS case.

If one accepts this second interpretation, it is appropriate to suggest the development of a more diversified child welfare system. For the first 18 months following referral, all families would be provided with a comprehensive assessment and, if warranted, the provision of intensive casework and support services. As discussed below, this 18-month treatment period should be sufficient to determine if the family has the potential to improve such that the child can eventually be safely reunited with his or her parents. Parents who fail to make any significant progress during this initial treatment phase will be unlikely to demonstrate a reduced propensity for maltreatment even if intensive services continued. However, for parents who do realize significant progress during this initial phase but who may still require some assistance in order to guard against future maltreatment, continued service on a more limited basis may be warranted.

Consequently, three options should be open to protective service workers at the end of the 18-month treatment period: (1) reunification and no further child welfare services, (2) termination of parental rights and establishment of a long-term placement alternative, or (3) reunification of the child with the family and retention on the agency's caseload in a less intensive service program. While this system would continue to allocate public resources to families that may not be among the most needy, it may also allow for reunification in those cases in which the safest 18-month decision option for the child would have been long-term placement in foster care. Anecdotal evidence suggests that merely keeping a case open may have a policing effect or halo effect on parents in that they perceive themselves still under the watchful eye of protective services. If this strategy results in further reduction in the reincidence of maltreatment and in a higher reunification rate without drawing substantial resources away from other child welfare functions, it is a strategy worth pursuing at least on an experimental basis. Given the differential needs of the child maltreatment population, it seems a worthwhile and equitable course of action to consider.

Enhancing Service Planning

Outside of CPS agencies, a wide range of community-based agencies have developed therapeutic and support service strategies for maltreating families. Often working in tandem with and receiving funding from local protective service agencies, these efforts represent considerable investments on the part of hospitals, schools, family counseling centers, and local professionals in addressing the diverse needs of abusive and neglectful families. Collectively, they can be considered the community's reponse to child maltreatment.

The most common service elements in these systems include *multidisciplinary teams* to review reports and assess initial treatment needs (Green, 1975; Green, 1976; Schmitt and Beezley, 1976; Blumberg, 1977; Brant and Tisza, 1977; Grazio, 1981; Galleno and Oppenheim, 1982), *direct services to maltreating parents* such as parenting education (Green, 1976; Applebaum, 1977; McKeel, 1978), counseling of new parents while they are still in the hospital (Schmitt and Beezley, 1976; Moore, 1982), group therapy (Bean, 1971; NcNeil and McBride, 1979), home-visitor services (Green, 1976; Moore, 1982), and services from lay therapists and self-help groups (Green, 1975; Powell, 1979; Blizinsky, 1982); and *direct services for maltreated children* such as therapeutic day care (Green, 1975), outpatient psychiatric treatment for school-aged children (Green, 1976), and special services for abused adolescents (Garbarino and Jacobson, 1978). In addition, greater coordination of the medical, psychiatric, social, and legal systems is also cited as strengthening a community's response to child maltreatment (Jones, 1982). Finally, *crisis intervention services* which facilitate the system's immediate response to families in stress, such as a 24-hour hotline (Green, 1976), crisis nursery or respite care (Green, 1975), and community-based family resource centers (Green, 1975; Cherry and Kirby, 1971) are also encouraged.

The majority of program evaluations that have been conducted on these strategies have suffered from the limitations of small, nonrepresentative samples; measurement of a very narrow range of behaviors, physical conditions, or attitudes; and poorly defined control or comparison groups. Further, for purposes of the current discussion, rarely has an explicit attempt been made to consider outcomes in terms of maltreatment subpopulations. Despite the methodological limitations inherent in applied research, a number of service components have consistently emerged as offering more productive avenues for effectively confronting child abuse. These features include:

a multidisciplinary approach including professionals from the legal, medical, social welfare, and educational fields;

provision of services from a family perspective rather than from an individual perspective;

expansion of interventions to include direct therapeutic services to abused or "at risk" children;

provision of concrete assistance to families in resolving problems having to do with inadequate income, poor housing, lack of medical care, and lack of formal and informal supports; and

integration of professional services and lay volunteer or self-help groups into the treatment plan.

Of all of these components, one of the most promising yet controversial areas involves the use of paraprofessionals or lay therapists in working with abusive families. The first major evaluation of federally-funded child abuse and neglect treatment programs concluded that, relative to any other discrete services or combination of services, lay services—lay counseling and Parents Anonymous—resulted in the most positive treatment outcomes. The study also noted that the use of supplemental services such as group therapy and parent education classes had positive effects, particularly for the physical abuser (Cohn, 1979). Although the authors cautioned that the lay services provided by the projects participating in the demonstration effort involved intensive on-the-job training and ongoing professional back-up and supervision, the study was one of the first evaluations to document the need to expand services beyond strictly therapeutic or professional counseling.

The continued growth of Parents Anonymous (PA) chapters and the positive responses reported by program participants further support the effectiveness of the lay therapy model (Junewicz, 1983; Moore, 1983; Fritz, 1986). These groups provide participants with an opportunity to validate their sense of frustration in being unable to effectively cope with the many and varied demands of parenting. The weekly meetings not only offer participants support and friendship but also knowledge regarding child development and positive parenting practices. Although directed by the participants themselves and a lay volunteer leader, the group has ongoing access to a clinical professional. This professional volunteer coordinates service referrals for those group participants needing more structured counseling or formal therapy.

While an expanding intervention model, the technique is not without its difficulties. Over one-quarter of the PA groups operating in the State of Washington between 1980 and 1982 ceased functioning because of the loss of their volunteer professional sponsors (Blizinsky, 1982). In the majority of these cases, the volunteers simply felt overwhelmed by the demands of the group, noting that a greater percentage of the group than they had anticipated required some form of counseling or service referrals. This high demand for therapeutic services among group participants have led others to conclude that the self-help method offers families only limited support and should never be construed as an adequate substitute for professional intervention (Powell, 1979).

To combat the "burnout" problem among volunteers and their professional sponsors, the majority of PA chapters maintain formal ties to existing service organizations with multiple professional staff rather than relying upon a single professional. Such a partnership ensures adequate supervision of the self-help group and lay volunteers as well as the long-term continuation of local chapters. While professionals continue to question the therapeutic limitations of lay therapy in particular and the self-help concept in general, the unpredictable nature of maltreatment suggests that the ongoing support of a peer around the everyday issues of parenting is an effective method for teaching skills and protecting children.

Adult Service Outcomes by Subpopulation

The National Clinical Evaluation Study offered a unique opportunity to explore the relative merits of these service components with families involved in different types of maltreatment. Under this initiative, 19 projects located throughout the country were funded by the federal National Center on Child Abuse and Neglect to demonstrate the effects of specialized clinical interventions targeted to five distinct abuse and neglect subpopulations. All of the 19 grants were awarded to existing public or private social service agencies to augment an existing service strategy, to test a new intervention, or to target a new client population. The demonstration effort included four projects targeting sexual abuse; four projects targeting adolescent maltreatment; three projects targeting substance-abuse-related child maltreatment; four projects targeting child neglect; and four projects targeting remedial services to maltreated children. While the child neglect and sexual abuse projects served a more homogeneous population in terms of presenting problems and family characteristics, the remaining 11 projects served families involved in the full range of maltreatment. The overall evaluation effort included both a systematic analysis of data on the projects' clients, services, and client outcomes and an analysis of the relationship among these three elements and project organization, case management practices, and staff characteristics. The major goals of the evaluation were:

> to determine if there were indeed distinct subpopulations of abuse and neglect and, if so, to identify the important differences;

to test whether families experiencing different patterns of abuse or neglect required unique investigative and treatment approaches; and

to provide direction on which particular strategies demonstrated by the projects were best suited to replication.

As presented below, these analyses confirmed that families involved in different types of maltreatment did indeed represent unique subpopulations.

The specific projects included in this evaluation encompassed a broad array of intervention strategies ranging from narrow, individual therapeutic services with the primary perpetrator to multiple service models in which all members of the family received therapeutic services. While certain of the projects emphasized the remediation of individual and family problems through the exclusive use of counseling, others stressed the importance of integrating counseling with specific supportive or concrete services. Table 4.1 summarizes the affiliation, client population, and theoretical model implemented by each of the 19 projects. The adults and children served by these 19 projects exhibited a full range of socioemotional and physical problems, as well as environmental difficulties generally found among maltreating parents and the victims of maltreatment. As such, the sample is an accurate reflection of the types of families child abuse treatment programs can expect to see on their caseloads.

At all of the projects, clinicians were asked to rate their clients at termination on three measures of success:

client's overall progress—a three-point scale on which clinicians judged the client's overall progress during the treatment period as having gotten worse (a rating of 1), having improved (a rating of 3), or having had no change (a rating of 2);

propensity toward future maltreatment—a four-point scale on which clinicians judged the client, in the absence of further interventions, to be very likely to maltreat in the future (a rating of 1), somewhat likely (a rating of 2), somewhat unlikely (a rating of 3), or very unlikely (a rating of 4); and

the number of different types of reincidence occurring during treatment—a five-point scale on which clinicians recorded the number of different types of maltreatment committed by the client during treatment, with a zero value indicating no reincidence, a rating of 1 indicating a single type of maltreatment, a rating of 2 indicating two different types of maltreatment, and so on.

The reliability and validity tests conducted on these indicators and the uniformity with which the data were collected ensured the comparability of these ratings, both within as well as across the 19 projects.[4]

The reliance upon clinical judgments of success was necessary because of the diversity in service structure and philosophy represented by the 19

Table 4.1

Descriptions of the 19 Demonstration Projects

Project Name	Project Affiliation
Family Resource Center, Team III Albuquerque, New Mexico	Team III is the sexual abuse treatment unit of the Family Resource Center (FRC), an organization housed within the New Mexico Department of Human Services, the state's mandated child abuse and neglect agency
Child Abuse Unit for Studies, Education, and Services (CAUSES) Chicago, Illinois	CAUSES is located within the Illinois Masonic Medical Center complex but is a private nonprofit organization entirely financially independent of the Medical Center.
Family Sexual Abuse Project (FSAP) Edina, Minnesota	The host agency of the NCCAN demonstration project is the Family Renewal Center, a chemical dependency family treatment program in the Fairview-Southdale Hospital.
Project Against the Sexual Abuse of Appalachian Children (PASAAC) Knoxville, Tennessee	PASAAC is affiliated with the Child and Family Services of Knox County, Inc. (CFS), a multiservice, voluntary, nonprofit agency funded by a variety of sources
Atlantic County Adolescent Maltreatment Project Atlantic City, New Jersey	The demonstration project is located administratively within the New Jersey Division of Youth and Family Services (DYFS).

Client Population	Theoretical Model
FRC refers only to families with a substantiated history of sexual abuse to Team III. Typically, these families are disorganized, unable to communicate, lack clearly-defined parent-child roles, appear to be functioning better than they are, and have a family dynamic of secrecy.	Team III employs a multidisciplinary approach to the treatment of sexual abuse, combining social support services with psychiatric and psychological therapy in an effort to improve family members' behavior and functioning by manipulating the dysfunctional environment.
CAUSES' research sample consists of all the substantiated sexual abuse cases which have been referred to the mandated child protection agency. In the past, 69.3% of the offenders have been natural parents or stepparents, usually fathers. The abused children are 88.9% female, with most being between 6 and 17 years of age.	Because the project sees the primary treatment need of their clients as being help with the immediate crisis of disclosure, supportive psychotherapy is favored over exploratory therapy. This treatment approach emphasizes symptom relief and overt behavioral change rather than modification of personality or resolution of psychological disturbances. Once the immediate situation is stabilized, the client becomes "treatable" in the traditional sense.
Due to project perceptions about the nature of intrafamily sexual abuse, FASP accepts only families. The definition of "family" started out as nuclear, but later broadened to include surrogate and quasi-family situations. The typical family served by the project consists of a father, mother, a teenage female incest victim, and at least one other child.	The project sees sexual abuse as a family systems problem with its roots firmly planted in the family's history. Thus, the primary causal factors associated with this form of maltreatment are generational and socioemotional. Since sexual abuse is primarily a family problem, the family must be treated as a unit. Therefore, the project has modified the 12 steps of Alcoholics Anonymous to accommodate sexual abuse cases.
The project treats clients on a priority basis according to need, with much of its client population being white and of a rural background. These clients can be described as having a long history of isolation, with many having deficits in social and relational skills. An adversarial model of parenting is also common, in which children are viewed as wild and evil by nature.	PASAAC's model for intervention and treatment combines a social casework model with the PLISSIT model of sex therapy. This model is based upon the belief that family life is the central value focus for many rural clients, even if the family is dysfunctional. Social casework rests on a holistic theory where concrete and educational services are integral parts of therapy.
The population served by this project includes families where the stress of raising an adolescent (12-17 years) results in physical or sexual abuse. This abuse should be reasonably substantiated and unique to the adolescent period.	The operating hypothesis of this project is that juvenile delinquency and adolescent behavior problems are due more to maltreatment than any other cause. Maltreated adolescents can be helped more by treating and strengthening the family, rather than by breaking it up. Project staff found adolescents reluctant to be placed in foster care, and quick to get involved in the "placement-replacement" syndrome.

Table 4.1 continued

Project Name	Project Affiliation
Diogenes Youth Services Sacramento, California	The project's host agency is Diogenes Youth Services, Inc., a series of youth crisis programs administered and supported from the business office located in Davis, California.
Youth in Need (YIN) St. Charles, Missouri	The NCCAN demonstration project for maltreated adolescents is located within the more general Youth in Need House, a shelter providing counseling and advocacy services for young persons in the St. Charles area.
Project Response Waterville, Maine	The parent agency for Project Response is Community Justice Programs, Inc. (C.J.P.), a nonprofit organization emphasizing the issues of justice and social redress.
Child Abuse and Neglect/ Substance Abuse Family Evaluation and Therapy Investigation Ann Arbor, Michigan	The project is a part of the Youth Outpatient Program of the Youth Service Division of the Department of Psychiatry, University of Michigan.
Arkansas Alcohol/Child Abuse Demonstration Project (ALCAN) Little Rock, Arkansas	The demonstration project is sponsored by the Graduate School of Social Work, University of Arkansas, Little Rock.
Parent and Child Treatment Program (PACT) New York, New York	PACT is one of a number of community-oriented health care programs of the Center for Comprehensive Health Practice (CCHP) which was founded in 1974 by New York Medical College to provide comprehensive care for general and high-risk populations.

Client Population	Theoretical Model

Most families are nuclear, with an increasing number of single-parent families. The client population has been primarily white, representing an upper-lower-class to lower-middle-class socioeconomic strata. The primary type of abuse seen is physical abuse from slapping to closed-fisted punching, as well as sexual abuse.

The project uses a casework model centering on family counseling. The counseling is eclectic, based on ego psychology, transactional analysis, Gestalt techniques, role-playing, and communication skill-building. Diogenes believes the family to be the best resource and context to deal with maltreatment problems.

The project's client population consists of adolescents 12-18 years old with 65% being female and 35% male. The majority of clients are white and are from two-parent households -- most are reconstituted families with an average income between $10,000 and $13,000 a year.

YIN employs a family systems approach which utilizes a psychodynamic base. This approach looks at the family as a system of dynamic interactions, with each family member contributing behaviorally to both the health and dysfunction of the family system.

The client population has been primarily white and approximately 75% of the families involved have been the recipients of AFDC or other forms of public assistance. On average, five family members per case have been involved with the project. Seventeen of 42 families had no parent involvement at all.

The model employed by Project Response postulates that parents who abuse and/or neglect their children are ineffective. The approach with parents is, therefore, to assist them in becoming more effective. The model seeks to put parents in control of their lives and to be competent in life situations.

The families receiving services from the Ann Arbor project have limited educations, tend to be working class, and are usually experiencing marital or other personal problems as well as problems with their children. The children demonstrate such problems as truancy, poor school performance, and drug abuse.

The Ann Arbor project has been founded on the belief that structural family therapy can be used effectively to reduce child abuse and neglect within families where substance abuse is also found. This approach views all individual behavior within the context of the family system. By altering the family's pattern of interaction, the abuse can be overcome.

The emphasis of the project is on the treatment of abused adolescents. Many of these clients have a long history of severe maltreatment, usually physical neglect and emotional abuse, by the time they reach adolescence. The parents of these victims tend to marry and have children at an early age. About one-third of the parents are currently single, and many families have been reconstituted. Alcohol abuse is a major problem, along with low education, low income, and social isolation.

The diagnostic method employed by ALCAN is inconsistent with the typical medically-derived model of diagnosis. Diagnosis is an ongoing process beginning with the first client contact and extending through the completion of treatment. Treatment options are constantly redefined as family or individual conditions change.

The educational attainment of adult clients averages about the middle of high school. Almost none of the clients are employed, so welfare is their chief means of support. About 45% of the clients are black, 45% Hispanic, and 5% white. The child clients are under seven years of age and evenly divided as to sex. The most common problem confronting these children is neglect.

PACT's basic premise is that the target population is in need of comprehensive services. The problems confronting clients are multiple and tend to reinforce one another in a syndrome of substance abuse, child maltreatment, emotional problems, ill health, and poverty. A combination of medical, social, psychological, and concrete services incorporated into a comprehensive outlook is needed to break this cycle.

Table 4.1 continued

Project Name	Project Affiliation
Project Respite and Remediation (R & R) Colorado Springs, Colorado	The host agency of Project R & R is the Urban League of the Pikes Peak Region, Inc.
Early Stimulation Project (ESP) New Haven, Connecticut	The parent organization for ESP is the Hill Health Center, which provides health services to all age groups in the community.
Children's Trauma Center Oakland, California	The Trauma Center is affiliated with Children's Hospital and Medical Center, the major pediatric facility in Northern California.
Project Begin Again Pittsburgh, Pennsylvania	The NCCAN-funded project is housed within the Parental Stress Center (PSC), which shares its facilities as well as staff and other resources with the project. The host institution of PSC is the Children's Hospital of Pittsburgh, which offers a comprehensive service program including both medical and social services.
Specialized Treatment of Child Neglect Project Auburn, Washington	The Muckleshoot Indian Tribe is the parent organization of the NCCAN project. The project is overseen by the Muckleshoot Child Welfare committee, which is appointed by the Tribal Council.

Client Population	Theoretical Model

Families participating in project services are primarily low-income families with children age 1 to 6. The current caseload is racially mixed and includes both single- and two-parent families, half of which are connected with one of the area's military bases. Most of the children display an average 8-1/2 month developmental delay, with severe difficulties in speech and language.

The assumption underlying Project R & R is that if neglectful or abusive parents are taught the parenting skills they lack, the family situation will improve. While the parents are being educated, children's developmental delays and behavior problems can be corrected through structured remedial services. The project minimizes the use of foster care placements, with the child generally remaining at home during the treatment period.

Most of the families receiving services are single parents with one or more children. Few parents have completed high school, and most are on welfare. The racial composition of the clients is approximately 50% black, 40% Hispanic, and 10% other. Typically, these children are emotionally and physically neglected as well as physically abused.

The basic premise underlying ESP is that a child cannot be treated effectively without treating the parent as well. Therefore, the thrust of services is to educate both, emphasizing remediation for children and reparenting for the parents. These two foci are combined into a family systems approach which gives the clinician an understanding of how one family member's behavior affects the other members.

The clients currently being served by the Center are primarily low-income, minority families who live relatively close to the hospital. The parents are often separated or in marital situations that are extremely stressful. Seventy percent of the adults receiving services are females 19-32 years old, 80% are blacks, and 60% are unemployed. All children in the program have been physically abused or are the siblings of a physically abused child.

The therapeutic preschool, established in 1977, emphasizes combining education and skill development with psychotherapy in the treatment of abused children. More recently, however, staff found that the program needed to work more on parent-child interaction and the integration of child and adult services.

The client population is divided between two service components, the Residential Nursery and the Parent Training Component. The residential component serves infants under six months old who have been physically injured, victims of failure-to-thrive, or living in a high-risk situation. The training component serves children up to 2-1/2 years old who have been victims of neglect.

The treatment plan used at the project has a multiple emphasis, which focuses on the child while also working with the parents and emphasizing the interaction between parent and child. The goal of services is to get the parents to the point where they are able to teach the child and help him or her through the various developmental stages. In addition, the project uses a social work model in providing basic emotional and physical support, and a family systems approach in assessing how family members interact.

The families served by the project are usually extremely poor and live in overcrowded, inadequate housing. Most parents have less than a high school education and lack employment skills. Most families are single-parent and lack the support provided by extended family relationships. The most prevalent types of child neglect include lack of supervision, poor nutrition, and emotional neglect.

The project feels that the general mistreatment of Indians makes it extremely difficult for them to provide for their children. Added to this problem is the fact that many of the parents in the project were placed outside the reservation as children, and thus lack support systems. The project's philosophy is that the individual project staff members must take over the role of the elders for these parents, and serve as an extended family. The approach is to support the family, teach the parents child care skills, and help resolve problems.

Table 4.1 continued

Project Name	Project Affiliation
Child Neglect Demonstration of the Dallas Children and Youth Project (DC&Y) Dallas, Texas	The DC&Y Project has been providing comprehensive medical services to high-risk and non-high-risk cases since 1968. The NCCAN funding is used to document the existing services program for neglect cases and evaluate this program's effectiveness.
Hospitalized Infants with Nonorganic Failure to Thrive Denver, Colorado	The Failure to Thrive Project is one of the activities of the C. Henry Kempe Center for Prevention and Treatment of Child Abuse and Neglect of Denver.
Project Time for Parents St. Louis, Missouri	Project Time for Parents is a component of the Family Resource Center, established in 1974 to reduce child abuse by providing a therapeutic and educational environment for both parents and children.

demonstration projects. Given that not all projects agreed on the specific behavioral or attitudinal changes they were seeking in clients, it was impossible to utilize standardized assessment measures of such concepts as self-esteem, parenting skills, child development knowledge, coping strategies, or social isolation. Further, the study captured only those changes in client functioning which occurred during treatment. Consequently, the study measured the likelihood for future maltreatment, not whether, in fact, future abuse or neglect occurred. Measuring longer-term client impact remains one of the most critical needs in child abuse and neglect research.

Within these limitations, the National Clinical Evaluation Study allowed for the systematic assessment of a sizable sample of families who were involved in different patterns of maltreatment and who received different types of intervention. Comparable data were collected, not only with respect to clinical judgments of the three outcome measures, but also

Client Population	Theoretical Model
The majority of neglect cases referred to the project involve children 3 years old or less exhibiting medical problems due to poor nutrition or infections, socioemotional problems, and cognitive delays. Most of the maltreators are extremely young single mothers with at least three children, the first of which was born while the mother was in her early teens.	The fundamental philosophy of the DC&Y Project is that all individuals deserve quality health services. A system of neighborhood clinics staffed by a multidisciplinary team offering a wide range of specialized services enables the project to reach out to the isolated neglect families and provide comprehensive medical, support, and social services to address the overwhelming needs of both mother and children.
Parents of infants with nonorganic failure to thrive served by the project are typically young adults (14–31 years) with one or two children, living with a spouse or common-law partner. Nearly all of the cases are low-income households.	The primary intervention of the project's treatment program is the lay health visitor, who acts as an empathic listener friend to the client, in an effort to reduce environmental stresses, isolation, and lack of a support system.
The main characteristic of neglecting parents is a limited capacity to cope with the stress of daily living, coupled with the additional stress of poverty, lack of social supports, several children, and a chaotic household. Neglect cases differ from the abuse cases within FRC in that neglect families appear to have fewer resources, social skills, and supports, and are more withdrawn. The children involved in these cases tend to be passive, withdrawn, and developmentally delayed.	The treatment approach of the project is based on the combination of two models, the Social Learning Approach and the Family Systems Theory. Social Learning focuses on inappropriate client behavior and attempts to change the environmental stimulus and/or teach the appropriate behavior. The Family Systems Theory attempts to resolve family dysfunction by focusing on the different roles assumed by each member, the interactional and communication patterns, and the family's general structure.

with respect to client characteristics and service profiles. The specific data collected on the adult clients included:

demographic characteristics—including age, sex, race, marital status;

problems noted at intake—including the number of presenting problems noted and the presence of a substance abuse problem;

maltreatment characteristics—including the primary type of maltreatment, the range of maltreatment which the client had been involved with at intake, and the severity of harm to the child resulting from this maltreatment;

compliance index—a composite score summarizing the extent to which the client acknowledged harm to the child resulting from the maltreatment, the client's willingness to change, and the client's acceptance of project services; and

service variables—including the client's length of time in treatment, the number of different types of service the client received, and

whether or not the client received individual counseling, group counseling, family counseling, educational and skills development classes,
parenting education, casework counseling, concrete services (e.g.,
food, clothing, transportation, medical care, etc.), or support services
(e.g., advocacy, legal assistance, recreational, lay therapy, etc.).

Each set of factors was assessed individually in the order outlined above.
This analytic method was selected in order to enter and control for all
variation in the outcomes which might be explained by nonservice-related
factors such as client characteristics and attitudes. If a significant degree
of variation in outcomes can be explained by the services after the influence of other factors has been accounted for, it would suggest that the
services played a meaningful and unique role in determining client outcomes.

In interpreting the study's findings, a number of factors should be kept
in mind. Because of the inevitable correlation between certain client characteristics and specific services, the analytic method employed in this
study represents a very conservative approach to identifying service impacts. To compensate for the lack of a formal control or comparison group,
the method assumes that there is no consistent relationship between client
characteristics and the provision of services. Individuals can be offered
only the services that an agency or individual practitioner has available,
and the range is usually quite narrow. To be sure, the services provided to
a given client are indeed partially determined by the client's characteristics
or, in the case of this study, by the type and severity of the initial maltreatment. When this type of selective service assignment exists, some of the
observed impact is shared between services and nonservice factors. By initially controlling for differences in client characteristics and presenting
problems in explaining positive outcomes, the analyses have potentially
contributed some service effects to client characteristics.

Only those services that made a statistically significant contribution to
client outcomes after considering the impacts of various nonservice factors
are discussed below. While such a stringent test is useful for highlighting
the most salient contributions to client outcomes, this strategy may overlook the influence of services that were more highly correlated with client
characteristics or that failed to pass tests of statistical significance. To investigate the extent to which certain types of clients systematically received or did not receive certain services, a series of multivariate analyses
were conducted on the adult client sample. As discussed in Appendix A,
these methods found very little correlation between a client's demographic
characteristics, presenting problems, or maltreatment patterns and a given
set of services. Consequently, the positive client impacts reported with respect to the evaluation's three outcome measures appear to be the result
of a number of unique and independent factors. Further, the relative im-

portance of these factors differed for the three maltreatment subpopulations studied.

Exploring the impact of different maltreatment patterns on overall client outcomes is an important factor in identifying true service impact. In order to determine if different factors contributed to the achievement of positive outcomes for clients involved in different types of maltreatment, individual analyses were conducted on three subgroups within this adult client sample—the 234 adults primarily involved in emotional maltreatment; the 291 adults primarily involved in neglect; and the 154 adults primarily involved in sexual abuse. Because too few adults were identified as being primarily involved in physical abuse (i.e., less than 150), an insufficient sample existed to support independent analysis of this subpopulation.

As summarized in Table 4.2, variation in success among clients experiencing different types of maltreatment was very evident in this client sample. Greater success in terms of overall client gains as well as in a reduced propensity toward future maltreatment was realized more often among those clients primarily involved in sexual abuse than among clients primarily involved in child neglect. For example, 64% of the adults primarily involved in sexual abuse were judged by their clinicians to be unlikely to maltreat their children further, an assessment given to only 30% of the adults primarily involved in child neglect. This success rate with the sexual abuse cases was even more dramatic among the four projects focusing specifically on sexual abuse, where clinicians judged over 70% of their client families to be unlikely to experience reabuse in the future. While the four projects that focused on child neglect also experienced better than average success in reducing the likelihood for further neglect among their caseloads (i.e., a 40% success rate on this measure), interventions targeted to this subpopulation have had largely disappointing results. The most notable difference across the three groups involved the reincidence measure. Over 80% of the adults involved in sexual abuse had no reincidence of any type of abuse during treatment, a situation which applied to only 34% of the neglect sample and 25% of the emotional maltreatment sample.

The initial success with families involved in sexual abuse achieved by the demonstration projects parallels the findings others have noted in working with this population (Giarretto, 1976; Anderson and Schafer, 1979; Bander et al., 1982; Sgroi, 1982).[5] In generalizing these findings to all cases of sexual abuse, it is important to bear in mind that the vast majority of these cases involved father-daughter or stepfather-daughter incest. A sizable number of perpetrators served by all of these projects admitted their guilt and accepted responsibility for their actions. As discussed below, this level of compliance was unique among the three subpopulations analyzed and may well differentiate this group from the total universe of molesters. It is also important to remember that, to date, only limited follow-up stud-

Table 4.2

Client Outcomes by Subpopulation

| | By Primary Type of Maltreatment | | | | | | | |
| | All Adults | | Emotional Maltreatment | | Neglect | | Sexual Abuse | |
	%	n	%	n	%	n	%	n
Clinical Judgment of Progress								
Client Got Worse	6	70	9	22	7	20	4	5
Client Stayed the Same	35	401	37	83	39	107	27	35
Client Improved	59	668	54	122	53	145	69	89
TOTAL	100	1,139	100	227	100	272	100	129
Likelihood for Future Maltreatment								
Very Likely	30	344	44	100	38	108	18	29
Somewhat Likely	24	282	29	65	32	89	18	28
Somewhat Unlikely	21	241	15	34	18	51	34	49
Very Unlikely	25	293	12	27	12	34	30	42
TOTAL	100	1,160	100	226	100	282	100	141
Number of Maltreatment Types Occurring During Program Enrollment								
No Reincidence	51	610	25	58	34	96	81	114
One Type of Reincidence	25	301	32	75	33	94	12	17
Two Types of Reincidence	18	212	27	63	30	86	6	8
Three Types of Reincidence	5	63	12	29	3	10	<1	1
Four Types of Reincidence	1	12	4	9	--	--	<1	1
TOTAL	100	1,198	100	234	100	286	100	141

ies have been conducted on incestuous families and that the very positive gains noted at termination with these families may not be sustained over time. Those follow-up studies that have been conducted suggest eventual reincidence rates of more than 20% (Able et al., 1984). Also, certain types of offenders, such as those who abuse boys, those who are more exclusively pedophilic, and those who have an "ideological" commitment to offending, show great propensity to reoffend (Groth and Burgess, 1979; Abel et al., 1984).

Table 4.3 summarizes the extent to which a client's progress on each of the three outcome measures utilized in this study was explained by different client characteristics and services. While the full results of the regression model used to determine these percentages are presented in Appendix B, the table highlights the different roles each of the five factors summarized on page 101 played in determining a client's response to treatment. Collectively, these factors accounted for between 23% and 51% of the variance observed in the study's three outcome measures. These levels of explained variance were statistically significant in all cases and validated the study's initial hypothesis regarding the relative importance of different client characteristics and services in explaining outcomes. As outlined in Table 4.3, the importance of the compliance index, the client's initial presenting problems, and the severity of the client's initial maltreatment in explaining positive outcomes varied across the three subpopulations assessed.

Over 30% of the variation in the client's overall progress and almost 17% of the variation in the clinician's assessment of the client's propensity for future maltreatment was explained by the compliance index for the sexual abuse subpopulation. In contrast, this factor explained less than 6% of the variation on any of the outcome measures for those adults involved in emotional maltreatment and less than 8% on these measures for clients involved primarily in child neglect. This pattern suggests that initial recognition of the harm associated with maltreatment and a commitment to change behaviors at the point of service intake may be a far more salient factor in achieving clinical success in cases of sexual abuse than in cases of either emotional maltreatment or child neglect. Secrecy with respect to the maltreatment is a powerful and unique force to overcome in the identification and treatment of sexual abuse. Bruises, broken bones, poor school attendance, or persistent illnesses frequently indicate the presence of maltreatment long before any family member is willing to admit that a problem exists. Although individual family members will certainly vary in terms of their recognition of the abuse and in their acceptance of services, referral to the treatment program for sexual abuse occurs because someone has told the secret and, in so doing, has removed one of the major barriers to successful intervention. On average, the adults involved in sexual abuse scored 2.5 on the five-point compliance index in comparison to an average

Table 4.3

Percent of Variance in Client Outcomes Explained by

Key Service and Client Characteristics by Subpopulation

	Demographic Characteristics	Problems at Intake	Maltreatment Characteristics	Compliance Index	Service Variables	Total Variance Explained by All Factors
Clinical Judgment of Client's Overall Progress						
Emotional Maltreatment	3%	1%	1%	5%	13%	23%
Child Neglect	4%	8%	1%	6%	16%	35%
Sexual Abuse	1%	1%	3%	30%	16%	51%
Clinical Judgment of Client's Likelihood for Future Maltreatment						
Emotional Maltreatment	4%	4%	7%	4%	9%	28%
Child Neglect	3%	8%	5%	7%	8%	31%
Sexual Abuse	3%	5%	10%	17%	6%	41%
Incidence of Reabuse or Reneglect During Treatment						
Emotional Maltreatment	6%	9%	14%	1%	10%	40%
Child Neglect	2%	2%	9%	4%	7%	24%
Sexual Abuse	6%	1%	13%	--	9%	29%

score of 1.8 for those adults involved in emotional maltreatment and 1.6 for those adults involved in child neglect.

Of the three subpopulations, the client's initial set of presenting problems had far more influence in predicting outcomes for the child neglect sample than for either the emotional maltreatment or sexual abuse sample. Specifically, the presence of a substance abuse problem proved a more formidable barrier to overcome when the family was involved primarily in child neglect. In general, these adults were judged to have made less overall progress in treatment and to have a higher likelihood for future maltreatment. Although clients who were involved in substance abuse fared less well overall in treatment than those who were not, and approximately equal percentages of the three subsamples were identified as having a substance abuse problem, this difficulty proved a consistent barrier to treatment only in the cases of child neglect. This finding suggests that programs targeting their services to a neglect population may be particularly well advised to include staff trained in the identification and treatment of substance abuse problems.

For all three subpopulations, the severity of the initial maltreatment was the best predictor of abuse or neglect during treatment. Those adults involved in multiple forms of maltreatment or who had a longer history of mistreating their children were more likely to continue this behavior while in treatment regardless of their primary form of abuse or neglect. Again, it is important to bear in mind that wide variation existed in the frequency of repeated maltreatment among the three subpopulations. Only 19% of the sexual abuse sample was involved in repeated abuse in contrast to 66% of the neglect sample and 75% of the emotional maltreatment sample. Although the use of placement or requiring the perpetrator to leave the home was an effective prevention strategy in cases of sexual abuse and severe physical abuse, foster care placement was not a critical variable in stopping repeated neglect or emotional maltreatment. In fact, placement had a significant impact on reincidence rates only for the younger children in the sample. Whereas over 32% of the adolescents who were in foster care placement during the treatment period were identified as repeated victims of maltreatment, only 17% of the children under 13 who resided in foster care were identified as experiencing repeated abuse or neglect. The ability to stop maltreatment simply may be far more difficult in cases of emotional maltreatment and neglect, even if the adult is in an intensive treatment program and sees the child for only limited periods of time.

Of the three outcome measures utilized in this study, the provision of specific services had the strongest impacts with respect to a client's overall progress in treatment. With the exception of the sexual abuse subpopulation, projects were generally more successful in improving their clients' overall functioning than they were in reducing a client's likelihood for future maltreatment or avoiding new abusive episodes while the family was in treatment. Clinicians noted improvements in their clients with respect to self-esteem, management of anger, use of social supports, child development knowledge, appropriate roles and responsibilities within the family and achievement of various employment and vocational objectives. In certain cases, particularly those involving sexual abuse, such improvements were seen as significantly reducing a client's propensity toward future maltreatment. Cases of chronic neglect, emotional maltreatment or severe physical abuse were rated more cautiously. Even when their clients exhibited these types of short-term gains, clinicians were not convinced that reabuse would not occur, particularly if the parent faced increased stress or the child's behavior became more problematic.

All of the projects conducted a careful assessment of the family as the initial step in the treatment process. While each of the demonstration projects approached this task somewhat differently, the most common procedure involved a series of personal interviews either with the individual clients or with the family as a unit and the administration of one or more standardized assessment instruments. While the four child neglect projects and the four projects targeting services to families involving very young victims focused particularly on the child's health and developmental needs and on the quality of the home environment and support system, all 19 projects adopted an ecological treatment approach and most commonly considered their clients to be the "family" unit as opposed to either the individual adult or child member.

Independent of the number or types of services the client received, the length of time a client was involved with the project proved a significant contributor to positive outcomes. Adult clients included in this study sample who received services for six months or less were less likely to make overall progress in treatment and to demonstrate a reduced propensity for future maltreatment than were clients who received services for longer than 18 months. While the predictive strength of this measure varied across the three subpopulations studied, the direction of this measure was consistent. In the case of the neglect sample, 13 to 18 months emerged as the most effective treatment period. The strongest outcomes in the emotional maltreatment and sexual abuse samples were noted among those receiving services between seven and 18 months. These patterns, while not always statistically significant, suggest that simply retaining a client in a program for an extended period of time may not produce more positive outcomes. The potential for intervention strategies like those supported by federal demonstration efforts may diminish after 18 months. For clients not making any significant progress after a year and a half of services, clinicians would be wiser to refer the family to another type of intervention or to terminate parental rights than to continue offering more of the same service. In fact, the clients retained for longer periods in these types of intensive therapeutic services actually appear to lose ground over time.

As for specific services, the most effective interventions differed for the three populations. While clients in all three subsamples benefited from a combination of therapeutic, support, and basic care services, the relative importance and utility of these service modalities differed across the three groups. Compared to the other two subpopulations studied, those involved in sexual abuse made impressive gains in terms of reduced propensity. Overall, only 36% of the adults primarily involved in sexual abuse were determined by their clinicians to be likely to reabuse their children in the future. While no individual service consistently emerges as a statistically significant explanation for this performance, the four projects that focused specifically on sexual abuse provided a particularly successful package of services including individual, group, and family therapy. Following an intensive psychosocial assessment and diagnostic process, most of the clients served by these projects were involved in individual therapy, initially weekly and then diminishing in frequency as other therapeutic modes were introduced. The primary objective of this service was to address specific problems that were not easily handled in a family or group therapy session. In only rare instances, however, was individual therapy the sole intervention utilized.

Group therapy was considered by the projects to be extremely useful in confronting issues shared by a number of clients, providing a support system for them, developing interpersonal skills and empathy, and in socialization. Individual groups were established for the male offenders, for the mothers of the victims, and for the victims themselves. In the male offenders group, the primary issue was taking responsibility for the sexual abuse and moving beyond vows that the abuse would not happen again to wanting to understand the underlying causes behind the initial maltreatment. Although the men usually entered the group minimizing the sexual abuse, having strong suicidal tendencies, and idealizing their families of origin, the group process proved helpful in confronting not only the sexual abuse but also this idealization. Participants often were able supportively to tell one another that the childhood experiences they described were abusive even when they could not label their own experiences as maltreatment. Such support was viewed by project staff as critical in reducing suicidal feelings and enhancing positive ego development. Staff saw reflective reformation (i.e., learning more through what you teach than through what you are taught) as being of central importance in achieving positive client outcomes.

Group therapy was also provided to the mothers of sexually abused children. Because a significant percentage of these mothers had themselves been sexually abused as children, these women also were encouraged to participate in adult victim groups operated by the projects. Such groups assisted these mothers in dealing first with their own victimization before addressing the needs of their daughters. In one instance, an attempt was made to combine adult victims with the mothers of current victims. It was initially thought that the ex-victims' anger toward their own mothers and the mothers' denial of responsibility and lack of empathy for their daughters could be addressed in a group setting to the advantage of both parties. However, despite staff efforts, the prior victims were excessively support-ive and nonconfrontative of the mothers and mothers seemed removed from the legacy of distress evidenced by the prior victims. This effort high-lighted the degree of intra- and interpersonal damage that can result from incest and the degree of rigidity, interpersonal distancing, and resistance to therapy that can initially characterize the mothers of incest victims. Overcoming these therapeutic barriers was more effectively achieved by establishing separate groups.

Family therapy involving all family members was usually the final coun-seling service provided prior to termination. Family sessions were held twice a month and focused on improving the family decision-making proc-ess and making ths process overt, identifying the role of normal sexual tension inherent in family life and learning to use it to ensure cohesion rather than destruction of the family, strengthening roles and clarifying role boundaries, and improving communications. One of the projects also staged multiple family group therapy sessions. The entire patient commu-nity met for two hours in a family workshop to teach the incest families to relate to a larger system and to reduce social isolation.

While the demonstration effort identified a combination of services that appear successful in working with sexual abuse cases, only partial service guidelines were generated with respect to the other forms of maltreatment examined. Family counseling to enhance positive outcomes proved partic-ularly effective with families involved in child neglect. The demonstration projects that centered their interventions on family therapy shared a com-mon commitment to resolving an adult's presenting problems within the context of his or her family sphere. The involvement of the entire family in treatment enhances each individual's chance for personal recovery. By addressing problems within a family context, the harmful beliefs and val-ues that have permitted abuse to occur are appropriately challenged and alternative models of discipline, showing affection, and demonstrating re-spect can be defined and practiced. In situations in which reunification of the family is considered the preferred clinical outcome, strengthening the family unit through the provision of family counseling would appear to be a critical first step in achieving this goal.[6]

Although 15 of the 19 projects served a sizable percentage of families involved in neglect, the four projects that specifically targeted this problem produced the most notable gains. Among the unique service characteris-tics represented by the four projects focusing on the problem of child ne-glect was the use of a broad range of community service referrals in provid-ing supportive services to almost two-thirds of their clients. As discussed in Chapter 6, these projects devoted significant resources both to assessing a family's need for a variety of basic care needs, such as food, clothing, emergency shelter, medical services, transportation, and legal assistance, and to providing these services either directly or through referral. This process was useful not only in addressing the family's immediate needs but also in familiarizing the family with the community's service network. Clients served by these projects were also provided an opportunity to participate in group therapy sessions. The primary focus of these sessions was the changing conditions in the client's living environment and improving the client's knowledge with respect to parenting and child development. This focus was in sharp contrast to the emphasis taken by those projects addressing the problem of sexual abuse, where the primary objective was to change the perpetrator's behavior and to improve the interpersonal relationships among all family members.

While not always statistically significant, the provision of casework counseling and educational and skill development classes was positively correlated with successful client outcomes for the neglect sample. Casework counseling, or basic problem solving, appeared to be uniquely effective with families involved in this type of maltreatment. Neglectful parents, generally single mothers, responded well to weekly casework counseling sessions which focused on resolving their immediate parenting problems or personal crises. Often involving in-home visits, this service provided projects with the flexibility to respond to the many and varied basic care needs often demonstrated by this subpopulation. This particular group of clients also responded well to the provision of education and skill development classes, which provided basic knowledge regarding the care of children, developed the clients' powers of reasoning and judgment, and improved their practical skills with respect to home management and social interactions. While specific child care tasks, such as diapering an infant, were covered in these classes, the instruction was not comprehensive with respect to parenting education or child development. In fact, the neglect sample generally did not respond favorably to formal parenting education classes and responded best when presentations on this topic were extremely concrete. These clients wanted to be shown exactly what steps needed to be taken in managing their households or in caring for their children. Attempts to ground these behaviors in the theoretical context of a child's different developmental stages and needs was not successful with these clients.

In contrast, those adults involved in emotional maltreatment had a positive response to more formal parenting education classes and group therapy. While not always statistically significant, these services contributed to the overall progress of these clients and to clinical judgments of reduced propensity for future maltreatment. Often the provision of these two services was conducted in tandem. Weekly two- to three-hour meetings of five to ten clients were held, with the initial portion of the meeting covering the basic stages of child development and specific parenting practices. Particular attention was paid during this period on providing parents with nonphysical methods of discipline. Following this instructional period, the parents would meet as a group to discuss both parenting and nonparenting issues such as poor impulse control, empathy, depression, and social isolation. Although this approach was not particularly successful with the neglect families, the adults primarily involved in emotional maltreatment made better use of this service package in effectively addressing their problems.

The differential success rates noted among the 19 projects may have more to do with the characteristics of families involved in different forms of maltreatment than with differences in the service delivery system. All of the 19 demonstration projects provided a full array of therapeutic as well as nontherapeutic services to their clients. Parenting education classes, assistance in securing welfare benefits and health care services, recreational activities to reduce social isolation, homemaker services, and vocational and job training assistance were provided by these projects along with at least one therapeutic service modality. The primary focus on the therapeutic process noted among those projects working specifically with sexual abuse, and the success of this approach, may not be transferable to other maltreatment subpopulations. To the extent that families involved in other forms of maltreatment are, on average, more resistant to change, face a greater number of financial and external family stresses, and are involved in multiple forms of maltreatment, these families may not be best served through intensive combinations of individual, group, and family therapy. Strategies that rely solely upon costly professional therapy without augmenting it with other supportive or remedial services offer less opportunity for maximizing clinical gains with these other subpopulations.

Service Effectiveness for Children

The National Clinical Evaluation Study identified a number of effective direct services for children and adolescents. Although the eight projects specifically funded to serve maltreatment victims implemented the broadest array of diagnostic and treatment methods for adolescents and children, all 19 of the demonstration projects adopted a family treatment focus rather than an individual one. Over 80% of all families served by the 19 projects received direct services for both the perpetrators and the victims of maltreatment. All told, over 1,600 children and adolescents were provided a wide range of direct services including individual therapy, group counseling, therapeutic day care, speech and physical therapy, and medical care. This rich array of services correlated with improved functioning for children and adolescents who had experienced a variety of abusive and neglectful behaviors. Unlike the difficulties noted in effectively working with adults involved in different maltreatment patterns, gains with maltreated children were more universal. Over 70% of the young children and adolescents served by the eight projects focusing specifically on these client populations demonstrated gains across all functional areas during treatment.[7]

The size of the infant, children and adolescent samples generated by the latest round of federal demonstration projects allowed for the application of the same type of multiple regression techniques conducted on the adult sample in order to identify those factors that accounted for positive outcomes. In the case of the adolescent and children samples, services had a unique and significant impact on all three of the study's outcome measures (i.e., the client's overall progress, clinician assessments of the likelihood of reabuse, and the extent of reincidence during treatment). In the case of infants (i.e., clients who were 18 months or less), the provision of specific services did not explain a significant percentage of the variance in either the measures of overall progress or of the likelihood for future maltreatment, although the provision of such services as medical care, supervised parent-child interactions, and infant stimulation was associated with lower reincidence rates.

Several of the projects, particularly those focusing on remedial services to young children and on child neglect included ample opportunities for supervised parent-child interactions in which parents were encouraged to develop more nurturing ways of relating to their children. These observations were conducted at the project's offices as well as in the client's home. These sessions, which lasted from one and a half to two hours, allowed staff to observe the extent to which parents implemented those behaviors discussed during more formal parenting classes and the extent to which children responded to the remedial services being provided to them in other settings. These sessions also served as an opportunity for the staff to model positive behavior, often demonstrating through direct interaction with the child such techniques as positive instructions and praise.

The provision of personal skill development classes, temporary shelter, and group counseling were all identified as contributing to positive client outcomes with the adolescent sample. As might be expected, adolescents who received temporary shelter experienced significantly less reabuse or reneglect during treatment than those who did not receive this service. Generally provided by the two adolescent treatment projects which also operated service programs for runaway and homeless youth, temporary shelter offered protection for the adolescent, appropriate caretaker modeling and the opportunity to build trust with staff. While in the shelter, the youths attended workshops on a variety of topics, depending upon the specific knowledge base and needs of the current residents. The most common topics addressed during these workshops included academic difficulties, the youths' future educational plans, peer pressure, drugs and alcohol, the location of part-time employment, and, for those youths who would be moving into independent living situations, the issues of finding an apartment, securing full-time employment or job training, and managing a household budget. The residents met as a group each evening for an hour and a half to two hours. In general, five to ten such meetings were usually called over any given two-week period. Project staff considered this service to be particularly effective in providing feedback to adolescents from their peers on their approaches to solving problems and in giving each youth an opportunity to experience positive, nondestructive confrontation.

Whether provided within the context of a shelter program or independently, group counseling and personal skill development classes were identified as particularly useful in achieving positive outcomes in terms of the adolescent's overall progress in treatment and in reducing his or her likelihood for future maltreatment. As has been noted by others, group therapy can serve a critical function in the treatment process for adolescent victims of sexual abuse (Porter et al., 1982). In this context, these sessions provide adolescents an arena in which the youth can resolve issues of "difference," guilt, misplaced responsibility, sexuality, peer relationships, parental and sibling reactions, and separation/individuation. Emphasis is placed on gaining control over one's body, assertiveness, socialization skills, and skills for living, including how to listen and how to give and take affection. Since the majority of adolescents seen by the demonstration projects had poor ego boundaries, attention was given to helping them learn to focus, to differentiate between those issues they could control and those they could not and to turn off outside stimulation. Rather than depending on the participants to define the agendas of these sessions, the groups were structured, including specific "exercises" to ensure that everyone participated and that all critical issues were addressed. Touch between the therapists and participants as a nonsexual positive experience was initiated slowly and cautiously by the staff, depending upon the ability of individual clients to accept normal displays of affection and caring.

For maltreated children, the provision of both individual counseling and group counseling has been shown by others to be successful interventions, particularly in cases of sexual abuse. For example, Delson and Clark (1981) instituted a weekly play therapy group for children under 12 years of age that involved art therapy, role playing, and drama; the children's group became an integral part of the family's ongoing treatment program. In a group for four to seven-year-old girls described by Beezley (1977), each weekly session included a talking and sharing time, a structured activity to initiate further fantasy and discussion, free play, and a snack. While the bulk of these activities did not focus on sexual abuse, Beezley felt that the girls came to be able to acknowledge the sexual trauma that had occurred and to discuss their feelings. These outcomes represent the judgments of staff; more objective outcome measures were not obtained. Haase and colleagues (1982) describe a similar treatment program for sexually abused children under the age of five years in a preschool play therapy setting. Through structured and unstructured play, the program provides a safe, nurturing, consistent environment for children three mornings per week.

Although developmental and psychological outcome data are currently being collected, the therapists report very beneficial initial effects.

The provision of therapeutic day care proved the most effective service for the physically abused and neglected children served by the 19 clinical demonstration projects, having a significant impact on reducing a child's likelihood for future maltreatment during and after treatment. In fact, the development of a successful therapeutic day care model is perhaps one of the most useful by-products of the overall demonstration. While significant variations existed in the range of activities provided for children within the context of this service, the typical daily array and sequence of activities included the following:

> *arrival:* children put their coats away, greet one another;
>
> *social time:* group activity geared toward cognitive and social tasks for self-awareness and awareness of other children;
>
> *clean-up and snack preparation:* mats are put away, children wash their hands, help pass out cups, spoons, bowls;
>
> *snack time:* foods low in sugar and salt and high in protein including fresh fruits and vegetables, are planned, recognizing the dietary deficiencies and types of food not available in children's homes; new foods are introduced, and the children have the option of *not* eating (no force-feeding);
>
> *clean-up:* snack things are put away, table is wiped;
>
> *bathroom activities:* diapers are changed, hands washed, teeth brushed, mouths rinsed, etc.;
>
> *structured free play:* art activity, fine motor activities, or sensory area depending upon each child's individual goals;
>
> *group activity:* small groups for older children to work on cognitive and social skills;
>
> *clean-up:* mats put away;
>
> *gross motor activities* (coats on, if going outside);
>
> *music session* (occasionally);
>
> *departure:* children escorted to the bus;
>
> *staff activities:* do final clean-up, complete daily logs, discuss issues with one another, telephone parents (if necessary), evaluate and redefine each child's goals.

Throughout the day, all activities were structured and children were required to verbalize, vocalize, or gesture for each activity. An individualized written plan was prepared for each child, with long-term (one-year) and short-term (under-six-month) goals. For each day the child was present, the assigned teacher recorded how she or he was on arrival, as well as descriptions of the child's daily emotional, behavioral, and physical status, and personal interactions throughout the day with peers, adults, the environment, and the materials. About twice a week in a formal session with the child, the teacher worked one-to-one on specific goal areas in the child's plan. During those sessions the teacher made observations of the child's progress and recorded them. Goals were revised every three months, or whenever there was a gap between the goal and the child's development. In addition to the information exchange at the end of each session among teachers and assistant teachers, staff were encouraged to request a multidisciplinary team meeting if needed.

The intense contact between project staff and abused children enrolled in daily therapeutic services offered an excellent opportunity to identify specific strategies for dealing with a variety of the developmental problems generally presented by this client group. While a more detailed discussion of the problems associated with the design and implementation of therapeutic services for abused children is presented elsewhere,[8] Figure 4.2 highlights the methods staff found particularly useful in addressing problems with attachment, self-concept, speech and language, emotional behavior problems, and physical problems with an abused and neglected population. Although these problems are found among non-maltreated children, they are particularly pronounced and seemingly intractable in children who have experienced long-standing physical abuse, neglect and emotional maltreatment. The costs of providing the intensity and quality of services implied by these methods is significant. (This point is discussed in Chapter 6.) On the other hand, the short- and long-term social costs associated with *not* intervening with the victims of maltreatment are even more substantial.

Again, it is important to underscore the need for a further analysis of service impacts, particularly with respect to how services provided to infants, children, and adolescents complement the services provided to their parents. While children and adolescents do indeed make significant progress in resolving their presenting problems during treatment, sustaining these gains and remaining free from future abuse depend not only on their own progress in treatment, but also on their parents' progress. It is interesting to note that at the time of termination, only 40% of the children and adolescents in these samples were residing in the same household and with the same caretaker they had had at intake. This finding speaks to the difficulty treatment programs have in changing family functioning such that children can safely be returned home once patterns of maltreatment are well established.

Summary and Practice Implications

Protective service agencies will continue to be the primary source of treatment services for the nation's maltreating families. Although these agencies have greatly expanded their intervention strategies through direct ser-

Figure 4.2

Suggested Intervention Strategies with Children by Problem Area

SERVICE STRATEGIES FOR ATTACHMENT PROBLEMS

Leave child alone awhile in the therapeutic setting to allow him or her to feel comfortable with the other children

Attempt to develop the child's attachment to a staff person

Assign one person to pay special attention to the child (if the problems are severe, this person should be a full-time staff member for continuity, rather than a part-time volunteer)

Provide nurturing, encouragement of positive behavior; set up situations with success built in, consistent demands (predictability), limit-setting

Develop challenging tasks with support built in

Slowly include more physical contact (typically, when they realize they will not be hit, these children will want a lot of physical contact)

Encourage consistent attendance of children

Keep staff-child ratio low, so time can be spent developing relationships with the child

Take children of different ages, since some children who are older or who have been in the program awhile will give comfort to the ones who are younger or newer

Encourage the caregiver to hold the child, meet the child's needs

Sensitize foster parents to the special needs of the child

Encourage foster parents to form attachment and not to hold back their affection for fear of removal

Tell foster/birth parents specific ways to foster attachment

Review the children's behaviors with birth/foster parents

SERVICE STRATEGIES FOR EMOTIONAL PROBLEMS

Develop attachments between staff and individual children

Create a supportive, nurturing environment

Implement consistent behavior management and limit-setting techniques (e.g., social isolation for aggression, verbal warnings, sitting the child down, etc.)

Model appropriate social behaviors

Work on making the child more attractive to parents by extinguishing "buggy" behaviors and punishing aggressive behaviors

Gear expectations placed upon the child to his or her level of understanding

Develop trust; be there for the child, even when angry; unconditionally accept him or her. Staff stability is very important in gaining trust

Figure 4.2 continued

Nurture children through the use of praise, physical affection, presentation of highly enjoyable activities, positive reinforcement for coping and staying within limits, small rewards (like the privilege of picking the song, going with the teacher for a snack, etc.)

Implement consistent behavior intervention techniques (e.g., time out for aggression, social isolation for aggression, prompt praise for behaviors incompatible with aggression)

Provide individualized attention and programming to develop skills, encourage development and awareness, etc.

Explain rules

Reinforce foster parents' efforts

Try to teach the same techniques to birth parents

SERVICE STRATEGIES FOR SPEECH AND LANGUAGE PROBLEMS

Exposure to other children

Designate language time in curriculum

Individualize objectives to remediate deficits

Ongoing assessment of language skills (expressive and receptive) of each child

Model appropriate vocalization, gestures, verbalization

Talk to the child, respond to the child

Reduce language (direction-giving, explanations, predicting, etc.) of teaching staff to appropriate levels geared to individual children's comprehension levels

Praise and reward appropriate language (e.g., encourage children to ask for what they want and give it to them whenever possible)

Encourage, request, and, at times, demand appropriate language

General exposure to appropriate materials and activities with an emphasis on language throughout (e.g., gross motor, fine motor, social play, etc.)

SERVICE STRATEGIES FOR PHYSICAL PROBLEMS

Program individual activities to strengthen and develop child's skills, with an emphasis placed on providing challenging experiences within a supportive environment

Conduct ongoing assessments of progress and needs

Provide a variety of experiences including gross motor, fine motor, perceptual skills, etc. (e.g., swings, playground, art supplies, walks in the neighborhood, etc.)

Figure 4.2 continued

During play and play therapy, acknowledge feelings, try to get through to the child

Disseminate information to parents/guardians regarding the child's treatment plan, intervention strategies, and child development in general

Work with foster/birth parents regarding the child's special needs

Match the child's coping skills to the parents'

For children traumatized by experiences, try to desensitize them by exposing them to the fire house, fire engines, hospitals, and animals through field trips and borrowing SPCA pets

Talk to older children to try to clear up their confusion

SERVICE STRATEGIES FOR SELF-CONCEPT PROBLEMS

Establish a child's attachment to one adult staff member

Individualize program, geared to challenge and "built-in" success with emphasis on self-awareness issues

Encourage parent-child interaction through parents' visits to the classroom to learn how to do what the teachers are doing with the children)

Provide for parenting the parents. Family treatment is crucial to work with parents on their own self-concept

Educate parents on what happens in the child when self-concept improves (i.e., the child moves from passivity to assertiveness and the parents have to be ready for it)

Group children by abilities and present appropriate tasks (not age-determined, but developmentally-determined) in which they can experience small successes

Shape and model social interaction to modify withdrawn behaviors

Label feelings, needs, and wants

Help foster/birth parents understand the special needs of the child

Encourage productive play and experimentation

Nurture

SERVICE STRATEGIES FOR BEHAVIOR PROBLEMS

Be consistent with demands, limit-setting (both over time), and promote consistency between staff members

Start with a few demands, increase slowly

Help child with self-control and learning to cope with feelings of hostility and aggression within established limits

Train the child to verbalize feelings (e.g., in cases of physical aggression, the progression is usually from feeling anger to hitting, then to verbalizing "I'm mad" and hitting, then to verbalizing the cause "I'm mad because . . . " and hitting, and finally to "I'm mad because . . . and this is what I want")

119

Figure 4.2 continued

Provide good nutrition in an unpressured atmosphere. Give children
the choice of whether they want to eat or not

Provide a variety of foods, since fears of new foods are broken
down by watching other children eat

Encourage use of medical services by birth/foster parents

Refer to appropriate staff/consultants (nutritionists, doctors)
when necessary

Educate parents on hygiene

Help foster/birth parents understand why problems may exist and
reinforce appropriate behaviors in caregivers

vices and third-party contracts, successfully channeling these services to those families most in need is hampered by an unwillingness of families to cooperate and a shortage of those services most frequently demanded by clients. Efforts to reduce reincidence and placement rates have met with mixed results, although gains have been realized with some severely dysfunctional families. Targeting services to those families who face immediate placement of their children has certain advantages in that these parents are more willing to experiment with new behaviors than are those who are not threatened with the loss of their child. Allowing family situations to reach such a point, however, places the child at great risk for severe and perhaps permanent damage to his or her physical or emotional development. Concern for the safety of the child will continue to result in the use of temporary and, if necessary, permanent foster care placement. Whether such placement is harmful or helpful, both parents and children can benefit from enhanced services prior to and following placement. The consequences of separation need not be negative, depending upon what the child experiences following the separation. The enhancement of traditional protective service interventions should include not only expanded therapeutic and supportive services for maltreating families but also expanded services to foster parents and group home counselors to sensitize them to the implications of maltreatment on the child's perception of himself and his birth parents.

The collective results of federally-funded research and demonstration efforts provide some important policy insight and guidance for practice. Specifically, the most heartening findings include:

greater clarity in understanding the different treatment needs of families experiencing various types of maltreatment;

expanded intervention models which include direct service to *both* adults and children;

improved client outcomes, especially in the areas of individual and family functioning with increasingly more severe cases of maltreatment; and

notable success in initially reducing the risk for future maltreatment among families involved in sexual abuse.

The studies also provide some cause for concern; notably, that treatment efforts in general are still not very successful. Child abuse and neglect continue despite early, thoughtful, and often costly intervention. Clinicians reported very little consistent progress in reducing the future likelihood of maltreatment in the most severe cases of physical abuse, chronic neglect, and emotional maltreatment. Overall, these pattens of abuse continued to occur with alarming frequency in families served by the demonstration projects, even while these families received intensive services. This finding suggests that, in the short run, existing treatment efforts have not been terribly successful in protecting children from further harm.

On the other hand, reincidence during treatment is not, in and of itself, a very good predictor of eventual progress in treatment and may not be a good predictor of the propensity for future maltreatment. The National Clinical Evaluation Study reported a relatively weak correlation among its three outcome measures.[9] In every respect, the projects most successful in eliminating reincidence were projects that generally separated the children from the abusive parent either by placing the child in temporary foster care or requiring the maltreating parent to move out of the home.[10] These findings suggest that greater emphasis on monitoring parent-child interactions will be necessary to protect the child against continued maltreatment if out of home placement options are not utilized.

It is of interest to note that while reincidence during treatment continues to be a problem, clinicians reported making progress in reducing the propensity for future maltreatment and in improving overall client functioning. This pattern of improvement is even more remarkable when one considers the fact that the caseloads of the more recent treatment projects have included larger percentages of families experiencing severe maltreatment and multiple problems.[11] Expansions in the service package and the better targeting of services to specific child maltreatment subpopulations are among the factors that have contributed to these successes.

Assessing the overall success rate one can hope to achieve in working with abusive and neglectful families, Kempe and Kempe (1978) estimated that regardless of the interventions used, 20% of the parents will be treatment "failures" such that the child will not be returned home,[12] 40% of the parents will grow and develop and eventually permanently change their parenting behaviors, and 40% of the parents will no longer physically abuse or neglect their children, but will continue to be emotional maltreators. While combined therapeutic and supportive services such as group and family therapy, educational and skill development classes, in-home lay therapists, and self-help groups have enhanced overall perform-ance with families agreeable to intervention, it appears the Kempes were correct in assuming that a sizable core of parents will remain unchanged and their children at risk despite our best efforts.

Collectively, the program evaluations reviewed suggest the need to con-tinue the search for effective treatment efforts. More importantly, they underscore the need to increase efforts to identify and widely implement child abuse prevention strategies. Working with families once they have established abusive and neglectful parenting patterns is akin to construct-ing a flimsy fence at the base of a hill once the rains have started in the hopes of stopping a landslide. Advocates of expanded child abuse preven-tion efforts argue that child maltreatment can only be successfully ad-dressed through the careful identification of the weaknesses in families or adults and the correction or shoring up of these weaknesses before envi-ronmental or personal stress overruns the family's frail resistance. "How useful is it in the long run," asked one author, "to concentrate social ser-vices at the point where a family is referred for protective services or a child is diagnosed as a candidate for residential treatment?" (Magura, 1981:209). In answer to this question, policy and program planners have established a wide range of child abuse and neglect prevention strategies and, in recent years, have passed a number of legislative initiatives targeted directly at prevention. These efforts and their impact on overall child abuse and neglect policy planning are discussed in the following chapter.

Chapter 5

Improving Practice: Prevention Strategies

Similar to the history of child abuse treatment, the early conceptualization of child abuse prevention also drew heavily upon standard medical practice. Prevention, in the context of health planning, can occur at three levels: primary prevention—targeting services to the general population with the objective of stopping any new reports of a given disease or condition; secondary prevention—targeting services to specific high-risk groups in order to avoid the continued spread of the disease or condition; and tertiary prevention—targeting services to victims of the disease or condition with the intent of minimizing its impact or negative consequences (Blum, 1974). Following this medical framework, initial child abuse prevention efforts focused on intensive education and support services for first-time mothers to improve parent-child bonding and on broad-scale media campaigns to increase public awareness of child abuse and neglect and to generate public support for expanded reporting laws (Gray and DiLeonardi, 1982).

While it has been argued that the lack of definitional clarity surrounding child abuse has made it difficult to define precisely what constitutes primary, secondary, and tertiary prevention, the field has successfully identified different programs for each of these intervention levels. In applying the medical model of prevention to child maltreatment, primary prevention has been limited to those services or social policies aimed at individuals (primarily infants) or to a socially defined subset of individuals for the purpose of ensuring that abuse never occurs; secondary prevention to those services targeted to an individual or group of individuals identified as "high risk" for purposes of ensuring the individual's offspring are not abused; and tertiary prevention to those services initiated after maltreatment has occurred to prevent reincidence of abuse or neglect (Helfer, 1982).

Although Helfer's model provides an interesting classification framework for prevention programs, it does not address the more problematic question of how to measure the effectiveness of these efforts or if these efforts represent an appropriate use of public resources. On the one hand, the limited success of treatment efforts in halting reincidence and in reducing propensity for future maltreatment support policies for early intervention. Also, research regarding the causal factors of child abuse, while far from decisive, has provided practitioners with a number of individual functioning and social variables which can be used to define "at risk" populations. Finally, increased coordination among various elements of the social service system and the expanded use of informal supports in shoring up weaknesses in the family are strategies being promoted in a variety of social service areas and are, therefore, likely to be socially and politically acceptable.

On the other hand, there are convincing arguments for curbing prevention expenditures. First, the demands on protective service systems by multiproblem families and the responsibility of this system to protect children at imminent risk of abuse and possible death focus social workers' energies on the most serious abusive cases. Faced with the need to choose between protecting a battered child and preventing harm to a child who *may* be abused in the future is a difficult choice, but one in which the present victim's needs generally will receive priority over the needs of a potential future victim. Second, while current research has given some insights into the life changes and environmental stresses that increase the likelihood of maltreatment, accurate prediction of future maltreatment within any population remains a challenging task. Third, intervening in a family or with an individual before abuse or neglect occurs runs the risk of violating the privacy of the family and the right of parents to determine the well-being of their children. A commonly-recognized barrier to primary prevention is the right of people to be left alone. Without concrete evidence identifying a given condition as leading to maltreatment, prevention efforts are limited to serving families who have defined themselves as being at risk of abusing or neglecting their children. However, these families may be less at risk than those unable to identify this potential in themselves.

All of these reasons confound efforts to show whether prevention programs are successful and thus to justify prevention expenditures. Because prediction of maltreatment, at best, is an uncertain science and because prevention efforts often serve families who have sought out assistance, low incidence rates among a prevention project's clientele have little internal validity. In the absence of intervention, abuse or neglect may still not have occurred. Measuring the effectiveness of prevention programs when the point of onset cannot be established and where the "at risk" population is small and amorphous is, indeed, a formidable task. To overcome this diffi-culty, assessment of prevention programs has generally followed a three-step process with evaluators (1) stipulating the conditions known to in-crease the likelihood for abuse or neglect (2) measuring the ability of programs to improve on these conditions, and (3) examining the impacts of these improvements on the rate of child abuse and neglect (Giovannoni, 1982).

Very thin evidence exists that current prevention efforts do indeed re-duce the incidence of child abuse and neglect. However, there is an ex-panding body of research which suggests that efforts such as parenting education, parent support groups, and in-home visitor programs are suc-cessful in altering adverse parenting behaviors and attitudes such that the child's living environment includes fewer of the factors perceived as pre-conditions for maltreatment. Similarly, instructing a child in how to pre vent assault has been found to improve the child's knowledge with respect to personal safety and body ownership. Such evidence is not trivial in an emerging field where the most effective and efficient service delivery sys-tems for various target populations are still being determined. As discussed below, these evaluative findings make a compelling case for expanding pre-vention efforts while seeking more rigorous assessments of long-term pro-gram impacts.

The Child Abuse Prevention Environment

A wide range of child abuse prevention strategies are currently employed in programs around the country, many of which stem from specific causal theories of child maltreatment (Newberger and Newberger, 1982). Psycho-dynamic theories of abuse support the training of medical personnel to recognize the mental health indicators of abusive or potentially abusive behavior, while learning theory suggests the expansion of parenting educa-tion classes. Attachment theorists advocate enhancement of the parent-child bonding process while stress theorists lobby for expanded supportive services including hot lines, homemaker services, health care for children, mental health care, child care, and enhancement of informal supports. Fi-nally, those who believe that child abuse or neglect is not limited to a single subpopulation or to a type of parent seek social reforms to reduce societal violence and other "social" causes or justifications for maltreatment which place all children at risk. At present, strategies representing virtually all of these theoretical orientations are found among local child abuse preven-tion efforts. In some communities, these efforts represent disjointed, indi-vidual attacks on the problem, while in other communities they represent a coordinated effort.[1]

Today, the clinical and political climate for prevention is quite positive. While disappointment in the overall effectiveness of treatment services has contributed to the increased interest in prevention among practitioners, the availability of funding for prevention efforts most certainly has influenced the rapid development and dissemination of these strategies. In the past several years, a number of states have passed legislation to support prevention programs in general[2] or to ensure the universal provision of a specific intervention.[3]

One of the most innovative and widely disseminated sources for child abuse prevention funding is the Children's Trust Fund, a concept conceived in the late 1970s by Dr. Ray Helfer of Michigan State University, School of Medicine. A pioneer in the area of child abuse identification and treatment. Dr. Helfer designed the Fund as a way of securing support for prevention efforts in an era of diminishing governmental budgets and increased scrutiny of public responsibilities. Currently operating in 41 states, the Children's Trust Fund raises money for child abuse prevention programs by building in surcharges on marriage licenses, birth certificates, or divorce decrees or through specially designated tax refunds. The funds range in size from $25,000 to over $2 million. Each state establishes an advisory committee to determine priorities and to oversee the allocation of these resources to ensure that the objectives articulated in the enabling legislation are honored. The guidelines adopted by the individual state trust funds reflect a strong emphasis on volunteerism, collaboration, community need and support, evaluation, innovation, and the potential for replication.

The projects funded by these funds represent the full spectrum of prevention strategies including support programs for new parents, parenting education services, life skills training for children and young adults, self-help groups and other neighborhood supports, family support services, programs for abused children, early and regular child and family medical screening and treatment, child care opportunities, community organization activities, public awareness efforts, and program evaluations (Scott and Birch, 1986). In addition to taking the pressure off regular state social service budgets to fund these types of prevention efforts, the strategy promotes a community solution to the problem of maltreatment and focuses public attention on the need for prevention. This focus has been further sharpened by the Child Abuse Prevention Federal Challenge Grant program which provides fiscal incentives for states to establish Children's Trust Funds or other similar legislation to support child abuse prevention projects. For every $4 a state allocates for prevention, the federal government provides $1 in matching support, up to an amount equal to 50 cents per child in the state.

Funding for prevention efforts has emerged not only in the public sectors, but also in the work place as evidenced by expanding fringe benefit packages and industrial social welfare. Among the prevention strategies currently being developed by employers around the country are employer-supported child care; flexible work time options; employee assistance programs for working parents, covering such issues as marital problems, child management, consumer and financial issues, stress reduction, and substance abuse; and educational programs and support networks for parents (Coolsen, 1982). While generally designed to reduce the tension between employment demands and family demands, these efforts also have been viewed as reducing the type of parental stress that can bring on abusive situations.

Regardless of the impetus for or funding of prevention efforts, it is clear that wide-scale acceptance of the need to intervene before a child is harmed exists and is an important element of child abuse policy planning. In a sense, the absence of clear guidelines as to what specifically will avert future maltreatment has given practitioners, policy makers, citizen groups, and employers license to try a number of interventions and to foster collaborative arrangements among a number of disciplines and governmental entities.

Child Abuse Prevention and Subpopulations

Because child abuse prevention efforts generally target those behaviors or situations that are believed to enhance positive parenting or to improve individual functioning, less emphasis has been placed on designing prevention models for specific maltreatment subpopulations. Prevention efforts focus more on the skills one needs to be an effective parent and less on the specific type of maltreatment being avoided. To be sure, the various causal explanations for different types of maltreatment indicate that some strategies may be more promising or appropriate with certain subpopulations than with others. Research that links the lack of certain parenting skills and knowledge of child development to an increased risk for physical abuse or emotional maltreatment supports the expansion of parenting education services as a means of preventing these types of maltreatment. Similarly, if poverty and its related stresses increase the likelihood for child neglect, efforts to reduce poverty and increase the range of support services available to families with limited incomes would be necessary if one hoped to reduce the incidence of neglect. Finally, the lack of appropriate boundaries with respect to sexual behavior, the inability of vulnerable children to withstand inappropriate sexual advances, and the tendency of victims to remain silent once molestation has occurred have led to the development and expansion of a number of child assault prevention curricula aimed at empowering the potential victim to say no and to tell someone.

Despite theoretical differences in the causal factors and treatment barriers associated with different maltreatment subpopulations, very few prevention strategies define their target population in terms of a specific form of maltreatment. Even the developers of child assault prevention curricula, a program which has the strongest identification with a single maltreatment subpopulation, have been expanding their programs to include other forms of maltreatment, most notably physical abuse and emotional maltreatment. The true utility of maltreatment subpopulations in informing our approach to preventing child abuse, therefore, may be less in identifying specific prevention efforts and more in increasing our awareness of the total range of prevention services necessary for effectively confronting child abuse and the variety of service delivery systems needed to engage all at-risk parents. Just as one treatment strategy is insufficient for all maltreating families, no one prevention effort can adequately address the various causal factors of maltreatment or provide effective inroads to all families at risk of different forms of maltreatment. Some families will respond to educational efforts, while other families initially will be more responsive to offers of material support. While some families will welcome a service provider into their homes, others will prefer to attend classes or support group meetings in a local community center or church. Certain at-risk families or individuals, recognizing that they need assistance, will voluntarily enter a prevention program; other families will need more encouragement. Effectively preventing child abuse is a tall order and one that requires a differential and flexible local response system. The most useful systems will be ones that address the multiple causal factors associated with various types of maltreatment, target services to both the potential perpetrator and the potential victim, and build on the experiences of others in designing specific prevention services.

There is little solid empirical evidence to support claims that child abuse prevention efforts are effective in reducing the incidence of maltreatment. Based upon a comprehensive review of the literature, Helfer (1982) noted that 85% of the prevention research articles he reviewed dealt with proposals and/or trials of programs on an experimental basis. Since his review, prevention efforts have mushroomed and efforts to assess their effectiveness have become more numerous. Although there continues to be only limited evidence that these efforts reduce maltreatment rates, the studies that have specifically measured this variable suggest, as discussed below, that current efforts may have a greater initial impact in reducing the incidence of physical abuse than the incidence of child neglect. The real strength of this collective body of knowledge, however, is the repeated documentation of initial and very positive service outcomes in terms of enhanced parenting skills and more positive parent-child interactions. In addition to documenting that services can effectively improve knowledge levels and alter parental behavior, these evaluations are extremely useful in identifying those adults and children who appear more amenable to voluntary prevention efforts and, conversely, those families that require more concerted efforts to engage in services.

On balance, two major prevention avenues have generated the most interest in terms of the number of providers and researchers they have attracted. The first group, the parenting enhancement models, includes efforts targeted to parents perceived to be at higher than average risk of physical abuse or neglect. As discussed below, evaluations of these programs have produced encouraging findings with respect to improving parenting skills and child development knowledge, particularly with teenage mothers. This body of research also includes the best empirical evidence of a reduction in actual child abuse rates resulting from such early interventions. The second group, the child empowerment service models, is a more homogeneous cluster of strategies that target their efforts to the potential victims of abuse, enabling them to resist threats of maltreatment, particularly sexual assault. In contrast to the gradual development of parenting enhancement services, the proliferation of child assault prevention curricula and related materials has outpaced research findings. The remainder of this chapter reviews the empirical evidence on these two prevention strategies and the implications of this research on practice and policy.

Parenting Enhancement Service Models

Much of what we know with respect to the individual causes of child maltreatment suggests that direct interventions with parents, preferably as close to the birth of their first child as possible, are excellent strategies for reducing levels of physical abuse, neglect, and emotional maltreatment. Programs offering instruction in specific parenting skills such as discipline methods, basic child care, and infant stimulation; child development education; familiarity with local support services; and linkages to other new parents in the community address a number of interpersonal and situational difficulties which are precursors to abusive and neglectful behavior. While the content and structure of these programs vary, ranging from in-home visitor programs to center-based services, the most effective of these efforts include the following service goals:

> increasing the parent's knowledge of child development and the demands of parenting;
>
> enhancing the parent's skill in coping with the stresses of infant and child care;
>
> enhancing parent-child bonding, emotional ties, and communication;
>
> increasing the parent's skills in coping with the stress of caring for children with special needs;
>
> increasing the parent's knowledge about home and child management;
>
> reducing the burden of child care; and
>
> increasing access to social and health services for all family members (Cohn, 1983).

On balance, programs that incorporate these objectives rely upon a mixture of therapeutic and supportive services. While there are no specific standards for structuring these programs, the most common service elements include routine health screening and developmental testing for the child, instruction in or modeling of basic child care techniques either through clinic-based classes or regular home visits, identification and enhancement of the mother's system of formal and informal supports, and, if appropriate, case management and advocacy services. Staffing patterns may include the use of multidisciplinary teams for both assessment as well as service delivery or may rely heavily upon the skills of a single service provider. This second approach is most common in those programs utilizing a home visitor approach.

In certain instances, such as the program developed and evaluated by David Olds and his colleagues, the provider is a health care professional or trained social worker. In other cases, such as the Ford Foundation's Fair Start Initiative, specifically trained paraprofessionals are utilized. Independent of professional training or education, the provider's personal skills play a central role in engaging and retaining families in their programs. Among the characteristics considered most essential are an active interest in new ideas, an active interest in people and an ability to engage people socially, an ability to accept people's life situation without prejudging them, an ability to relate to a family's experiences without becoming enmeshed in the family's problem cycles, and relative stability in his or her own personal life (Halpren and Larner, forthcoming).

Comprehensive programs that have incorporated these program objectives and staff skills through intensive weekly contact with participants over a period of one to three years generally have been found to produce the most positive gains. Both home-based and center-based programs have demonstrated a wide range of positive client outcomes. Specific gains have included improved mother-infant bonding and maternal capacity to respond to the child's emotional needs (Dickie and Gerber, 1980; Field et al., 1980; O'Connor et al., 1980; Affholter et al., 1983); demonstrated ability to care for the child's physical and developmental needs (Love et al., 1976; Gutelius et al. 1977; Gabinet, 1979; Field et al., 1980; Larson, 1980; Travers et al., 1982; Gray, 1983; Olds et al., 1986); fewer subsequent pregnancies (McAnarney et al., 1978; Badger et al., 1981; Olds et al., 1986); more consistent use of health care services and job training opportunities (Powell, 1986); and lower welfare use, higher school completion rates, and higher employement rates (Gutelius et al., 1977; Badger et al., 1981; Seitz et al., 1985; Powell, 1986; Polit, 1987). In identifying the types of parents most likely to benefit from these educational and supportive services, several researchers have noted particular success with young, relatively poor mothers (Gabinet, 1979; Badger, 1981; Olds et al., 1986), and with mothers who felt confident in their lives prior to enrolling in the program (Powell, 1986). Others have observed less positive gains when the client population included a sizable percentage of middle-class parents (McGuire and Gottlieb, 1979; Wandersman et al., 1980; Levant and Doyle, 1983).[4]

At least one ten-year longitudinal study suggests not only that comprehensive parenting services produce initial gains but that these gains are retained and possibly enhanced over time. Seitz and her colleagues (1985) successfully tracked, ten years later, 15 of 17 matched sets of families, half of whom had received a coordinated set of medical and social services, including day care for their children (Provence et al., 1977; Provence and Naylor, 1983). While not specifically identified as being at risk of maltreatment, these families all had household incomes below the federal poverty level and were expecting their first child. In targeting the intervention, impoverished families were chosen under the assumption that chronic stress is a significant impediment to effective family functioning and that poverty both increases the likelihood of such stress and restricts the resources available to families to cope with it. Following the birth of the baby, the team pediatricians saw the mother and baby daily in the hospital and scheduled an initial home visit following discharge. Each treatment family received 13 to 17 well-baby visits; an average of 28 home visits by a social worker, psychologist, or nurse; and two to 28 months of day care services over the entire treatment period. Families were enrolled from pregnancy through 30 months postpartum.

Although the sample is small and was limited to first-time mothers, repeated follow-up studies on the treatment families have noted a steady improvement from termination, to five years later, to the current ten-year posttermination study. Specific differences were noted at each of the follow-up periods between the two groups in the mother's level of education, the family's financial independence, and the child's school performance. Average educational achievement for treatment mothers ten years after the intervention was 13.0 years while the control sample had an average of only 11.7. The study team found 13 of the 15 treatment families had at least one full-time wage earner or full-time equivalent between both adult partners in the home, a situation found in only eight of the 15 control families. Significant differences were also noted in the school performance of the two groups of children. Only four of the 15 control children were judged by their teachers to have good school adjustment, a rating given to ten of the 16 treatment children.

On balance, these findings show a slow and steady increase in the economic growth of the treatment families and a static picture for the controls. Translating these gains into social service savings, the authors noted that an additional $40,000 in welfare costs and documented school services were needed by the 15 control families in the single year in which the ten-year follow-up study was conducted (Seitz et al., 1985). While not specifically documenting a reduction in abuse or neglect, the study clearly demonstrates the elimination of certain factors associated with higher rates of neglect such as low income and poor social adjustment and the positive effects early family-based interventions can have on both parents and children.

While such studies are useful in advancing our understanding of how best to enhance general parenting skills, the work of David Olds and his colleagues has provided some of the best empirical evidence to date that the provision of a specific service model does indeed reduce the incidence of child abuse and neglect. The participants in this study, all of whom were first-time mothers, were randomly assigned to one of four groups in which the most intensive level of services involved regular pre- and postnatal home visits by a nurse practitioner.[5] The nurse home visitors carried out three major activities, parent education regarding fetal and infant development, the involvement of family members and friends in child care and support of the mother, and the linkage of family members with other health and human services. Of the 400 women participating in the program, 47% were younger than 19 years of age, 62% were unmarried, and 61% had low socioeconomic status. Those who received the most intensive intervention had a significantly lower incidence of reported child abuse over the two-year postbirth study period. While 19% of the comparison group at greatest risk for maltreatment (i.e., poor, unmarried teens) were reported for abuse or neglect, only 4% of their nurse-visited counterparts were reported. Of these cases, 50% involved reports of neglect only and 50% involved reports of neglect and physical abuse. Although these results were not replicated for older program participants, the dramatic gains realized with first-time, teen mothers suggest that this group may benefit particularly from prevention services. In addition to having a lower reported rate of child abuse, those infants whose mothers received ongoing nurse home visits had fewer accidents and were less likely to require emergency room care. The mothers also reported less frequent need to punish or restrict their children (Olds et al., 1986).

The use of home visitors has been identified by others as achieving notable gains in parent-child interactions and in improving the child's developmental progress (Dawson et al., 1982; Affholter et al., 1983; Gray, 1983) and at least one study has suggested that such visits when conducted by a trained paraprofessional result in fewer instances of child abuse or neglect (Gray et al., 1979). A number of parenting enhancement models utlizing a center-based service delivery model have also produced positive gains in overall parenting skills and in the use of community resources (Dickie and Gerber, 1980; Badger et al., 1981; Andrews et al., 1982). One of the most widely disseminated models of this type is the Minnesota Early Learning Demonstration (MELD), an intensive two-year parenting education and support program. Since its inception in 1975, six specific programs have been developed: MELD for New Parents, MELD for Young Moms, MELD Plus for growing families, La Familia/MELD for Hispanic families, MELD Special for parents of children with special needs, and HIPP/MELD for hearing impaired parents. Each program's purpose is to provide the most useful information available in the most supportive environment that can be created. MELD's mission is to get families off to a good start and to eliminate the potential for maltreatment by never letting abusive or neglectful patterns begin. The MELD staff believe that there is no one right way to parent and participants are encouraged to make the child-rearing choices that are appropriate for them. The program demonstrates that if participants are supported in their efforts to be good parents, if they are exposed to good information and alternative ways of addressing child-rearing issues, they will be able to make the choices that enhance their children's well-being as well as their own.

A typical MELD group includes 10–20 mothers who meet for two to three hours weekly. While the program lasts for two years, the meetings are scheduled in four six-month phases that include 20 meetings each, led by extensively trained parent volunteers. The topics discussed during these meetings include health issues, child development, child guidance, family management, and personal growth. Specific techniques incorporated into the program include large group discussions, small group discussions, brainstorming, demonstrations, homework, roleplaying, minilectures, films, outside resources, facilitator presentations, parent presentations, sharing of experiences, and informal socializing during the meal provided at each meeting. All participants are provided with transportation assistance and child care to facilitate attendance at the meetings.

Although the program has never been evaluated in terms of child abuse prevention, the immediate outcomes demonstrated by program participants are encouraging. A recent evaluation of the MELD Young Moms program conducted by the Child Welfare League of America noted that 80% of the participants had finished or were completing high school compared to an overall school completion rate of only 20% for the general adolescent parent population. Also, while 25% of all teenage mothers experience a repeat pregnancy within a year of their first birth, MELD Young Moms participants had a repeat pregnancy rate of only 10% to 15%. Changes were also noted in the parents' use of discipline, where the percentage of parents who spanked their children decreased from 56% at the start of the program to only 12% at the conclusion of services. The evaluation also noted some difficulties with the program, particularly with respect to retaining participants for the full two-year period. Depending upon the group, only 25% to 40% of the participants stayed with the program for the full two years. Also, the CWLA evaluation found that an educational support group which met once a week was not sufficient to deal with the individual crises that young mothers face, such as establishing a household, securing day care, completing school, or finding employment. Addressing these needs required that the group leaders spend considerable time working with participants on an individual basis.

The collective results outlined above underscore the difficulty in addressing the myriad issues associated with an increased risk for maltreatment under the rubric of a single service framework. Offering services in a client's home has a number of distinct advantages, particularly when the objective is to reduce the likelihood of maltreatment. Such services offer the provider an excellent opportunity to assess the safety of the child's living environment and to work with the mother in very concrete ways to improve parent-child interactions. The method also affords the client a degree of privacy and the practitioner a degree of flexibility difficult to achieve in center-based programs. Individuals who may be reluctant to attend weekly sessions at a community-based service center or local hospital either because they are uncomfortable about sharing their experiences with other parents or because they find it difficult to travel to the center find home-based services a welcome alternative.

The method, however, is not without drawbacks. The costs of these programs can be quite significant, particularly if, as in the case of the Olds study, the home visitors are nurse practitioners or clinical social workers. Even if trained paraprofessionals or volunteers are used, the strategy is highly labor intensive and involves considerable transportation costs. Also, the one-to-one service model places a tremendous burden on the individual provider. The home setting makes it potentially more difficult to focus on parent-child relationships or on a given set of parenting skills. Often, clients are not prepared for the worker's visit although these appointments may be longstanding. A clinician may need to spend considerable time focusing the mother on the issues or tasks to be addressed during the visit and away from the normal, daily distractions found in home settings. Children crying, the telephone ringing, or an unexpected visitor are distractions that are more readily controlled in an office setting. Also, the method itself does not afford the practitioner the opportunity to draw on the benefits of a group service model, as discussed below, nor the client to work through his or her difficulties with others in similar circumstances. Further, although these clients initially will have tacitly agreed to participate in the program, having a stranger actually enter one's home can be extremely threatening. Consequently, clients may be particularly resistant to the home visitor during the first several contacts. In addition, these clients may be less outer-directed and socially skilled than those women who choose to attend parenting programs held outside their homes. Practitioners involved in this method of service delivery need to be sensitive to these fears and limitations and to work with these clients in developing a gradual nurturing, personal relationship with the mother. Several initial visits may be required to develop this level of trust before the client is able to discuss her parenting concerns openly and honestly and accept specific child care suggestions.

In contrast, parenting services offered through a community-based family service center or health care facility provide participants with an opportunity to share child-rearing and personal problems with other parents in similar situations. This exchange serves an important validation function for parents, allowing them to acknowledge their difficulties and stresses while accepting peer suggestions on how best to cope with the demands of young children. Strategies such as the MELD program establish an ongoing support group for parents to draw upon during and outside the actual service delivery process, further reducing the level of isolation. Often the physical location of the group meetings becomes identified as a general support center for all parents to utilize in addressing a wide range of issues. In this sense, the strategy serves as a foundation for a more universal child abuse prevention effort in which parents seeking assistance need not first be identified as requiring "special" services.

The difficulty these programs have, however, in successfully retaining a high percentage of their clients over an extended period of time suggests that the method requires a good deal of motivation on the part of participants. Drop-out rates of as high as 40% to 50% have been noted by several program reviewers (Lochman and Brown, 1980; Johnson and Breckenridge, 1982). Unlike the home-based models, continued participation in a center-based program is contingent upon a parent's willingness to cope with the transportation and child care demands inherent in attending any event outside of one's home. Also, weekly participation requires that these young mothers introduce a level of consistency and scheduling in their daily lives which generally has been absent. It is logical to assume that parents exhibiting this motivational level will be predisposed to taking full advantage of the support and educational services offered by center-based programs. However, parents lacking this motivation and who may be among those at greatest risk for maltreatment will be unlikely to sustain involvement with these programs long enough to achieve the most positive outcomes. This difficulty in retaining a sizable number of participants in center-based service programs has led some to suggest that satisfactory participation in these programs may require that parents already be functioning in a fairly healthy and adaptive manner (Halpren, 1984). At least one evaluation of a group service model noted that expressive mothers were significantly more likely to contribute verbally to the group discussions and to form friendships more readily with other participants (Powell, 1986).

Reaching the full spectrum of the "at-risk" population clearly requires some combination of both methods. Center-based services, particularly if they are associated with local junior high and high school programs for adolescent parents, offer excellent opportunities for a highly motivated teenage mother not only to improve her parenting skills but also to continue her education and to establish a stable life for herself and her infant. Home-based programs, with their more individualized and flexible service delivery systems, will be particularly useful with a more isolated population or those mothers lacking the interest or motivation to participate in a group service system. Regardless of the method employed, the empirical evidence strongly suggests that parenting enhancement services, as a child abuse prevention strategy, are most effective when provided to first-time mothers as early in their pregnancy as possible. To accomplish this client targeting goal, such services need to develop solid referral linkages with local hospitals, medical centers, adolescent health care programs, and schools. In the absence of firm knowledge as to which specific parents will abuse or neglect their children, at least some minimal parenting education and support services should be offered to all first-time parents. The duration and intensity of these services necessary to reduce the risk of maltreatment would depend upon the number of risk factors exhibited by a given parent. While no specific ideal length of time for these services has been determined, the most positive gains have been achieved by programs offering high-risk mothers at least one year of assistance. A successful parenting enhancement program also will need to draw upon a number of disciplines including, among others, medical experts, child development specialists, social workers, and educators in designing its curricula or service objectives and in training its service delivery staff. At a minimum, those offering assistance to parents should have specific knowledge with respect to alternative discipline methods, basic physical and emotional needs of young children, child development, local support services, and local child abuse reporting procedures.

Underscoring all of these efforts should be a concern for better documenting the immediate and long-term impacts of these efforts with parents and children. The work of Olds and Seitz, among others, testifies to the feasibility of documenting long-term outcomes and to measuring a reduction in maltreatment or the conditions associated with a higher risk of abuse or neglect over time. These studies also indicate that such gains may not be immediately apparent. Providers and policy makers alike need to be extremely patient and not discontinue programs because such evidence is not rapidly forthcoming. On the other hand, practitioners need to be open to the possibility that their interventions may not be as successful as their theories indicate. Even the most potent home-based interventions reviewed by Halpren accounted for only 10% of the variation in client outcomes. Other factors such as economic insecurity, limited access to services, maternal educational levels, and parental psychopathology were more powerful predictors of success or failure (Halpren, 1984).

If these factors are indeed significant barriers to the successful participation of certain high-risk parents in the types of programs outlined above, the focus and methods of service delivery need to be altered. Possible strategies for successfully engaging the most at-risk parents might include integrating these services with existing community organizations and housing improvement programs; advocating for the expansion of local health care facilities including pre- and postnatal care, well-baby clinics, and general family practice; mandating the provision of parenting and family life education to all high school students; and providing specific instruction and support for adolescent parents, including school-based support groups and day care programs. Hospitals that deliver babies to a significant percentage of high-risk mothers might be encouraged to alter their discharge planning process to incorporate specific service planning around the initial care of the baby. To the extent parenting services remain voluntary, a certain percentage of the parents most at risk of physical abuse, neglect, and emotional maltreatment will choose not to participate. Incorporating such services, however, into those institutions and service organizations with whom the mother or child has routine contact expands the possible points of entry and, it is hoped, captures a greater percentage of the at-risk group.

Child Empowerment Service Models

In response to concerns raised by parents and concerned professionals regarding increased reports of child sexual assault, state and federal administrators and local service agencies have developed a number of programs and policies to address the treatment needs of identified victims and perpetrators as well as the need to prevent such abuse from occurring. While prevention strategies for other forms of maltreatment frequently focus on changing the behaviors and attitudes of parents, one of the most popular sexual abuse prevention strategies focuses on changing the behavior of children. Developed initially by Women Against Rape in Columbus, Ohio in the late 1970's, this intervention, generally referred to as child assault prevention classes, provides classroom-based instruction for children of all ages on how to protect themselves from sexual assault by strangers as well as by family members. A national survey recently completed by the National Committee for Prevention of Child Abuse found that over 25% of all public schools provide this type of instruction to at least one grade level.

Methods for providing this instruction vary along a number of key dimensions, including the characteristics and background of the instructor, the frequency of the presentations, and specific content of the message. All of the programs, however, share a number of common goals and objectives. The most similar program features include:

> direct instruction to the child on the distinction between good, bad, and questionable touching;
>
> the concept of body ownership or the rights of children to control who touches their bodies and where they are touched;
>
> the concept of keeping secrets and the importance of the child to tell if someone touches him or her even if that person tells the child not to reveal the incident;
>
> the ability to act on one's intuition regarding when a touch or action makes a child feel uncomfortable even if the child does not know why he or she is uncomfortable;
>
> assertiveness skills, ranging from repeatedly saying "no" to someone who wants to do something that makes the child feel uncomfortable

to the use of various self-defense techniques (e.g., yelling, kicking, fighting back); and

the existence of support systems to help the child if he or she has experienced any form of maltreatment.

In addition, all of the programs include some type of orientation or instruction for both the parents and school personnel. These sessions cover a number of topics including a review of the materials to be presented to the children, a summary of the local child abuse reporting system, a discussion of what to do if you suspect a child has been mistreated, and a review of the local services available to victims and their families.

Intuitively, the notion of preventing child sexual abuse is attractive both from a humanitarian or child advocacy perspective as well as from a social cost perspective. Children have a right not to be molested and the society as a whole has a responsibility to protect the future generation from such harm at the hands of their parents or strangers. While intervention to remediate the negative consequences of maltreatment can be seen as society's minimal responsibility, policies aimed at avoiding the initial abuse are particularly attractive in that the child does not have to experience harm before services are available and the society is able to avoid the significant costs of long-term therapeutic interventions generally required in cases of sexual abuse. Prevention strategies that focus on empowering children to better protect themselves from harm also have a certain parsimonious appeal in that they avoid very costly and often intrusive interventions into the private family. Finally, incorporating this strategy in the context of an existing universal service system, namely primary and secondary public education, offers the dual attraction of reaching large numbers of children at very low per-unit costs and avoiding many of the stigmas commonly associated with secondary prevention services. Rather than identifying a specific child or family as being at particular risk of maltreatment, these interventions assume all children are at equal risk and, therefore, in need of the instruction. Also, children who have been mistreated have a safe and supportive environment in which to disclose the abuse and from which to accept assistance.

Despite the laudable goals of this intervention and its intuitive appeal, the rapid proliferation of these efforts has occurred in the absence of any empirical evidence that such instruction does indeed change a child's attitudes or behaviors or minimizes a child's risk for maltreatment. Unlike the relatively rich body of empirical evidence surrounding the development of the parenting enhancement service models, very few studies have employed experimental or quasi-experimental research designs in assessing the initial impacts of child assault prevention classes. No study completed to date has assessed the long-term effects of this intervention on such issues as a child's attitudes or perceptions of strangers, a teacher's willingness to have physical contact with a child, or a child's fear of being abused by his or her parents or other family members. Anecdotal and descriptive studies regarding specific incidents of success or failure are far more abundant than solid empirical evidence. While such descriptive studies are useful for raising public awareness of the issue and for demonstrating the need for a coordinated public response to the problem, they are far less useful in determining how best to allocate scarce public resources among competing alternatives.

The research conducted to date on the impact of child sexual assault prevention classes is inconclusive and leaves a number of critical program and policy questions unanswered. First, with the exception of Woods and Dean (1986), who compared the impacts of the "Talking About Touching" curriculum with reading the National Committee for the Prevention of Child Abuse's Spiderman comic book, all of the studies identified to date have assessed the impacts of a single curriculum or approach. Very few of these program evaluations have employed control or comparison groups as a means of determining if the gains noted among those children who received the instructions could be attributed to the program itself or might be explained by some other event which occurred between the pre- and posttest periods. While such comparisons are useful in determining if a specific curriculum has any notable impact on a child's attitudes, knowledge, or behavior, this research is less useful in informing educators, mental health professionals, and policy makers of the most appropriate strategy to employ with children of different ages or backgrounds. As documented in the educational literature, not all children learn at the same rate, nor do they respond in a similar manner to various teaching techniques. It is logical, therefore, to assume that the different philosophies and techniques found among the child assault prevention models may produce different effects on children. Identifying these differential effects, however, requires that the various models be evaluated in terms of a single set of outcome indicators. To date, this type of cross-curriculum comparison has not been done either within or across specific developmental age groups.

Second, the vast majority of the evaluations that have been completed have drawn their client samples from children between the ages of eight and eleven. Only three of the evaluations (Conte et al., 1985; Borkin and Frank, 1986; and Collins, 1986) studied the impacts of these curricula on preschoolers, and assessments of program impact on the high school population is even more limited. This almost exclusive focus on elementary school children makes it difficult to determine the most appropriate age group for these interventions. While anecdotal evidence suggests that even very young children (i.e., three- or four-year-olds) can be taught basic safety rules, the child development literature strongly suggests that concepts of "stranger" and "touch continuum" are too complex for preschoolers to comprehend, much less apply to a specific life situation. This lack of empirical data on the impacts of similar programs on children of different developmental ages, however, has not tempered the application of this specific prevention strategy to all age groups. To address the question of which children can best benefit from child assault prevention classes and which techniques are best-suited to a given developmental age group, research that looks at program effects on children of different ages is needed.

Several evaluations of these programs have noted that children who receive child assault prevention instruction demonstrate an increase in knowledge regarding various safety rules and are more aware of the local support system available to them if they have been or are abused (Downer, 1984, Plummer, 1984; Conte et al., 1985; Swan et al., 1985; Collins, 1986). Other findings are less convincing. Those studies which included preschoolers in their client sample noted significantly lower knowledge gains on the part of younger children. For example, Borkin and Franks (1986) found that virtually none of the three-year-olds interviewed retained any of the information presented after only one week and only 40% of the four- and five-year-olds retained any knowledge over this period. Similarly, Conte and his colleagues found significant differences in the level of information retained by the four- and five-year-olds in their sample versus the six-to-ten-year-olds whom they studied. In addition, Conte noted that even the best performers in this study grasped only 50% of the concepts taught in the program (Conte et al., 1985). Further, at least one evaluator discovered that while children have been found to retain increased awareness and knowledge of safety rules several months after receiving the instruction, they retain less information with respect to such key concepts as who can be a molester, the difference between physical abuse and sexual abuse, and the fact that sexual abuse, if it occurs, is not the victim's fault (Plummer, 1984).

Recently, a number of studies have noted that a significant percentage of children are familiar with many of the basic safety concepts presented in these classes prior to receiving formal instruction (Plummer, 1984; Swan et al., 1985; Collins, 1986). This finding suggests that many of the safety rules taught in these programs as well as a basic awareness of the existence of child sexual abuse may be far more familiar to children today than at the time these programs were initially designed. In the past five years, media attention to this issue has increased dramatically. Children receive the message that sexual abuse is wrong, and that it is not their fault if it has happened to them from myriad sources, including television, books, movies, and, increasingly, their parents. As public awareness of this issue increases, it is conceivable that the basic information presented in these classes might be available to large numbers of children through other media, thereby freeing the programs to focus more on developing specific skills to facilitate the child's use of the basic concepts being taught. For example, if children are expected to trust their judgments with respect to dangerous situations, additional classroom time could be spent in role-play activities where children would be confronted with a variety of circumstances requiring safety judgments. Examples could include potentially abusive situations as well as more general, age-appropriate safety tasks.

The studies that assessed the ability of children to apply the techniques they have been taught suggest that this type of skill-building is needed. For example, Downer noted that although the children who had received the instruction could provide the textbook definition of assertiveness, none of the children could provide a single example of how they would apply assertive behavior in their own lives (Downer, 1984). Similarly, Nelson and colleagues noted that the fifth and sixth graders receiving prevention instruction showed notable gains in safety knowledge and understanding of sexual abuse in comparison to a control sample, but that the intervention had no impact on such constructs as self-acceptance, autonomy, internal control, and external control (Nelson et al., 1986). While one might question the appropriateness of these outcome measures, they represent the essential changes child assault prevention programs strive to realize in children. Participants, even very young children, are asked to rely upon their own assessment skills and intuition in (1) judging the relative risk of a given situation and (2) acting in a manner that will avert possible harm or maltreatment. Children with strong self-concepts and a sense of autonomy and self-control are more likely to have the capacity to make these types of judgments and the character strength to act upon them.

Finally, at least one evaluation has noted a significant increase in the percentage of children who feel that sexual assault could occur within their own families following the workshop presentations. Swan, Press, and Briggs noted that, following a presentation of the play "Bubbylonian Encounter," 93% of the children recognized the potential within their own families for a coercive (i.e., nonviolent) episode of child sexual assault and 88% saw the potential for violent sexual assault (Swan et al., 1985). While this finding reflects the program's emphasis on making a child aware that sexual abuse is not necessarily something that occurs at the hands of a stranger, it also suggests that large numbers of children are questioning the safety of their own homes. Even if the incidence of child sexual abuse is as high as some researchers have claimed (i.e., one of every four girls and one of every seven or ten boys by the time they reach the age of 18), the vast majority of children will not experience sexual abuse by anyone, much less an immediate family member.

While yet to be documented in any systematic manner, anecdotal evidence suggests that children are not the only ones experiencing new fears and uncertainties. Fear of potential lawsuits led one suburban Chicago school superintendent to order his teachers to cease touching their students in any manner. Even parents, particularly those involved in custody disputes, are questioning if appropriate displays of affection could be misconstrued as precursors to sexual abuse. Many professionals and concerned policy makers are questioning whether or not such discomfort and concern among nonabusive parents and nonabused children is the unavoidable cost of reducing the incidence of sexual assault. To address this question, research is needed to determine (1) the extent to which individual behavior and attitudes have been altered as a result of collective efforts to raise public awareness regarding the incidence and consequences of child sexual abuse, (2) the extent to which these changes cause individuals any lasting discomfort or impinge upon healthy parent-child relationships or child development, and (3) whether or not these instructional programs do indeed serve to protect children.

The passage of legislation supporting the universal provision of child assault prevention classes in ten states and the serious consideration of similar legislation in several other states attests to the popularity of this specific prevention strategy. Legislators appear committed to supporting these efforts, potentially as an alternative to supporting other prevention strategies. The pool of prevention funding, while temporarily expanding, is not limitless. Also, as demonstrated in California, the costs associated with the universal provision of child assault prevention instruction is not trivial. Prevention advocates may well find themselves needing to choose between the continued expansion of this intervention and the expansion of other, well documented, prevention services such as parenting education for all teen parents or all first-time parents. Until all three of the research areas outlined above are systematically pursued, the appropriate role of child assault prevention education in the more general context of child abuse prevention cannot be determined.

Summary and Practice Implications

Effectively preventing child abuse requires activities in three spheres: an awareness of the specific policies and behaviors that constitute maltreatment or that result in harm to children, a knowledge of the personal and societal conditions that strengthen a parent's or child's ability to avoid maltreatment, and mechanisms for enhancing the ability of parents and children to adopt the positive practices and to avoid the negative practices. At present, the ability of research to clarify the components in each of these spheres varies greatly across the four major types of maltreatment. Empirical evidence with respect to the definition and causal factors associated with different types of maltreatment will shape the direction taken in the first two of these spheres, and progress in the third sphere will depend upon information gleaned from ongoing program evaluation efforts. Although not always conclusive, the present knowledge base, as summarized in Figure 5.1 is useful in outlining the range of activities which, if implemented, would produce a comprehensive and effective approach to child abuse prevention.

First, the prevention of all forms of maltreatment rests on the develop-

Figure 5.1

Prevention Strategies Suggested by
Empirical Research and Program Evaluation Findings

AN AWARENESS OF BEHAVIORS AND POLICIES THAT CONSTITUTE MALTREATMENT OR HARM CHILDREN

Public awareness campaigns to promote the following messages:

Use of severe corporal punishment by parents can harm children
Use of corporal punishment in the schools can harm children
Repeated yelling and swearing can result in emotional harm to children
Beating a child often results in serious and permanent physical harm
Leaving children unattended can lead to avoidable accidents
Failure to secure regular medical care can lead to serious illness or permanent damage
Deriving sexual satisfaction from children is always wrong
Pornography helps "normalize" sexual abuse
Violence in the media helps "normalize" violence
Poverty is detrimental to a child's healthy development

IDENTIFICATION OF THE PERSONAL OR SOCIETAL CONDITIONS THAT STRENGTHEN A PARENT'S OR CHILD'S ABILITY TO AVOID MALTREATMENT

Developing alternative, nonphysical methods of discipline

Strengthening a parent's formal and informal support network

Providing children with specific safety rules and prevention skills to avoid maltreatment

Developing stress management techniques

Identifying specific methods for improving a child's self-esteem

Promoting media presentations that deal honestly and sensitively with parenting and child maltreatment

MECHANISMS FOR ENHANCING A PARENT'S OR CHILD'S ABILITY TO INTEGRATE PREVENTIVE MEASURES INTO THEIR DAILY LIVES

Crisis intervention services:

Respite care
Hot lines/warm lines

Parenting enhancement services:

Parenting education classes
Support groups
In-home visitor programs
Perinatal support services (e.g., prenatal care, prenatal classes, postbirth home visits, and medical care)
Life skills training for all high school students

Child assault prevention services:

Classroom-based instruction
Media presentations
Books and other printed materials
Teacher training

Figure 5.1 continued

Parent training
Therapeutic services to adolescent perpetrators

Services to abused and neglected children:

Individual, family, group therapy
Physical rehabilitation service
Therapeutic day care
Support groups
Peer counseling

ment of an increased awareness among parents, practitioners, and administrators of the specific policies and behaviors that contribute to an increased incidence of child maltreatment. While a survey conducted for the National Committee for Prevention of Child Abuse in 1982 found that over 90% of the general public perceive child abuse to be a serious social problem warranting public intervention, it is not clear what the public's level of awareness is with respect to specific abusive or neglectful behaviors. Most individuals would agree that torturing a child is wrong or that using children for sexual gratification goes beyond the boundaries of appropriate behavior. Leaving infants unattended or in the care of young siblings or failing to secure needed medical care also are generally regarded as dangerous parenting practices. As one moves away from these extreme behaviors, public perception of the problem becomes less clear. There is less agreement among parents and the general public that the use of corporal punishment and the proliferation of violent and sexually suggestive television shows are uniquely detrimental to children. Although virtually all states prohibit prison guards or wardens from using physical punishment with inmates, 41 states still allow the use of corporal punishment in the schools. Concern over the growing number of children living in poverty or who do not have access to routine preventive medical care generally does not translate into specific child abuse prevention strategies.

Strengthening the empirical evidence linking these and other conditions to increased rates of child abuse and passing on this evidence to professionals and the general public alike is an important first step in creating a more informed context in which to develop and implement child abuse prevention efforts. As indicated in Figure 5.1, the prevention of all forms of maltreatment would be enhanced by expanded public awareness efforts. Because parents often repeat the child-rearing practices they experienced as children, or adopt the norms and parenting customs of the community in which they live, it will be necessary not only to raise awareness of negative parenting practices but also to suggest and promulgate positive alternatives. Efforts to define alternative, nonphysical methods of discipline, to strengthen a parent's formal and informal support network, to increase familiarity with and use of community medical care facilities, and to provide children with specific skills to strengthen their self-esteem and enhance their personal growth and development are equally useful for all parents and children. Offering examples of positive parenting would be a much-needed companion to campaigns that merely articulate what parents and children should not do. Perhaps more important than the glut of parenting books and parenting videos which offer scores of formulas on how to be a better parent is the growth of child care cooperatives and informal parenting support groups. These types of collective efforts encourage parents to pool their resources and knowledge in reducing the stress of parenting and establish a sense of communal responsibility for children. To the extent that parents come to accept outside assistance in the rearing of their children as the norm, the expansion of secondary prevention efforts becomes easier for at least two reasons. First, such a shift in attitudes would reduce the supremacy of the private family and the rights of parents to rear children in the manner they deem appropriate regardless of the impacts of such practices. Second, offering more directed assistance—such as requiring public health visits to all first-time mothers, requiring all first-time parents to enroll in monthly parenting classes until the child's first birthday, or requiring annual medical and developmental testing of all children through age five—would appear less of an infringement on parental rights and more an appropriate exercise for a soceity concerned about its future well-being. Such routine screening of newborns is currently done in other countries, including the United Kingdom, Sweden, and Israel.

Again, further research is needed to identify the specific parenting practices that will reduce the risk of all forms of maltreatment, the specific personal safety skills appropriate for children at different developmental stages, and the specific public policies that will strengthen families and best protect children. Teaching positive, nonphysical methods of discipline as well as stress management skills holds promise as a means of curbing physical abuse. Enhancing knowledge of and access to a variety of support services are promising avenues for reducing the isolation and lack of material resources generally associated with neglectful behavior. Teaching parents how to enhance their children's self-esteem through praise and positive verbal exchanges offers positive alternatives to emotionally abusive or neglectful exchanges between parents and children. Outlining clear safety rules for children and families to follow may reduce the likelihood for sexual or physical abuse. Promoting media presentations that deal sensitively with the trials and tribulations of parenting and promoting expanded financial support and medical services for low-income families with young children represent more global efforts to improve the general child-rearing environment.

Merely identifying and promulgating such positive practices may be helpful in preventing child abuse in many families. The prevailing evidence suggests, however, that a significant number of families will require specific assistance to integrate these suggestions into their daily behaviors. Furthermore, the victims of maltreatment will need assistance not only in remediating the immediate physical and emotional effects of such treatment but also in repairing their sense of self-worth and confidence such that they can effectively develop the personal and social skills necessary for a healthy transition to adult life. As summarized in Figure 5.1, a wide range of prevention services are currently in place throughout the country, including crisis intervention efforts, parenting enhancement models, child assault prevention services, and therapeutic services to child abuse victims. The number of individuals who would benefit from these services is unclear, although the two million families reported for suspected maltreatment annually might constitute the minimum target population.

Reducing the overall level of maltreatment, however, will be achieved not by promoting a single prevention strategy but rather by developing an integrated system in which each service is but one part of a coordinated service continuum. The complex nature of maltreatment and the ever-changing nature of children and, more recently, families, require that individual prevention efforts join forces to construct a child abuse prevention system that will address the many and varied needs of the at-risk population. For example, first-time parents or parents of young children require different interventions and parenting supports than do the parents of adolescents. Similarly, families with limited financial resources may require different levels of support and encouragement than families of average to above average means. Just as there is no single cause of child maltreatment, neither is there a single prevention strategy that will ensure, over time, a child's safety, a parent's competence, or a family's stability. In this respect, it will always be unreasonable, regardless of our methodological sophistication, to expect a single prevention program to eliminate forever the risk of maltreatment for a given child or to reduce the incidence of child abuse and neglect in a given community. It may not be unreasonable, however, to expect a coordinated local child abuse system to achieve this objective, as discussed in the concluding chapter.

Part III

Future Strategies

Chapter 6

The Costs of Prevention
and Intervention

An often unstated or understated aspect of social service planning is the real and potential costs associated with "doing good." Reducing the present and future pain caused children by abusive or neglectful parents is considered a worthy and humanitarian public policy objective, regardless of the costs. Attempts to quantify the value of an abuse-free environment for a child or for the society as a whole are generally viewed by the child welfare worker as insensitive at best and Draconian at worst. Confronting the child abuse crisis, however, is costly. Ignoring the direct and indirect expenditures associated with attempts to resolve this social problem will not make the task less costly nor will it result in the most efficient practice choices. While no one would argue that costs should be the sole determinant of policy, neither should costs be considered an inappropriate contributor to the decision-making process.

Expanded reporting laws, increased public and professional awareness of child maltreatment, intensive interventions with abuse victims and perpetrators, and comprehensive primary prevention efforts have commanded and will continue to command significant public funds. In light of fiscal constraints and increasing concern over the efficient and equitable use of scarce public resources, governments, like individuals, need to weigh the gains to be realized from a number of alternative investment strategies. Child maltreatment policies and programs will increasingly need to compete for social service dollars, not only with other legitimate social expenditures, but also with each other.

The purpose of this chapter is to examine the potential costs involved in addressing the issue of child maltreatment through a variety of treatment and prevention strategies. Following a general discussion of the common limitations found in cost-benefit and cost-effectiveness studies, the chapter compares the specific fiscal ramifications of adopting nonintervention, treatment, and prevention approaches to child maltreatment. While total dollar values are not always assigned to the costs and benefits raised in this initial discussion, the presentation identifies the categories of benefits and costs associated with different policies and highlights the tradeoffs that are implicit in decisions to spend money or to allocate resources among various alternatives. The chapter then presents the relative costs and cost-effectiveness of different intervention models drawing upon the results of two national evaluations (BPA, 1977, 1983). The section concludes with a discussion of implications and limits of cost-benefit and cost-effectiveness research in shaping future child maltreatment policy and practice.

Difficulties with Cost-Benefit Analysis

Cost-benefit analysis is the principal analytical framework used to evaluate public expenditures. Simply put, the analysis seeks to determine if the total benefits of a given public sector activity outweigh its total costs. Since its inception, critics have charged that this analytic approach has certain practical or definitional requirements that limit its utility in social service planning. First, the quantification of benefits and costs is extremely problematic for programs designed to improve the quality of life or to prolong it. The value that is placed on a human life has come, in practice, to be equated with that individual's contribution to the GNP or with his or her potential earnings, a standard that implicitly works against certain groups in the society who, on average, earn less than others, such as women, minorities, and those born into families of lower socioeconomic status (Scheffler and Paringer, 1980; Buxbaum, 1981). Given this standard, one would place less value on the outcome of a program designed to assist women rather than men or to assist a college graduate rather than a highschool dropout simply because one group can be expected to have greater lifetime earnings than the other.

Even if cost-benefit models were to use an average earning capacity for all program recipients, the definition of value of life remains problematic because individuals contribute more to society than their labor or than those functions for which they are reimbursed. Emotional support, voluntary assistance, and other nonmarket human interactions pose an insurmountable measurement task for any researcher seeking to quantify a person's absolute contribution and thus worth to the society. While one could resort to a "willingness to pay" criterion to set values on these services in determining a person's worth, (e.g., what would you be willing to pay for a friend's support?) such strategies do not reduce bias, since one's willingness to pay is largely determined by one's income, the degree to which society assigns a monetary value to the service, and the availability of other sources of the desired good. In addition, this approach introduces a new bias against those who lack a large network of friends or family who are willing "to pay" for, or need, their support.

Second, the method requires that future costs and benefits be discounted or be ascribed a current value generally below what they would be worth if they were accrued in the present. The basic rationale for this system is that everyone would prefer to have something now more than in the future, or that present gains are more valuable than the anticipation of future gains. The essence of discounting is that it reduces a stream of costs and benefits to a single amount comparable across different programs.[1] This system of evaluation, while a logicial and necessary one from an economic perspective, systematically favors programs that produce benefits sooner over those that produce the same overall benefits but do so over a longer period of time. For example, coupled with the notion of valuing human life in terms of potential earnings, cost-benefit analyses will show that programs that serve children generate fewer current benefits than programs serving adults, due to the low value assigned to the earnings of children who will not begin their labor force participation until ten to 20 years hence. All things being equal in terms of the total earnings preserved, programs targeted to individuals who are currently in their prime or closer to their prime working years will be identified as producing greater total present benefits than programs serving young children (Scheffler and Paringer, 1980).[2]

The third problematic issue is determining what specific benefits and costs to include. Evaluations of programs that have significant "intangible" benefits or costs (i.e., items difficult to value in dollar terms) tend to be more biased by subjective value judgments. A determination of whether someone is better off or has greater peace of mind depends on the analyst's or interest group's particular values and preferences. For example, a child placed in foster case may be considered by the system to be "better off" in the sense that he or she has been removed from an abusive or potentially abusive environment. From the point of view of the child and the child's parents, however, foster care placement may not be seen as the preferred state. For them, intervention has left them worse off, with the child deprived of his natural parents and the parents deprived of their child. Determining what constitutes an enhanced living situation becomes increasingly subjective as one moves further away from the most damaging and dangerous forms of child maltreatment.

Similar disagreement can exist over the short- and long-term benefits of primary prevention programs. While the prevention of child abuse and neglect is generally viewed as a laudable goal, there is room for honest disagreement in identifying which programs best achieve this goal. For example, the provision of child assault prevention classes in preschools is considered by some to represent a positive commitment to the protection of children from unwanted sexual and physical assaults. Proponents of these programs point to increased reports of sexual abuse and the notable number of self-disclosures by children following these presentations as indicators of success. Others, however, are less convinced of these programs' overall utility. As discussed in the previous chapter, some view these classes as unnecessary and unwelcomed intrusions into an area best explained by parents. In addition, these programs may inappropriately raise a child's expectations that disclosure will result in a formal investigation of the charges or protect them from further abuse. Other critics suggest that classes may leave children who have been victimized feeling even more anxious about their situation. Children unable to comply with the request to come forward may view themselves as failures and a disappointment to their teachers. Further, children who will not be abused by their parents may experience unnecessary anxiety as a result of this intervention. While the scope of the costs and benefits included in a given model can be expanded to capture conflicting values, ascribing dollar values to such factors as intrusion into the family versus a child's security and safety remains a very subjective process.

Finally, discretion also exists in identifying the groups that experience a benefit or a cost. Theoretically, cost-benefit models are concerned with identifying total costs and total benefits and pay little attention to who bears the costs and who shares in the benefits. As long as benefits exceed costs, it is assumed that society, as a whole, is better off. Those who find themselves with greater income following the construction of a new factory in town, for example, could share their new wealth with those who were displaced by the factory. Since this type of benefit exchange rarely, if ever, occurs in social service programs, an economically-beneficial social program could leave some groups considerably worse off than before. For example, a protective service agency may shift a sizable percentage of its program resources into its emergency response and family maintenance units in order to provide intensive services for families at risk of losing their children to foster care placement. Such a strategy may well result in fewer children entering foster care which, in turn, may produce a net savings in overall foster care payments. However, employing this strategy in the context of a decreasing budget means that fewer staff and service resources are now available to those families whose children are taken into the foster care system. These families are now deprived of resources that would have been available to them had the agency continued its prior allocation system. While theoretically the savings produced in foster care could be redirected toward enhanced service packages to assist in reunification of foster care children and their birth parents, it is far more likely that the savings will be viewed as an opportunity to reduce the total child welfare budget.

In order to avoid some of the shortcomings associated with cost-benefit analysis, social scientists often employ a truncated version of the analysis known as cost-effectiveness studies. This methodology, characterized by the measurement of costs and benefits in different terms, avoids the difficulty of having to place dollar values on intangibles. Generally, cost-effectiveness studies are pursued when (1) the costs of alternative programs are identical or a fixed amount is available for a given intervention and therefore only benefits need to be compared, or (2) the benefits of a program are identical and therefore only the costs need to be compared (Stokey and Zeckhauser, 1978). Because benefits and costs are measured in different units (e.g., dollars versus years of life), cost-effectiveness analysis provides no direct guidance for determining if benefits outweigh costs or if the optimal expenditure level for a given program or policy has been reached. If, however, one knows what needs to be accomplished or how much can be spent, cost-effectiveness offers a less complex but equally suitable methodology for enhancing the efficiency of the decision-making process.[3]

The structure of cost-benefit and cost-effectiveness analyses suggests that, at best, these methods offer practitioners and planners only partial assistance in determining best practice. As long as programs seek specific measurable outcomes such as fewer hospitalizations due to abuse-related injuries or fewer children needing services to remediate language delays or physical handicaps due to prolonged maltreatment, cost-effectiveness analysis offers a reliable way to assess the relative effectiveness of competing programs. However, child abuse treatment and prevention programs also seek less tangible goals such as improved parent-child relationships, higher levels of self-esteem, and greater social integration. Further, most of these programs directly or indirectly struggle with the appropriate balance between child protection and parental rights. In these cases, quantifying outcomes becomes a very value-laden process. Selecting the most effective program is determined less by objective standards of highest and best use and more by the personal concerns and professional preferences that governed the definition of benefits.

Within these limitations, however, the methods serve a heuristic value. Regardless of one's personal values as to the importance of confronting child maltreatment, the expansion of public policy in this area will result in very real costs. While the selection of inputs into a cost-benefit model is indeed value-laden and far less objective than advocates of the method suggest, the process does require the explicit recognition of the factors governing the selection of a given set of variables. This clarity, while influencing the outcomes, also provides those who wish to disagree with the outcomes specific assumptions to attack, a clarity not often present in less quantifiable methods of decision making.

Theoretical Costs and Benefits

Assuming a conservative national incidence rate of 11.8 per 1,000 children under 18, it can be estimated that approximately 739,000 children were maltreated by their parents in 1983 (AAPC, 1985). The first step in calculating the social costs of maltreatment is documenting the percentage of abused or neglected children who require treatment for specific health or emotional difficulties. The problems observed in those children under 13 included in the National Clinical Evaluation Study offers one estimate of these prevalence rates. For example:

> approximately 30% of the abused children had chronic health problems;
>
> approximately 30% of the abused children had some type of cognitive or language disorder;
>
> over one-half of the abused children had such socioemotional problems as low self-esteem, lack of trust, low frustration tolerance, and poor relationships with their parents;
>
> approximately 14% of the abused children exhibited self-mutilative or other self-destructive behaviors;
>
> over one-half of the abused children had difficulty in school, including poor attendance and misconduct; and
>
> over 22% of the abused children had learning disorders requiring special education services (BPA, 1983).

Similar difficulties were also noted among the 700 adolescents included in this same study. On balance, a greater percentage of the adolescents than the children studied exhibited a wider range of problems and a larger number of severe disorders at intake. For example, over 40% of these adolescents exhibited self-destructive behavior, over one-quarter had a serious drug and/or alcohol problem, and over 17% had attempted suicide. Over two-thirds showed poor academic performance. One-quarter of these youths had actual learning disorders, with the remainder demonstrating poor conduct or failing to attend school regularly. Overall, the severity and range of problems found among the adolescent sample suggested that the difficulties of abused and neglected children intensify over time, particularly when abuse is longstanding and no formal intervention occurs.[4]

In addition to the immediate consequences of maltreatment, exploratory research on this population suggests that these problems continue to manifest themselves as the child grows into adulthood. Among the difficulties noted for adults or adolescents who were maltreated as children are an increased prevalence of drug or alcohol dependency, increased rates of status offenses (i.e., running away, truancy, incorrigibility, etc.) as well as delinquent behavior and adult criminal behavior, and recurring health problems, both physical and mental. Perhaps most disturbing within the present context is the suggestion that, left unserved, abused or neglected children grow up to become the abusive or neglectful parents of the next generation. While we currently do not have conclusive evidence linking adult dysfunctioning to being victimized as a child, the exploratory evidence is strong enough to warrant consideration in any model concerned with estimating the total social costs of child maltreatment.

Addressing these and other problems resulting from maltreatment, both in the short and long run, places considerable fiscal demands on local public health, rehabilitation, criminal justice, and child welfare systems. Using very conservative estimates regarding both the incidence of abuse and the number of abused children requiring health and remedial services, Figure 6.1 summarizes some of these costs. As reported by the American Association for Protecting Children (1985), some 23,648 children were reported with serious physical injury due to maltreatment in 1983. This classification covers such impairments as brain damage, skull fractures, bone fractures, internal injuries, poisoning, and burns. Assuming that only half of these children required hospitalization for an estimated 5.2 days—the average length of stay for children with bone fractures—the immediate inpatient medical costs associated with maltreatment would exceed $20 million, the vast majority of which would be paid for through Medicaid. In addition to immediate hospitalization, the result of many of these injuries is long-term disability for the child or, at a minimum, several years of rehabilitation services. In FY 1984, it was estimated that local special education expenditures exceeded $2.7 billion, resulting in an annual cost of $655 for each child enrolled in school-based programs. Again, assuming that only half of the seriously injuried children required special education services, over $7 million would be required in the one year following maltreatment. In addition, these children might well become eligible for long-term disability payments and other community services for the developmentally disabled. The cost of these community services, estimated at $13 per day, would be increased by $1.1 million annually if only 1% of seriously abused children suffered permanent developmental disabilities as a result of maltreatment.

The final immediate cost implication of child maltreatment quantified in Figure 6.1 involves placement in foster care. While the number of children entering foster care and the average length of stay for these children in foster care steadily declined following passage of the Adoption Assistance and Child Welfare Reform Act of 1980 (PL 96-272) the annual costs of providing foster care services to children continued to increase. AAPC estimates that at least 18% of all confirmed cases reported to child protective services (CPS) agencies result in the child spending at least some amount of time in foster care (AAPC, 1986). Applying this estimate to the 1983 data suggests that 133,020 children were placed in foster care during or following the investigation of maltreatment charges. Based on the average length of stay in foster care noted by the American Public Welfare Association (APWA) in its assessment of the system in 1982, it can be estimated that during the year immediately following the maltreatment report, roughly 22% of these children will stay in foster care an average of three months and 78% will stay an average of nine months.[5] Assuming an aver-

Figure 6.1

Summary of the Immediate and Long-Term Costs Surrounding Child Maltreatment

(Based upon 739,000 Confirmed Cases of Maltreatment in 1983[1])

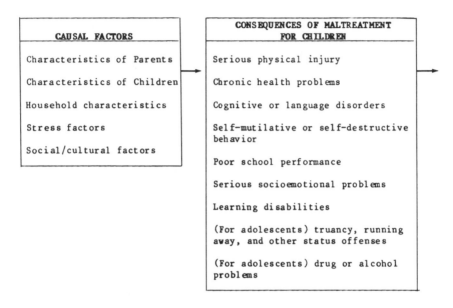

CAUSAL FACTORS	CONSEQUENCES OF MALTREATMENT FOR CHILDREN
Characteristics of Parents	Serious physical injury
Characteristics of Children	Chronic health problems
Household characteristics	Cognitive or language disorders
Stress factors	Self-mutilative or self-destructive behavior
Social/cultural factors	Poor school performance
	Serious socioemotional problems
	Learning disabilities
	(For adolescents) truancy, running away, and other status offenses
	(For adolescents) drug or alcohol problems

[1]American Association for Protecting Children, Highlights of Official Child Neglect and Abuse Reporting, 1983, Denver, CO: The American Humane Association, 1985.

age $450 per month maintenance payment (Gershenson, 1984), foster care costs relating to new reports of child maltreatment exceed $460 million annually.

In addition to the immediate costs associated with remediating the effects of child abuse and neglect, the fiscal impact of maltreatment continues throughout the child's lifetime. Increased rates of juvenile delinquency, leading to increased rates of adult crime, higher drug and alcohol abuse rates, and potential emotional and physical disabilities generate both direct costs for the service systems addressing these problems as well as indirect costs in terms of a reduction in the child's potential lifetime earnings.

Initially, the continued costs of maltreatment are shouldered by youth service systems. For example, assuming that those children remaining in foster care after the initial year following the maltreatment episode do so for an average of 1.8 additional years, the foster care costs associated with these children are an additional $646 million over the initial annual costs

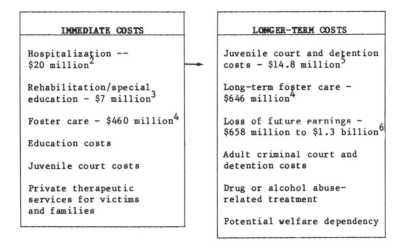

IMMEDIATE COSTS	LONGER-TERM COSTS
Hospitalization -- $20 million[2]	Juvenile court and detention costs - $14.8 million[5]
Rehabilitation/special education - $7 million[3]	Long-term foster care - $646 million[4]
Foster care - $460 million[4]	Loss of future earnings - $658 million to $1.3 billion[6]
Education costs	Adult criminal court and detention costs
Juvenile court costs	
Private therapeutic services for victims and families	Drug or alcohol abuse-related treatment
	Potential welfare dependency

[2] U.S. Bureau of the Census, Statistical Abstract of the United States: 1985 (105th Edition), Washington, DC, 1984, Tables No. 171 and 172.

[3] U.S. Bureau of the Census, Statistical Abstract of the United States: 1985 (105th Edition), Washington, DC, 1984, Table No. 231; David Braddock et al., Public Expenditures for Mental Retardation and Developmental Disabilities in the United States, Chicago: Institute for the Study of Developmental Disabilities, University of Illinois, 1985, p. 80.

[4] Charles Gershenson, "The Cost Saving Impact of Permanency Planning," Child Welfare Research Notes No. 6 (April 1984); Toshio Tatara, Characteristics of Children in Substitute and Adoptive Care: A Statistical Summary of the UCIS National Child Welfare Data Base, Washington, DC: American Public Welfare Association, 1983.

[5] U.S. Bureau of the Census, Statistical Abstract of the United States: 1985 (105th Edition), Washington, DC, 1984.

[6] U.S. Bureau of Labor Statistics, Table of Working Life: The Increment-Decrement Method, Bulletin 2135 (November 1982), Tables 3, 7; pp. 21, 28.

outlined above.[6] Similarly, the juvenile court and juvenile justice system are routinely involved with youth who have been abused or neglected. In 1982, it was estimated that it cost approximately $21,000 annually to care for a juvenile offender in either a public or private residential facility. Assuming a 20% delinquency rate among the 177,360 adolescent maltreatment victims identified in 1983 (Carr, 1977), one can estimate that over $14.8 million would be spent if these youth required only an average of two years in a correctional facility.

As an abused child matures, the social costs of maltreatment shift to the adult criminal justice system, rehabilitation services, and income maintenance systems. While estimating the exact amount of these costs is unclear, given the difficulty associated with ferreting out clear causal relationships over time, the types of problems exhibited in maltreated children clearly impede normal, healthy development and might well result in ongoing functioning problems and consequently, ongoing social costs. Also, maltreatment suffered as a child may establish parenting behaviors and expectations that lead to an increased likelihood for abusing or neglecting the next generation, actions that simply reinitiate the cycle of problems and related costs described above.

Finally, it is reasonable to assume that child maltreatment might reduce the lifetime productivity of its victims. Similar to a number of nonabuse-related factors which have been found to make significant contributions to one's ultimate lifetime earnings, such as the educational level and employment pattens of one's parents, socioeconomic status, race, sex, and one's own educational performance and attainment, child maltreatment might also be expected to influence one's earnings potential, particularly if the immediate consequences of maltreatment are serious physical injury, the development of school-related problems, or the loss of self-esteem. The calculations summarized in Table 6.1 suggest that even with very conservative estimates, significant losses in potential lifetime earnings may result from child abuse and neglect. Assuming that such losses would be experienced only by those children who suffered severe injuries as a result of maltreatment and that such impairments are limited to 5% or 10% of the child's total potential earnings, some $658 million to $1.3 billion in lost productivity might result each year because of early battering or severe neglect.

Consideration of lost future earnings complements simple, humanitarian arguments favoring intervention in cases of child maltreatment. Declining birth rates, particularly among whites, will result in an increasing discrepancy between the number of older Americans drawing social security payments and the number of workers contributing their earnings to support the system. By the time the baby boom retires, declining birth rates and the increasing rate of early retirement will shift the number of retirees supported by every 100 workers from 19 to 38 (Ozawa, 1985). Enhancing the productivity of the future generation requires not only improving basic health, education, and welfare services for all children but also providing more remedial services to all abused and neglected children, particularly in the areas of langauge and other cognitive skills essential to

Table 6.1

Estimated Loss of Earnings Due to Child Maltreatment

	Estimated Labor Force Participation (In Years)[a]	Estimated Median Annual Earnings[b]	Number of Maltreated Children With Serious Injuries[c]	Lifetime Earnings Potential of Children	Estimated Loss of Earning Potential due to Child Maltreatment	
					Assume 5% Loss	Assume 10% Loss
Male	38.5 years	$19,708	11,564	$8,774,277,500	$438,713,850	$877,427,750
Female	27.7 years	$13,104	12,084	$4,386,259,900	$219,312,950	$438,625,990
Total/ Average	33.0 years (average)	$16,330 (average)	23,648	$13,160,537,400	$658,026,800	$1,316,053,740

[a]SOURCE: U.S. Department of Labor, Bureau of Labor Statistics, Table of Working Life: The Increment Decrement Method, Bulletin 2135, November 1982, Tables 3, 7, pp. 21, 28.

[b]SOURCE: U.S. Bureau of the Census, Statistical Abstract of the U.S. 1985 (105th Edition), Washington, DC, 1984, Table 700.

[c]SOURCE: American Association for Protecting Children, Highlights of Official Child Neglect and Abuse Reporting, 1983, Denver, CO: American Humane Association, 1985.

the child's initial positive performance in school and future performance in the work place.

In determining the best intervention strategies, it is useful first to consider the potential benefits and costs associated with the generic categories of treatment versus prevention. Focusing solely on the treatment of identified child abuse and neglect cases offers little in the way of reducing the initial social costs of maltreatment. Theoretically, remediating the problems suffered by maltreated children through the provision of support and therapeutic services should protect against the worst consequences of nonintervention, such as reabuse, the intergenerational maltreatment cycle, and loss of adult productivity. In practice, however, treatment interventions are often not successful in preventing reabuse, particularly in cases of chronic neglect, emotional maltreatment, and serious physical abuse. Also, extensive treatment models such as those funded as federal demonstration projects are extremely costly. Since these interventions result in a reduced propensity for maltreatment in, at best, only half of the families they serve, intervening only after abuse has occurred may be too late in the process to significantly reduce the long-term problems of these families and children, and, consequently, the social costs associated with addressing these problems.

In contrast, prevention services, or intervening before maltreatment begins, offer the opportunity not only to reduce the long-term costs associated with abuse and neglect, but also significantly to reduce short-term costs. While solid empirical evidence linking the provision of prevention services to a reduction in the incidence of maltreatment is thin, treatment program evaluations have consistently found high-risk families more amenable to change and more likely to experience positive outcomes than those families who have already been involved in maltreatment (BPA, 1977, 1983). Even if early intervention had prevented only 20% of the abuse and neglect episodes reported in 1983, a minimum of $97 million might have been saved in initial hospitalization, remediation, and foster care costs, based upon the conservative cost estimates summarized in Figure 6.1.

The effectiveness of a prevention or early intervention emphasis in producing these types of cost savings within the child welfare system has been documented by at least one benefit-cost analysis. Reviewing the impact of permanency planning on foster care costs, Gershenson (1984) estimated that this reform, with its emphasis on family maintenance and family reunification, save state and federal governments between $3.8 and $5.4 billion in foster care maintenance payments.[7] These savings compared very favorably to the $5 million federal investment made in the demonstration, evaluation, and marketing effort on behalf of the permanency planning concept. "Far more significant," notes Gershenson, "is the unmeasurable impact on approximately 620,000 to 1,400,000 children and families who were the primary beneficiaries of permanency planning during the five-year period" (Gershenson, 1984:3). Among the benefits theoretically accruing to these families were a reduction in the frequency and duration of separations and the ability of these families to remain intact following a briefer and, it is hoped, less intrusive public intervention.

While Gershenson's analysis makes a persuasive case for prevention, it did not include all of the costs of implementing permanency planning. In addition to the costs incurred by the federal government through its demonstration efforts, individual states also experimented with different types of foster care management and placement systems prior to the passage of PL 96-272 and in implementing their own permanency planning legislation. Collectively these individual state efforts dwarf the federal investment effort. Further, Gershenson excluded the costs associated with the potential reabuse children experienced because they were not removed from their homes.[8] In order to project the total social savings realized through permanency planning, we must accurately assess the ability of child welfare services to offer protection to children in the absence of placement and to correctly determine when at least temporary placement is the most appropriate course of treatment. Recent investigations into child abuse fatalities have noted that between 25% and 50% of these cases involved children who were active or terminated cases of local child protective service agencies at the time of their death (Daro and Mitchel, 1987a). These cases, unfortunately, underscore the unavoidable difficulty of protecting children who continue to reside in volatile and chaotic environments. If children continue to experience maltreatment, either because they were initially not removed from the home or were returned home too soon, the estimated savings in foster care costs may simply reappear as an additional cost to other social service systems, resulting in, at best, zero net benefit or, at worst, an increase in total costs.

Independent of the success prevention efforts have in reducing the incidence or severity of maltreatment, the wide-scale implementation of these strategies raises serious questions regarding their potential costs and possible negative side effects. To say the society should be committed to preventing child abuse is one thing; to accomplish this goal within current fiscal constraints and with regard for a family's right to privacy is another. Prevention efforts need to address the multiple causal correlates of maltreatment if they are to maximize potential savings. Because current research has not produced very accurate predictive models of maltreatment at the individual client level, entire subgroups have been identified as being at greater than average risk of abuse or neglect. Providing such services as parenting education, in-home support services, or peer support groups to all young or first-time parents, single mothers, or low-income parents would place formidable demands on state and local social service budgets. For example, a 12-week parenting education course provided at a total per-client cost of $158 would have cost approximately $57 million to provide to every low-income mother who gave birth in 1982.[9] For this service to be most effective, however, some percentage of these women may have required in-home follow-up services for some period of time after the baby's birth or ongoing assistance in child care or in securing routine medical services. In short, establishing a comprehensive package of prevention services for a social problem with unclear and multiple causal paths generally results in the casting of several, often very thin, nets over a very large target population.

In addition to cost concerns, secondary prevention efforts carry with them a potential stigma. Parents receiving these services have been identified, often in the absence of any overt harm to their children, as potential maltreators. While no dollar value can be ascribed to a family's loss of privacy or to the social stigma of being viewed as a potential child abuser, these issues represent very real "costs" for early intervention. Even when such services are provided on a voluntary basis, recipients, particularly low-income women, may feel less able to refuse services for fear of losing their children to the foster care system or having certain public benefits taken from them if they fail to cooperate. Even primary prevention efforts may generate intangible costs for recipients. Raising the spectre of an ideal childhood or ideal parenting practices may make both children and parents more uncomfortable about their current situation, a situation they may be unable to alter. While one certainly can recognize extreme and harmful behaviors that should not be tolerated under the guise of parents' rights to rear their children as they see fit, it is not easy to identify the precise boundaries of what constitutes "good parenting." Individual parents' choices of certain snack foods, acceptable levels of cleanliness, and selective use of corporal punishment reflect a wide range of values and cultural practices; it is unlikely that any generic prevention program could accurately draw the line between acceptable and abusive choices in these and other areas. Forcing families to adhere to a single standard of care once one moves beyond very extreme acts of abuse or neglect cannot help but raise serious questions of parental rights, family privacy, cultural diversity, and, ultimately, individual freedom.

Two choices are open to advocates of prevention wishing to avoid the types of intangible costs outlined above. The first option is to make new prevention services available to all children and families regardless of need. This strategy, while removing the stigma from recipients, exacerbates the cost dilemmas and continues to threaten an individual's freedom to reject services. Another objection to this strategy is that, despite continued increases in the maltreatment reporting rates, child maltreatment remains a relatively rare event. Even if the AAPC incidence rate increased five-fold, less than 60 children in every 1,000 would require prevention services. Services to the other 940 children would be theoretically unnecessary and represent a waste of public dollars.

A second, and perhaps more fruitful, strategy would be to take advantage of existing formal and informal service systems in strengthening parents. A number of public health and nutritional programs, such as the

Women, Infants and Children (WIC) supplemental food program and the Early and Periodic Screening, Diagnosis and Treatment program (EPSDT), already serve large segments of those populations considered among the most at risk for maltreatment and have been found to be cost-effective.[10] In addition, general pre- and postnatal care programs present opportunities to make all parents aware of the universal potential for abuse and to provide services for those seeking education or assistance in establishing peer support groups. Voluntary associations, local community organizations, churches, and employers should be encouraged to establish parent support services to facilitate child-rearing for their members and employees. The elementary and secondary education systems offer the opportunity for the training of future parents in basic child development and caretaker tasks, and may also serve as a source of support and positive role models for children who are being maltreated.

In short, a number of public and private service vehicles already exist and can be used to expand prevention efforts without straining public coffers. The use of these existing service structures can reduce both program costs and the social stigma attached to secondary prevention. Also, this diversity in service settings allows for the development of more culturally sensitive and appropriate interventions at the individual community level. In this manner, the process of prevention becomes one of family, friends, or community members assisting parents to improve their child-rearing skills and expanding the support services available to them. Preventing maltreatment and ensuring the safety of the nation's 63 million children is a tall order for the entire community to fill and a virtually impossible order for only one segment of the social service network. Prevention, as opposed to treatment, offers a far broader platform for building the type of public-private coalition necessary to offer families sufficient education and support to reduce the incidence of maltreatment.

The establishment of this type of public-private partnership is a laudable long-term goal. In the short run, however, practitioners will need to select the most cost-effective interventions from among competing, fragmented service alternatives. Unfortunately, the data necessary to make these types of decisions is sorely lacking. Program managers rarely present their costs in terms of specific service components nor do they generally link costs in any direct way to eventual client outcomes. Such information gaps make it difficult for practitioners and program planners to make informed choices as to which services offer the most efficient use of resources. Addressing this problem, a method of cost accounting has been developed which identifies expenditures in terms of distinct service categories rather than in terms of more traditional budget line items such as rent, utilities, staff salaries, supplies, and capital purchases. Under this method of accounting, all program costs are assigned to discrete service categories either in total or in direct proportion to the time staff spent engaged in a given activity.

This method was used by Berkeley Planning Associates in the firm's evaluation of the 11 child abuse and neglect demonstration projects funded by the National Center for Health Services Research between 1974 and 1977 and again in the National Clinical Evaluation Study. These two efforts resulted in detailed cost data on over 30 different program models and discrete services. Analyses of these data and their policy implications are presented in the following section.

Cost-Effectiveness of Different Interventions

A direct comparison of the relative cost-effectiveness of different treatment programs was conducted by Berkeley Planning Associates (BPA) as part of its first national child abuse program evaluation (BPA, 1977). The cost and service data generated by the 11 demonstration programs evaluated under that effort produced average per-unit costs for various key services, as summarized in Table 6.2. These costs were then used to estimate the annual costs of applying five different service models to a hypothetical caseload of 100 clients.[11] These service models included an Individual Counseling/Social Work model, a Lay Therapy model, a Group Treatment model, a Children's Program model, and a Family Treatment model. While all of the models included the provision of intake and initial diagnosis, case management and regular case review, crisis intervention after intake, multidisciplinary team case review for 25% of the caseload, court case activities for 10% of the caseload, and follow-up, each model provided a unique package of counseling or support services. As summarized in Figure 6.2, the estimated costs of these models, without ancillary services or community education activities, ranged in 1977 dollars from $104,372 to over $800,000. Adding in the costs of such ancillary services as babysitting, transportation, and psychological testing, and community activities such as professional education, coordination, and policy activities, the annual costs for the models increased from less than $200,000 to well over $1 million.

In order to determine if the more expensive interventions were justified by being more effective per dollar of cost in producing positive client outcomes, the BPA study team compared the marginal increase in the probability of reduced propensity for future maltreatment given the provision of the various service models with the estimated per-client cost of each model. Reinforcing the recommendations that emerged from the study's client outcome analysis, this analysis found that the most effective services were also among the least expensive. Parent aid and lay therapy counseling, Parents Anonymous, and parent education classes emerged as more cost-effective in securing a small but significant increase in the probability of a successful family outcome from treatment than did the principal service of the Social Work model, individual counseling. Table 6.3 summarizes the relative cost-effectiveness of three of the service models depicted in Figure 6.2. As this table indicates, the annual costs per successful adult client outcome in a project serving 100 clients with the Lay Therapy model was estimated at $2,590, in contrast to an estimated cost of $4,081 with the Group Therapy model and $4,462 with the Individual Counseling/ Social Work model.

Similar to the approach taken in the BPA study, the National Clinical Evaluation Study also collected detailed cost data. Table 6.4 summarizes the average costs for various services as reported by the 19 clinical demonstration projects and adjusted to reflect 1983 cost levels. These demonstration projects offered a wider range of services to a more diversified client population than did the initial 11 projects evaluated by BPA. As might be expected, there was significant variation not only in the types of therapeutic and support services provided to adult clients exhibiting different maltreatment behavior or presenting problems but also in the types of concrete, supportive, and therapeutic interventions provided to maltreatment victims. For example, those programs targeting services to maltreated adolescents offered shelter care, vocational counseling, and household management in addition to family, group, and individual counseling. Therapeutic day care programs, infant stimulation, and special education classes were key interventions for those projects targeting services to the youngest victims of maltreatment. Overall, this diversity in service structure and target population made it possible to develop more elaborate service models and to estimate the costs of these models.

Table 6.5 estimates the annual costs associated with the provision of these various basic needs, support services, and therapeutic services in terms of the National Clinical Evaluation Study's five target populations. Of these five populations, only two—child neglect and sexual abuse—involved a specific type of maltreatment. As might be expected, the caseloads of the projects in these two categories were the most homogeneous with respect to their primary type of maltreatment. In contrast, the caseloads for the remaining three target areas were more diverse, with the adolescent projects serving families primarily involved in physical abuse or emotional maltreatment; the substance abuse projects serving families primarily involved in emotional maltreatment or neglect; and the remedial services projects serving roughly equal numbers of families involved in either physical abuse, neglect, or emotional maltreatment. This case distribution, while useful for identifying the relative effectiveness of services with different types of maltreatment, made it difficult to use these data to assess potential program costs in terms of the two subpopulations of maltreatment not specifically targeted in this demonstration effort. However, the variety of services and caseload characteristics represented by these 19 projects is indicative of the range of expenditures commonly found among the universe of child abuse treatment programs. As such, the findings provide useful cost estimates of various direct and indirect ser-

Table 6.2

Average Unit Costs Across All Projects for Direct Services

Service	Unit Measurement	$/Unit (Average Cost to Project)[a]	$/Unit Adjusted for 1983 Costs[b]	Number of Projects Providing Service
Outreach	Cases	25.25	46.78	7
Intake and Initial Diagnosis	Intakes	78.75	130.41	10
Court Case Activities	Cases	126.00	208.66	10
Crisis Intervention During Intake	Contacts	13.50	22.36	6
Multidisciplinary Review	Reviews	54.75	90.67	9
Individual Counseling	Contact hours	14.75	24.43	11
Parent Aide/Lay Therapy	Contact hours	7.25	12.00	8
Couples Counseling	Contacts	17.00	28.15	8
Family Counseling	Contacts	30.00	49.68	6
Alcohol, Drug, Weight Counseling	Session	7.50	12.42	2
24-Hour Hotline	Calls	7.50	12.42	2
Individual Therapy	Contacts	21.25	35.19	7
Group Therapy	Session	10.50	17.39	6
Parents Anonymous	Session	5.75	9.52	4
Parent Education Classes	Session	9.50	15.73	7

Service	Unit			
Crisis Intervention after Intake	Contacts	14.25	23.60	10
Day Care	Child sessions	7.75	12.83	2
Residential Care	Child days	37.75	62.51	1
Child Development Program	Child sessions	21.50	35.60	4
Play Therapy	Child sessions	11.75	19.46	4
Special Child Therapy	Contacts	54.25	89.84	1
Crisis Nursery	Child days	35.50	58.78	1
Homemaking	Contacts	22.75	36.67	3
Medical Care	Visits	23.50	38.92	7
Babysitting/Child Care	Child hours	3.50	5.80	4
Transportation/Waiting	Rides	8.75	14.49	8
Psychological & Other Tests	Person tests	36.25	60.03	8
Follow-Up	Pers. follow-ups	36.50	43.88	6

[a]These costs reflect raw data adjusted for wage/price differentials, project management, and overhead distribution.

[b]All costs have been inflated by a factor of 1.656 to reflect the average increase in state and local government service workers between the 1976 data collection period and 1983, as reported in the U.S. Bureau of the Census Statistical Abstract of the United States: 1985 (105th Edition), Washington, DC, 1984, Table No. 474.

SOURCE: Berkeley Planning Associates, Cost Report: Evaluation, Joint OCD/SRS National Demonstration Program in Child Abuse and Neglect, 1974-1977. Prepared for the National Center for Health Services Research under Contract No. 106-74-120 and Contract No. 230-75-0076, December 1977.

Figure 6.2

Annual Program Costs Estimated for Five Intervention Models Serving 100 Families

	Model Costs	With Ancillary Service[1]	With Community Education Services[2]
INDIVIDUAL COUNSELING/ SOCIAL WORK MODEL Basic services Individual counseling*	$135,897 ($225,045)[3]	$169,560 ($280,791)[3]	$211,950 ($350,989)[3]
LAY THERAPY MODEL Basic services Lay therapy counseling Parents Anonymous* (25% of caseload)	$104,372 ($172,840)[3]	$138,035 ($228,586)[3]	$172,543 ($285,731)[3]
GROUP TREATMENT MODEL Basic services Group therapy* (50% of caseload) Parent education classes (20 sessions) Individual counseling* (25% of caseload)	$124,672 ($206,457)[3]	$158,335 ($262,203)[3]	$197,919 ($327,754)[3]

BASIC SERVICES

Intake and initial diagnosis

Case management and regular case review

Crisis intervention after intake

Multidisciplinary team case review (25% of caseload)

Court case review (25% of caseload)

Follow-up

CHILDREN'S PROGRAM

Basic services

Child development program *

Special child therapy (10% of caseload)

$645,407 $608,070 $850,088

($1,070,450)[3]   ($1,006,964)[3]   ($1,407,775)[3]

FAMILY TREATMENT PROGRAM

Basic services

Children's program

Individual counseling *

Family counseling (50% of caseload)

Group therapy (50% of caseload)

$328,407 $862,070 $1,077,586

($1,372,842)[3]   ($1,427,588)[3]   ($2,784,481)[3]

*Assume weekly provision

[1] Ancillary services include babysitting/child care, transportation/waiting, and psychological and other testing.

[2] Community activities, estimated to result in a 25% increase over the costs of the basic model and ancillary services, include prevention, community education, professional education, coordination, and legislation and policy.

[3] These figures have inflated the costs by a factor of 1.656 to reflect the average wage increase for state and local government service workers between the 1976 data collection period and 1983, as reported by the U.S. Bureau of the Census Statistical Abstract of the United States: 1985 (105th Edition), Washington, DC, 1984, Table No. 474.

SOURCE: Berkeley Planning Associates, Cost Report: Evaluation, Joint OCD/SRS National Demonstration Program in Child Abuse and Neglect, 1974-1977. Prepared for the National Center for Health Services Research under Contract No. 106-74-120 and Contract No. 230-75-0076, December 1977.

Table 6.3

Cost-Effectiveness of Service Models

Service Model[a]	Probability of Reduced Propensity for Child Abuse/Neglect if a Client Receives Services[b]	Average Costs of Serving 100 Clients with Model	Average Cost per Successful Family Outcome
Lay Model	.533	$138,935 ($228,586)[c]	$2,590 ($4,289)[c]
Group Model	.388	158,335 (262,203)[c]	4,081 (6,758)[c]
Social Work Model	.380	169,560 (280,791)[c]	4,462 (7,389)[c]

[a]The specific services represented by these models are summarized in Figure 6.2.

[b]Calculated from a multivariate regression of each of the three service models against the clinician's judgment of the client's likelihood for reabuse.

[c]The figures have inflated the costs by a factor of 1.656 to reflect the average wage increase for state and local government service workers between the 1976 data collection period and 1983, as reported by the U.S. Bureau of the Census Statistical Abstract of the United States: 1985, 105th Edition, Washington, DC, 1984, Table No. 474.

SOURCE: Berkeley Planning Associates, Cost Report: Evaluation of the Joint OCS/SES National Demonstration Program in Child Abuse and Neglect, 1974-1977. Prepared for the National Center for Health Services Research under Contracts No. 106-74-120 and No. 230-75-0076, December 1977.

vices for those currently managing such programs or developing community-wide service systems to address the problem of maltreatment.

While the costs associated with indirect services such as intake and diagnosis, regular case review, multidisciplinary case review, project management, evaluation and research, and community activities would not necessarily vary among programs serving different subpopulations, the costs of most direct services will fluctuate, depending upon a project's caseload characteristics. On balance, the need for concrete services to address basic needs such as food, clothing, assistance in finding housing, and employment and job training assistance were more frequently requested by clients of the child neglect and remedial services projects than by clients of the sexual abuse treatment projects. The projected annual costs associated with the provision of these services to 100 families ranged from almost

$34,000 for clients served by the child neglect projects to less than $6,000 for clients served by the sexual abuse projects. This discrepancy is consistent with the differences in household incomes and family characteristics generally found among families involved in sexual abuse versus families involved in child neglect. As discussed in prior chapters, cases of sexual abuse include a higher proportion of two-parent households and fewer families on public assistance than do cases of child neglect. The typical neglect family is headed by a single, unemployed female. However, the higher use of basic care services by the child neglect projects may be only partially due to the type of maltreatment they addressed. As indicated in Table 6.5, those projects offering remedial services to young children had the highest expenditures with respect to this service category. This pattern suggests that families with very young children may be among the most needy in terms of basic care services independent of their presenting pattern of maltreatment.

Similarly, the provision of casework counseling (i.e., counseling that focuses on the client's initial presenting problems and on resolving immediate environmental difficulties) also differed across the five program areas. Projects working with adolescent victims used this intervention not only with the adults on their caseloads but also with their adolescent clients. Among the most common problems for youth addressed through these counseling sessions were the identification of alternative living arrangements, the resolution of school problems, and the need for medical care. In the case of those projects focusing on substance abuse, casework counseling served as a means of identifying a family's most immediate problems and the alternatives available in the community to address these problems. Rather than providing, directly, for a client's basic care needs, these projects utilized other local service providers. While this method may offer a more cost-effective means of meeting the basic care needs of maltreating families, the experiences of the demonstration projects suggest that determining a family's specific needs in these areas and locating appropriate service alternatives in the community is a time-consuming task for staff and an ultimately costly function for child abuse treatment programs.

As with the BPA evaluation, the National Clinical Evaluation Study also found services to children to be among the most costly strategies for confronting child abuse. Projects in all of the five program categories identified in Table 6.5 devoted some resources to supervision of parent-child interactions for purposes of assessing this relationship, monitoring change over time, and providing physical rehabilitation or special education services. The frequency with which these services were provided varied across the five program categories and depended largely on the number of young children found on each project's caseload. Services to remediate the developmental delays associated with maltreatment were most often provided by the projects that targeted their services to young children, projects working with families involved in child abuse and substance

Table 6.4

Summary of Average Costs for Various Services Provided by NCCAN-Funded Demonstrations

	Unit Measurement	Staff Cost Per Unit[a]	Total Per Unit Cost[b]	Number of Projects Providing Service
Crisis and Emergency Services				
Crisis Intervention	Per hour	$16.29	$21.18	15
Respite Nursery	Per child stay	19.38	25.19[c]	1
24-Hour Hotline	Per call	6.71	8.72	9
Concrete Services				
Clothing	Per 30 min. contact	2.06	2.68[c]	2
Day Care/Babysitting	Per client contact	13.06	16.98	2
Food	Per client week	3.97	5.16[c]	6
Medical Services	Per client hour	56.48	73.42	5
Money	Per 30 min. contact	4.08	5.30[c]	4
Recreational Services	Per client hour	9.50	12.35	9
Shelter -- Adolescents	Per client week	25.95	33.74[c]	2
Shelter -- Children	Per client week	14.56	18.93[c]	1
Transportation	Per client trip	15.91	20.68	17
Support Services				
Advocacy	Per 45 min. contact	10.00	13.00	18
Casework Counseling	Per client hour	10.23	13.30	16

Foster Placement Assistance	Per client hour	15.6?	20.40	7
Home Finding -- Adults	Per client hour	15.54	20.20	3
Home Finding -- Adolescents	Per client hour	5.0?	6.59	3
Job Finding -- Adults	Per client hour	11.3?	14.79	5
Job Finding -- Adolescents	Per client hour	6.1?	8.05	3
Lay Companion	Per 90 min. contact	18.7?	24.43	5
Legal Assistance	Per client contact	13.2?	17.20	9
Vocational Couns.-- Adolescents	Per client hour	2.81	3.65	2
Education and Skill Development				
Academic Education	Per client hour	10.79	$14.03	2
Cooking Instructions	Per 30 min. contact	7.84	10.19	4
Family Planning -- Adults	Per client hour	5.87	7.63	4
Family Planning -- Adolescents	Per client hour	9.78	12.71	1
Household Mgmt. -- Adults	Per 30 min. contact	6.98	9.07	4
Household Mgmt. -- Adolescents	Per 30 min. contact	7.09	9.22	4
Parenting Training	Per client hour	10.14	13.18	8
Vocational Skills Training -- Adolescents	Per client hour	3.93	5.11	2
Remedial Services for Children				
Infant Stimulation	Per client hour	20.81	27.05	5
Parent-Child Supervised Interactions	Per client hour	11.14	14.48	3
Physical Rehabilitation	Per client hour	15.67	20.37	3
Special Education	Per 90 min. contact	16.63	21.62	2
Therapeutic Day Care	Per child day	16.94	20.02[c]	3

Table 6.4 continued

Therapy				
Individual Therapy	Per client hour	22.41	29.13	17
Family Therapy	Per family hour	20.14	26.18	16
Adolescent Group Therapy	Per client hour	12.79	16.63[c]	4
Adult Group Therapy	Per client hour	14.73	19.15[d]	6
Play Therapy	Per child hour	20.76	26.99	7
Children Support Groups	Per child hour	5.74	7.46	6
Family Workshops	Per family hour	20.10	26.13	2
Diagnosis and Case Mgmt. Services				
Intake and Initial Diagnosis	Per week[e]	99.25	129.00	18
Multidisciplinary Team Case Review	Per week[e]	186.05	241.87	17
Psychological Testing	Per client contact	35.82	46.57	12
Regular Case Review	Per week[e]	408.50	530.47	19
Project Management and Research				
Daily Project Management	Per week[e]	648.50	843.05	19
Staff Development & Supervision	Per week[e]	214.05	278.27	19
Evaluation & Research	Per week	413.36	537.37	18
Community Activities				
Community Coordination	Per week	106.06	137.88	18

Community Education	Per week	136.17	177.02	18
Legislative Activities	Per week	12.42	157.85	7
Professional Education & Training	Per week	146.33	190.23	15

[a]All staff salaries have been inflated by a factor of 1.255 to reflect the average salary increase for state and local government service workers between the 1980 data collection period and 1983. U.S. Bureau of the Census, Statistical Abstract of the United States: 1985 (105th Edition), Washington, DC, 1984, Table No. 474.

[b]These costs include an estimated 30% increase to cover all nonpayroll expenditures such as rent, utilities and equipment. In general, payroll expenditures represent roughly 70% of a program's total costs.

[c]The total costs indicated for these services do not take into account the cost of the actual items provided as in the case of clothing, food, and money, or the start-up costs for the purchase of equipment necessary for establishing a respite nursery, shelter program, or therapeutic day care center. Consequently, actual program costs for these items would exceed the totals indicated.

[d]In computing the average cost for this category, data for all types of adult group therapy (e.g., mothers' groups, fathers' groups, parent groups, etc.) were pooled.

[e]These cost estimates are based upon an average caseload of 35 families.

Table 6.5

Estimated Annual Service Costs by Program Type

for Caseloads of 100 Families

	Sexual Abuse	Adolescent Maltreatment	Substance Abuse	Remedial Services	Child Neglect
Caseload Characteristics					
Number of Families	100	100	100	100	100
Number of Adults	120	120	160	130	120
Number of Adolescents	40	150	90	---	30
Number of Children:	50	30	150	140	250
(Infants 0 - 18 Months)	(—)	(—)	(33)	(42)	(78)
(Children 19 Months - 12 Years)	(50)	(30)	(117)	(98)	(172)
Service Volume and Costs[a]					
Crisis Intervention					
Average Cost per Week	$372	$372	$372	$372	$372
TOTAL ANNUAL COST	$19,344	$19,344	$19,344	$19,344	$19,344
Concrete Services					
Number of Families	13	30	50	73	67
Average Caseload Cost Per Week	$110	$253	$421	$651	$565
TOTAL ANNUAL COST	$5,720	$13,156	$21,892	$33,852	$29,380
Shelter Care - Adolescents					
Number of Adolescents Served		150			
Average Weekly Caseload Costs		$5,060			
TOTAL ANNUAL COST		$263,120			

Support Services – Adult					
Number of Adults Served	59	101	99	110	101
Average Weekly Caseload Costs	$280	$479	$469	$521	$479
TOTAL ANNUAL COST	$14,560	$24,908	$24,388	$27,092	$24,908
Support Services – Adolescents					
Number of Adolescents Served	16	138	36	––	12
Average Weekly Caseload Costs	$28	$242	$63		$21
TOTAL ANNUAL COST	$1,456	$12,584	$2,268		$1,092
Casework Counseling					
Number of Adults Served	94	103	115	111	62
Number of Adolescents Served	32	137	45	––	6
Average Annual Costs Per Client	$692	$692	$692	$692	$692
TOTAL ANNUAL COSTS	$87,192	$166,080	$110,720	$76,812	$47,056
Educational and Skill Development – Adults					
Number of Adults Served	40	36	56	62	68
Average Weekly Caseload Costs	$196	$177	$275	$304	$334
TOTAL ANNUAL COST	$10,192	$9,204	$14,300	$15,808	$17,368
Educational and Skill Development – Adolescents					
Number of Adolescents Served	14	69	––	––	6
Average Weekly Caseload Costs	$45	$222			$19
TOTAL ANNUAL COST	$2,340	$11,544			$988

Table 6.5 continued

Estimated Annual Service Costs by Program Type

for Caseloads of 100 Families

	Sexual Abuse	Adolescent Maltreatment	Substance Abuse	Remedial Services	Child Neglect
Parent Education Classes					
Number of Adults Served	54	49	69	109	71
Annual Per Client Cost for 52 Sessions	$753	$753	$753	$753	$753
TOTAL ANNUAL COST	$40,662	$36,897	$51,957	$82,077	$53,463
Infant Stimulation					
Number of Infants Served	--	--	--	42	38
Annual Per Client Cost for 26 Sessions				$704	$704
TOTAL ANNUAL COST				$29,568	$26,752
Supervised Parent-Child Interactions					
Number of Clients Served	21	11	62	119	135
Annual Per Client Cost for 52 Sessions	$753	$753	$753	$753	$753
TOTAL ANNUAL COST	$15,813	$8,283	$46,686	$89,607	$101,655

Physical Rehabilitation or Special Education

Number of Children Served	46	25	132	129	248
Annual Per Client Cost for 26 Sessions	$546	$546	$546	$546	$546
TOTAL ANNUAL COST	$25,116	$13,650	$72,072	$70,434	$135,408

Therapeutic Day Care

Number of Children Served	--	--	--	98	--
Average Annual Per Client Cost				$5,205	
TOTAL ANNUAL COST				$510,090	

Individual Therapy

Number of Adults Served	90	106	136	65	102
Number of Adolescents Served	33	144	18	--	27
Number of Children Served	28	20	23	78	--
Annual Per Client Cost for 52 Sessions	$1,515	$1,515	$1,515	$1,515	$1,515
TOTAL ANNUAL COST	$228,765	$409,050	$268,155	$216,645	$195,435
TOTAL ANNUAL COST -- ADULTS ONLY	(136,350)	(160,590)	(206,040)	(98,475)	(154,530)

Family Therapy

Number of Families Served	100	100	100	100	100
Annual Per Family Cost for 52 Sessions	$1,361	$1,361	$1,361	$1,361	$1,361
TOTAL ANNUAL COST	$136,100	$136,100	$136,100	$136,100	$136,100

Table 6.5 continued

Estimated Annual Service Costs by Program Type

for Caseloads of 100 Families

	Sexual Abuse	Adolescent Maltreatment	Substance Abuse	Remedial Services	Child Neglect
Group Therapy -- Children					
Number of Children Served	39	4	29	10	--
Annual Per Child Cost for 52 Sessions	$358	$358	$358	$358	
TOTAL ANNUAL COST	$13,962	$1,432	$10,382	$3,580	
Group Therapy -- Adolescents					
Number of Adolescents Served	39	96	16	--	--
Annual Per Client Cost for 52 Sessions	$865	$865	$865		
TOTAL ANNUAL COST	$33,735	$83,040	$13,840		
Group Therapy - Adults					
Number of Adults Served	118	16	34	122	43
Annual Per Client Cost for 52 Sessions	$996	$996	$996	$996	$996
TOTAL ANNUAL COST	$117,528	$15,936	$33,864	$121,512	$42,828

Intake and Initial Diagnosis					
Average Weekly Cost	$369	$369	$369	$369	$369
TOTAL ANNUAL COST	$19,188	$19,188	$19,188	$19188	$19,188
Regular Case Review					
Average Weekly Cost	$1,514	$1,514	$1,514	$1,514	$1,514
TOTAL ANNUAL COST	$78,728	$78,728	$78,728	$78,728	$78,728
Multidisciplinary Case Review					
Number of Families Served	25	25	25	25	25
Average Weekly Cost	$688	$688	$688	$688	$688
TOTAL ANNUAL COST	$35,776	$35,776	$35,776	$35,776	$35,776
Psychological Testing					
Number of Adults Served	12	12	16	13	12
Number of Adolescents Served	4	15	9	---	3
Number of Children Served	5	3	15	14	25
Average Cost Per Contact	$47	$47	$47	$47	$47
TOTAL ANNUAL COST	$987	$1,410	$1,880	$1,269	$1,880
Project Management					
Average Weekly Cost	$2,409	$2,409	$2,409	$2,409	$2,409
TOTAL ANNUAL COST	$125,268	$125,268	$125,268	$125,268	$125,268

Table 6.5 continued

Estimated Annual Service Costs by Program Type

for Caseloads of 100 Families

	Sexual Abuse	Adolescent Maltreatment	Substance Abuse	Remedial Services	Child Neglect
Staff Development					
Average Weekly Cost	$794	$794	$794	$794	$794
TOTAL ANNUAL COST	$41,288	$41,288	$41,288	$41,288	$41,288
Evaluation and Research					
Average Weekly Cost	$537	$537	$537	$537	$537
TOTAL ANNUAL COST	$27,924	$27,924	$27,924	$27,924	$27,924
Community Activities					
Average Weekly Cost	$663	$663	$663	$663	$663
TOTAL ANNUAL COST	$34,476	$34,476	$34,476	$34,476	$34,476

[a]Estimates of the number of families or individuals receiving each of the identified service types were based upon the actual percentage of clients provided the service by the specific demonstration projects within each of the five treatment cells. The estimated annual costs for each service were calculated based upon the average costs per client session experienced by the demonstration projects.

abuse, and projects working with families involved in child neglect. Over 90% of the children under five served by the projects in these three program categories were provided some type of remedial services. While all of the programs offered individual, family, or group counseling to the children on their caseloads, the most extensive and costly services for children and youth were limited to those projects specifically targeting victims. Therapeutic day care, as provided by the demonstration projects, cost programs over $510,000 annually for every 100 families they served. Similarly, the provision of shelter care for adolescents cost projects offering this service an estimated $263,120 annually.

While the costs for individual services are useful in highlighting key service similarities and differences across various child maltreatment subpopulations, clients are generally provided a package or combination of services. Drawing upon the experiences of the 19 demonstration projects, Table 6.6 summarizes the costs of providing various service packages to five distinct client populations: families involved in sexual abuse, families with adolescent victims, families involved in both substance abuse and child abuse, families involved in child neglect, and families with young children requiring remedial services due to maltreatment. While these annual cost estimates are based upon the per unit cost experiences of the 19 clinical demonstration projects, they tend to exceed the total actual costs of the demonstration effort for several reasons. First, average case management and project management costs have been adjusted to reflect the costs associated with maintaining an average caseload of 100 families as opposed to the average caseload of 35 families carried by the demonstration projects. Second, these estimates again assume an "ideal" service delivery system and, as such, assume clients do indeed receive the full service levels indicated by each model. In reality, clients will often not receive all of the services originally planned due to scheduling problems, client or staff illness, or client resistance to regular intervention.

Third, the most costly of these service models assumes an intensive level of service to all family members, a reality rarely achieved by the demonstration projects. There was wide variation in the number and types of service options provided to the individual adults, adolescents, and children served by the projects, although most projects perceived their primary client to be the family. In reality, only the remedial services, adolescent maltreatment projects, and, to a lesser extent, the sexual abuse projects provided an equally diverse and intensified service package to all family members. In order to reflect the cost of each service level, Table 6.6 includes individual cost estimates within each program area for a Minimal Service model, Nontherapeutic Service model, Therapeutic Service for Adults model, and Therapeutic Service for Children model.

Finally, all service models assume that resources also would be allocated to community activities, as well as to program evaluation and research efforts such as community coordination, professional education and training,

Table 6.6

Service Models and Associated Costs for Serving 100 Families

| | SEXUAL ABUSE PROJECTS | | | | |
| | | | Therapeutic Service Models | | |
	Minimal Service Model	Nontherapeutic Service Model	Individual Counseling	Individual and Family Counseling	Group Counseling
Basic Service Package					
Intake and Diagnosis	X	X	X	X	X
Regular Case Review	X	X	X	X	X
Multidisciplinary Case Review (30% of all families)	X	X	X	X	X
Project Management and Staff Development	X	X	X	X	X
TOTAL COMPONENT COSTS	$300,248	$300,248	$300,248	$300,248	$300,248
Minimal Service Package					
Crisis Intervention	X	X	X	X	X
Casework Counseling	X	X	X	X	X
Concrete Services	X	X	X	X	X
Support Services -- Adults	X	X	X	X	X
Support Services -- Adolescents	X	X	X	X	X
Remedial Services for Children	X	X	X	X	X
TOTAL COMPONENT COSTS	$153,389	$153,389	$153,389	$153,389	$153,389
Nontherapeutic Ancillary Services					
Educational and Skill Development -- Adults		X		X	X

Educational and Skill Development -- Adolescents	X	X	X	X	
Parent Education	X	X	X	X	
Supervised Parent-Child Interactions					
TOTAL COMPONENT COSTS	$53,194	$53,194	$53,194	$53,194	--
Therapeutic Services					
Individual Counseling		X	X		
Family Counseling		X			
Group Counseling	X				
TOTAL COMPONENT COSTS	$225,225	$364,865	$228,765	--	--
Intensive Children/Adolescent Services					
Temporary Shelter	X	X	X	X	X
Therapeutic Day Care	X	X	X	X	X
Infant Stimulation	X	X	X	X	X
TOTAL COMPONENT COSTS	$453,637	$453,637	$453,637	$453,637	$453,637
Indirect Services					
Program Evaluation	X	X	X	X	X
Community Activities	X	X	X	X	X
TOTAL COMPONENT COSTS	$62,400	$62,400	$62,400	$62,400	$62,400
TOTAL COST FOR SERVICE MODEL	$794,456	$934,096	$797,996	$569,231	$516,037

Table 6.6 continued

ADOLESCENT MALTREATMENT PROJECTS

| | Minimal Service Model | Nontherapeutic Service Model | Therapeutic Service Models | | | |
| | | | Counseling Only | | Plus Youth Services | |
			Family Counseling	Individual Counseling	Family Counseling	Individual Counseling
Basic Service Package						
Intake and Diagnosis	X	X	X	X	X	
Regular Case Review	X	X	X	X	X	X
Multidisciplinary Case Review (30% of all families)	X	X	X	X	X	X
Project Management and Staff Development	X	X	X	X	X	X
TOTAL COMPONENT COSTS	$300,248	$300,248	$300,248	$300,248	$300,248	$300,248
Minimal Service Package						
Crisis Intervention	X	X	X	X	X	X
Casework Counseling	X	X	X	X	X	X
Concrete Services	X	X	X	X	X	X
Support Services -- Adults	X	X	X	X	X	X
Support Services -- Adolescents	X	X	X	X	X	X
Remedial Services for Children	X	X	X	X	X	X
TOTAL COMPONENT COSTS	$249,722	$249,722	$249,722	$249,722	$249,722	$249,722
Nontherapeutic Ancillary Services						
Educational and Skill Development -- Adults		X			X	

Educational and Skill Development -- Adolescents		X	X	X	X	X
Parent Education		X	X	X	X	X
Supervised Parent-Child Interactions						
TOTAL COMPONENT COSTS	--	$57,645	$57,645	$57,645	$57,645	$57,645
Therapeutic Services						
Individual Counseling			X	X	X	X
Family Counseling				X		X
Group Counseling						
TOTAL COMPONENT COSTS	--	--	$136,100	$409,050	$136,100	$409,050
Intensive Children/Adolescent Services						
Temporary Shelter					X	X
Therapeutic Day Care						
Infant Stimulation						
TOTAL COMPONENT COSTS	--	--	--	--	$263,120	$263,120
Indirect Services						
Program Evaluation	X	X	X	X	X	X
Community Activities	X	X	X	X	X	X
TOTAL COMPONENT COSTS	$62,400	$62,400	$62,400	$62,400	$62,400	$62,400
TOTAL COST FOR SERVICE MODEL	$612,370	$670,015	$806,115	$1,079,065	$1,069,235	$1,342,185

Table 6.6 continued

SUBSTANCE ABUSE PROJECTS

	Minimal Service Model	Nontherapeutic Service Model	Therapeutic Service Models	
			Family Counseling	Individual Counseling
Basic Service Package				
Intake and Diagnosis	X	X	X	X
Regular Case Review	X	X	X	X
Multidisciplinary Case Review (30% of all families)	X	X	X	X
Project Management and Staff Development	X	X	X	X
TOTAL COMPONENT COSTS	$300,248	$300,248	$300,248	$300,248
Minimal Service Package				
Crisis Intervention	X	X	X	X
Casework Counseling	X	X	X	X
Concrete Services	X	X	X	X
Support Services -- Adults	X	X	X	X
Support Services -- Adolescents	X	X	X	X
Remedial Services for Children	X	X	X	X
TOTAL COMPONENT COSTS	$250,684	$250,684	$250,684	$250,684
Nontherapeutic Ancillary Services				
Educational and Skill Development -- Adults			X	X
Educational and Skill Development -- Adolescents				

Parent Education	X	X		
Supervised Parent-Child Interactions				
TOTAL COMPONENT COSTS	$66,257	$66,257	--	--
Therapeutic Services				
Individual Counseling	X	X		
Family Counseling		X		
Group Counseling	X			
TOTAL COMPONENT COSTS	$268,155	$136,100	--	--
Intensive Children/Adolescent Services				
Temporary Shelter				
Therapeutic Day Care				
Infant Stimulation				
TOTAL COMPONENT COSTS	--	--	--	--
Indirect Services				
Program Evaluation	X	X	X	X
Community Activities	X	X	X	X
TOTAL COMPONENT COSTS	$62,400	$62,400	$62,400	$62,400
TOTAL COST FOR SERVICE MODEL	$947,744	$815,689	$679,589	$613,332

Table 6.6 continued

REMEDIAL SERVICE PROJECTS

| | Minimal Service Model | Nontherapeutic Service Model | Therapeutic Service Models | | | |
| | | | Counseling Only | | Plus Children's Services | |
			Family Counseling	Family & Group Counseling	Family Counseling	Family & Group Counseling
Basic Service Package						
Intake and Diagnosis	X	X	X	X	X	X
Regular Case Review	X	X	X	X	X	X
Multidisciplinary Case Review (30% of all families)	X	X	X	X	X	X
Project Management and Staff Development	X	X	X	X	X	X
TOTAL COMPONENT COSTS	$300,248	$300,248	$300,248	$300,248	$300,248	$300,248
Minimal Service Package						
Crisis Intervention	X	X	X	X	X	X
Casework Counseling	X	X	X	X	X	X
Concrete Services	X	X	X	X	X	X
Support Services -- Adults	X	X	X	X	X	X
Support Services -- Adolescents						
Remedial Services for Children	X	X	X	X	X	X
TOTAL COMPONENT COSTS	$227,534	$227,534	$227,534	$227,534	227,534	$227,534
Nontherapeutic Ancillary Services						
Educational and Skill Development -- Adults		X	X	X	X	X

Service Component						
Educational and Skill Development -- Adolescents						
Parent Education		X	X	X	X	X
Supervised Parent-Child Interactions		X	X	X	X	X
TOTAL COMPONENT COSTS	--	$187,492	$187,492	$187,492	$187,492	$187,492
Therapeutic Services						
Individual Counseling			X	X	X	X
Family Counseling				X	X	X
Group Counseling				X	X	X
TOTAL COMPONENT COSTS	--	--	$136,100	$257,612	$257,612	$257,612
Intensive Children/Adolescent Services						
Temporary Shelter						
Therapeutic Day Care					X	X
Infant Stimulation					X	X
TOTAL COMPONENT COSTS	--	--	--	--	$539,658	$539,658
Indirect Services						
Program Evaluation	X	X	X	X	X	X
Community Activities	X	X	X	X	X	X
TOTAL COMPONENT COSTS	$62,400	$62,400	$62,400	$62,400	$62,400	$62,400
TOTAL COST FOR SERVICE MODEL	$590,182	$777,674	$913,774	$1035,286	$1453,432	$1574,944

Table 6.6 continued

CHILD NEGLECT PROJECTS

	Minimal Service Model	Nontherapeutic Service Model	Therapeutic Service Models			
			Counseling Only		Plus Children's Services	
			Individual Counseling	Family Counseling	Individual Counseling	Family Counseling
Basic Service Package						
Intake and Diagnosis	X	X	X	X	X	X
Regular Case Review	X	X	X	X	X	X
Multidisciplinary Case Review (30% of all families)	X	X	X	X	X	X
Project Management and Staff Development	X	X	X	X	X	X
TOTAL COMPONENT COSTS	$300,248	$300,248	$300,248	$300,248	$300,248	$300,248
Minimal Service Package						
Crisis Intervention	X	X	X	X	X	X
Casework Counseling	X	X	X	X	X	X
Concrete Services	X	X	X	X	X	X
Support Services -- Adults	X	X	X	X	X	X
Support Services -- Adolescents						
Remedial Services for Children	X	X	X	X	X	X
TOTAL COMPONENT COSTS	$257,188	$257,188	$257,188	$257,188	$257,188	$257,188

		1	2	3	4	5	6
Nontherapeutic Ancillary Services							
Educational and Skill Development -- Adults				X	X	X	X
Educational and Skill Development -- Adolescents							
Parent Education				X	X	X	X
Supervised Parent-Child Interactions				X	X	X	X
TOTAL COMPONENT COSTS		--	$172,486	$172,486	$172,486	$172,486	$172,486
Therapeutic Services							
Individual Counseling				X	X	X	
Family Counseling				X		X	
Group Counseling							X
TOTAL COMPONENT COSTS		--		$195,435	$136,100	$195,435	$136,100
Intensive Children/Adolescent Services							
Temporary Shelter							
Therapeutic Day Care							
Infant Stimulation						X	X
TOTAL COMPONENT COSTS		--	--	--		$29,568	$29,568
Indirect Services							
Program Evaluation		X	X	X	X	X	X
Community Activities		X	X	X	X	X	X
TOTAL COMPONENT COSTS		$62,400	$62,400	$62,400	$62,400	$62,400	$62,400
TOTAL COST FOR SERVICE MODEL		$619,836	$792,322	$987,757	$928,422	$1017,325	$957,990

and legislative activities. While the vast majority of the demonstration projects did indeed devote a percentage of their resources to these functions, any of the service models outlined in Table 6.6 could be adopted without the suggested level of nonclient services.

These caveats aside, the total annual costs of providing the service models listed in Table 6.6 to 100 families range from $516,037 to $1.6 million. As had been true for the initial demonstration projects, the most costly of these service models involve daily, direct therapeutic services to young children. Service models that do not augment their service package with intensive services to adolescents or children or do not include therapeutic services such as individual, family, or group counseling are less costly. On balance, family and group counseling are less costly to provide than individual counseling, particularly when the subpopulation caseload includes a larger than average number of adults and adolescents.

The total costs of the service models outlined in Table 6.6 tended to fall between the first demonstration project's very expensive Family and Children's Service model and its very moderately priced Lay Therapy model. One possible explanation for this pattern is that by targeting services to a specific subpopulation, as opposed to trying to provide all of the services needed by a very diverse maltreating population, projects were able to fine tune their service strategies, offering only those supportive and therapeutic services most needed by their particular clientele. Since the Lay Therapy model was not adopted by any of the 19 projects funded under the second demonstration, it is not possible to assess whether its costs could be further reduced through more efficient client targeting.

Although specific analyses were not done to determine the marginal increase in reduced propensity for future maltreatment associated with the provision of these various service models,[12] the client outcome findings reported earlier offer some tentative conclusions regarding cost-effectiveness. Controlling for client characteristics and severity of the initial maltreatment, group and family counseling made significant contributions to positive outcomes for all adults, with family counseling being particularly useful in achieving success with adults involved in child neglect. Also, the provision of personal skill development classes, temporary shelter, and group counseling all contributed to more positive outcomes with adolescent clients, the majority of whom were victims of physical abuse and emotional maltreatment. Children who were victims of severe physical abuse and neglect responded well to individual counseling, group counseling, and therapeutic day care.

Considering the cost data in tandem with these outcome data the findings suggest that the increased costs associated with therapeutic services, particularly family and group counseling, are well worth the added expense in terms of realizing greater client benefits. While the provision of support services and basic educational services enhanced client outcomes, the experiences of the 19 demonstration projects suggest that the provision of these services alone would be insufficient for addressing the full array of presenting problems and interpersonal difficulties common among abusive and neglectful families. The higher costs associated with Individual Therapy models versus Group or Family Therapy models, however, does not seem warranted given the generally poor showing of this service in the client impact analysis. Of these three therapeutic strategies, the Individual Therapy model demonstrated the least impact on client outcomes. While the use of individual therapy may play a useful role in helping clients understand the underlying causes of their behaviors or attitudes and in improving a client's ability to engage in other forms of therapy or supportive services, the method, on its own, failed to produce significant positive outcomes.

The cost and outcome data associated with the provision of therapeutic day care for children and shelter care for adolescents pose a more difficult choice for program managers. While these services produced among the most notable gains achieved by the clinical demonstration projects, the sizable budgets associated with these services suggest they may have limited utility to public or private service agencies. Even the majority of the federally-funded demonstration projects were unable to incorporate these strategies into what CPS workers might consider to be very generous operating budgets. The use of volunteers and donated resources is one way to reduce the overall costs of these services. Certainly the experiences of the National Runaway Youth Program suggest that costs associated with the provision of emergency shelter care can be significantly curtailed through developing a system of volunteer homes (BPA, 1979). Therapeutic day care is more difficult to provide without significant resources. However, total costs might be reduced by offering specific remedial services to abused children in the context of an existing day care program or augmenting hospital or school-based speech and language programs with a parent education component.

A critical element in determining the success of any individual service or service package will be the characteristics of the adults and children the program serves. Specifically, the severity of the initial maltreatment and the receptiveness of the family to project services will influence the extent to which even the most promising strategies will realize positive client outcomes. Although individual projects can enhance their overall cost-effectiveness by including those service strategies identified as particularly effective and less costly, expectations for success must be tempered by the characteristics of a given caseload.

Summary and Practice Implications

The limited number of cost-benefit and cost-effectiveness studies available to social planners makes it difficult to assess the potential utility of these analytic methods in shaping child maltreatment service delivery systems.

Nevertheless, the above discussion demonstrates the value of these methods in identifying and assessing the short-and long-term consequences of action or nonaction and in selecting the most cost-effective therapeutic or support services. It goes without saying that such analytic methods can never be the sole determinant in allocating services to individual clients. They can, however, be useful for practitioners and policy makers in making some very critical choices in the short run and for clarifying their long-run objectives.

Specifically, the cost analyses outlined above illustrate the utility of maintaining budgets by service category. At a minimum, this accounting method allows program managers to see exactly where staff are spending their time and what types of services are most frequently provided to clients. While staff time and client demand are generally highly correlated, the method highlights those occasions when a service modality is consuming significant staff time but is being utilized by relatively few clients. For example, staff may have spent considerable time developing and advertising a support group for adolescent parents. Despite their thorough recruiting efforts, however, only three youths have agreed to participate. Consequently, the service has a much higher per-client cost than originally planned. By maintaining program expenditures in terms of the specific costs associated with providing each service to clients, a manager can then make an informed decision regarding whether the continuation of this service is warranted, given total resources and total service demand among the program's client population. While one can envision a host of reasons for retaining a service modality utilized by only a limited number of clients, recording expenditures by service category provides more precise and timely data for identifying the most and least efficient services.

In addition to offering a method for monitoring current expenditures, the development of cost profiles for specific services can assist program managers in planning new service components or more efficiently managing existing resources. Practitioners operating with a fixed budget can use the method to identify the specific tradeoffs between the number of families they will serve and the intensity of the services they can provide. Those operating with limited funds will need to severely limit the number of families they serve if they choose to provide the most extensive of the service packages outlined in Table 6.6. Programs that must provide services to large numbers of families may want to consider strategies such as group services or educational and skill development programs, which have relatively low costs per client. Further, the data suggest that programs targeting families involved in specific types of maltreatment will face caseloads with a unique set of characteristics and service demands. The structure of the National Clinical Evaluation Study makes it difficult to estimate the specific costs associated with a physically abusive or emotionally maltreating population, but specific guidelines can be gleaned from the experiences of those projects that target their interventions to either child neglect or sexual abuse. The most cost-effective treatment plan in instances of child sexual abuse involving family members seems to be a combination of family and group counseling for the victim, the victim's siblings, the perpetrator, and the perpetrator's spouse. In cases of child neglect, the most efficient interventions will combine family counseling with parenting education and basic care services such as babysitting, medical care, clothing, and housing assistance. Regardless of the presenting type of maltreatment, at least minimal services should be made available to the victims of maltreatment. Even if the provision of extensive therapeutic day care programs or shelter care for adolescents might lie beyond the fiscal means of all child abuse treatment programs, administrators would be well-advised to include assessment services for maltreatment victims in their service planning and work with other local service providers to expand the therapeutic and support services available to children and youth.

Finally, the type of cost data generated by the National Clinical Evaluation Study also has utility in improving the development and monitoring of community-wide service systems. From a cost-effectiveness pespective, programs that provide parenting education, educational and skill development classes, lay therapy, peer support groups, and group and family therapy offer the best avenues for achieving maximum client benefits, often at the lowest possible per-client costs. Agency administrators and legislators concerned with funding programs that will maximize positive client outcomes for large numbers of families would be well advised to direct service dollars to these types of programs. However, maximizing total client outcomes may not be the only policy objective of concern. Developing innovative strategies for hard-to-serve clients or those who have failed to demonstrate any significant gains with existing service strategies may require a shift of revenues to programs that are, for the moment, less cost-effective. In determining budget levels for these types of research and development projects, legislative analysts and agency administrators can draw on the types of cost data outlined in Figure 6.2 and Table 6.6 to establish realistic caseload targets and expenditure patterns.

The total costs associated with intervention are far from minimal. On balance, the experiences of these two national evaluation efforts suggest that replicating the various treatment models will cost between $2,860 per family per year for the provision of lay therapy to $28,000 per family per year for the provision of comprehensive therapeutic and support services. Providing this level of service to the close to one million families identified each year as having experienced some form of child maltreatment would cost public and private service systems between $2.8 billion and $28 billion annually. For the most part, these costs would be in addition to the very significant social costs incurred by the social welfare, medical, and judicial systems in simply investigating and managing these cases. If these expenditures successfully remediated the consequences of maltreatment so that the long-term costs associated with continued dysfunctioning were reduced, these expenditures would indeed be recouped in terms of higher productivity, less welfare dependency and, ultimately, less child abuse. However, the prevailing evidence suggests that treatment efforts, at best, are successful with only half of their clients and that the poorest, most dysfunctional families are least likely to achieve successful outcomes.

Given the high cost of treatment services and their limited promise for remediating the consequences of maltreatment, prevention efforts appear to be a more efficient alternative. Approximately $1.3 billion would purchase two years of weekly parenting education and supervised parent-child interactions for *all* adolescent mothers.[13] By way of contrast, this amount would be insufficient to cover even one year of lay therapy for all families reported to CPS last year for maltreatment. Supporting families through the birth of their first child carries the potential for a significant reduction in the health care and therapeutic service costs associated with maltreatment, savings that would most certainly cover the costs of such prevention efforts.

Whether these treatment or prevention expenditure levels are an appropriate use of public resources will depend on their ability ultimately to reduce the incidence of maltreatment and, correspondingly, the social costs of child abuse. The National Clinical Evaluation Study suggests that targeting services in terms of primary type of maltreatment is one method for reducing costs and improving outcomes. Prevention services linked to existing universal service systems, such as the public schools, public health care providers, community-based family service agencies, or churches, will be more efficiently delivered than services that require a new institutional system. Building upon these strategies in jointly expanding our treatment and prevention efforts is a more cost-effective practice and policy path to pursue than simply dealing with the growing number of victims the current system is certain to produce.

Chapter 7

Planning for the Future by Building on the Past

Child maltreatment is less of a mystery today than it was at the time of Kempe's landmark research in 1962. Over the last two decades, the field has made great progress from its initial starting point in terms of reporting statutes, legislative initiatives, treatment programs, and prevention efforts. Overall, child advocates have constructed a service system that offers a significant degree of protection for children who have been harmed or who potentially may suffer harm at the hands of their parents or other adults. Despite these gains, many unanswered practice and policy questions remain in the way we define and respond to cases of child maltreatment.

Notable signs of progress include federal initiatives and state statutes which have created a vast reporting and investigatory network, providing protection to millions of children at risk. Mandatory reporting systems and federal laws against child abuse were virtually nonexistent in 1962 and the importance of their rapid implementation following Kempe's research should not be minimized. It has been suggested that the existence of these laws has partially accounted for a dramatic reduction in deaths due to maltreatment and in the overall level of violence suffered by children in their own homes (Besharov, 1986; Gelles and Straus, 1986). As gatekeepers to the child welfare system, reporting laws have offered professionals and private citizens alike the means to channel those parents needing assistance in safely rearing their children to a service system theoretically designed to offer such assistance. While this model may be an effective and efficient one, its broad scale and ever expanding implementation has not been without controversy. Historically, a disproportionate share of families "captured" by the reporting system have been low-income, minority and single-parent households, a phenomenon due in part to the higher risk for maltreatment within this population and in part to the higher surveillance of this group by public agencies. To the extent that this pattern reflects differential treatment rather than differential risk, serious equity problems emerge that are further exacerbated by the tendency of professionals, particularly those in private practice, not to report maltreatment among their white, middle-class caseloads.

More recently, this concern over reporting bias has given way to a new set of problems fueled by a very rapid increase in the number of reports, particularly those involving sexual abuse. This exponential growth in reports, often involving middle-class families embroiled in divorce and custody battles, has intensified concerns over the appropriateness of current reporting statutes. The roughly 50% substantiation rate for child abuse reports has been remarkably consistent over the past ten years and is well within the confirmation rate experienced by other emergency response systems.[1] While concern over the unjust removal of children from the care of their parents has always existed, the sheer number of unsubstantiated reports, approximately 1,036,200 in 1984 compared to 692,400 reports in 1980, has created a growing pool of individuals who feel that their parenting skills have been inappropriately questioned. Further, charges of sexual abuse carry a unique need for vindication. The accused child molestor faces more serious social isolation or stigmatization than does a "simple" child abuser. The devastating personal and sometimes professional impacts levied by charges of sexual abuse on the accused perpetrator have highlighted the reporting system's imperfect nature and pose a serious challenge to its broad conceptualization of maltreatment.

Concern over the appropriateness of the reporting laws is found concurrently among practitioners both within and outside public protective service agencies. As summarized earlier, a growing number of professionals have lost or are losing faith in the ability of child protective service agencies to respond to reports in an efficient and effective manner. As a result, only a fraction of the cases known to practitioners are actually reported and processed through the system. Professional dissatisfaction with the present child welfare system is certainly understandable. Serious delays in initially investigating reports of maltreatment and often haphazard monitoring of the families accepted onto CPS caseloads leave some number of children at risk or suffering potentially avoidable harm. To a certain extent, these delays in conducting initial investigations and the perceived poor quality of these investigations stem from a lack of adequate staff. For example, caseworkers in California's emergency response units, the units responsible for such investigations, carry average caseloads of 32.8 families as opposed to the recommended caseload of 15.8 (*Child Welfare Services*, May 1985). Such staff shortages exist throughout these systems, as the majority of CPS budgets have not kept pace with the increased number of reports.

Even if caseloads were reduced, however, increasing concern is being raised over the competence of CPS workers to handle sensitive investigations, particularly around issues of sexual abuse, which may result in formal prosecution. The standards of evidence and proof of guilt used in criminal court proceedings are far more narrow than the reasonable cause criterion used to justify a child abuse report. Interviewing techniques that are appropriate in the course of treatment may confound attempts to bring a case to trial. Just as the growing number of unsubstantiated reports has magnified longstanding imperfections in the child abuse reporting laws, the criminalization of child abuse magnifies the inherent contradictions in a system that seeks to protect children while honoring the rights of parents.

In an effort to achieve balance between these two missions, a number of reforms have been suggested by practitioners and policy makers alike. These include larger child welfare budgets, or at least a shifting of resources to intake and investigatory units; comprehensive training and support services for workers throughout the CPS system, particularly with respect to the system's legal responsibilities; the use of the most knowledgeable and trained personnel to investigate child abuse reports; improved methods for prioritizing cases such that the most immediate investigations can be targeted to the most serious cases; and rewriting the child abuse reporting laws so as to reduce the number of reports requiring investigation. While the careful implementation of such reforms may well improve the accuracy and timeliness of the child abuse reporting system, some number of maltreating families will avoid the system and some number of innocent families will be investigated. The scope of future child abuse reporting laws will be shaped both by the realities of what a child welfare system can accomplish and the extent to which practitioners and policy makers are comfortable erring on the side of either protecting family privacy or protecting children.

As reflected in the expanded reporting laws, the many faces of child maltreatment are more recognizable and better defined today than in 1962. Extensive research on abusive and neglectful families has consistently identified at least four unique subpopulations—physical abuse, physical neglect, sexual abuse, and emotional maltreatment. The identification of specific client characteristics that correlate highly with different forms of maltreatment has been useful in developing more accurate assessment and intake procedures; in identifying certain client behaviors and attitudes which practitioners will need to modify in the couse of treatment; in defining high-risk populations for purposes of better targeting prevention efforts; and, paradoxically, in illustrating the universal potential for maltreatment, given that virtually every family will fall into at least one high-risk group during its child-rearing years. Perhaps the clearest distinction for purposes of defining treatment strategies can be made between physically neglectful families and families involved in sexual abuse. These two groups usually represent very different family structures, socioeconomic conditions, and presenting problems. While therapeutic service models that gradually engage all family members have demonstrated solid progress with the victims and perpetrators of sexual abuse, general support and in-home services have produced more positive gains with neglect cases. To the extent that this type of definitional clarity can be achieved, practitioners and service agency administrators will be able to target interventions to specific client groups and offer more effective assistance to each particular family.

The method, however, is not without drawbacks. Great diversity is found in the characteristics and presenting problems of families experiencing physical abuse and emotional maltreatment. The fact that a sizable percentage of cases currently reported for maltreatment involve multiple forms of abuse and neglect limits the widespread application of this new definitional clarity. Overburdened workers and limited fiscal resources also constrain the kind of differential assessment and treatment suggested by consistent application of the subpopulation paradigm. Nevertheless, the conceptualization of child maltreatment as consisting of a number of discrete parenting practices is essential, as discussed below, for improving general practice and enhancing intervention systems.

Finally, the treatment and prevention of child abuse has expanded beyond the narrow range of psychodynamic and medical services that initially dominated the field. In developing specific treatment plans, prevention strategies, and public policies, practitioners and legislators alike have a broader array of therapeutic and support services from which to choose. Recognizing the limits of intervention after a child has already experienced serious abuse, family and child welfare practitioners also have advanced the cause of prevention. Today, most would agree that programs that enhance parents' abilities to meet their children's basic needs and to support their children's healthy and productive development are essential components in any policy that would claim to be effective in confronting child abuse.

What is perhaps most surprising about the current expansion of child abuse prevention programs, however, is that it has occurred largely in the absence of substantial empirical data that early intervention is effective in reducing the level or severity of maltreatment within a given population or within the general community. While many of the parenting enhancement models identified in Chapter 5 have shown solid success in improving parenting practices and personal functioning, evidence that such efforts reduce the total rate of abuse, although growing, is limited. Better integration of research and practice, therefore, has its clearest application in the prevention arena. Unless those concerned with prevention are more aggressive and effective in documenting the impacts of their efforts, continued enthusiasm for this critical program component may dampen.

Addressing the First National Conference on Child Abuse in 1976, Edward Zigler questioned the advisability of the then newly-passed federal child abuse legislation, labeling it "little more than putting a band aid on a cancer." "Social change," he went on to note, "is produced not by the stroke of a pen but by intensive and persistent efforts to change the human ecology within which the social target is embedded" (Zigler, 1976:65). Fortunately, those who sought the passage of federal and state legislation in this area and practitioners who provide direct services to maltreating families did not and do not rely upon "a stroke of the pen" to resolve the problem. They labor long and hard to identify and implement effective treatment interventions and to alter the belief that the only role for protective service agencies and family-based interventions is to repair the damage once abuse has occurred. Practitioners and policy makers now believe, and correctly so, that effective action can be taken before a child is harmed. Such efforts attest to the collective gains that can be made through what some may believe to be limited, incremental changes. As with most social problems, practitioners seeking to confront child maltreatment will need to measure their success in the short run—not by the ultimate elimination of the problem, but rather by their increased understanding of its dimensions and causal correlates and by developing and assessing strategies for reducing its prevalence and mitigating its consequences.

Formulating sound practice to achieve these gains, however, will involve more than merely making incremental changes in current laws and practice standards based upon the field's growing body of knowledge. For future efforts to benefit most from past and ongoing research, findings need to be assessed in terms of three broader criteria. First, recognizing that unique subpopulations of maltreatment exist, care must be taken to ensure that current practice and child welfare policy in this area are sensitive to the differing presenting problems and service needs of these groups. Second, those concerned with expanding child abuse prevention efforts need to be explicit in identifying the appropriate balance between treatment and prevention efforts and in defining the specific activities that are essential to reducing the incidence and severity of child maltreatment. Finally, those working with abused and neglected children and their families need to consider how best to channel their growing body of knowledge to those in positions to enact legislative and administrative changes.

Considering Subpopulations in Shaping Child Maltreatment Practice and Policy

The conceptualization of child maltreatment in terms of recognizable subpopulations is useful in a number of ways. While overlapping membership most certainly occurs, the paradigm protects practitioners and policy makers from identifying a single causal correlate, a single treatment strategy, or a single prevention strategy as a singular solution to all maltreatment. A father who gives his seven-year-old son welts on his legs and buttocks by disciplining him with a belt; a single mother who leaves her four-year-old unattended while she goes shopping for several hours; the stepfather who has intercourse with his wife's 14-year-old daughter; and overbearing parents who continuously belittle their daughter for failing to achieve extraordinarily high standards—the diversity of these cases highlights the complexity of child maltreatment and underscores the necessity for multiple treatment and prevention efforts. If practitioners and policy makers have learned only one thing over the past two decades, it should be that allowing one type of maltreatment to dominate our thinking leaves us with a response system and practice standards inappropriate for the full range of concerns represented by this serious social welfare dilemma.

The initial focus on physical abuse and serious forms of child neglect produced a response system that depended upon the identification of certain physical signs of maltreatment and the reporting of these cases to protective services. The fact that advocates sought a formal reporting system and that the public endorsed this system was not surprising for a number of reasons. First, the link between the physical signs of maltreatment and certain parental behaviors had a solid empirical base in the general medical literature. Second, judgments as to a parent's involvement in these cases were primarily being made by professionals assumed to have unique knowledge and skills. Third, while thought to be significant, the number of abuse and neglect cases was not perceived as overwhelming. One could envision a protective service system with sufficient resources to thoroughly investigate all reported cases of maltreatment. Finally, the treatment and prevention services that emerged from this conceptualization of maltreatment were well within the existing service technology and were supported by child development and learning theories.

Unfortunately, as this system expanded and our collective wisdom grew, so did our conceptualization of maltreatment. Not only did this new pool of reports include less obvious cases of physical abuse and neglect, it increasingly included reports of emotional maltreatment and sexual abuse. Investigation protocols that had been used to determine if a child needed to be placed in foster care began to be used, in cases of sexual abuse, to determine if criminal charges would be filed. A response system initially designed for the rapid assessment of physical abuse and neglect reports and for addressing the problem in a social service rather than criminal context has proven ill-suited to the task of investigating complex and often very vague charges of parental misconduct. Furthermore, the intervention methods developed in tandem with the reporting system, namely the provision of therapeutic and support services to parents such that their children could remain with them or be safely returned to their care, assumed that the number of cases requiring such intervention was limited. The present number and diversity of maltreatment reports has proven this assumption fallacious. While child protective service agencies will continue to play a central role in receiving and responding to reports of maltreatment, responsibility for effective intervention must rest with the broader community. Either significant additional resources must be allocated to child welfare efforts or some method must be developed to better balance the scope of their mission with their current budgets.

The ultimate utility of the subpopulation concept may be in its ability to direct our thinking regarding this new balance such that we do not foresake the gains already achieved. Each of the four major types of maltreatment discussed throughout this book has a unique contribution to make to future policy and practice. The presence of physical abuse reinforces the need for the existing reporting system and the importance of having a mechanism through which concerned professionals and private citizens can report specific acts of abuse. The public has the right and the responsibility to act swiftly and decisively in cases where children have suffered or are at risk of suffering serious physical injury at the hands of their parents or caretakers. Any effort to narrow the range of reportable offenses with respect to this type of maltreatment runs the risk of increasing a child's likelihood of suffering serious and potentially irreversible harm. In addition to maintaining an aggressive reporting system, key strategies in the effort to reduce physical abuse include parenting education programs that emphasize stress management and a variety of discipline methods, hotlines and respite care centers, campaigns to increase public awareness of the difficulties inherent in child-rearing, and expanded support services for first-time parents.

Child neglect also underscores the importance of the current reporting system and the need for public intervention in cases where parents are not ensuring their child's health and well-being. In addition, the investigation of neglect cases needs to focus not only on the behaviors of individual parents but also on the environmental context in which a child lives. The importance of this expanded focus, coupled with the resistance of chronic neglect to successful intervention, reveals the inadequacies of a response system limited to working with the social and fiscal resources neglectful parents bring with them. A significant reduction in the incidence of child neglect depends upon reforms in the quality of housing, medical care, schools, and employment opportunities available to poor families. Ideally, such a coordinated response to the poverty problem would create a network of services sufficient to support poor families and to allow protective service agencies to focus only on those cases that pose an immediate and serious threat to a child's well-being. In the short run, however, a truly sufficient support system is unlikely to be developed and local CPS agencies will continue to serve as gatekeepers to the limited range of services currently available to poor families. Progress with this subpopulation will be made not by focusing solely on the most severe cases, as some would suggest, but rather by establishing a referral mechanism to channel into local, community-based service programs those young mothers who have been reported, and whose support systems are limited. Early intervention in these cases is the only way in which limited resources can be effective in curbing growing rates of child neglect. Once serious and chronic neglect patterns are established, such limited assistance will continue to be ineffective.

The rapid increase in the number of child sexual abuse reports and the difficulty surrounding the identification and prosecution of these cases highlight the complexity of confronting child abuse in the absence of physical evidence. Intervention into the private family is a delicate issue made even more delicate when the charge is sexual abuse. More than any other form of maltreatment, sexual abuse requires that investigators operate with circumstantial evidence often hinging on the ability of the young victim to be convincing and consistent in recalling the alleged events. Further, the child's testimony often must withstand legal scrutiny in criminal court, a standard that even adults find difficult to meet. While cases of physical abuse, neglect, and emotional maltreatment generally involve the primary caretaker, charges of sexual abuse increasingly involve stepparents, noncustodial parents involved in volatile divorce proceedings, family friends, extended family members, older siblings, and day care providers. Even the prevention of this type of maltreatment differs from efforts to prevent other forms of maltreatment. Rather than targeting specific behavioral changes in potential perpetrators, the prevention of child sexual abuse has focused on empowering children to protect themselves better and to disclose actual or attempted molestations immediately.

Significant controversy currently exists over the ability of protective service workers to investigate cases of sexual abuse and the utility of relying upon children to protect themselves from assault. This first concern has led some to suggest that the standards for reporting suspected cases of maltreatment should be narrowed and that these investigations should resemble the same procedures followed in determining the validity of other criminal charges. While such changes may be necessary at this juncture to ensure the fair and full prosecution of these cases, they would not be helpful in addressing the vast majority of maltreatment cases where the major objective is not criminal prosecution but rather family reunification. Regarding the second concern, targeting prevention services to potential victims rather than to potential perpetrators may also be a necessary short-term strategy for reducing the risk of sexual abuse. In the long run, however, significantly reducing the incidence of all forms of maltreatment will require reducing the prevalence of those individual and social conditions that lead to, or allow us to tolerate child maltreatment. Rather than seeking to empower children to better protect themselves, child assault prevention classes need to focus on making children aware of the potential for maltreatment and making adults aware of their responsibility for protecting children from these situations. Children should certainly be made to realize that if abuse occurs, it is never their fault. They should not be made to feel, however, that it is solely their responsibility to protect themselves from harm.

In addition to refocusing prevention efforts, confronting child sexual abuse can be effectively addressed through the expansion of the type of multifaceted treatment strategies represented by the federal demonstration programs evaluated in the National Clinical Evaluation Study. Once a child has disclosed abuse it may be far more important for the child's recovery and future development to receive quality therapeutic services than it will be to prosecute the case through the criminal courts. In the long run, reducing child abuse will not be accomplished by a treatment philosophy that relies upon the courts to define abuse or by a prevention philosophy that relies upon the empowerment of children. Practitioners and policy makers need to guard against incorporating what might be necessary short-term adjustments for dealing with sexual abuse into system-wide changes that would have lasting and potentially-negative consequences on our ability to combat other forms of maltreatment.

The emergence of emotional maltreatment as a unique subpopulation emphasizes a very different set of issues in the battle to confront all aspects of child abuse. Although there is growing evidence that emotional maltreatment has longstanding and serious impacts on a child's development and social functioning, public intervention in these cases is limited. Unless a child exhibits serious behavioral problems, or the emotional maltreatment is only one part of a complex package of physical abuse or neglect, it is unlikely that professionals or private citizens will report this type of maltreatment or, if they do, that such cases will be accepted on to CPS caseloads. The behaviors captured under the broad rubric of emotional maltreatment are simply too diverse and too prevalent and the consequences too diffuse to expect that they could be captured adequately under a single definition which could be equitably applied.

In a sense, this form of maltreatment, more so than the other most common forms, highlights the limits of the reporting system and the child welfare system in identifying and providing direct intervention in all cases of child maltreatment and it emphasizes the need for primary prevention. While the National Clinical Evaluation Study noted limited gains with families involved in emotional maltreatment, the gains which were realized underscore the utility of universal parent education. Unlike the child neglect population, families experiencing emotional maltreatment make greater progress in terms of resolving their own problems as well as in reducing the likelihood for future maltreatment when specific parenting practices are integrated into broader theories of child development and human behavior. This finding suggests that primary prevention efforts such as public awareness campaigns, parenting education classes for all first-time parents, and child development and parenting training in the high schools could, over time, significantly reduce maltreatment levels.

To limit our conceptualization of maltreatment only to behaviors that merit explicit public intervention into the private family after the fact is to limit unnecessarily our efforts to improve the quality of life for children. Reducing the rate of emotional maltreatment, as well as all other forms of abuse and neglect, will require not only an improved child welfare system but also a basic community-wide commitment on the part of adults to stop those behaviors that damage children. Certainly an efficient and equitable child abuse reporting and response system is critical if children are to be protected from the worst and most damaging forms of mistreatment. Research on abusive and neglectful individuals, however, suggests that relatively few of these adults become involved in serious forms of maltreatment without first demonstrating less volatile behaviors. What initially begins as occasional neglect, acceptable corporal punishment, or periodic yelling or swearing at a child can and does escalate into more serious and consistent patterns of child abuse. While local child welfare workers and private practitioners can minimize the risk of serious abuse in specific cases by referring families exhibiting these behaviors to community-based service programs, altering public opinion will require a more concerted effort on the part of child and family practitioners. Teachers, health care professionals, social workers, and day care providers, among others, have a responsibility to define for themselves and their clients a child abuse threshhold that pertains to behaviors that stifle a child's development. Practitioners can confront child abuse not only by reporting all known or suspected cases of maltreatment, but also by accepting a leadership role in informing the general public about all forms of mistreatment, not merely those acts that constitute reportable child abuse offenses. A reduction in the rate of child abuse will be achieved not by focusing solely on the most damaging end of the child maltreatment continuum—a child with broken bones, the sexually-molested child, or the failure-to-thrive infant. Real gains will be made only when individual parents recognize the harmful effects of routinely striking their child, swearing at their child, or ignoring their child, and, once recognizing this fact, cease these behaviors.

Balancing Treatment and Prevention: Developing a Coordinated Response

One of the most commonly debated issues in setting any social policy and developing intervention programs is the correct allocation of resources between those currently experiencing a certain social problem and those at risk of becoming its next victims. Child maltreatment is no exception to this dilemma. Proponents of a treatment emphasis argue that the need for public intervention into maltreating families is obvious and that past research suggests positive outcomes can be realized through thoughtful interventions. To the extent that maltreated children can be expected to grow up to become maltreating adults, intensive intervention with abused children offers the most logical and noncontroversial path to ultimate reduction of the problem. Shifting resources from these efforts into a cauldron of unproven prevention strategies represents, treatment advocates argue, not only a misapplication of scarce public resources, but also an unnecessary intrusion into the private family.

In reality, the choice between treatment and prevention is more a matter of degree and balance than of kind. In the short run, some combination of both strategies is needed if the problem of maltreatment is to be effectively confronted. Treatment strategies and long-term foster care will continue to be needed for maltreating families and for abused and neglected children unable to be reunited with their parents. While lower incidence rates might well be realized in the long run through the provision of comprehensive prevention strategies, such strategies will never completely eliminate maltreatment. On the other hand, there is much knowledge regarding the causal correlates of maltreatment that can be used to begin identifying and assisting those families at greater than average risk for various types of maltreatment.

In advocating prevention, it is important to clarify the costs of these efforts. While many of the most common prevention strategies (e.g., hotlines, respite care, public service announcements, parenting education, etc.) are relatively inexpensive compared to therapeutic services, they can represent sizable public expenditures. For example, California spends over $30 million annually specifically on child abuse prevention, $11 million of which is allocated to the universal provision of a single primary prevention effort (i.e., child assault prevention classes). To the extent that the demand for public dollars continues to grow faster than revenues, tradeoffs between treatment and prevention become sharper both for policy makers as well as for practitioners. If prevention advocates are to hold their own in the budget allocation process, they will need to develop accurate assessments of the short- and long-term benefits of early intervention.

The other practical problem with prevention, particularly secondary prevention efforts, is the potential stigma it may place on recipients. Some have avoided this issue by calling for the universal provision of selected educational and supportive services to all parents, children, and adolescents regardless of their present or potential need for them. It may be wiser, however, to change the rationale for offering services such as parenting education, respite care, and support groups than merely to expand the pool of recipients. Services could be promoted not under the rubric of "child abuse prevention" but rather as more general efforts to assist families in parenting or child-rearing. Families would be encouraged to participate in services not because they are seen as personally inadequate, but rather, due to a variety of circumstances, that they have fewer resources than other families to cope with the demanding task of parenthood. To the extent that the provision of these services could be expanded within particularly high-risk communities and provided through existing community-based organizations or voluntary agencies, much of the stigma associated with present child welfare interventions might be minimized.

This issue aside, a broader philosophical question regarding the overall advisability of prevention remains. It can be argued that prevention is extremely problematic within any reasonable scope of fiscal effort and within the values of a free society that gives people the right to be left alone (Gaylin et al., 1978; Gilbert, 1983). Also, to promote "happiness" is dangerous in that it requires practitioners and policy makers to make value judgments as to what constitutes a "higher quality of living." Despite these difficulties, responding only after the fact ensures the continuous need for society to deal with the victims dysfunctional families will inevitably produce. Just as the hallmark of good leaders is the ability of their followers to operate efficiently without them, one might argue that the best child welfare system will be one that eventually is able to reduce its overall size and scope not by definition (i.e., by ignoring the precursors of specific social ills), but rather by reducing the number of abused and neglected children through thoughtful and coordinated early intervention.

Having made a commitment to preventing child abuse, the final remaining question is how best to accomplish this task. Preventing child abuse will require more than a well-functioning child welfare system and a number of effective parenting programs or public awareness campaigns. The multifarious nature of maltreatment, in terms of both its precursors and consequences, makes it unrealistic to expect that a single program, no matter how successful, will eliminate the complete risk for future abuse or neglect with any given family. Some have addressed this problem by clamoring for broad-scale social change as the only means of altering those individual, cultural, and political practices deemed harmful to children (Gil, 1981). With an eye toward eventual social change, others have articulated short-range plans which identify the key attributes of a successful child abuse prevention strategy (Helfer, 1982; Cohn, 1983). Such systems, if fully implemented, provide a continuum of support for families and victims of maltreatment such that the burden of prevention is no longer shouldered by a single effort. Prevention, in the broadest sense, becomes the combined responsibility of practitioners working with maltreating families in both public and private contexts, legislators and administrators establishing policies that shape the social context in which families live, and families themselves.

While our knowledge of child abuse is not perfect, current practice and research findings suggest that some components may be more necessary than others and that some specific interventions may be more promising than others. Confronting physical abuse, child neglect, emotional maltreatment, and sexual abuse, will require a coordinated system of primary, secondary, and tiertiary prevention efforts, augmented by better professional training and child welfare practice. Among the specific primary prevention efforts that need to be included in such a continuum of care are:

> public awareness campaigns and media presentations and speakers programs to voluntary organizations and civic groups;

24-hour hotline/crisis intervention;

adequate day care facilities (i.e., adequate in terms of both quantity and quality);

adequate after-school programs (i.e., again, adequate in terms of both quantity and quality);

general family workshops on selected parenting topics (e.g., discipline, sex education, having fun with your child);

child assault prevention training in the schools emphasizing self-esteem (kindergarten through grade 12);

improved medical care for children, including routine medical check-ups and expanded access to medical care;

improved public housing and welfare benefits; and

development of community-based organizations which incorporate parenting education, child care, and family support services into their overall goals and objectives.

Beyond these broadly targeted interventions, specific secondary and tertiary prevention services for parents who are at risk for maltreatment or who have already mistreated their children need to be designed and disseminated in all local communities. Such services include:

for parents/families

parenting education classes,

household management classes,

self-help groups,

in-home visitor programs,

prenatal care,

family workshops,

respite care (in and out of the home),

hospital follow-up after birth,

rooming in, and

services to reduce isolation and to facilitate service delivery (e.g., transportation, day care, emergency assistance, housing assistance);

for children (preadolescents)

therapeutic day care, preschool,

play therapy,

group therapy,

remedial services (speech therapy, skill development, reading skills), and

recreational services;

for adolescents (who are not yet parents)

temporary shelter.

self-help groups,

counseling (individual and group),

remedial services and educational assistance, and

independent living programs/skills development;

for adolescents (who are parents)

parenting education,

household management,

family planning,

in-home visitor program,

employment training and/or assistance in obtaining GED or high school diploma, and

self-help groups.

In addition, professional educational services specific to child maltreatment need to be provided to local practitioners covering such topics as:

in-service training on child abuse reporting laws;

in-service training on recognition of abusive/neglectful families or children;

in-service training on how to improve service coordination and expand service capacity; and

multidisciplinary team review planning and implementation guidelines.

Finally, the relationship among specific programs and the extent to which county and state officials systematically monitor programs are also critical to a well-functioning prevention system. Key elements of an ideal child welfare system include:

clear, agreed-upon definitions of maltreatment;

stable and secure funding for prevention services;

knowledge of the specific parenting practices of cultural groups represented in the population;

identified intake point(s) for all reported cases;

a centralized information and referral source regarding all services available for abusive and neglectful families and individuals;

clear legal procedures governing the reporting of cases and the investigation of these reports to ensure consistency and due process;

agreement on service boundaries for the system as a whole and for each individual component within the system (e.g., protective services, police, juvenile court);

multidisciplinary case review teams, including representatives from such key disciplines as medicine, social welfare, and law, as well as minority representatives;

qualified personnel within all agencies serving abusive and neglectful families (i.e., staff with both professional training and/or experience in working with these families);

opportunities for staff to expand their clinical skills and personal professional growth; and

a coordinated method for regular evaluation of the system's performance, including

> clear and solid baseline data.
>
> records of the number of families/individuals served by the system,
>
> records of the number of volunteers participating in the system;
>
> records of the number of agencies participating in the system.
>
> measurement of changes in the number and characteristics of the cases reported for maltreatment;
>
> clarity as to the specific target population(s) to be reached and the extent to which the system is serving these populations,
>
> clear methods of obtaining follow-up data on clients, and
>
> clear methods for assessing the range of referrals being made to the system.

The planning challenge facing practitioners is less in identifying the necessary service and practice components of a successful child abuse intervention continuum and more in achieving new levels of coordination among their colleagues. The success of multidisciplinary teams in investigating and monitoring cases of child abuse has shown that representatives from a variety of disciplines, including medicine, law, mental health, social welfare, and education, can indeed draw on each other's expertise and the skills of lay volunteers in developing effective treatment plans for individual families. A similar level of cooperation needs to be employed in developing a network of coordinated services and policies to ensure that the procedures governing performance in each of these subsystems are tempered by the needs of the overall prevention model. Also, increased support for prevention efforts, as demonstrated by the Children's Trust Fund and the growth of work-based social services, bodes well for the expansion of existing prevention services and the development of innovative strategies to reach particularly vulnerable populations. While full implementation of the model outlined above does not guarantee a reduction in the levels and severity of child maltreatment, it does offer a concrete future course of action.[2]

Integrating Research and Practice

Society has an obligation to protect children from the extreme consequences of physical or emotional trauma, such as broken bones, sexual assault, and nonorganic failure to thrive. However, wide disagreement exists over the need to protect children from milder forms of mistreatment. Even more disagreement exists over the rights of society to overrule parental authority in those cases where present or future harm to the child is not evident. The diversity in cultural values and parenting norms represented in the American social fabric, not to mention the diversity in children's needs, may best be protected by allowing parents to rear their children in the manner they see fit so long as the basic health and well-being of the child is not compromised.

As such, child abuse and neglect intervention systems will continue to be developed in light of our broader image of family life and the rights of parents, not society, to determine what is in their child's best interest. In any policy context, but particularly with regard to such subjectively defined phenomena as child maltreatment, practitioners must accept the limited role empirical data will play in shaping public policy. Rather than dictating the outcomes of policy debates, the real strength of field research and the experience of practitioners may be in our ability to establish a perspective or framework within which a wide range of information can be carefully synthesized.

Properly constructed and implemented, clinical assessments and program evaluations can go a long way toward clarifying objectives, determining impacts, and defining the paradigms within which future policy or programs will be determined. For example, past research efforts have successfully expanded the conceptualization of maltreatment to include acts other than physical abuse and neglect. The influence of carefully-documented clinical experiences on public attitudes is reflected in increased public awareness of the incidence of child sexual abuse and its long-term consequences, and with the potential damaging effects of prolonged emotional maltreatment. Also, research regarding the impact of poverty in limiting the choices parents have with respect to housing, medical care, and educational opportunities for their children and the poor quality of those opportunities that are available to these families, have reshaped thinking regarding the appropriate scope for child abuse and neglect interventions, shifting interventions away from a strict focus on client-level solutions and toward consideration of more widespread systematic reforms.

Careful field research also can assist individual workers, administrators, and policy makers in selecting among competing alternatives. Expanded cost effectiveness studies identifying the most economical and successful treatment strategies, and expanded clinical research on the short- and long-term costs and benefits of various prevention strategies can help determine how best to allocate scarce public resources. Such efforts can pinpoint, particularly in the prevention sphere, the different roles nonpublic entities such as community organizations, churches, and voluntary associations can play in reaching different "at risk" populations.

In order to play a role in shaping the normative debate or in the selection of specific intervention strategies, practitioners will need to be more aggressive in making their findings available in a format that policy makers can understand and rapidly assimilate into the decision-making process. Unless clinical findings are more accessible to policy makers than they have been in the past, such efforts will continue to have less of an influence than they warrant. Withholding clinical findings until they are perfect or until they have been proved time and time again will not slow down the pace of decision making in this field; it will simply result in policy choices being made with less knowledge than the situation warrants or the field deserves.

Appendix A

The National Clinical
Evaluation Study:
Data Characteristics
and Methodology

Overview of the National Evaluation

A three-and-one-half-year demonstration program in the field of child abuse and neglect was initiated by the U.S. Department of Health and Human Services, National Center on Child Abuse and Neglect (NCCAN) during the fall of 1978. Nineteen projects located throughout the country were funded to demonstrate the effects of specialized clinical interventions targeted to five distinct abuse and neglect subpopulations. These subpopulations included sexual abuse, adolescent maltreatment, substance-abuse-related child maltreatment, child neglect, and remedial services to maltreated children. A comprehensive evaluation of the NCCAN demonstration program was conducted under the direction of this author by Berkeley Planning Associates (BPA) with the assistance of the Urban and Rural Systems Associates (URSA). The major goals of this evaluation were:

> to determine if there were indeed distinct subpopulations of abuse and neglect and, if so, to identify the important differences;
>
> to test whether families experiencing distinct child abuse and neglect problems (i.e., subpopulation-related) required unique investigative and treatment approaches; and
>
> to provide direction on which particular strategies demonstrated by the projects were best suited for replication in other communities.

The evaluation's various components fell into one of two principal groups: those which collected information on the families receiving services and those which collected information on the individual 19 demonstration projects. First, the three components that assessed client impact and service outcomes included:

> the collection of baseline, service, and outcome data on approximately 1,000 families served by the demonstration projects between October 1979 and October 1981;

> the use of clinicians not from the demonstration projects to assess the status of a subsample of the projects' adult clients by interviewing these clients at the time services were terminated; and

> a qualitative and descriptive review of a subsample of the projects' most successful and least successful client families.

Second, the study components that focused on the characteristics of the projects and their respective staff included:

> an overview of each project's host agency, organization, and staffing structure;

> an in-depth look at each project's case management process and service delivery system;

> a review of the cultural values of each project's clinical staff;

> a review of the type and nature of each project's service linkages with both its host organization and with other community agencies; and

> a systematic review of the way in which each project allocated its staff resources among a range of direct and indirect client services.

In selecting these specific areas for further exploration from among the many possible aspects of a project's management and service structures, the anticipated importance of each factor on client outcomes was considered as well as the extent to which each factor lent itself to review and analysis by an outside evaluator.

Finally, because the analysis of the client data as well as the project variables was geared toward testing specific hypotheses and documenting the effects of specialized treatment strategies on the various subpopulations, the evaluation also included cell-specific components to further explore those client, project, and community factors identified by the projects within a given treatment cell as being critical to fully understanding the issues related to the treatment of their particular subpopulation. Therefore, the majority of the policy issues addressed in these five cell-specific studies were suggested by the projects themselves, with the evaluator playing a facilitating role.

The findings from the majority of the studies outlined above have been presented in individual reports devoted solely to each particular topic. These reports are summarized in Attachment A and are available from both NCCAN and the evaluator.

Key Research and Policy Questions

In funding this round of demonstration projects as well as the corresponding evaluation, NCCAN identified five primary objectives, as follows:

> to generate additional knowledge about the nature, causes, effects, and promising preventive, treatment, and child protective approaches to the specific forms of child maltreatment;

> to develop new or to refine existing service techniques for dealing with the unique needs of the children and families involved in the specific forms of maltreatment;

> to develop and test new or revised approaches to the delivery of services needed by the children and families involved in specific forms of child maltreatment;

> to meet the preventive, treatment, and child protective service needs as well as other identified service needs of the children and families served by the projects; and

> to identify resource needs associated with specific forms of child maltreatment including staff qualifications and configuration, staff training, management and administrative processes, and program funding.

Underlying all of these objectives was the assumption that different types of families experience different stresses which result in different forms of child maltreatment and that these different forms of maltreatment require unique, tailored intervention strategies in order to be treated successfully.

As the study moved into the final phase, the purpose of the research and policy questions became more focused and was governed not by what one might want to say, but by what, indeed, one could say to the field about the nature and treatment of child abuse and neglect. Four critical areas of exploration were identified:

> definitional issues,

> differential or specialized treatment issues,

> client treatability issues, and

> cost issues.

Each of these areas represented a concern not only of federal and state policy makers, but also of practitioners and researchers. While great gains have been made in identifying the precursors and impacts of child maltreatment on the perpetrator and the victim, additional information was still needed regarding exactly what attributes characterize families involved in child maltreatment, what types of services achieve greatest success with what types of families, what kinds of families are and are not being helped by existing intervention strategies, and the relative costs associated with each of these strategies. The specific questions outlined in Figure A.1 represent those aspects of each of the areas addressed in the study.

The Data Collection Process

The data base for the core client evaluation consists of information on the clients served by each of the 19 demonstration projects during the data collection period extending from October 1979 to October 1981. The data collection instruments were organized to record data on four different client groups (i.e., families, adults, adolescents, and children and infants) at two different time periods (at project intake, and at termination). Service data were collected on all individual clients at the time they were terminated.

In general, the forms were completed by the person on the project's clinical staff who had the most direct contact with the client. For some projects, different people completed the various forms or sets of forms for individuals in the same family. For example, the staff member working most closely with the parents would complete the adult client forms while another working with the child in the family would complete the infant and child client forms. However, in projects that provided services to both parents and children from the same family, the person completing the adult client forms on the maternal figure was also responsible for completing the family form. For cases in which no parent was served, the individual working with the youngest maltreated child completed the family form.

Because the purpose of the baseline forms was to capture the attributes and functioning of clients at the time of first contact with the project, this data was recorded at project intake. However, because it was understood that a client's functioning is often not discernible until after some time has elapsed, the baseline forms were completed when the project's intake and diagnostic process was completed, but in no case later than 30 days after first contact with the client. The services forms and outcomes forms were completed within one week of termination from the project. Termination, for the purposes of the study, was defined as the point when project services ended. For those projects that did not officially terminate clients or that terminated cases long after services ended, termination was defined as that time when a client had received no project services for two months, there was no specific plan for future services.

Table A.1 summarizes the key dependent and independent variables for the families, adults, adolescents, and children included in the data base. As this table indicates, information was collected on a wide range of client and service variables, allowing for the testing of numerous hypotheses regarding successful treatment.

Data Reliability and Validity

In order for the client data being collected from the 19 demonstration projects to be useful for analysis and for generalization about the projects and their clients, it was imperative that the data were reliable; that is, the responses provided were internally consistent as well as consistent across individuals who were presented with the same information. Concern for this issue was present in all stages of the BPA client impact analysis including the initial development of the instruments, the refinement of the instruments, and the conceptualization of the analysis plan. During these activities, questions or terminology that the projects found confusing or ambiguous were removed from the instruments or were sufficiently clarified so as to ensure proper interpretations by all project personnel. Also, a detailed instruction guide was developed, providing the projects with a clear frame of reference for completing the forms. Throughout the data collection period, constant attention was given to this topic. Training and retraining the project staff responsible for completing the forms took place on each site visit, and included a review of the definitions contained in the instruction guide, as well as the procedures required to complete the forms properly. Regular telephone contact was maintained with the projects to monitor any problems. Common problems that emerged at a number of the projects were clarified through written memoranda distributed to all 19 sites.

As part of BPA's concern for high-quality data, a number of formal and informal reliability tests were built into the study design and evaluation procedures. The first reliability test was conducted by the BPA Data Management Team during special visits to the majority of the 19 demonstration projects early in 1980, and involved two or more caseworkers at a project completing forms on the same family. The test served as an overall indicator of the extent to which the forms were being completed accurately by the projects and the extent to which appropriate procedures were being followed. The test also served to troubleshoot, identifying those questions or instructions which were, at that time, unclear and therefore subject to further clarification.

While this initial reliability test did provide a certain degree of feedback regarding the reliability of the forms, the test was hampered by a number of factors. First, the staff members at the projects often did not share information regarding a particular family, and caseworkers had detailed knowledge only of those families with which they had direct, ongoing contact. Second, the approach did not assess interrater reliability across projects because the "sample case" used at each site was taken from each project's specific caseload. Finally, because BPA personnel had no factual or background information on the family other than what the caseworkers had reported it could not be determined if the responses were "accurate" given the specific definitions outlined in BPA's instruction guide.

Figure A.1

Final Research Questions for the Evaluation
of the Clinical Demonstration Projects

A.   Definitional Issues

A-1.   How do we define different child abuse and neglect subpopulations? Is "type of abuse" the most useful way to stratify clients or do we want to stratify clients along a different set of dimensions (i.e., family structure, presenting problems, age of parents, etc.)?

A-2.   What family and other problems characterize parents who commit different types of abuse and/or neglect?

A-3.   What are the developmental and functioning problems characterizing children and youth experiencing different kinds of maltreatment?

A-4.   What are the different community coordination issues faced by projects working with different child abuse and neglect subpopulations? Are different local agencies involved, are different costs associated with these coordination efforts, and are different types of personnel required to effectively achieve a well-coordinated system?

B.   Differential or Specialized Treatment Issues

B-1.   Do different diagnoses (by type of abuse and presenting problems) lead to very different treatment strategies within the same project as well as across projects, and if so, how different are these strategies? Do they involve different services, different ordering of similar services, different focuses within similar services, different types of staff providing similar services, etc?

B-2.   Is specialized treatment to different subpopulations by type of abuse effective?

B-3.   What types of services or service mix work best for different client subpopulations such as ethnic groups, family structure, income, etc.?

B-4.   What "innovative" services do the projects offer?

B-5.   To what extent does the organizational structure, management, and staffing pattern help explain the differences in performance and attainment of service delivery goals among the projects?

C.   Client Treatability Issues

C-1.   Who are the priority clients for services under a system operating with too few resources, and how do you ensure that projects focus on these priority groups?

C-2.   Are there some groups of families who, for whatever reasons, do not make progress within current identified treatment modalities, and if so, what new types of intervention strategies would we propose trying with these families?

C-3.   Are the projects intervening with the most severe cases?

C-4.   Do all family members need to be treated, or does working with just the perpetrator and/or the child suffice?

C-5.   Under what circumstances should a child be removed from the home, and what guidelines should be used in determining when it is in the best interest of the child to seek placement options?

D.   Cost Issues

D-1.   How much does it cost to implement the treatment intervention strategies used by the demonstration projects?

D-2.   Are different treatment strategies more or less cost-effective?

D-3.   Which of the most affordable services are most effective?

D-4.   How do you cut the costs of service models that work so that they can become affordable to a wider variety of community and organizational settings?

Table A.1

Listing of Variables

Unit of Analysis	Dependent Variables
Families	Clinician judgment of overall progress Reincidence rate, timing, and severity of neglect, physical abuse, and emotional maltreatment Improvement on various functioning problems exhibited at intake
Adult Clients	Relative difficulty in treatment Clinician judgment of overall progress Likelihood for future maltreatment Reincidence rate, timing, and relative severity of types of abuse/neglect Improvement on various functioning problems exhibited at intake

Independent Variables	
Client Characteristics	Service Variables

Household composition
Number of children
Age of children
Whether family was court-ordered
into treatment
Whether criminal charges were filed
Prior abuse/neglect reports
Household income
Welfare status
Description of abuse or neglect,
including characteristics of mal-
treatment and duration
Overall severity of case
High-risk status
Primary type of maltreatment
Functioning status on range of
family problems
Stresses noted for family
Strengths noted for family

Length of time in treatment
Maltreator's residence during treatment
Child's residence during treatment

Age
Sex
Race
Marital status
Educational level
Employment status
Relationship to youngest child
Residence at time of abuse
Description of abuse or neglect,
including role in abuse, charac-
teristics of abuse, and duration
Explanation for maltreatment
Acknowledgement of harm to child
Attitude toward services
Motivation to change
Likelihood for reabuse in the
absence of services
Substance abuse problem
Functioning status on range of
problems
Primary type of abuse/neglect
Overall severity of maltreatment

Nonproject services prior to intake
Nonproject services after intake
List of support services provided
during treatment
Medical services provided
Provision of casework counseling
frequency of in-home casework
frequency of in-office casework
Experience of primary caseworker
Lay therapy provided
Educational or skill development
services provided
Parenting education provided
Types of therapy provided (for each
type, frequency, duration, and skill
level of provider is noted as are
specific counseling techniques employed)
Length of time in treatment
Residence during treatment
Court action during treatment
Reason for terminating services

Listing of Variables

Unit of Analysis	Dependent Variables
Adolescent Clients	Relative difficulty in treatment Clinician judgment of overall progress Likelihood to be reabused in future Reincidence rate, timing, and relative severity of types of abuse/neglect Improvement on various functioning problems exhibited at intake
Children and Infant Clients	Relative difficulty in treatment Clinician judgment of overall progress Likelihood to be reabused in future Reincidence rate, timing, and relative severity of types of abuse/neglect Improvement on various functioning problems exhibited at intake

With these difficulties in mind, a second reliability test was scheduled during the regular March–April 1980 site visits to the projects. During these site visits, the BPA and URSA site liaisons asked staff members to read a common "sample case study" and complete the baseline forms based on this information. While certain factual items, such as the number of children in the family and the presence of physical abuse, were clearly documented in the sample case, many variables were treated in a way that required professional judgment and interpretation. No answer to any ques-

Independent Variables	
Client Characteristics	Service Variables
Age	Nonproject services prior to intake
Sex	Nonproject services after intake
Residence at intake	List of supportive services provided
Prior out-of-home placements	during treatment
Reason for referral	Number of nights temporary shelter
Description of abuse or neglect,	was provided
including characteristics of abuse	Medical services provided
and duration	Provision of casework counseling
Likelihood for reabuse in absence	Frequency of in-home casework
of services	Frequency of in-office casework
Overall severity of harm done as	Experience of primary caseworker
a result of abuse	Provision of education and skill
Primary type of abuse/neglect	development services
	Types of therapy provided (for each
	type, frequency, duration, and skill
	level of provider is noted, as are
	specific counseling techniques employed)
	Length of time in treatment
	Residence during treatment
	Court action during treatment
	Reason for terminating services
Age	Nonproject services prior to intake
Sex	Nonproject services after intake
Residence at intake	List of supportive services provided
Prior out-of-home placements	during treatment
Description of abuse or neglect,	Number of nights temporary shelter
including characteristics of	was provided
abuse and duration	Medical services provided
Likelihood for reabuse in absence	Frequency of therapeutic day care
of services	services
Overall severity of harm done as	Frequency of other remedial services
a result of abuse	Frequency, duration of infant
Primary type of abuse/neglect	stimulation
	Frequency, duration of supervised
	parent-child interactions
	Types of therapy provided (for each
	type, frequency, duration, and skill
	level of provider is noted, as are
	specific counseling techniques employed)
	Length of time in treatment
	Residence during treatment
	Court action during treatment
	Reason for terminating services

tion in each questionnaire was embedded in the case study. Clinicians were asked to review the information presented in the case study and record their "clinical judgments" of the family and its individual members on the appropriate baseline forms.

As with the previous reliability test, the procedures undertaken during the March–April 1980 site visit found most project staff to be familiar with the forms and to be following the indicated skip patterns. Project personnel had little or no difficulty in accurately recording the various factual information asked for on the family, adult, adolescent, and infant and child forms—virtually 100% of the respondents answered these types of questions correctly. Also, as found in our previous reliability tests, the projects' staff members showed less agreement on the more judgmental questions, with certain functioning indicators proving more problematic than others.

A third reliability-validity test was administered at the clinical demonstration projects during the September 1980 site visits. To test reliability, four different example case histories ("vignettes") were constructed to illustrate either physical neglect, emotional maltreatment, physical abuse, or sexual abuse. These vignettes were followed by selected questions drawn from the actual data collection instruments. Some of the questions were selected specifically for the subject matter of the vignettes; others were chosen as "dummy" questions to serve as a further check on how clinicians responded to a question when no specific information relating to it was included in the case file. Put together, the four vignettes and their attendant questions became a test package, to be administered at the projects to the clinicians who regularly filled out the client impact forms.

To test the validity of the data generated by this study (i.e., any "systematic bias"), it was decided to vary three descriptions in each type of vignette that might theoretically tend to bias the responses. The decision on the amount of variation to introduce was based on the constraints of orthogonally balanced test design and estimates of the total number of respondents who would take the test. The "randomization" technique involved creating dichotomies for each of these three factors, creating "either-or" versions of the same vignette. The first dichotomy chosen for investigation was that of *race*, in order to determine if the clinicians showed a systematic bias in responses about a case according to the client's race. This was structured as a black and white division—in half of each of the four vignettes the subject family was black; in the other half, they were white.

The second dichotomy chosen was *employment status*, to see if clinicians gave evidence of systematic bias in similar cases where a family's employment status differed. Thus, half of all the black family vignettes concerned working families, and half covered welfare families; the same division occurred in the white family vignettes.

The third dichotomy selected was specific to the type of abuse or neglect illustrated by the particular vignette. In the "physical neglect" vignette, we probed as to whether substance abuse on the part of the adult maltreator resulted in clinician bias; in the "emotional maltreatment" case, we attempted to see whether clinician perceptions were altered depending on the victim's sex; where "physical abuse" was involved, we altered the mother and father as perpetrator to see if there were any differences in perception; and in the "sexual abuse" vignette, we varied the maltreator from the biological father to a stepfather.

In order to capture each possible variation, eight versions of each vignette were prepared. Each respondent then received a test package containing four different vignettes, one of each of the four types of maltreatment: two described white families, and two described black families, with half of each group working and half unemployed. This procedure guaranteed the greatest possibility for generalization regarding the data findings. Respondents were told only that the test was a reliability test and were not told they were completing different versions of each vignette.

Taken together, the results of these reliability tests suggest that the information collected on the core client instruments presents, in general, a reliable and valid picture of the family's initial problems, services, and outcomes. When faced with similar information, clinicians showed little variation in their assessment of the family's overall progress, the reincidence of abuse, and the likelihood of future maltreatment. Slightly more variation was found in the clinicians' assessments of the family and individual performance on the various functioning indicators, although significant differences were noted on only a few of the functioning indicators.

The Data Base

The total number of families included in the study sample is 986, as shown in Table A.2. Across the 19 demonstration projects, six of the projects (i.e., Albuquerque, Atlantic City, Knoxville, New York, Sacramento, and St. Louis) provided 75 cases or more to the sample, while only three projects (Auburn, Denver, and New Haven) completed forms on 25 cases or less. The treatment cell that provided a slightly higher proportion of families is the adolescent maltreatment cell. To ensure that this did not bias the overall findings in any significant way, the characteristics of families served by the projects in this treatment cell were compared with the families served by the other four cells to see if they differed in terms of such critical dimensions as severity of maltreatment, income, functioning, progress in treatment, and propensity for future maltreatment.

In terms of the types of clients on which data were gathered, the largest category of clients in the sample was the adult population, totaling 1,250 individuals, versus only 701 adolescents and 975 infants and children. The adult clients represent the majority of individuals on which information was recorded in three of the cells, while more data was collected on infants and children in the child neglect cell and on adolescents in the adolescent maltreatment cell.

It should be stressed that, although this sample most likely represents the majority of families receiving services from the 19 projects, it does not include all the individuals served during the demonstration period. Because most of the projects began serving clients prior to the onset of the data collection process in October 1979 and continued intake of new cases after termination of data collection in October 1981, the families served during these time periods were not included in the study's data base. In

Table A.2

Number of Cases in the Study Sample

Cell/Project	Number of Families	Number of Adults	Number of Children/ Infants	Number of Adolescents
SEXUAL ABUSE				
Albuquerque	84	110	47	48
Chicago	34	49	23	22
Edina	59	113	63	79
Knoxville	76	85	38	49
CELL TOTAL	253	357	171	198
ADOLESCENT MALTREATMENT				
Atlantic City	76	104	15	98
Sacramento	101	91	14	117
St. Charles	65	47	2	72
Waterville	40	35	33	72
CELL TOTAL	282	277	64	359
SUBSTANCE ABUSE				
Ann Arbor	28	57	50	41
Little Rock	41	58	20	50
New York	87	111	141	6
CELL TOTAL	156	226	211	97
REMEDIAL SERVICES				
Colorado Springs	33	47	45	--
New Haven	24	17	36	--
Oakland	29	32	29	--
Pittsburgh	48	66	51	--
CELL TOTAL	134	162	161	--
CHILD NEGLECT				
Auburn	18	22	36	1
Dallas	40	57	93	3
Denver	25	26	25	--
St. Louis	78	123	213	43
CELL TOTAL	161	228	367	47
SAMPLE TOTAL	986	1,250	975	701

addition, a significant number of families received some services from the project but did not stay in the treatment program long enough (i.e., at least one month) to give project staff adequate information to complete an accurate assessment of the family's presenting problems or to engage them in the therapeutic process. Because the study design measured the change families and individual family members underwent between intake and termination, completion of the forms on those families for whom an initial assessment was not possible would not yield particularly useful data. Also, the individuals included in the study sample represent only those clients served by the projects' NCCAN-funded treatment components. For some projects, families were served via several different treatment programs of which only one received NCCAN funding and therefore only a limited number of cases were included in the study's data base. Finally, only those individuals considered to be actively involved in a given case were included in the sample. Therefore, if a project provided a service on a one-time basis to an extended family member of one of their clients, information on this individual would not have been collected.

The study's data base also included some cases that had not completed the treatment program and were still receiving services as of the end of the data collection period. For these cases, the projects were required to "artificially" terminate these families and complete the services and outcomes forms. For the purposes of the analysis, these artificially-terminated cases were handled in the following manner:

> client baseline information was reported for all clients in the sample, whether they were official or artificial termination;

> for each project, all "artificially" terminated clients who received services for at least 80% of the average length of time services were provided to its officially terminated clients were merged with the officially terminated clients in analyzing the services data; and

> a comparison was made between the officially terminated and the "artificially" terminated cases on each of the key outcome indicators to determine if significant differences existed. In those instances in which differences were found to exist, the outcomes for the "artificially" terminated clients have been reported separately from the outcomes for the officially terminated clients.

On balance, relatively few of the clients who were artificially terminated had been in treatment a short period of time. Overall, 20.9% of the adult sample, 10.8% of the adolescent sample, and 36.2% of the infant and children sample were still receiving service at the end of the data collection period. However, more important for the purposes of the analysis, over two-thirds of all these individuals had been receiving services for over a six-month period. For any given project, the number of artificially terminated clients who had not received services for at least 80% of the project's average treatment period were so small that their inclusion in the study does not bias, to any significant degree, the project's overall results.

Analytic Approach

Initial analyses of these data, conducted during the summer of 1982, included univariate distributions of all key client, service, and outcome variables; bivariate analyses which explored the association between client outcomes and various client characteristics and service variables as well as relationships among different descriptive variables; and multiple regressions to explain successful performance on the adult client outcome variables. Additional multivariate analyses were completed in 1985.

This study employed a multiple group comparison design in which the outcomes achieved by any one project's service strategy was compared to the outcomes achieved by others utilizing a different service approach with similar types of families. In all of the multiple regressions conducted on the data, client characteristics and other nonservice variables were entered first to control for their unique impacts on client outcomes.

This method, while representing a very conservative approach to identifying significant service impacts, is one of the few analytic methods that can be used to determine service impact in the absence of a formal control or comparison group. To compensate for the lack of a true experimental research design, the method assumes services were randomly assigned to clients (i.e., no consistent relationship existed between client characteristics and the provision of services). Client characteristics and other nonservice variables are entered into the model first under this method as a means of controlling for their specific contribution to differential outcomes. Service impact is then determined to be the additional variance in the dependent variable of interest explained by the introduction of specific service variables.

However, the reality of social service systems is that the services provided to a given client are indeed partially determined by the client's characteristics or, in the case of the present study, by the type and severity of the initial maltreatment. When this type of selective service assignment exists, some of the observed client impact is shared statistically between services and client characteristics. Assignment of this shared variance, particularly if it is substantial, can have rather dramatic impacts on what, if any, services are found to be significant contributors to positive or negative client outcomes. If one attributes all of this shared variance to service impacts, as would be the case if the nonservice variables were not included in the regression models or were entered into the model only after the service variables had been allowed to explain all of the variance they could, one would risk overestimating the true impact of the intervention. Certain services may be associated with more positive outcomes because they were systematically provided to families or individuals who made progress in treatment because they entered a service program with a greater likelihood for success (e.g., their problems were more amenable to treatment, they were more willing to change or more open to services, etc.). If one assigns all of the shared variance to the nonservice factors, as was done in the current analyses, the reverse problem may emerge. By initially controlling for client characteristics and presenting problems in the regression models, the analyses have potentially controlled for a large part of the effects of services, leaving the service variables to explain the variance in outcome due to other, as yet undefined, problems or client characteristics.

The true impact of services lies somewhere between the total variance explained by services alone and the unique variance explained by services, controlling for nonservice factors. Without a formal control group, it is not possible to tell precisely where the true level lies. However, one can identify the potential range of service impacts partially by determining the size of the shared variance, as has been done in Table A.3 for the adult client sample.

As this table indicates, the shared variance in the case of the overall progress measure was quite small, suggesting that service assignment was indeed a rather random event and that specific services were not routinely assigned to specific types of clients. In terms of the other two dependent

Table A.3

Comparison of Unique and Shared Variance

Between Service and Nonservice Variables.

All Adult Sample

	Dependent Variables		
	Client's Overall Progress	Likelihood for Future Maltreatment	Reincidence
Variance explained by services model alone	.1055	.0994	.1709
Variance explained by nonservice model alone	.1364	.3811	.3009
Variance explained by combined model	.2161	.4157	.3580
Variance unique to service (Line 3 minus Line 2)	.0797	.0346	.0571
Shared variance between service and nonservice variables (Line 1 minus Line 4)	.0258	.0648	.1138

variables, likelihood for future maltreatment and reincidence, the shared variance is larger, most likely due to the effects of the client's initial maltreatment history on eventual client progress in both of these areas. Clients involved in more severe types of maltreatment or multiple types of maltreatment at intake generally demonstrate a greater number of functioning problems and are far more resistant to project services than clients without these characteristics. Also, it is logical to assume that the ability of a project to prevent reincidence during treatment may be more influenced by the use of placement (i.e., physically separating the maltreator from the victim) than through the provision of any specific therapeutic or supportive service. While the correlation coefficients between individual service variables and client chracteristics were generally low (i.e., less than .15), as a group, client and service factors did overlap. Consequently, the analytic method employed here may underestimate the true impact of services in terms of progress on these two dependent variables. Even with this conservative strategy, however, a number of services were found to have a significant impact on outcomes, a point that suggests that certain services, independent of a wide range of client characteristics and presenting problems, are more effective with various types of maltreators.

Attachment A: Study Reports

Evaluation of the Clinical Demonstrations of the Treatment of Child Abuse and Neglect. Berkeley Planning Associates, under contract to the National Center for Child Abuse and Neglect, Office of Human Development Services, DHHS (HEW 105-78-1108), June 1983.

Vol. 1: Executive Summary

Vol. 2: The Exploration of Client Characteristics, Services, and Outcomes: Final Report and Summary of Findings

Vol. 3: A Qualitative Study of Most Successful and Least Successful Cases

Vol. 4: Child Neglect Cell-Specific Study

Vol. 5: Therapeutic Child Care: Approaches to Remediating the Effects of Child Abuse and Neglect

Vol. 6: Resource Allocation Study

Vol. 7: Overview of each Project's Internal Evaluation Methodology

Vol. 8: Final Analysis Plan and Methodology for the Exploration of Client Characteristics, Services, and Outcomes

Vol. 9: Historical Case Studies

The National Clinical
Evaluation Study:
Multiple Regression Results

Table B.1

Multiple Regression Results on Adult Neglect Subsample:

Full Model

Independent Variables	Dependent Variable: Overall Progress[a]		
	Parameter Estimate	Standard Error	t-Value
Married	-.0990	.0805	-1.23
Client Aged 31-40	.1236	.1296	.95
Female	-.0840	.1079	-.78
Client Less Than 21	.0902	.1562	.58
White	.0929	.0850	1.09
Client Aged 21-30	.2297	.1244	1.85*
Number of Presenting Problems	-.0352	.0199	-1.77*
Substance Abuse Problem	-.2023	.0891	-2.27**
Moderate Harm Resulting from Maltreatment	.1444	.1057	1.37*
Number of Types of Maltreatment Committed by Client	-.0264	.0541	-.49
Severe Harm Resulting from Maltreatment	.0537	.1190	.45
Compliance Index	.0778	.0275	2.83***
In Treatment 6 Months or Less	-.1698	.1253	-1.36*
Client Received Support Services	.1083	.0922	1.17
Client Received Individual Counseling	.1252	.1186	1.06
Client Received Group Counseling	.1248	.1372	.91
Client Received Parenting Education	-.2091	.1277	-1.64*
Client Received Concrete Services	.0039	.1261	.03

In Treatment 13-18 Months	.0723	.1382	.52
Client Received Family Counseling	.4350	.1279	3.40***
Client Received Casework Counseling	.0285	.1156	.25
Client Received Educational or Skill Development Training	.1630	.1242	1.31*
In Treatment 7-12 Months	.0488	.1282	.38
Number of Different Service Types Provided to Client	.0293	.0839	.35
Constant	-1.8843	.2315	-8.14***

R^2: .3446

F-Ratio: 4.65

Significance: $p < .000$

Key: * $p < .20$
      ** $p < .05$
     *** $p < .01$

[a]Variable values range from 1 to 3:
  1 = client got worse
  2 = client remained the same
  3 = client improved

Table B.1 continued

Independent Variables	Dependent Variable: Propensity[b]		
	Parameter Estimate	Standard Error	t-Value
Married	-.1604	.1341	-1.20
Client Aged 31-40	-.0597	.2160	- .28
Female	-.0694	.1798	- .39
Client Less Than 21	-.2901	.2603	-1.11
White	.0830	.1417	.59
Client Aged 21-30	-.0599	.2073	- .29
Number of Presenting Problems	-.0529	.0332	-1.60*
Substance Abuse Problem	-.3730	.1486	-2.51***
Moderate Harm Resulting from Maltreatment	-.0092	.1762	- .05
Number of Types of Maltreatment Committed by Client	-.1469	.0902	-1.63*
Severe Harm Resulting from Maltreatment	-.2790	.1983	-1.41*
Compliance Index	.1829	.0458	3.99***
In Treatment 6 Months or Less	-.2384	.2089	-1.14
Client Received Support Services	-.0643	.1537	- .42
Client Received Individual Counseling	.1297	.1976	.66

Client Received Group Counseling	.3905	.2287	1.71**
Client Received Parenting Education	-.0595	.2127	- .28
Client Received Concrete Services	.1164	.2101	.55
In Treatment 13-18 Months	.1549	.2303	.67
Client Received Family Counseling	.4136	.2131	1.94**
Client Received Casework Counseling	-.1351	.1926	- .70
Client Received Educational or Skill Development Training	.2417	.2069	1.17
In Treatment 7-12 Months	-.1622	.2136	- .76
Number of Different Service Types Provided to Client	-.0388	.1398	- .28
Constant	2.6327	.3858	6.82***

R^2: .3108

F-Ratio: 3.98

Significance: $p < .000$

Key:　　* $p < .20$
　　　** $p < .05$
　　　*** $p < .01$

[b] Variable values range from 1 to 4:
1 = very likely to reabuse
2 = somewhat likely to reabuse
3 = somewhat unlikely to reabuse
4 = very unlikely to reabuse

Table B.1 continued

Independent Variables	Dependent Variable: Reincidence[c]		
	Parameter Estimate	Standard Error	t-Value
Married	.1307	.1222	1.07
Client Aged 31-40	-.3010	.1970	-1.53*
Female	-.0767	.1639	- .47
Client Less Than 21	-.2589	.2373	-1.09
White	-.0227	.1292	-1.18
Client Aged 21-30	-.2970	.1890	-1.57
Number of Presenting Problems	.0356	.0302	1.18*
Substance Abuse Problem	-.0898	.1354	- .66
Moderate Harm Resulting from Maltreatment	.2769	.1607	1.72*
Number of Types of Maltreatment Committed by Client	.2380	.0822	2.89***
Severe Harm Resulting from Maltreatment	.4197	.2144	2.32*
Compliance Index	-.1001	.0418	-2.40*

In Treatment 6 Months or Less	-.5201	.1904	-2.73***
Client Received Support Services	-.0111	.1402	-.08
Client Received Individual Counseling	-.1155	.1802	-.64
Client Received Group Counseling	-.5616	.2085	-2.69***
Client Received Parenting Education	-.0995	.1940	-.51
Client Received Concrete Services	-.1135	.1916	-.59
In Treatment 13-18 Months	-.3112	.2099	-1.48*
Client Received Family Counseling	-.1662	.1943	-.86
Client Received Casework Counseling	.0225	.1756	.13
Client Received Educational or Skill Development Training	-.3037	.1887	-1.61*
In Treatment 7-12 Months	-.4027	.1947	-2.07**
Number of Different Service Types Provided to Client	.1424	.1275	1.12
Constant	.9959	.3518	2.83***

R^2: .2278

F-Ratio: 2.61

Significance: p < .000

Key: * p < .20
    ** p < .05
    *** p < .01

cVariable values range from 0 to 4:
0 = no reincidence by client during treatment
1 = client committed one type of maltreatment during treatment
2 = client committed two types of maltreatment during treatment
3 = client committed three types of maltreatment during treatment
4 = client committed four types of maltreatment during treatment

Table B.2

Multiple Regression Results for Adult Emotional Maltreatment Subsample:

Full Model

	Dependent Variable: Overall Progress[a]		
Independent Variables	Parameter Estimate	Standard Error	t-Value
Married	.0891	.1017	.88
Client Aged 31-40	-.1692	.1174	-1.44*
Client Less Than 21	-.2308	.3050	- .76
Female	-.0142	.1160	- .12
White	.1594	.1088	1.47*
Client Aged 21-30	-.1654	.1475	-1.12
Number of Presenting Problems	-.0198	.0275	.72
Substance Abuse Problem	-.0783	.1177	- .67
Moderate Harm Resulting from Maltreatment	.0039	.2302	.02
Number of Types of Maltreatment Committed by Client	-.0743	.0588	-1.26*
Severe Harm Resulting from Maltreatment	-.0060	.2426	- .03
Compliance Index	.0930	.0332	2.79***
In Treatment 7-12 Months	-.3124	.1634	-1.91**
Client Received Family Counseling	.0031	.1505	.02
In Treatment 13-18 Months	-.0524	.1852	- .28
Client Received Support Services	-.0324	.1226	- .26
Client Received Group Counseling	.2389	.1687	1.42*
Client Received Individual Counseling	.0491	.1532	.32

Client Received Casework Counseling	-.1044	.1739	.60
Client Received Educational or Skill Development Training	.0242	.1688	.14
Client Received Parenting Education	.1010	.1714	.60
Client Received Concrete Services	.0456	.1761	.26
In Treatment 6 Months or Less	-.5982	.1569	-3.81**
Number of Different Service Types Provided to Client	-.0341	.1075	-.32
Constant	-1.0273	.3693	-2.78***

R^2: .2346

F-Ratio: 2.25

Significance: p < .001

Key: * p < .20
       ** p < .05
      *** p < .01

[a]Variable values range from 1 to 3:
  1 = client got worse
  2 = client remained the same
  3 = client improved

Table B.2 continued

Independent Variables	Dependent Variable: Propensity[b]		
	Parameter Estimate	Standard Error	t-Value
Married	.0958	.1545	.62
Client Aged 31-40	-.2294	.1785	-1.29*
Client Less Than 21	-.3010	.4634	-.65
Female	-.0467	.1763	-.27
White	-.0896	.1652	-.54
Client Aged 21-30	-.4361	.2241	-1.95**
Number of Presenting Problems	-.0443	.0417	-1.06
Substance Abuse Problem	-.0489	.1788	-.27
Moderate Harm Resulting from Maltreatment	-.0613	.3498	-.18
Number of Types of Maltreatment Committed by Client	-.2550	.0894	-2.85***
Severe Harm Resulting from Maltreatment	-.1937	.3687	-.53
Compliance Index	.1403	.0506	2.77***
In Treatment 7-12 Months	-.3515	.2483	-1.42*
Client Received Family Counseling	-.0685	.2287	-.30
In Treatment 13-18 Months	-.0138	.2813	-.05
Client Received Support Services	.0173	.1863	.09
Client Received Group Counseling	.6011	.2562	2.35**
Client Received Individual Counseling	-.0622	.2327	-.27
Client Received Casework Counseling	-.0327	.2642	-.12
Client Received Educational or Skill Development Training	-.0386	.2566	-.15

Client Received Parenting Education	.1189	.2604	.45
Client Received Concrete Services	-.0883	.2676	- .33
In Treatment 6 Months or Less	-.5893	.2385	-2.47***
Number of Different Service Types Provided to Client	-.0887	.1633	- .54
Constant	3.4224	.5611	6.10***

R^2: .2798

F-Ratio: 2.82

Significance: $p < .000$

Key: * $p < .20$
   ** $p < .05$
   *** $p < .01$

[b]Variable values range from 1 to 4:
1 = very likely to reabuse
2 = somewhat likely to reabuse
3 = somewhat unlikely to reabuse
4 = very unlikely to reabuse

Table B.2 continued

Independent Variables	Dependent Variable: Reincidence[c]		
	Parameter Estimate	Standard Error	t-Value
Married	-.1876	.1487	-1.26*
Client Aged 31-40	.2024	.1718	1.18
Client Less Than 21	.1679	.4462	.38
Female	-.1190	.1698	-.70
White	.0935	.1591	.59
Client Aged 21-30	-.2375	.2158	-1.10
Number of Presenting Problems	.0429	.0402	1.07
Substance Abuse Problem	.0223	.1722	.13
Moderate Harm Resulting from Maltreatment	-.1479	.3368	-.44
Number of Types of Maltreatment Committed by Client	.4080	.0861	4.71***
Severe Harm Resulting from Maltreatment	.0371	.3550	.11
Compliance Index	.0847	.0487	1.74*
In Treatment 7-12 Months	-.4691	.2391	-1.96**
Client Received Family Counseling	-.0383	.2202	-.17
In Treatment 13-18 Months	-.3717	.2709	-1.37*
Client Received Support Services	-.0498	.1794	-.28
Client Received Group Counseling	-.6714	.2468	-2.72***
Client Received Individual Counseling	-.0473	.2241	-.21
Client Received Casework Counseling	-.2140	.2544	-.84
Client Received Educational or Skill Development Training	-.0055	.2471	-.02

Client Received Parenting Education	-.0583	.2508	- .23
Client Received Concrete Services	.1884	.2577	.73
In Treatment 6 Months or Less	-.4788	.2297	-2.09**
Number of Different Service Types Provided to Client	.1771	.1572	1.13
Constant	.5178	.5403	.96

R^2: .3941

F-Ratio: 4.85

Significance: $p < .000$

Key: * $p < .20$
     ** $p < .05$
    *** $p < .01$

cVariable values range from 0 to 4:
0 = no reincidence by client during treatment
1 = client committed one type of maltreatment during treatment
2 = client committed two types of maltreatment during treatment
3 = client committed three types of maltreatment during treatment
4 = client committed four types of maltreatment during treatment

Table B.3

Multiple Regression Results for Adult Sexual Abuse Subsample:

Full Model

Independent Variables	Dependent Variable: Overall Progress[a]		
	Parameter Estimate	Standard Error	t-Value
Married	-.0481	.1097	- .44
Client Aged 21-30	-.0782	.1503	- .52
Female	.1147	.1383	.83
White	-.1245	.1041	-1.20
Client Aged 31-40	-.1830	.0956	-1.91**
Client Less Than 21	-.1044	.2607	- .40
Number of Presenting Problems	-.0359	.0205	-1.76*
Substance Abuse Problem	.1380	.1046	2.31*
Moderate Harm Resulting from Maltreatment	-.2070	.1499	-1.38*
Number of Types of Maltreatment Committed by Client	.1243	.0591	2.10**
Severe Harm Resulting from Maltreatment	-.2824	.2155	-1.31*
Compliance Index	.1795	.0270	6.65**
Client Received Support Services	-.2408	.0980	-2.45***
In Treatment 7-12 Months	.0410	.1284	.32
Client Received Casework Counseling	-.0334	.1306	- .25
Client Received Family Counseling	-.1495	.1411	-1.06
Client Received Educational or Skill Development Training	-.0665	.1322	- .50

Client Received Individual Counseling	-.1055	.1292	-.82
Client Received Group Counseling	.1148	.1280	.90
Client Received Parenting Education	-.1720	.1513	1.14
In Treatment 6 Months or Less	-.2448	.1303	-1.88**
Number of Different Service Types Provided to Client	.0906	.0791	1.15
Constant	-1.3229	.2892	-4.57***

R^2: .5129

F-Ratio: 4.55

Significance: p < .000

Key: * p < .20
        ** p < .05
        *** p < .01

[a]Variable values range from 1 to 3:
1 = client got worse
2 = client remained the same
3 = client improved

Table B.3 continued

Independent Variables	Dependent Variable: Propensity[b]		
	Parameter Estimate	Standard Error	t-Value
Married	.4053	.2299	1.76*
Client Aged 21-30	-.3546	.3151	-1.13
Female	.3488	.2899	1.20
White	.0937	.2183	.43
Client Aged 31-40	-.1841	.2005	- .92
Client Less Than 21	.3093	.5467	.56
Number of Presenting Problems	-.1014	.0429	-2.37***
Substance Abuse Problem	.0444	.2193	.20
Moderate Harm Resulting from Maltreatment	.5062	.3144	1.61*
Number of Types of Maltreatment Committed by Client	-.0246	.1240	- .20
Severe Harm Resulting from Maltreatment	-.0493	.4517	- .11
Compliance Index	.2595	.0566	4.59***
Client Received Support Services	-.1090	.2054	- .53
In Treatment 7-12 Months	-.1224	.2692	- .45
Client Received Casework Counseling	.1178	.2738	.43
Client Received Family Counseling	.0285	.2958	.09
Client Received Educational or Skill Development Training	.3364	.2771	1.21
Client Received Individual Counseling	.2803	.2710	1.03
Client Received Group Counseling	.0821	.2684	.31
Client Received Parenting Education	-.0994	.3173	- .31

250

In Treatment 6 Months or Less	-.4598	.2732	-1.68*
Number of Different Service Types Provided to Client	-.1153	.1657	-.70
Constant	2.3858	.6064	3.93**

R^2: .3978

F-Ratio: 2.97

Significance: $p < .000$

Key: * $p < .20$
       ** $p < .05$
       *** $p < .01$

[b] Variable values range from 1 to 4:
1 = very likely to reabuse
2 = somewhat likely to reabuse
3 = somewhat unlikely to reabuse
4 = very unlikely to reabuse

Table B.3 continued

Independent Variables	Dependent Variable: Reincidence[c]		
	Parameter Estimate	Standard Error	t-Value
Married	-.0877	.1569	-.56
Client Aged 21-30	-.2381	.2150	-1.11
Female	.4532	.1978	2.29**
White	.0745	.1489	.50
Client Aged 31-40	.0205	.1368	.15
Client Less Than 21	-.4063	.3730	-1.09
Number of Presenting Problems	-.0154	.0293	-.53
Substance Abuse Problem	.1575	.1496	1.05
Moderate Harm Resulting from Maltreatment	-.1691	.2145	-.79
Number of Types of Maltreatment Committed by Client	.3241	.0846	3.83***
Severe Harm Resulting from Maltreatment	-.3699	.3082	-1.20
Compliance Index	-.0312	.0386	-.81
Client Received Support Services	.2272	.1401	1.62*
In Treatment 7-12 Months	-.1967	.1836	-1.07
Client Received Casework Counseling	-.2212	.1868	-1.18
Client Received Family Counseling	.1510	.2018	.75
Client Received Educational or Skill Development Training	.0905	.1891	.48
Client Received Individual Counseling	.2092	.1849	1.13
Client Received Group Counseling	.1572	.1831	.86
Client Received Parenting Education	-.2752	.2165	-1.27*

In Treatment 6 Months or Less	-.1105	.1864	- .59
Number of Different Service Types Provided to Client	.0678	.1131	.60
Constant	-.0156	.4137	- .04

R^2: .2874

F-Ratio: 1.82

Significance: p < .025

Key: * p < .20
    ** p < .05
    *** p < .01

[c]Variable values range from 0 to 4:
0 = no reincidence by client during treatment
1 = client committed one type of maltreatment during treatment
2 = client committed two types of maltreatment during treatment
3 = client committed three types of maltreatment during treatment
4 = client committed four types of maltreatment during treatment

Table B.4

Block Regression Findings for Adult Clients
By Primary Type of Maltreatment

	Model R^2	F-Ratio for Model	Signifi-cance	Change on R^2	F-Ratio for Change	Significance of Change
EMOTIONAL MALTREATMENT						
Dependent Variable:						
Clinical Judgment of Overall Progress						
Independent Variables:						
Block 1: Demographic Characteristics	.0253	.84	.540	--	--	--
Block 2: Problems at Intake	.0344	.85	.556	.0090	.90	.409
Block 3: Maltreatment Characteristics	.0454	.82	.623	.0110	.73	.536
Block 4: Compliance Index	.0998	1.74	.062	.0543	11.35	.010
Block 5: Service Variables	.2346	2.25	.001	.1349	2.58	.003
Dependent Variable:						
Likelihood for Future Maltreatment						
Independent Variables:						
Block 1: Demographic Characteristics	.0359	1.19	.312	--	--	--
Block 2: Problems at Intake	.0807	2.08	.039	.0448	4.63	.011
Block 3: Maltreatment Characteristics	.1490	2.98	.001	.0683	5.01	.002
Block 4: Compliance Index	.1921	3.69	.000	.0431	9.92	.002
Block 5: Service Variables	.2798	2.82	.000	.0877	1.76	.052
Dependent Variable:						
Range of Reincidence During Treatment						

254

Independent Variables:

Block 1: Demographic Characteristics	.0595	2.08	.058	---	---	---
Block 2: Problems at Intake	.1453	4.14	.000	.0858	9.79	.000
Block 3: Maltreatment Characteristics	.2832	6.90	.000	.1380	12.32	.000
Block 4: Compliance Index	.2962	6.70	.000	.0130	3.52	.062
Block 5: Service Variables	.3941	4.85	.000	.0979	2.41	.006

CHILD NEGLECT

Dependent Variable:

Clinical Judgment of Overall Progress

Independent Variables:

Block 1: Demographic Characteristics	.0381	1.52	.172	---	---	---
Block 2: Problems at Intake	.1196	3.87	.000	.0814	10.54	.000
Block 3: Maltreatment Characteristics	.1324	3.12	.001	.0128	1.11	.347
Block 4: Compliance Index	.1881	4.33	.000	.0558	15.38	.000
Block 5: Service Variables	.3446	4.64	.000	.1565	4.22	.000

Dependent Variable:

Likelihood for Future Maltreatment

Independent Variables:

Block 1: Demographic Characteristics	.0273	1.08	.378	---	---	---
Block 2: Problems at Intake	.1081	3.45	.001	.0808	10.33	.000
Block 3: Maltreatment Characteristics	.1614	3.94	.000	.0533	4.77	.003
Block 4: Compliance Index	.2338	5.70	.000	.0724	21.17	.000
Block 5: Service Variables	.3108	3.98	.000	.0769	1.92	.028

Table B.4 continued

	Model R^2	F-Ratio for Model	Significance	Change on R^2	F-Ratio for Change	Significance of Change
Dependent Variable:						
Range of Reincidence During Treatment						
Independent Variables:						
Block 1: Demographic Characteristics	.0186	.73	.628	--	--	--
Block 2: Problems at Intake	.0343	1.01	.429	.0156	1.84	.161
Block 3: Maltreatment Characteristics	.1212	2.82	.002	.0869	7.42	.000
Block 4: Compliance Index	.1574	3.49	.000	.0362	9.62	.002
Block 5: Service Variables	.2278	2.61	.000	.0704	1.61	.090

SEXUAL ABUSE

	Model R^2	F-Ratio for Model	Significance	Change on R^2	F-Ratio for Change	Significance of Change
Dependent Variable:						
Clinical Judgment of Overall Progress						
Independent Variables:						
Block 1: Demographic Characteristics	.0072	.13	.992	--	--	--
Block 2: Problems at Intake	.0163	.23	.986	.0091	.51	.605
Block 3: Maltreatment Characteristics	.0501	.51	.894	.0338	1.26	.293
Block 4: Compliance Index	.3504	4.72	.000	.3003	48.53	.000
Block 5: Service Variables	.5129	4.55	.000	.1625	3.17	.002

Dependent Variable:

Likelihood for Future Maltreatment

Independent Variables:

Block 1: Demographic Characteristics	.0252	.50	.810	--	--	--
Block 2: Problems at Intake	.0767	1.17	.322	.0514	3.15	.047
Block 3: Maltreatment Characteristics	.1721	2.08	.028	.0955	4.23	.007
Block 4: Compliance Index	.3414	4.71	.000	.1692	28.01	.000
Block 5: Service Variables	.3978	2.97	.000	.0564	.93	.511

Dependent Variable:

Range of Reincidence During Treatment

Independent Variables:

Block 1: Demographic Characteristics	.0582	1.18	.320	--	--	--
Block 2: Problems at Intake	.0648	.98	.456	.0067	.40	.669
Block 3: Maltreatment Characteristics	.1974	2.46	.009	.1326	6.06	.001
Block 4: Compliance Index	.1979	2.24	.014	.0005	.07	.795
Block 5: Service Variables	.2874	1.82	.025	.0895	1.24	.273

Table B.5

Regression Within Blocks for Adult Clients by Primary Type

Using Stepwise Selection Techniques

	Parameter Estimates	Standard Error	t-Value	Signifi- cance
EMOTIONAL MALTREATMENT				
Dependent Variable:				
Clinical Judgment of Overall Progress				
Independent Variables:				
Block 3: Range of Maltreatment Perpetrated by Client	-.1048	.0521	-2.01	.046
Block 4: Compliance Index	.0999	.0307	3.25	.001
Block 5: 6 Months or Less in Treatment	-.3830	.0886	-4.32	.000
Constant:	-1.3980	.1321	-10.58	.000

R^2: .1552

F-Ratio: 12.06 d.f. 3/197

Significance: p < .000

	Parameter Estimates	Standard Error	t-Value	Signifi- cance
Dependent Variable:				
Likelihood for Future Maltreatment				
Independent Variables:				
Block 2: Count of Presenting Problems	-.0524	.0345	-1.52	.130
Block 3: Range of Maltreatment Perpetrated by Client	-.2723	.0815	-3.34	.001
Block 4: Compliance Index	.1225	.0473	2.60	.010
Block 5: 6 Months or Less in Treatment	-.4050	.1378	-2.94	.004
Client Received Group Counseling	.5937	.1809	3.28	.001
Number of Different Service Types Provided	-.1138	.0457	-2.49	.014

Constant:

R²: .2399

F-Ratio: 10.10 d.f. 6/192

Significance: p < .000

Dependent Variable:

Range of Reincidence During Treatment

Independent Variables:

Constant:	3.0084	.2783	10.81	.000
Block 1: Married	-.1768	.1325	-1.33	.184
Block 2: Count of Presenting Problems	.0382	.0331	1.15	.250
Block 3: Range of Maltreatment Perpetrated by Client	.4076	.0778	5.24	.000
Block 5: Number of Different Service Types Provided	.1942	.0448	4.34	.000
Client Received Group Counseling	-.7612	.1764	-4.32	.000
	-.0487	.2394	-.20	.839

Constant:

R²: .3385

F-Ratio: 20.26 d.f. 5/198

Significance: p < .000

Table B.5 continued

	Parameter Estimates	Standard Error	t-Value	Significance
CHILD NEGLECT				
Dependent Variable:				
Clinical Judgment of Overall Progress				
Independent Variables:				
Block 1: Client 20-30 Years Old	.1428	.0709	2.02	.045
Block 2: Substance Abuse Problem Present	-.3134	.0714	-4.39	.000
Block 3: Compliance Index	.0997	.0250	3.99	.000
Block 4: Client Received Family Counseling	.3754	.0767	4.90	.000
6 Months or Less in Treatment	-.2119	.0734	-2.89	.004
Constant:	-1.6797	.0794	-21.15	.000
R^2: .2784				
F-Ratio: 17.83 d.f. 5/231				
Significance: p < .000				
Dependent Variable:				
Likelihood for Future Maltreatment				
Independent Variables:				
Block 1: White	.0644	.1228	.53	.600
Block 2: Substance Abuse Problem Present	-.4617	.1197	-3.86	.000
Block 3: Severe Harm Resulting from Initial Maltreatment	-.2020	.1354	-1.49	.137
Range of Maltreatment Perpetrated by Client	-.1472	.0829	-1.78	.077
Block 4: Compliance Index	.2000	.0432	4.63	.000
Block 5: Client Received Family Counseling	.4041	.1290	3.13	.002
13-18 Months in Treatment	.3668	.1460	2.51	.013
	1.9404	.1891	10.26	.000

Constant:

R^2: .2636

F-Ratio: 11.71   d.f. 7/229

Significance: p < .000

Dependent Variable:

Range of Reincidence During Treatment

Independent Variables:

Block 3: Range of Maltreatment Perpetrated by Client	.2359	.0764	3.09	.002
Block 4: Compliance Index	-.1254	.0392	-3.20	.001
Block 5: Client Received Group Counseling	-.4037	.1507	-2.68	.008

Constant:

R^2: .1382

F-Ratio: 12.46   d.f. 3/233

Significance: p < .000

.9692	.1483	6.54	.000

Table B.5 continued

	Parameter Estimates	Standard Error	t-Value	Significance
SEXUAL ABUSE				
Dependent Variable:				
Clinical Judgment of Overall Progress				
Independent Variables:				
Block 4: Compliance Index	.1489	.0226	6.59	.000
Block 5: Client Received Supportive Services	-.3271	.0817	-4.00	.000
6 Months or Less in Treatment	-.2213	.0826	-2.68	.008
Constant:	-1.4702	.0841	-17.47	.000
R^2: .4083				
F-Ratio: 26.23 d.f. 3/114				
Significance: p < .000				
Dependent Variable:				
Likelihood for Future Maltreatment				
Independent Variables:				
Block 2: Substance Abuse Problem Present	-.2608	.1735	-1.50	.135
Block 3: Moderate Harm Resulting from Initial Maltreatment	.4497	.2175	2.07	.041
Block 4: Compliance Index	.2624	.0489	5.36	.000

Constant: 1.8806 .2249 8.36 .000

R^2: .2778

F-Ratio: 15.13 d.f. 3/118

Significance: p < .000

Dependent Variable:

Range of Reincidence During Treatment

Independent Variables:

Block 3: Range of Maltreatment Perpetrated by Client	.2356	.0650	3.62	.000
Block 5: Client Received Supportive Counseling	.2556	.1170	2.18	.031
Constant:	-.1440	.1184	-1.22	.226

R^2: .1252

F-Ratio: 8.52 d.f. 2/119

Significance: p < .000

Table B.6

Multiple Regression Results for All Adolescents:

Full Model

Independent Variables	Dependent Variable: Overall Progress[a]		
	Parameter Estimate	Standard Error	t-Value
White	.0381	.0602	.63
Client Aged 14	-.0779	.0717	-1.09
Female	-.0383	.0590	- .65
Client Aged 15	-.0941	.0722	-1.30*
Client Aged 11-13	-.1492	.0642	-2.32**
Number of Physical Problems	.0164	.0268	.61
Number of Socioemotional Problems	-.0075	.0052	-1.43*
Number of Educational Problems	-.0120	.0229	- .53
Primary Type: Physical Abuse	-.1248	.0826	-1.51*
Moderate Harm Due to Maltreatment	-.0825	.0740	-1.12
Primary Type: Neglect	-.2862	.0963	-2.97***
Number of Different Types of Maltreatment Experienced	-.0124	.0292	- .42
Primary Type: Emotional Maltreatment	-.2109	.0699	-3.02***
Severe Harm Due to Maltreatment	-.1799	.1050	-1.71*
Client Received Support services	.0956	.0688	1.39*
Client Received Personal Skill Development Classes	.0533	.0589	.90
Client Received Medical Services	-.2058	.0805	-2.56***
Client Received Casework Counseling	-.0305	.0667	- .46

Client Received Temporary Shelter	.0234	.0863	.27
Client Received Concrete Services	.0714	.0744	.96
In Treatment 13-18 Months	.0591	.1225	.48
Client Received Family Counseling	(dropped from model)		
In Treatment 7-12 Months	-.0545	.1081	-.51
Client Received Group Counseling	.0891	.0652	1.37*
Client Received Individual Counseling	.0597	.0633	.95
In Treatment Six Months or Less	-.1868	.1081	-1.73*
Constant	-.9821	.1564	-6.28***

R^2: .1172

F-Ratio: 2.53

Significance: $p < .000$

Key: * $p < .20$
       ** $p < .05$
      *** $p < .01$

[a]Variable values range from 1 to 3:
1 = client got worse
2 = client remained the same
3 = client improved

Table B.6 continued

Independent Variables	Dependent Variable: Propensity[b]		
	Parameter Estimate	Standard Error	t-Value
White	.0520	.1028	.51
Client Aged 14	-.2977	.1224	-2.43***
Female	-.0506	.1008	-.50
Client Aged 15	-.2002	.1234	-1.62*
Client Aged 11-13	-.4400	.1097	-4.01***
Number of Physical Problems	-.0101	.0458	-.22
Number of Socioemotional Problems	-.0289	.0090	-3.22***
Number of Educational Problems	-.0413	.0391	-1.06
Primary Type: Physical Abuse	-.2866	.1411	-2.03**
Moderate Harm Due to Maltreatment	-.2567	.1264	-2.03**
Primary Type: Neglect	-.3724	.1645	-2.26**
Number of Different Types of Maltreatment Experienced	-.1489	.0499	-2.98***
Primary Type: Emotional Maltreatment	-.5461	.1195	-4.57***
Severe Harm Due to Maltreatment	-.3653	.1793	-2.04**
Client Received Support services	.0015	.1174	.01
Client Received Personal Skill Development Classes	.1302	.1005	1.29*
Client Received Medical Services	.0096	.1376	.07
Client Received Casework Counseling	-.2186	.1140	-1.92**
Client Received Temporary Shelter	.2049	.1474	1.39*
Client Received Concrete Services	-.0759	.1271	-.60
In Treatment 13-18 Months	.0856	.2092	.41

Client Received Family Counseling	-.0702	.0904	-.78
In Treatment 7-12 Months	.0564	.1846	.31
Client Received Group Counseling	.2180	.1115	1.96**
Client Received Individual Counseling	.0256	.1081	.24
In Treatment Six Months or Less	-.3123	.1847	-1.69*
Constant	4.0817	.2672	15.28**

R^2: .2481

F-Ratio: 6.55

Significance: $p < .000$

Key: * $p < .20$
       ** $p < .05$
      *** $p < .01$

[b]Variable values range from 1 to 4:
  1 = very likely to be reabused
  2 = somewhat likely to be reabused
  3 = somewhat unlikely to be reabused
  4 = very unlikely to be reabused

Table B.6 continued

Independent Variables	Dependent Variable: Reincidence[c]		
	Parameter Estimate	Standard Error	t-Value
White	-.0977	.0756	-1.29*
Client Aged 14	.1368	.0900	1.52*
Female	.0116	.0741	.16
Client Aged 15	.1475	.0907	1.63*
Client Aged 11-13	.1694	.0807	2.10**
Number of Physical Problems	-.0153	.0337	-.45
Number of Socioemotional Problems	.0099	.0066	1.50*
Number of Educational Problems	-.0351	.0288	-1.22
Primary Type: Physical Abuse	.1862	.1037	1.80*
Moderate Harm Due to Maltreatment	.0760	.0929	.82
Primary Type: Neglect	.2977	.1210	2.46***
Number of Different Types of Maltreatment Experienced	.2216	.0367	6.04***
Primary Type: Emotional Maltreatment	.6434	.0878	7.33***
Severe Harm Due to Maltreatment	.4035	.1318	3.06***
Client Received Support services	.0469	.0863	.54
Client Received Personal Skill Development Classes	.1811	.0739	2.45***
Client Received Medical Services	.1594	.1011	1.58*
Client Received Casework Counseling	-.0358	.0838	-.43
Client Received Temporary Shelter	-.4030	.1083	-3.72***
Client Received Concrete Services	.1669	.0934	1.79*
In Treatment 13-18 Months	-.3262	.1538	-2.12**

Client Received Family Counseling	.0708	.0664	1.07
In Treatment 7-12 Months	-.5573	.1358	-4.11***
Client Received Group Counseling	-.9045	.0820	-1.15
Client Received Individual Counseling	.0748	.0795	.94
In Treatment Six Months or Less	-.6430	.1358	-4.73***
Constant	.1944	.1965	.99

R^2: .4361

F-Ratio: 15.38

Significance: $p < .000$

Key:
* $p < .20$
** $p < .05$
*** $p < .01$

[c]Variable values range from 0 to 4:

0 = experienced no reincidence during treatment
1 = experienced a single type of abuse during treatment
2 = experienced two types of abuse during treatment
3 = experienced three types of abuse during treatment
4 = experienced four types of abuse during treatment

Table B.7

Multiple Regression Results for All Children:

Full Model

Independent Variables	Dependent Variable: Overall Progress[a]		
	Parameter Estimate	Standard Error	t-Value
White	.0576	.0538	1.07
Client Aged 6-8	-.0536	.0640	- .84
Female	-.0163	.0479	- .34
Client Aged 19 Months - 2 Years	-.1753	.1051	-1.68*
Client Aged 2-5 Years	-.0695	.0687	-1.01
Number of Developmental Problems	.0179	.0162	1.10
Number of Educational Problems	-.0242	.0267	- .91
Number of Socioemotional Problems	-.0165	.0066	-2.50***
Number of Health Problems	-.0245	.0162	-1.52*
Primary Type: Physical Abuse	-.1684	.0948	-1.78*
Moderate Harm Due to Maltreatment	.0506	.0608	.83
Primary Type: Emotional Maltreatment	-.3216	.0798	-4.03***
Number of Different Types of Maltreatment Experienced	.0336	.0298	1.13
Severe Harm Due to Maltreatment	.0078	.0926	.08
Primary Type: Neglect	-.1336	.0793	-1.68*
Client Received Support Services	.0507	.0499	1.02
Client Received Medical Services	-.0979	.0630	-1.55*
Client Received Supervised Parent-Child Interactions	.1482	.0537	2.76***

Variable	Coefficient	Std. Error	t-Ratio
Client Received Therapeutic Day Care	.3172	.0928	3.42***
In Treatment Six Months or Less	-.3264	.0628	-5.20***
Client Received Family Counseling	.0332	.0454	.61
Client Received Individual Counseling	.1674	.0750	2.23***
Client Received Group Counseling	.2431	.0879	2.77***
In Treatment 7-12 Months	-.2014	.0598	3.37***
Constant	-1.1589	.1123	10.32***

R^2: .1964

F-Ratio: 5.07

Significance: $p < .000$

Key: * $p < .20$
      ** $p < .05$
     *** $p < .01$

[a]Variable values range from 1 to 3:
1 = client got worse
2 = client remained the same
3 = client improved

Table B.7 continued

Independent Variables	Dependent Variable: Propensity[b]		
	Parameter Estimate	Standard Error	t-Value
White	.1768	.0995	1.80*
Client Aged 6-8	-.0108	.1185	- .09
Female	-.0334	.0887	- .38
Client Aged 19 Months - 2 Years	.0338	.1934	.18
Client Aged 2-5 Years	-.1204	.1272	- .95
Number of Developmental Problems	.0332	.0300	1.11
Number of Educational Problems	-.0851	.0493	-1.73*
Number of Socioemotional Problems	-.0425	.0122	-3.48***
Number of Health Problems	-.0746	.0300	-2.49***
Primary Type: Physical Abuse	.1629	.1755	.93
Moderate Harm Due to Maltreatment	-.1465	.1126	-1.30*
Primary Type: Emotional Maltreatment	-.5981	.1475	-4.05***
Number of Different Types of Maltreatment Experienced	-.2049	.0552	-3.71***
Severe Harm Due to Maltreatment	.2601	.1714	1.52*
Primary Type: Neglect	-.5657	.1468	-3.85***
Client Received Support Services	-.0320	.0923	- .35
Client Received Medical Services	-.1372	.1166	-1.18
Client Received Supervised Parent-Child Interactions	-.0784	.0993	- .79
Client Received Therapeutic Day Care	.5950	.1717	3.46***
In Treatment Six Months or Less	-.3186	.1162	-2.74***
Client Received Family Counseling	.1074	.1010	1.06

Client Received Individual Counseling	.0216	.1389	.16
Client Received Group Counseling	.0118	.1626	.07
In Treatment 7-12 Months	-.0090	.1107	-.08
Constant	3.5866	.2078	17.26***

R^2: .2481

F-Ratio: 7.30

Significance: $p < .000$

Key: * $p < .20$
      ** $p < .05$
      *** $p < .01$

[b]Variable values range from 1 to 4:
1 = very likely to be reabused
2 = somewhat likely to be reabused
3 = somewhat unlikely to be reabused
4 = very unlikely to be reabused

Table B.7 continued

Independent Variables	Dependent Variable: Reincidence[c]		
	Parameter Estimate	Standard Error	t-Value
White	-.0508	.0746	-.68
Client Aged 6-8	-.0197	.0888	-.22
Female	.0731	.0665	1.10
Client Aged 19 Months - 2 Years	-.1251	.1450	-.86
Client Aged 2-5 Years	.0732	.0954	.77
Number of Developmental Problems	-.0476	.0225	-2.12**
Number of Educational Problems	.0413	.0369	1.12
Number of Socioemotional Problems	.0293	.0092	3.20***
Number of Health Problems	.0895	.0224	3.99***
Primary Type: Physical Abuse	.0857	.1316	.65
Moderate Harm Due to Maltreatment	-.0239	.0844	-.28
Primary Type: Emotional Maltreatment	.9090	.1106	8.22***
Number of Different Types of Maltreatment Experienced	.3511	.0413	8.49***
Severe Harm Due to Maltreatment	-.0677	.1285	-.53
Primary Type: Neglect	.5865	.1100	5.33***
Client Received Support Services	.0741	.0692	1.07
Client Received Medical Services	.1692	.0874	1.94**
Client Received Supervised Parent-Child Interactions	.0609	.0745	.81
Client Received Therapeutic Day Care	-.2968	.1287	-2.31**
In Treatment Six Months or Less	-.2040	.0871	-2.34***
Client Received Family Counseling	.0350	.0757	.46

Client Received Individual Counseling	.0449	.1041	.43
Client Received Group Counseling	.0810	.1219	.66
In Treatment 7-12 Months	-.3457	.0830	-4.17***
Constant	-.3850	.1558	-2.47***

R^2: .4630

F-Ratio: 19.07

Significance: $p < .000$

Key: * $p < .20$
        ** $p < .05$
        *** $p < .01$

[c]Variable values range from 0 to 4:
0 = experienced no reincidence during treatment
1 = experienced a single type of abuse during treatment
2 = experienced two types of abuse during treatment
3 = experienced three types of abuse during treatment
4 = experienced four types of abuse during treatment

Table B.8

Multiple Regression Results for All Infants:

Full Model

Independent Variables	Dependent Variable: Overall Progress[a]		
	Parameter Estimate	Standard Error	t-Value
White	-.0638	.1373	-.46
Infant Less Than 2 Months	-.1245	.1748	-.71
Female	.1434	.1070	1.34*
Infant Aged 7-11 Months	-.0226	.1636	-.14
Infant Aged 2-3 Months	.1581	.1746	.91
Infant Aged 4-6 Months	.2278	.1568	1.45*
Number of Cognitive Development Problems	-.0264	.0663	-.40
Number of Health Problems	.0033	.0396	.08
Number of Affect Development Problems	-.0324	.0450	-.72
Moderate Harm Due to Maltreatment	.2618	.1612	1.62*
Primary Type: Emotional Maltreatment	-.6772	.7214	-.94
Primary Type: Physical Abuse	-.5431	.7672	-.71
Number of Different Types of Maltreatment Experienced	.0210	.0918	.23
Severe Harm Due to Maltreatment	.3180	.1921	1.66*
Primary Type: Neglect	-.5318	.7030	-.76
Client Received Support Services	.0517	.1213	.43
Client Received Medical Services	-.1226	.1215	-1.01
Client Received Supervised Infant-Parent Interactions	.0285	.1242	.23

In Treatment 7-12 Months	-.1538	.1428	-1.08
In Treament 6 Months or Less	-.3235	.1372	-2.36**
Constant	-.9681	.6918	-1.40

R^2: .1819

F-Ratio: 1.35

Significance: p < .165

Key: * p < .20
         ** p < .05
         *** p < .01

[a]Variable values range from 1 to 3:
    1 = client got worse
    2 = client remained the same
    3 = client improved

Table B.8 continued

Independent Variables	Dependent Variable: Propensity[b]		
	Parameter Estimate	Standard Error	t-Value
White	.3901	.2221	1.76*
Infant Less Than 2 Months	-.3148	.2826	-1.11
Female	-.2671	.1730	-1.54*
Infant Aged 7-11 Months	.0876	.2646	.33
Infant Aged 2-3 Months	-.1081	.2824	-.38
Infant Aged 4-6 Months	-.3448	.2536	-1.36*
Number of Cognitive Development Problems	-.2046	.1073	-1.91**
Number of Health Problems	.1018	.0640	1.59*
Number of Affect Development Problems	.0176	.0728	.24
Moderate Harm Due to Maltreatment	.0251	.2608	.10
Primary Type: Emotional Maltreatment	1.2792	1.1667	1.10
Primary Type: Physical Abuse	2.4266	1.2407	1.96**
Number of Different Types of Maltreatment Experienced	-.5109	.1485	-3.44***
Severe Harm Due to Maltreatment	.0381	.3107	.12
Primary Type: Neglect	1.0150	1.1368	.89

Client Received Support Services	.0178	.1962	.09
Client Received Medical Services	-.1085	.1966	- .55
Client Received Supervised Infant-Parent Interactions	.0801	.2009	.40
In Treatment 7-12 Months	-.0963	.2309	- .42
In Treatment 6 Months or Less	.0354	.2218	.15
Constant	1.7428	1.1188	1.56*

R^2: .2784

F-Ratio: 2.56

Significance: $p < .001$

Key: * $p < .20$
      ** $p < .05$
      *** $p < .01$

[b] variable values range from 1 to 4:
1 = very likely to be reabused
2 = somewhat likely to be reabused
3 = somewhat unlikely to be reabused
4 = very unlikely to be reabused

Table B.8 continued

	Dependent Variable: Reincidence[c]		
Independent Variables	Parameter Estimate	Standard Error	t-Value
White	.2094	.1638	1.28*
Infant Less Than 2 Months	.0080	.2085	.04
Female	-.0682	.1276	-.53
Infant Aged 7-11 Months	-.3621	.1952	-1.86*
Infant Aged 2-3 Months	-.2743	.2083	-1.32*
Infant Aged 4-6 Months	-.2456	.1871	-1.31*
Number of Cognitive Development Problems	-.0565	.0792	-.71
Number of Health Problems	.0395	.0472	.84
Number of Affect Development Problems	.0824	.0537	1.53*
Moderate Harm Due to Maltreatment	-.2441	.1924	-1.27*
Primary Type: Emotional Maltreatment	-1.1539	.8606	-1.34*
Primary Type: Physical Abuse	-2.4681	.9153	-2.70***
Number of Different Types of Maltreatment Experienced	.4423	.1096	4.04***
Severe Harm Due to Maltreatment	-.2298	.2292	-1.00
Primary Type: Neglect	-1.2828	.8386	-1.53*

Client Received Support Services	.0056	.1447	.04
Client Received Medical Services	.5136	.1450	3.54***
Client Received Supervised Infant-Parent Interactions	.1838	.1482	1.24
In Treatment 7-12 Months	.1375	.1703	.81
In Treament 6 Months or Less	-.0328	.1636	-.20
Constant	1.3923	.8253	1.69*

R^2: .3633

F-Ratio: 3.79

Significance: $p < .000$

Key: * $p < .20$
       ** $p < .05$
       *** $p < .01$

[c]Variable values range from 0 to 4:
0 = experienced no reincidence during treatment
1 = experienced a single type of abuse during treatment
2 = experienced two types of abuse during treatment
3 = experienced three types of abuse during treatment
4 = experienced four types of abuse during treatment

Table B.9

Block Regression Findings for Adolescent, Infant and Children Samples

	Model R^2	F-Ratio for Model	Significance	Change on R^2	F-Ratio for Change	Significance of Change
ADOLESCENTS						
Dependent Variable:						
Clinical Judgment of Overall Progress						
Independent Variables:						
Block 1: Demographic Characteristics	.0173	1.82	.108	--	--	--
Block 2: Problems at Intake	.0271	1.79	.077	.0098	1.73	.160
Block 3: Maltreatment Characteristics	.0598	2.30	.005	.0327	2.94	.008
Block 4: Nontherapeutic Services	.0935	2.58	.000	.0337	3.11	.005
Block 5: Length of Time in Treatment and Therapeutic Services	.1172	2.53	.000	.0236	2.21	.041
Dependent Variable:						
Likelihood for Future Maltreatment						
Independent Variables:						
Block 1: Demographic Characteristics	.0351	3.91	.002	--	--	--
Block 2: Problems at Intake	.1107	8.31	.000	.0756	15.12	.000
Block 3: Maltreatment Characteristics	.2047	9.71	.000	.0940	10.40	.000
Block 4: Nontherapeutic Services	.2175	7.25	.000	.0128	1.42	.205
Block 5: Length of Time in Treatment and Therapeutic Services	.2481	6.55	.000	.0306	3.50	.002

Dependent Variable:

Range of Reincidence During Treatment

Independent Variables:

Block 1: Demographic Characteristics	.0351	3.92	.002	--	--	--
Block 2: Problems at Intake	.0930	6.85	.000	.0578	11.37	.000
Block 3: Maltreatment Characteristics	.3549	20.78	.000	.2619	35.79	.000
Block 4: Nontherapeutic Services	.4023	17.60	.000	.0474	6.92	.000
Block 5: Length of Time in Treatment and Therapeutic Services	.4361	15.38	.000	.0338	5.16	.000

INFANTS

Dependent Variable:

Clinical Judgment of Overall Progress

Independent Variables:

Block 1: Demographic Characteristics	.0672	1.62	.146	--	--	--
Block 2: Problems at Intake	.0895	1.44	.177	.0223	1.08	.361
Block 3: Maltreatment Characteristics	.1411	1.38	.167	.0516	1.26	.279
Block 4: Nontherapeutic Services	.1442	1.15	.312	.0031	.15	.931
Block 5: Length of Time in Treatment	.1819	1.35	.165	.0376	2.78	.066

Dependent Variable:

Likelihood for Future Maltreatment

Independent Variables:

Block 1: Demographic Characteristics	.1133	3.13	.006	--	--	--
Block 2: Problems at Intake	.1469	2.76	.005	.0366	1.89	.134

283

Table B.9 continued

	Model R^2	F-Ratio for Model	Signifi-cance	Change on R^2	F-Ratio for Change	Significance of Change
Block 3: Maltreatment Characteristics	.2733	3.46	.000	.1264	4.00	.001
Block 4: Nontherapeutic Services	.2767	2.87	.000	.0034	.21	.888
Block 5: Length of Time in Treatment	.2783	2.57	.001	.0017	.16	.857

Dependent Variable:
Range of Reincidence During Treatment
Independent Variables:

	Model R^2	F-Ratio for Model	Signifi-cance	Change on R^2	F-Ratio for Change	Significance of Change
Block 1: Demographic Characteristics	.0324	.82	.555	--	--	--
Block 2: Problems at Intake	.1319	2.43	.013	.0995	5.50	.001
Block 3: Maltreatment Characteristics	.2907	3.77	.000	.1588	5.15	.000
Block 4: Nontherapeutic Services	.3584	4.19	.000	.0676	4.74	.004
Block 5: Length of Time in Treatment	.3633	3.79	.000	.0049	.51	.600

CHILDREN

Dependent Variable:
Clinical Judgment of Overall Progress
Independent Variables:

	Model R^2	F-Ratio for Model	Signifi-cance	Change on R^2	F-Ratio for Change	Significance of Change
Block 1: Demographic Characteristics	.0196	2.06	.069	--	--	--
Block 2: Problems at Intake	.0300	1.77	.072	.0105	1.39	.238
Block 3: Maltreatment Characteristics	.0771	2.83	.000	.0471	4.31	.000
Block 4: Nontherapeutic Services	.1203	3.62	.000	.0431	6.16	.000
Block 5: Length of Time in Treatment and Therapeutic Services	.1964	5.07	.000	.0761	9.43	.000

Dependent Variable:

Likelihood for Future Maltreatment

Independent Variables:

Block 1: Demographic Characteristics	.0188	2.11	.063	--	--	--
Block 2: Problems at Intake	.1004	6.77	.000	.0816	12.38	.000
Block 3: Maltreatment Characteristics	.2121	9.69	.000	.1117	12.76	.000
Block 4: Nontherapeutic Services	.2300	8.43	.000	.0179	3.11	.015
Block 5: Length of Time in Treatment and Therapeutic Services	.2481	7.30	.000	.0181	2.56	.027

Dependent Variable:

Range of Reincidence During Treatment

Independent Variables:

Block 1: Demographic Characteristics	.0224	2.52	.029	--	--	--
Block 2: Problems at Intake	.2024	15.40	.000	.1800	30.81	.000
Block 3: Maltreatment Characteristics	.4215	26.23	.000	.2191	34.09	.000
Block 4: Nontherapeutic Services	.4444	22.56	.000	.0228	5.51	.000
Block 5: Length of Time in Treatment and Therapeutic Services	.4629	19.07	.000	.0186	3.67	.003

Table B.10

Regression Within Blocks for Adolescent, Infant, and Children Clients

Using Stepwise Selection Techniques

	Parameter Estimates	Standard Error	t-Value	Signifi-cance
ADOLESCENT CLIENTS				
Dependent Variable:				
Clinical Judgment of Overall Progress				
Independent Variables:				
Block 2: Number of Educational Problems	-.0518	.0182	-2.84	.005
Block 4: Client Received Medical Services	-.1720	.0689	-2.50	.013
Client Received Personal Skill Development Services	.1192	.0516	2.31	.021
Block 5: 6 Months or Less in Treatment	-.1289	.0510	-2.53	.012
Constant:	-1.2477	.0496	-25.14	.000
R^2: .0496				
F-Ratio: 6.74 d.f. 4/517				
Significance: p < .000				
Dependent Variable:				
Likelihood for Future Maltreatment				
Independent Variables:				
Block 1: Client 11 to 13 Years Old	-.3987	.0973	-4.10	.000
Client 14 Years Old	-.2350	.1100	-2.14	.033
Block 2: Number of Socioemotional Problems	-.0308	.0083	-3.70	.000
Number of Educational Problems	-.0482	.0370	-1.30	.193

Block 3: Primary Type - Emotional Maltreatment	-.5318	.1073	-4.96	.000
Range of Maltreatment Noted at Intake	-.1950	.0455	-4.29	.000
Primary Type - Physical Abuse	-.1982	.1284	-1.54	.123
Primary Type - Neglect	-.3413	.1461	-2.34	.020
Block 4: Client Received Personal Skill Development Services	.1691	.0915	1.85	.065
Client Received Casework Counseling	-.2071	.1046	-1.98	.048
Block 5: 6 Months or Less in Treatment	-.3134	.0864	-3.63	.000
Client Received Group Counseling	.2429	.1042	2.33	.020
Constant:	3.8713	.1428	27.10	.000

R^2: .2307

F-Ratio: 13.24 d.f. 12/530

Significance: $p < .000$

Dependent Variable:

Range of Reincidence During Treatment

Independent Variables:

Block 1: Female	-.0216	.0699	-.31	.757
Block 2: Number of Socioemotional Problems	.0047	.0056	.83	.407
Block 3: Primary Type - Emotional Maltreatment	.5902	.0748	7.89	.000
Range of Maltreatment Noted at Intake	.2234	.0345	6.47	.000
Experienced Severe Harm from Maltreatment	.3277	.0922	3.55	.000
Primary Type - Neglect	.2388	.1042	2.29	.022
Block 4: Client Received Temporary Shelter	-.3070	.0950	-3.23	.001
Client Received Concrete Services	.2439	.0818	2.98	.003

Table B.10 continued

	Parameter Estimates	Standard Error	t-Value	Significance
Client Received Personal Skill Development Services	.1298	.0700	1.85	.065
Block 5: 6 Months or Less in Treatment	-.6673	.1333	-5.01	.000
7-12 Months in Treatment	-.6183	.1325	-4.67	.000
13-18 Months in Treatment	-.3688	.1508	-2.45	.015
Constant:	.4328	.1595	2.71	.007

R^2: .4149

F-Ratio: 31.38 d.f. 12/531

Significance: p < .000

INFANT CLIENTS

Dependent Variable:

Clinical Judgment of Overall Progress

Independent Variables:

	Parameter Estimates	Standard Error	t-Value	Significance
Block 1: Infant One Month or Less	-.2930	.1424	-2.06	.041
Block 5: 6 Months or Less in Treatment	-.2396	.1105	-2.17	.032
Constant:	-1.3189	.0652	-20.22	.000

R^2: .0642

F-Ratio: 4.76 d.f. 2/139

Significance: p < .009

Dependent Variable:

Likelihood for Future Maltreatment

Independent Variables:

Block 1: White	.4842	.2064	2.35	.020
Block 2: Number of Cognitive Problems	-.0799	.0707	-1.13	.261
Block 3: Primary Type - Physical Abuse	1.2058	.3405	3.54	.000
Range of Maltreatment Noted at Intake	-.3476	.1077	-3.23	.002
Constant:	2.5300	.1501	16.86	.000

R^2: .2127

F-Ratio: 10.06 d.f. 4/149

Significance: p < .000

Dependent Variable:

Range of Reincidence During Treatment

Independent Variables:

Block 2: Number of Affect Development Problems	.0745	.0368	2.03	.044
Block 3: Range of Maltreatment Noted at Intake	.3590	.0839	4.28	.000
Primary Type - Physical Abuse	-1.0159	.2319	-4.38	.000
Block 4: Client Received Medical Services	.4690	.1231	3.81	.000
Constant:	.1761	.1214	1.45	.149

R^2: .2961

F-Ratio: 15.67 d.f. 4/149

Significance: p < .000

Table B.10 continued

	Parameter Estimates	Standard Error	t-Value	Signifi-cance
CHILD CLIENTS				
Dependent Variable:				
Clinical Judgment of Overall Progress				
Independent Variables:				
Block 1: White	.0978	.0496	1.98	.049
Block 3: Primary Type - Emotional Maltreatment	-.2843	.0624	-4.55	.000
Primary Type - Neglect	-.0696	.0616	-1.13	.260
Block 4: Client Received Parent-Child Supervision	.1287	.0503	2.56	.011
Client Received Therapeutic Day Care	.1835	.0750	2.45	.015
Block 5: 6 Months or Less in Treatment	-.2690	.0591	-4.55	.000
7-12 Months in Treatment	-.1615	.0558	-2.89	.000
Client Received Individual Counseling	.1859	.0701	2.65	.008
Client Received Group Counseling	.2113	.0804	2.62	.009
Constant:	-1.3368	.0681	-19.63	.000

R^2: .1565

F-Ratio: 10.57 d.f. 9/513

Significance: p < .000

Dependent Variable:

Likelihood for Future Maltreatment

Independent Variable:

| Block 1: White | .2314 | .0886 | 2.61 | .009 |

Block 2: Number of Socioemotional Problems	-.0418	.0116	-3.59	.000
Number of Health Problems	-.0871	.0284	-3.06	.002
Number of Cognitive Problems	.0327	.0294	1.11	.267
Number of Educational Problems	-.0470	.0448	-1.05	.295
Block 3: Primary Type - Physical Abuse	.2073	.1673	1.24	.216
Range of Maltreatment Noted at Intake	-.2423	.0494	-4.91	.000
Severe Harm Due to Maltreatment	.3791	.1367	2.77	.006
Primary Type- Emotional Maltreatment	-.5817	.1397	-4.16	.000
Primary Type - Neglect	-.5061	.1309	-3.87	.000
Block 4: Client Received Therapeutic Day Care	.4931	.1584	3.11	.002
Constant:	3.2859	.1368	24.02	.000

R^2: .2233

F-Ratio: 14.22 d.f. 11/544

Significance: p < .000

Dependent Variable:

Range of Reincidence During Treatment

Independent Variables:

Block 1: Child 2-5 Years of Age	.1030	.0749	1.38	.169
Block 2: Number of Socioemotional Problems	.0304	.0035	3.57	.000
Number of Health Problems	.0879	.0213	4.12	.000
Number of Cognitive Problems	-.0450	.0219	-2.06	.040
Number of Educational Problems	-.0494	.0348	1.42	.156
Block 3: Range of Maltreatment Noted at Intake	.3510	.0359	9.78	.000
Primary Type - Emotional Maltreatment	.8481	.0866	9.79	.000
Primary Type - Neglect	.5010	.0820	6.11	.000

Table B.10 continued

	Parameter Estimates	Standard Error	t-Value	Signifi-cance
Block 4: Client Received Medical Services	.1792	.0806	2.22	.027
Client Received Therapeutic Day Care	-.3048	.1195	-2.55	.011
Block 5: 7-12 Months in Treatment	-.3379	.0799	-4.23	.000
6 Months or Less in Treatment	-.2112	.0836	-2.53	.012
Constant:	-.2735	.1023	-2.67	.008

R^2: .4568

F-Ratio: 30.05   d.f. 12/543

Significance: $p < .000$

Appendix C

Legislative and Service Resources for Improving Program Planning

Model State Legislation and Policies

California AB 2443

Passed in 1984, this initiative authorizes the State Office of Child Abuse Prevention to fund two regional training centers and 82 local service providers for the purpose of offering child assault prevention instruction to all public school children K-12 and to all children enrolled in state-funded preschools. The bill appropriated $11.25 million annually from the State's General Fund for a four year period. Reauthorization hearings will begin in July, 1988.

CONTACT: Director
State Office of Child Abuse Prevention
744 P Street
Sacramento, CA 95814
(916) 323-2888

California AB 1733

This legislation provides an annual allocation of $10 million for such child abuse prevention services as respite care, therapeutic services for abused and neglected children, parenting education classes, parent aide and home visitor programs and individual, group and family counseling. This initiative supported 167 programs in FY 1986–87. The state distributes funding to individual counties on a per capita basis with no county receiving less than $50,000.

CONTACT: Director
State Office of Child Abuse Prevention
744 P Street
Sacramento, CA 95814
(916) 323-2888

Oklahoma Senate Bill 559

Passed in May, 1984, this bill created a State Office of Child Abuse Prevention within the Department of Health and authorized the allocation of $1 million annually from the State's General Fund to support a wide range of child abuse prevention services. A state-wide child abuse prevention plan, developed by OCAP in January, 1986, governs the allocation of all resources and divides the state into 17 planning districts. In FY 1986–87, 45 programs were funded under this initiative.

CONTACT: Director
State Office of Child Abuse Prevention
Oklahoma Department of Health
P.O. Box 53551
Oklahoma City, OK 73152
(405) 271-4477

Ounce of Prevention Fund

This unique public-private initiative was launched in 1982 through an agreement between the State of Illinois's Department of Children and Family Services and Irving Harris, Chairman of the Pittway Corporation Charitable Foundation. Each entity agreed to allocate $400,000 to create new service models to prevent the cumulative family problems that can result in child abuse and neglect, infant mortality, and teenage pregnancy and parenthood. The Ounce develops, monitors and evaluates projects designed to addressed these problems, conducts research to aid in identifying causes and potential solutions, and provides training and technical assistance to enable community organizations such as churches, social service agencies, health clinics and other organizations to carry out prevention programs.

CONTACT: The Ounce of Prevention Fund
188 W. Randolph, Suite 2200
Chicago, IL 60601
(312) 853-6080

Massachusetts Child Abuse Prevention Steering Committee

The Joint efforts of the Massachusetts Legislature and the State Office of Human Services established a state wide planning body in 1986 and charged them with the responsibility of writing a child abuse prevention plan. The specific goals of the Child Abuse Prevention Steering Group are to promote the development and expansion of informal support systems; to promote programs within corporations and small businesses which strengthen families; to expand child abuse prevention services within the public and private human services sectors; to insure that health care institutions fulfill their vital role in child abuse prevention; to insure the integration of child abuse prevention and family life education within local school systems; and to develop policies and procedures in the courts and law enforcement which support families and prevent child abuse.

> CONTACT: Child Abuse Prevention Steering Group
> Special Commission on Violence Against
> Children
> State House
> Boston, MA 02133
> (617) 722-1627

Children's Trust Funds

As of 1987, 44 states had passed Children's Trust Funds or child abuse prevention initiatives, thereby establishing a specific funding mechanism for community-based child abuse and neglect prevention programs. A variety of funding mechanisms are used to finance this legislation including surcharges on marriage licences, birth certificates, divorce decrees or death certificates, special income tax check-offs or direct appropriations from a State's General Fund. Wide variation also exists among the funds in the level of funding, administrative auspice, advisory board composition and authority, and program priorities.

> CONTACTS (Alphabetized by State):
> Sue McInnish
> Executive Director
> Children's Trust Fund
> P.O. Box 4251
> Montgomery, AL 36103
> (205) 261-5710
>
> Candee Stanton
> Department of Economic Security-
> ACYF-940A
> 1400 West Washington
> Phoenix, AZ 85007
> (602) 255-3981

Lewis Leslie, Chairman
Children's Trust Fund
P.O. Box 1437
Little Rock, AR 72203
(501) 371-2651

Beth Hardestry-Fife
Chief, Office of Child Abuse
 Prevention
California State Department of Social
 Service
744 P. St.-MS 9-100
Sacramento, CA 95814
(916) 323-2888

Mike Burns
Staff, Children's Trust Fund
D.A.T.A. Inc.
880 Asylum Ave.
Hartford, CT 06105
(203) 278-2477

James Kane
Criminal Justice Council
820 N. French
Wilmington, DE 19805
(302) 571-3430

Anne Nolan
Child Abuse & Neglect Prevention
 Specialist
Dept. of Health & Rehabilitative Serv.
Children, Youth & Families Prg. Ofc.
1317 Winewood Blvd.
Tallahassee, FL 32301
(904) 488-5881

Jack Harden
Governor's Office
245 State Capitol
Atlanta, GA 30334
(404) 656-1794

Jane Pang
Dept. of Health
P.O. Box 3378
Honolulu, HI 96801
(808) 548-5519

Edward Van Dusen
Department of Health and Welfare
Division of Welfare

Statehouse
Boise, ID 83720
(208) 334-5688

Glennanne Farrington
Chief, Office of Program Development
  and Support
Illinois Dept. of Children & Family
  Services
1 North Old State Capitol Plaza
Springfield, IL 62706
(217) 785-2459

Audie Gilmer
Indiana Department of Human Services
251 North Illinois Street
P.O. Box 7083
Indianapolis, IN 46207-7083
(317) 232-1749

Norm Ostbloom
Iowa Chapter NCPCA
1200 University
City View Plaza
Des Moines, IA 50314
(515) 281-6327

David O'Brien
Youth Services
Smith Wilson Bldg.
2700 W. 6th Street
Topeka, KS 66606
(913) 296-7030

Leo Hobbs
Victims Advocacy Division
909 Leawood Drive
Frankfort, KY 40601
(502) 564-5900

Larry J. Hebert, M.D.
Chairman, Louisiana Children's Trust
  Fund
Professor, Pediatrics, LSUMC
Chief, Pediatrics, EKLMH
Medical Director, Louisiana Child
  Protection Programs
5825 Airline Highway
Baton Rouge, LA 70805
(504) 358-1098
(504) 358-1063

Raymond C. Cook
Executive Director
Children's Trust Fund Board
2 Central Plaza
Augusta, ME 04330
(207) 289-2044

Diane Madoni
Governor's Office for Children
    and Youth
301 West Preston Street, Room 21201
Baltimore, MD 21201
(301) 225-1290

David Mills
Executive Director
Children's Trust Fund
P.O. Box 30026
Lansing, MI 48909
(517) 373-4320

Maureen Cannon
Executive Director
Children's Trust Fund
333 Sibley, Suite 567
Transportation Building
St. Paul, MN 55101
(612) 296-5437

Patty Wolfe
Executive Director
Children's Trust Fund
P.O. Box 1641
Jefferson City, MO 65102
(314) 751-6511

Richard Kerstein
Social and Rehabilitation Services
1211 Grand Ave.
Billings, MT 59102
(406) 252-5601

Mona Way
Nebraska Department of Social Services
301 Centennial Mall South
Lincoln, NE 68509
(402) 471-3121

Carol Johnston
Acting Assistant Chief of Program
  Services
2527 N. Carson Street
Capitol Complex, Room 203
Carson City, NV 89710
(702) 885-4967

Deborah Dickinson, Chairperson New
  Hampshire Children's Trust Fund
Civil Practice Clinic
Two White Street
Concord, NH 03301
(603) 225-3350

Jacqueline Crawford
Children's Trust Fund
CN 711
Trenton, NJ 08625
(609) 633-3992

Pat Good
Human Service Department
PERA Bldg., Room 513
Old Pecos Trail
Santa Fe, NM 87501
(505) 827-4047

Joy Griffith
Project Director
Children and Family Trust Fund
Department of Social Services
40 N. Pearl Street, Eleventh Floor
Albany, NY 12243
(518) 474-3963

Jan Shafer
Coordinator of Child Abuse Prevention
Department of Public Instruction
Education Building
116 West Edenton Street
Raleigh, NC 27603-1712
(919) 733-0139

Beth Wosick
North Dakota Children's Trust Fund
Department of Human Services
State Capital
Bismarck, ND 58501
(701) 224-4807

Jeannette Birkhoff
Coordinator, Children's Trust Fund
Governor's Office of Criminal Justice
    Service
65 East State St., Suite 312
Columbus, OH 43215
(614) 466-1832

Terri Gallmeier, Ph.D.
Director, Special Projects Division
Office of Child Abuse Prevention
P.O. Box 53551
1000 N.E. 10th
Oklahoma City, OK 73152
(405) 271-4477

Robin Karr-Morse
Children's Services Division
Department of Human Resources
198 Commercial Street, S.E.
Salem, OR 97310
(503) 378-3016

Nancy Harrington
Department of Children and Their
    Families
610 Mt. Pleasant Avenue
Providence, RI 02908
(401) 457-4519

Harriet Ferguson
Director, Children's Trust Fund
P.O. Box 12468
Columbia, SC 29211
(803) 256-7146

Denny Bendt
Program Administrator
Children, Youth & Family Services
700 N. Illinois St. Kneip Building
Pierre, SD 57501
(605) 773-3227

Diane Craver
Program Specialist
Department of Human Services
400 Deaderick
Nashville, TN 37219
(615) 741-5947

Janie Fields
Executive Director
Children's Trust Fund of Texas
P.O. Box 160610
Austin, TX 78716-0610
(512) 345-9218

Marilyn Sandberg
Chairperson
Utah Children's Trust Fund
P.O. Box 349
Ogden, UT 84402
(801) 626-3300

Ted Mabels
Vermont Children's Trust Fund
Agency of Human Services
103 South Main Street
Waterbury, VT 05676
(802) 241-2242

Ann Childress
Virginia Department of Social Services
8007 Discovery Drive
Richmond, Va 23229-8699
(804) 281-9081

Peggy Friedenberg
Virginia Department of Social Services
8007 Discovery Drive
Richmond, VA 23229-8699
(804) 281-9217

Kip Tokuda
Executive Director
Washington Council for Prevention
   of Child Abuse and Neglect
1507 Western Ave., Suite 605
Seattle, WA 98101
(206) 464-6151

Thomas Llewellyn
Executive Director
Commission of Youth & Children
1900 Washington St., E.
Charleston, WV 25305
(304) 348-0258

Elaine Olson
Executive Director
Children's Trust Fund
110 E. Main St., Room 520
Madison, WI 53703
(608) 266-6871

National Resources and Research Centers

National Center on Child Abuse and Neglect (NCCAN)

Established in 1972 with passage of the Child Abuse and Neglect Treatment and Prevention Act, NCCAN serves as the lead federal agency in monitoring and evaluating existing child abuse treatment and prevention efforts as well as funding annually a number of innovative treatment and research projects.

CONTACT: NCCAN
PO Box 1182
Washington, D.C. 20013
(202) 245-2856

National Child Abuse Coalition (NCAC)

NCAC is composed of national organizations with a significant interest in the field of child abuse prevention and treatment. Among the objectives of the coalition are ensuring the ongoing national focus on the child abuse problem and coordinating the activities implemented by state and local groups within each organization's national network system. In addition, the coalition coordinator keeps the member organizations informed concerning federal legislation specifically relating to child abuse.

CONTACT: Tom Birch, Coordinator
NCAC
1116 F St. N.W.
Washington, D.C. 20004
(202) 347-3666

National Committee for Prevention of Child Abuse (NCPCA)

NCPCA is a volunteer-based organization of concerned citizens working with community, state and national groups to expand and disseminate knowledge about child abuse prevention and to translate that knowledge into community action through sound policies and prevention programs.

Specifically, the committee has a goal to reduce child abuse 20% by 1990. In addition to its national publications and public awareness campaign, NCPCA also implements its mission through the coordinated efforts of 68 local chapters throughout the country.

> CONTACT: NCPCA
> 332 S. Michigan Ave. Suite 950
> Chicago, IL. 60604
> (312) 663-3520

National Center on Child Abuse Prevention Research

In 1986, NCPCA established the National Center on Child Abuse Prevention Research to facilitate the exchange of information between academic researchers and program managers. Guided by a Scientific Advisory Committee, the Center's activities include conducting or facilitating comprehensive evaluations of key prevention strategies; establishing an agenda of critical research questions facing the child abuse prevention field; measuring the extent to which NCPCA realizes its 20% reduction goal; and facilitating the exchange of program and policy relevant information between researchers and policy makers.

> CONTACT: National Center on Child Abuse Prevention Research
> 332 S. Michigan Ave. Suite 950
> Chicago, IL 60604
> (312) 663-3520

Family Resource Coalition (FRC)

FRC is a membership organization composed of social service agencies concerned with family issues and strengthening families through prevention services. FRC maintains a clearinghouse for information on family resource programs throughout the United States and Canada, publishes a quarterly newsletter and program directory, sponsors conferences and workshops, and provides technical assistance to family-based service programs.

> CONTACT: FRC
> 230 N. Michigan Ave. Suite 1625
> Chicago, IL 60601
> (312) 726-4750

Harvard Family Research Project

The Harvard Family Research Project was begun in 1983 in an effort to collect, review, synthesize and dissiminate information about a burgeoning and very promising set of prevention programs designed to provide support and education to families with pre adolescent children. In addition to tracking the development and dissimination of these programs, gathering evidence of their effectiveness, and making recommendations about appropriate evaluation strategies, the project has conducted a national review of family support and educational program evaluations.

> CONTACT: Harvard Family Research Project
> Gutman Library 301
> Appian Way
> Cambridge, MA 02138
> (617) 495-9108

American Association for Protecting Children (AAPC)

A division of the American Humane Association, AAPC is a national center for promoting and creating child protective services in every community. It provides program planning, community planning, consultation, education and training. As part of its role as the Federal National Resource Center for Child Abuse and Neglect, AAPC conducts an annual survey and analysis of child abuse reports nationwide.

> CONTACT: AAPC
> 9725 East Hampden Ave.
> Denver, CO 80231
> (303) 695-0811

ACTION for Child Protection

ACTION is a private non-profit organization dedicated to the reduction of child abuse and neglect and the improvement of child protection efforts nationwide. ACTION offers training and technical compentency building to all child abuse public and private agencies and conducts research on the current and needed standards of best practice in local child protective service agencies. For example, the organization recently conducted a 35 state survey of the guidelines used by states to determine when a child will be removed from his or her birth parents. Most recently, in association with the North Carolina Division of Social Services, ACTION produced a protocal to provide social service departments with a specific method for investigating alleged intrafamilial child sexual abuse.

CONTACT: ACTION For Child Protection
319 E. Worthington Ave.
Charlotte, NC 28203
(704) 332-1030

National Association of Public Child Welfare Administrators (NAPCWA)

NAPCWA, an affiliate of the American Public Welfare Association, was established in December, 1983 to enhance and improve public policy and administration of services to children and their families. In 1986, the NAPCWA Executive Committee accepted the charge from its members to develop a model system for child protective services. Final guidelines, based upon the input of numerous state and local public child welfare administrators, are anticipated by the end of 1987.

CONTACT: NAPCWA
1125 Fifteenth St. NW
Washington, D.C. 20005
(203) 293-7550

National Conference of State Legislatures (NCSL)

NCSL's Children, Youth and Families Program is designed to meet the needs and interests of state legislatures in developing policy and programs related to children and families. Technical assistance offered by the program include testimony at committee hearings, briefings for state legisla tors and their staffs, and actual bill drafting and analysis. The program areas emphasized are child care and early childhood education, child support and paternity, and child welfare services.

CONTACT. National Conference of State
Legislatures
1050 17th St. Suite 2100
Denver, CO 80265
(303) 623-7800

National Parent Aide Association

Initiated by a core group of parent aides and parent aide supporters throughout the country, the Association's purpose is the promotion of parent aide activities which strengthen families, offer support to parents, and prevent child abuse and neglect. The Association has available a comprehensive inventory of existing parent aide programs across the country and is fostering the development of state and regional networks of parent aide programs.

> CONTACT: National Parent Aide Association
> c/o Massachusetts Committee
>   for Children and Youth
> 14 Beacon St. # 706
> Boston, MA 02108
> (617) 742-8555

Child Welfare League of America (CWLA)

CWLA is an organization composed of direct-service agencies throughout the United States and Canada. Members include both public and private agencies. CWLA sets standards for its members to help them provide high-quality social services for children and their families. A catalog of publications and audiovisual materials is available free upon request.

> CONTACT: Child Welfare League of America
> 440 First St. N.W.
> Washington, D.C. 20001
> (202) 638-2952

Children's Defense Fund (CDF)

CDF's primary goal is to educate the nation on the needs of children and encourage prevention investment in children before they get sick, drop out of school or get into trouble. Rather than focusing on helping families on an individual, case by case basis, CDF monitors and evaluates national and state policy and programs that affect large numbers of children. Through its Adolescent Pregnancy Prevention Initiative, CDF has gathered and analyzed a wide range of data on the critical service needs of adolescent parents.

> CONTACT: CDF
> 122 C Street, NW
> Washington, D.C. 20001
> (202) 628-8787
> For Information on Federal Legislation:
>   (800) 424-9602

C. Henry Kempe Center for the Prevention and Treatment of Child Abuse and Neglect

Long considered one of the key practice and policy leaders in this field, the Kempe Center emphasizes the development of treatment programs for abused children, conducts training programs, and offers technical assistance. At present, the Center also serves as the Federal National Child Abuse Clinical Resource Center.

> CONTACT: Kempe Center
> University of Colorado
> Health Sciences Center
> 1205 Oneida St.
> Denver, CO 80220
> (303) 321-3963

National Resource Center on Family-Based Services

Located at the University of Iowa, the Center has been funded by the Federal Children's Bureau to assist state and county social service agencies in implementing home-based family-centered services. Since 1981, the Center has collaborated with a consortium of social service agencies, providing technical assistance and training in family-centered services as an alternative to foster care placement. The Center has produced a model design and implementation system for state administrators interested in initiating or expanding family-based services.

> CONTACT: National Resource Center on Family-Based Services
> School of Social Work
> University of Iowa
> N-240A Oakdale Hall
> Iowa City, Iowa 52242
> (319) 353-5076

Parents Anonymous (PA)

PA self-help groups serve parents under stress and abused children. There are over 1,500 groups throughout the United States, Canada, and Europe. Volunteer opportunities include forming new PA groups, conducting fundraising and publicity events, providing child care service, and working with abused children.

> CONTACT: Parents Anonymous
> 6733 S. Sepulveda Blvd
> Los Angeles, CA 90045
> (213) 410-9732
> Toll Free (Outside California):
> (800) 421-0353
> Toll Free (Inside California):
> (800) 352-0386

National Legal Resource Center for Child Advocacy and Protection

A program of the American Bar Association's Young Lawyers Division, the Resource Center began in 1978 to increase the legal community's professional awareness and competency in the area of child welfare issues and to function as a national legal clearinghouse on matters related to child welfare. The Center also serves as the Federal National Legal Resource Center for Child Welfare Programs, providing training and technical assistance directly to the child advocacy and protection community. A list of the Resource Center's publications is free upon request.

> CONTACT: American Bar Association
> 1800 M. Street N.W. Ste.200
> Washington D.C. 20036
> (202) 331-2250

Model Child Abuse Prevention Programs

Parenting Enhancement Services

The programs listed below are a representative sample of the types of interventions commonly used with families at risk of physical abuse and neglect. As discussed in Chapter 5, the most promising strategies include home health visitor programs, hospital-based perinatal services, parenting education classes, and peer support groups.

> Exchange Club Parent-Child Center
> Greater Jackson Mississippi
> Becky Williams
> 2906 N. State St., Suite 401
> Jackson, MS 39216
> (601) 366-0025
>
> First Steps
> Georgia Council on Child Abuse
> Sandra Wood
> 250 Georgia Ave. S.E., Suite 203
> Atlanta, GA 30312
> (404) 688-0581
>
> Friendly Connection
> Piedmont Council for Prevention
>   of Child Abuse, Inc.
> Ilene Shapiro
> 844 E. Washington
> Greenville, S.C. 29601
> (803) 232-2434

Infant-Parent Clinical Program
University of California, San Francisco
J. H. Pawl
Ward 95, San Francisco General
  Hospital
1001 Potrero
San Francisco, CA 94110
(415) 821-5289

MELD
Ann Ellwood
123 E. Grant St.
Minneapolis, MN 55403
(612) 870-4478

Nurse Home Visitation
University of Rochester
Department of Pediatrics
David Olds
601 Elmwood Ave.
Box 777
Rochester, NY 14642
(716) 275-3738

Parent Linking Project III
New Jersey Chapter—NCPCA
Mary Beth Pavelec
17 Academy St. Suite 709
Newark, NJ 07102
(201) 643-3710

Parents Too Soon
Illinois Department of Children
  and Family Services
Tonya Baise
One N. Old State Capitol Plaza
Springfield, IL 62706
(217) 785-0825

Proud Parents at Park School
Alfreda Clay-Canaday
100 W. Baker St.
Richmond, VA 23220
(804) 780-1746

Teen Parent Connection
San Antonio CARE

Mary Taylor
1101 W. Woodlawn
San Antonio, TX 78201
(512) 732-1051

Young Parents Program
The Boys and Girls Aid Society
    of Oregon
Anne Mundal
2301 N.W. Glisan St.
Portland, OR 97210
(503) 222-9661

Child Assault Prevention Curricula

Over the past several years, dozens of curricula have been developed to teach children how to protect themselves from sexual abuse. The programs listed below represent the most established and most frequently evaluated of these materials.

Bubbylonian Encounter:
    A Play for Children
    About The Sense of Touch
Bubbylonian Productions
7204 W. 80th
Overland Park, KS 66204
(913) 648-4600

Child Assault Prevention Project/
    Women Against Rape
Sally Cooper
P.O. Box 02084
Columbus, OH 43202
(614) 291-2540

Children's Self-Help Project
Phenia Tobin
170 Fell St., Room 34
San Francisco, CA 94102
(415) 552-8304

Personal Safety Curriculum: Prevention
    of Child Sexual Abuse
Geraldine A. Crisci
Franklin/Hampshire Community Mental
    Health Center
50 Pleasant St.
Northampton, MA 01060
(413) 586-8680

Preventing Sexual Abuse: Activities and
  Strategies for Those Working with
  Children and Adolescents
Carol A. Plummer
Learning Publications
3030 S. 9th St.
Kalamazoo, MI 49009
(616) 372-1045

Red Flag Green Flag Program
Rape and Abuse Crisis Center
P.O. Box 1655
Fargo, ND 58107
(701) 293-7273

Talking About Touching
Committee for Children
P.O. Box 15190
Seattle, WA 98115
(206) 522-5834

Touch
Illusion Theater
304 N. Washington Ave.
Minneapolis, MN 55401
(612) 339-4944

You're In Charge
1618 Yale Ave.
Salt Lake City, UT 84105
(801) 582-2398

A comprehensive listing of these and other audiovisual and printed materials which have been developed on the subject of child sexual abuse is available from the National Committee for Prevention of Child Abuse, 322 S. Michigan Ave. Suite 950, Chicago, IL 60604.

Notes

Chapter 1

1. The authors themselves have suggested a number of alternative explanations for the reported 47% decrease in the level of serious violence toward children. First, the method of data collection differed in the two studies. Because in-person interviews were conducted with the first sample of families and telephone interviews were utilized in the most recent effort, direct comparisons of the findings are subject to debate. Second, parents may be less likely to report serious use of force or violence toward their children today than they were in 1975. Increased public awareness regarding child abuse and its consequences may partially account for this reluctance. In addition, it could be argued that the pool of two-parent families from which the sample was drawn is different today than in 1975. Two-parent families, as a group, may indeed be less violent today. Higher divorce rates and a growing network of support services for battered women suggest that two-parent families may include fewer of the most extreme cases of violence. To the extent the children in these more violent families now live in single-parent families but continue to have contact with the primary perpetrator, the apparent 47% reduction may be more a variant of sampling characteristics than real. Repeated application of the methodology to single-parent families will be necessary to identify the existence or scope of this transfer effect.

2. These percentages add to more than 100 because several cases involved multiple types of maltreatment.

3. These percentages add to more than 100 because several cases involved multiple types of maltreatment.

4. In response to such criticism, the National Incidence Study team revised their estimates of the number of children suffering serious physical or emotional

damage as a result of "purposive acts or extreme inattention by a parent or other in-home adult caretaker" to an annual rate of 1.1 million. This revision was based on the fact that the National Incidence Study had not included any reports or interviews with nonprofessionals (i.e., private citizens), the group responsible for over 39% of all reports made to local protective service agencies. (Leishman, 1983:24). Other concerns with this study, including the representativeness of the sample counties, have prompted the federal government to commission a new incidence study to be completed in 1987.

5. Based on a comparison of substantiated and unsubstantiated maltreatment reports, Jason and her colleagues found that urban residence, early childhood, early motherhood, and maltreatment by mothers are not more dominant in either group, suggesting that identification of these factors may very well reflect a bias in who is reported rather than who is abusive or neglectful. In contrast, the study did identify a disproportionately high number of large families and households without a natural mother or without a natural father (i.e., either single-parent families or stepparent/live-in-partner families) among the confirmed cases, suggesting that these may be true risk factors or caseworkers may be more predisposed to "confirm" child abuse in single-parent families. Also, the study confirmed a higher percentage of families known to AFDC caseworkers among the confirmed cases, although current AFDC recipients were not overrepresented in the control group. The similar proportion of families known to AFDC workers in both samples is not surprising, given the recent findings generated by the University of Michigan's Panel Study of Income Dynamics which stated that fully one-quarter of the nation's families drift on and off the welfare caseloads over a ten-year period. The more interesting finding in Jason's study is the *absence* of a disproportionate number of current AFDC recipients in the maltreatment sample. This suggests that the provision of welfare benefits may reduce the level of stress in the family or mitigate against maltreatment in other, undefined, ways. For a full discussion of the mobility of the welfare population, see Greg J. Duncan, *Years of Poverty, Years of Plenty*, Ann Arbor: The University of Michigan, Institute for Social Research, 1984.

A secondary analysis of the National Incidence Study data to determine what differences existed in the characteristics of children formally reported to protective service agencies and those children not reported identified similar biases. Although hospital personnel reported cases of abuse and neglect to local authorities more frequently than did other professionals, they failed to report almost half of the cases they believed to involve maltreatment. Most alarming were the racial and socioeconomic differences noted between those cases which medical personnel did report and those which they did not. A disproportionate number of unreported cases were victims of emotional abuse, in families of higher income, whose mothers were alleged to be responsible for the injuries and who were white. The severity of harm resulting from the maltreatment was found to be a significant discriminating factor between reported and unreported cases only when income level was excluded from the analyses, suggesting that class and race, not severity, define who does and who does not get reported (Newberger, 1983).

Chapter 2

1. Investigating 99 families identified by the Los Angeles County Department of Social Services, Kent analyzed 251 characteristics over nine categories. These categories included the immediate circumstances of the incident, the characteristics of the abused child prior to the incident, the characteristics of the caretaker, the family's social and economic circumstances, the court disposition of the case, the child's placement history, the child's behavior and development following the incident, and the parent's attitude toward placement and casework goals.

2. The frequency with which victims of physical abuse report themselves to authorities may increase with the expanded provision of child assault prevention training in the schools. These programs place a heavier emphasis on sexual abuse, but physical abuse and the right of children not to be beaten by their parents are also addressed in certain presentations. Some providers in California have noted that reports of physical abuse are increasing as their programs spend more time on this topic.

3. Cultural differences clearly exist in discipline techniques, the use of young children as caretakers for their younger siblings, and the use of medical care. Over and above the differences in culture, the variety of family forms and the wealth of information on how best to rear a child make setting absolute standards of care far more difficult today than in an era when parental roles and responsibilities were more universally accepted and the care of children was done principally by the mother in the home.

4. For example, segregating families in terms of the age of their children has been one of the central principles incorporated into the expansion of the Minnesota Early Learning Demonstration (MELD) program. Initially developed for first-time parents, this parent-education support group intervention has developed a progressive service component that provides parents an opportunity for regular group meetings each time their child achieves a new developmental milestone.

5. The most common forms of maltreatment included physical neglect (39%), psychological abuse (20%), abandonment (18%), and physical abuse (15%). All of the other forms listed in this typology were found in less than 5% of the cases, suggesting that further attempts to differentiate among families falling within these more narrow categories may be difficult due to limited sample size unless data are pooled across multiple sources (Bedger et al., 1976).

Chapter 3

1. Burland et al. (1973) identified six such types of psychotic parents: the violent borderline schizoid mother; the dependent, narcissistic, insecure mother or father; the depressed mother who generally requires parenting by the child; the anxious and chaotic parent who fosters anxious and chaotic children; the father who is inadequate as a man and feels threatened by his son and therefore requires total submission; and the mother devoid of narcissistic resources who gives nothing to her infant child.

2. For example, Evans (1979) noted significant differences between abusive and nonabusive mothers in terms of Erikson's initial six stages of development. In his comparison of 20 AFDC mothers reported for physical abuse and 20 AFDC mothers who were not abusive, he found that the abusive mothers were less likely to have trust, autonomy, initiative, industry, self-identity, and intimacy. The author attributed these differences to consistent early trauma in the abusive mother's childhood, trauma that was generally absent in his sample of nonabusive mothers.

    In a similar study, Rosen (1978) compared 60 abusive and nonabusive mothers to determine if abusive mothers have a lower self-concept, higher self-concept incongruence and higher self-concept inconsistency than those who have not abused their children. While no significant demographic differences existed between the two groups, the abusive mothers did express more ambivalence toward their children, were less successful in achieving desired responses from their children, and were less certain about their own life goals. These specific disorders within the abusive mothers were viewed by Rosen as enhancing their frustration with their children which, in turn, led to maltreatment.

3. Commenting on their findings, the authors noted that young mothers in the sample had received a significant number of social services and that receipt of such services may have been key in the low rate of maltreatment noted for this group.

4. These scales included the MMPI, the Schedule of Recent Experiences, the Downstate Childrearing Questionnaire, the Family Life Form, and the number of days the child remained in the hospital following birth.

5. Reluctance to implement such a system is evident in the recent controversy over the establishment of a national registry of individuals who have been charged with child sexual abuse. The ACLU and other civil libertarians moved quickly to testify against this legislation when it was introduced by Senator Paula Hawkins (R-Florida).

6. For example, native-born Spanish-speaking mothers were more likely to be neglectful than Spanish-speaking mothers born in Central America or Mexico. While young mothers were more predominant within the neglectful white sample, older women were more predominant among the black and Spanish-speaking neglectful mothers. White mothers, as a group, were better-informed than the sample black or Spanish-speaking mothers on local politics and on general services, recreational and medical care systems, while black mothers were better informed than white and Spanish-speaking mothers on the local housing, welfare, and school systems. This knowledge, however, was not found to explain differences in the parenting levels within any of the three groups.

7. For example, Barth and Blythe (1983), in their study of stress factors relating to child maltreatment, noted that whether a parent will be abusive will depend upon his or her personal skills and (1) the immediate conditions preceding the event (e.g., phenomenological stress), (2) the prolonged series of changes that the adult is experiencing (e.g., life changes), and (3) the impacts of poverty and deprived social supports (e.g., social stress).

8. The effective use of such a checklist, however, may require more concerted

effort by clinicians. Specifically addressing the interplay between sociological variables such as environmental stress, community discipline standards, and social isolation, and psychological variables such as the lack of emotional maturity, psychiatric illness, inadequate personalities, and so forth, Sze and Lamar (1981) studied a sample of 76 randomly-selected cases from an urban protective services caseload. While both types of causal factors were noted among all of the investigated cases, sociological factors were more often identified by caseworkers as secondary or contributing causes to maltreatment. The most common primary cause cited by the caseworkers was the parent's lack of emotional maturity and patience. However, when the authors looked at the sample in terms of first offenders versus repeat offenders, a sharp difference was noted in the frequency of the two types of causal explanations. On balance, caseworkers noted significantly more sociological or stress factors in their initial assessment of the families while psychological problems dominated the subsequent assessments of these families. The authors concluded that the "de-emphasis of psychological factors [for the first-time offenders] was greater than the reality warranted," adding that the personal functioning problems noted at the time of the reassessments were most likely present at the time of the families' first assessments (Sze and Lamar, 1981:23).

Chapter 4

1. Both Illinois and San Francisco child welfare officials reported an alarming increase in the number of deaths due to maltreatment which involved children who were current or recently-terminated child protective service clients. In Illinois, 19 of the 82 deaths due to maltreatment occurring between July 1985 and June 1986 were or had been under the supervision of local child protective service workers. In August 1986, San Francisco Mayor Diane Feinstein ordered a full investigation of ten suspected abuse-related deaths involving children who were living in county-supervised emergency shelters or foster care at the time of their death. The investigators concluded that in eight of the ten cases inaction or inappropriate action on the part of protective services contributed to the child's death. Similarly, an investigation by the *New York Times* into child maltreatment fatalities in that city noted that 50% of the cases were on CPS caseloads.

2. This figure assumes that the child would be in foster care a total of eight years, the average length of stay for the Maryland caseload, and that the family-based services would be provided for a total of 15 months, with intensive intervention occurring during the initial three months. In making these estimates, the authors projected a 3% annual salary increase pool and employed a 5% discount rate.

3. For example, between 1977 and 1979, the UCLA Medical Center referred 419 families to its Child Abuse Screening Program which involved evaluation by a number of medical, legal, and social service experts. The team confirmed abuse or neglect in 41% of the cases and provided these cases with immediate supportive and counseling services as well as two years of follow-up services.

During the follow-up period, only 9% of the cases experienced reincidence. Evaluating these results, Galleno and colleagues noted that the "concept of a Child Abuse Team is valid and results in a higher index of suspicion, earlier recognition, and hence judicious rescue and prevention" (Galleno and Oppenheim, 1982:18).

Reporting on a similar use of multidisciplinary teams with physical abusers, Barnes and colleagues (1974) noted a 10% reincidence rate and a 100% improvement rate in parenting skills with a sample of 30 families. Elements of the process which the authors cited as contributing to the program's success were the careful screening for those most likely to respond well to treatment (i.e., families who were open to change and willing to have a lay volunteer come to their home); a thorough review and assessment of needs and difficulties unique to each family; and a commitment on the part of all team members to follow through on team-determined recommendations.

Similar assessment procedures and the use of multidisciplinary teams have also been advocated in cases of child sexual abuse (Brant and Tisza, 1977; Giarretto, 1978; Anderson and Shafer, 1979; Faller and Ziefert, 1981; Prochaska, 1984; Hochstadt and Harwicke, 1985).

4. A detailed summary of these procedures is included in Appendix A.

5. Success in treating families experiencing incest and other forms of sexual abuse has also been reported by a number of researchers working with this population. Anderson and Shafer (1979) noted only a 3% reincidence rate among the 62 families participating in a multiple component intervention strategy. The program included initial individual therapy for the perpetrator to address various functioning problems, particularly substance abuse; peer group therapy for the daughter; behavior modification for the parents; and family therapy, initiated while the offender was out of the home and continuing after reunification occurred. Key to the program's success was the coordination of all professionals involved in the case and the establishment of an authoritative position with the family through the courts.

One of the most widely publicized intervention programs for sexual abuse is Henry Giarretto's program in Santa Clara County, California. From the outset, Giarretto and his colleagues have reported significant success in working with incest victims and their families (Giarretto, 1976, 1978). Treatment for participants proceeds through several stages, beginning with individual therapy for all family members, then moving to dyad counseling involving the mother and daughter, mother and father, and father and daughter. This stage is then followed by family therapy, with the treatment package finally expanding to include self-help groups (e.g., Parents United, Daughters-Sons United). Of the first 500 families served by the project, 95% of the victims were reunited with their families, the vast majority (90%) of these being reunited within the first treatment month, and 90% of the couples continued their marriages (Giarretto, 1976). Based on the strong coordination among the project and the county's social service and legal systems, conviction rates for sexual abuse were significantly higher than they had been prior to the project. Of the cases brought to trial, only 4% were acquitted (Giarretto, 1978).

Similar to the Giarretto program, Suzanne Sgroi of Connecticut's Sexual Trauma Treatment Program uses a multiple-modality, multiple-therapist approach to families involved in child sexual abuse (Sgroi, 1982). In her program, the first step is to assign to each family member a separate individual therapist. Dyadic therapy for mother and daughter may follow, and may occur simultaneously with group therapy. An assessment of the effectiveness of this approach reports that the greatest gains were noted with respect to the victim feeling safe from reabuse by the perpetrator (62% of the cases), in social relationships (58%), and in intrapersonal difficulties (53%). In 46% of the cases, the perpetrator admitted guilt and accepted responsibility. Of couples involving perpetrators, 42% were separated or divorced during involvement with the program (Bander et al., 1982).

6. These service findings are consistent with other research in this area. For example, Bean (1971) reported no reincidence of abuse in the 23 physically abusive families provided a combination of group therapy (for parents) and supervised day care and medical care (for children). McNeil and McBride (1979) also reported no reincidence among U.S. Air Force couples identified as physically abusing their children and who participated in six to 15 months of weekly group therapy. During these group meetings, emphasis was placed on developing mutual support systems and on enhancing the parents' decision-making and parenting skills. In addition to reporting no reincidence by group participants, the authors also noted a general improvement in couples' marital relationships.

7. The responsiveness of abused and neglected children to direct intervention consistently has been documented in the literature. In a study of 20 abused children ages five to 15, Green (1978b) found that psychoanalytically-oriented play therapy and psychotherapy helped to improve the child's presenting symptoms, cognitive functioning, impulse control, control over aggressive and destructive behavior, school performance, and self-esteem and trust. In an evaluation of the Bowen Center Project in Chicago, the Juvenile Protection Association (1975) found that the children served by this multipurpose community-based center showed more dramatic social and cognitive gains than did their parents. Specifically, the children, all of whom suffered from chronic neglect, demonstrated a better handling of aggression, less acting-out behavior, clearer articulations of feelings, and improved cognitive development and learning skills.

Working with failure-to-thrive infants and their families, Moore (1982) developed a three-part program including (1) supportive services to parents during the infant's hospitalization, (2) assessment of the family's environmental needs and securing services to meet these needs either through service referrals or enhancement of the family's informal support system, and (3) semiweekly home visits following the infant's discharge. Of the 28 babies served by the project, none were rehospitalized over a 12-month observation period and all of the babies realized significant weight gains.

More recently, Culp and his colleagues achieved significant developmental progress with a sample of 35 maltreated children through the provision of intensive therapeutic day care and group therapy. The treatment strategy involved a six-hour-a-day program for five days a week. Children remained in the program between 4.4 and 15.9 months, with the average length of stay being 7.6 months. The adult-to-child ratio was one to two. Compared to a matched control group, the treatment group, two-thirds of whom were victims of child neglect, showed significant pre-and posttest gains in all developmental areas tested, including fine motor skills, cognitive development, gross motor skills, social and emotional functioning, and language development. Of these areas, greatest gains were realized in gross motor skills and social and emotional development (Culp et al., 1987).

8. Berkeley Planning Associates, *Therapeutic Child Care: Approaches to Remediating the Effects of Child Abuse and Neglect.* Prepared for the National Center for Child Abuse and Neglect under contract No. 105-78-1108. February, 1982b.

9. For example, adult clients included in the National Clinical Evaluation Study produced the following correlation matrix for the study's dependent variables:

	Reincidence	Overall Progress in Treatment	Likelihood for Future Maltreatment
Reincidence	1.000		
Overall Progress	−.442	1.000	
Likelihood for Future Maltreatment	−.272	.456	1.000

10. For treatment projects committed to working with the entire family and maintaining the family unit throughout the treatment process, this intervention strategy is less viable. Breaking the cycle of maltreatment is a difficult treatment issue that involves not only breaking the abusive or neglectful patterns but also cultivating different, more appropriate patterns of interaction and discipline. Prior to the completion of this process, it is likely that parents will fall back into those patterns that are familiar and comfortable. As each of these evaluations has pointed out, reincidence in this context is not solely an outcome indicator, but rather a continuum along which a family's progress may be monitored.

11. The increased percentage of severe maltreatment cases being served by the demonstration projects has both positive and negative aspects. It is certainly encouraging to see that solid success can be achieved with multiproblem families. Where ten years ago the children in such families might have automatically been removed and parental rights terminated, these families are now viewed as viable candidates for treatment and eventual reunification. On the other hand, the focus on the more severe cases places child abuse and neglect treatment projects in the difficult position of working with families that have fewer and fewer material and personal resources. This increase in caseload severity has been noted by each subsequent federal demonstration effort not only among its substantiated cases but also among its "high risk" cases. In the most recent demonstration effort, the "high risk" families were as likely as the substantiated cases to exhibit financial difficulties, physical violence, disruptive conflict between spouses and extended family members, and social isolation

These similarities suggest that child abuse and neglect prevention programs which target their services to "high risk" parents may, in fact, be serving as complex and as difficult a population as those programs targeted toward actual maltreators. By the time families have moved into a "high risk" classification, they have already established behavior patterns and developed functioning difficulties that make efforts to prevent actual maltreatment extremely difficult. One conclusion from this finding is that the prevention of child abuse requires not only a focus on families considered high risk but also a focus on the range of problems that push a family into a "high risk" situation.

12. Of this 20%, roughly half of the cases are those in which the child should be removed immediately. These include cases of alcohol or drug addiction, severely retarded caretakers, and families where serious injury or death has already occurred with one child. The Kempes also note that if a parent fails to make any progress in six months of treatment, the child should most likely be removed.

Chapter 5

1. For example, SCAN (Supportive Child Abuse Network) is a community-wide intervention model developed in Arkansas and based upon the primary use of lay therapists and self-help groups to foster an abuse-free community. The system involves the formulation of clear objectives to sensitize and mobilize public response to families at risk through (1) an increase in community awareness regarding the nature of maltreatment and the existing protective service system, (2) the development of broad-scale community support for expanded, comprehensive services, (3) the development of community standards for acceptable parenting, and (4) the enhancement of local primary prevention efforts (Grazio, 1981). SCAN advocates the use of multidisciplinary teams to assess cases and to train professionals on existing reporting laws; the use of the media to educate, inform, and motivate the general public; and the use of primary prevention strategics to reduce the level of violence in the community, physical punishment of children, and inappropriate parenting.

2. For example, the State of California passed legislation in 1982 (AB 1733) that appropriates $10 million annually for child abuse prevention, with each county receiving a minimum of $50,000. Programs funded under this effort have included community awareness programs, such as community education, media campaigns, professional education, and technical assistance and consultation; general casework activities, such as intake and initial diagnosis, clinical supervision, case management, multidisciplinary case reviews and follow-up; treatment services, such as counseling, parents anonymous, parenting education, therapeutic day care, child development services, and medical care; and support services such as homemaker services, child care, transportation, advocacy and information, and referral (California Consortium of Child Abuse Councils, 1984).

3. The California General Assembly passed the Maxine Waters Child Abuse Prevention Training Act (AB 2443) in response to growing concern among parents and the general public regarding the increase in reports of child sexual assault. The bill, passed in 1984, provides $11.4 million annually to ensure "comprehensive and effective prevention education" to all of California's public school children four times in their school career, including once each in preschool, elemen-

tary school, junior high school, and senior high school. The dual purpose of this training will be to prevent the occurrence of physical abuse, sexual assault, and neglect and to reduce the general vulnerability of children to such attacks. Direct appropriations have been made to 82 direct service providers and two regional resource centers. While no other state has authorized funding for the universal provision of this service, Texas, Wisconsin, Tennessee, Minnesota, and Massachusetts, among others, have passed legislation supporting this concept.

4. Middle-class parents have been found to respond positively, however, to classroom-based training in social competence. Dickie and Gerber reported that parents who received eight weeks of parenting training recorded higher ratings in all categories than members of a randomly-determined control group. All participants were college graduates with normal four-to-twelve-month-old infants. For parents, improved competency was defined as anticipating the infant's needs, reading infant cues, and responding, contingently, as well as initiating contacts with the infant. For the infants, competency was defined as providing readable, predictable cues to parents, eliciting responses from the environment, and responding often and appropriately to parents and the environment. Overall, mothers were judged by observers as better in reading infant cues than fathers. Interestingly, the parents did not consider themselves more competent but did consistently note improvement in their spouses. The authors suggested that a possible side effect of the instruction is raising the awareness of participants such that they evaluate their own behaviors more harshly (Dickie and Gerber, 1980).

5. Olds's methodology involved the random assignment of first-time mothers to one of four conditions: (1) the control group who received only health screening of their children at one year and two years of age; (2) those who, in addition to the screening, were provided free transportation to regular prenatal and well-child care at local clinics and physicians' offices; (3) those who, in addition to the screening and transportation services, received biweekly nurse home visitor services throughout their pregnancy; and (4) those who received all of the services provided to the third group and who continued to receive the nurse home visitor services until the child reached age two. During infancy, the babies were brought to the project office at six, 12, and 24 months for weighing and measuring and were administered developmental tests, using the Bayley scales at 12 months and the Cattell scales at 24 months. During these visits, the mothers were interviewed concerning how they handled common infant behavioral problems, such as feeding difficulties and crying. When the infants were ten and 22 months, the mothers were interviewed in their homes and the Caldwell Home Observation checklist and interview procedure was completed. These provided a uniform assessment of the quality of the child's living environment and parental care on such dimensions as the mother's avoidance of restriction and punishment and the provision of appropriate play materials.

Chapter 6

1. For example, if one anticipated that a given program would provide $100 of benefits to Mr. Jones today and $100 to Mr. Jones a year from now, the total present value of the program to Mr. Jones would be $190—$100 from Year

One and $90 from Year Two, assuming a 10% discount rate for not having the $100 in benefits during Year One.

2. Given this difficulty, the discount rate has a very important influence on the overall results of most benefit-cost analyses. The higher the discount rate, the lower the net values of future benefits. While there is an extensive literature on the appropriate basis for the choice of a given discount rate, current policy analysts tend to choose rates based upon opportunity costs or short-term market indications of social time preferences and thus to emphasize fairly high discount rates (e.g., 10% to 15%). These rates create systematic bias against programs with benefits not realized in the immediate future. For example, assume there were two programs, one of which offered $900 in total benefits (Program A) and another which offered $1,000 in total benefits (Program B) over a three-year period. Program A offered the largest payoff in Year One while Program B yielded the majority of its benefits in Years Two and Three. As the following table illustrates, the selection of one of these programs over the other could depend on the discount rate utilized. A 5% discount rate would favor selection of Program B while a 15% discount rate would favor the selection of Program A.

	Year 1	Year 2	Year 3	Total
Program A				
Total Projected Benefits	$500	$350	$ 50	$900
Benefits Assuming a 5% Discount Rate	500	333	45	878
Benefits Assuming a 15% Discount Rate	500	304	38	842
Program B				
Total Projected Benefits	$100	$400	$500	$1,000
Benefits Assuming a 5% Discount Rate	100	380	455	935
Benefits Assuming a 15% Discount Rate	100	348	385	833

3. As discussed in the following section, this methodology can successfully be used to compare the relative cost-effectiveness of different child abuse and neglect treatment strategies. At least one researcher, however, has applied this methodology in estimating the net benefits and costs of a child abuse prevention project. Armstrong (1983) estimated that a net social savings of $227,880 was realized as a result of a child abuse prevention program which provided the high-risk parents with parenting education and support services and that a net benefit of 112 "healthy child years" (i.e., the absence of time spent in outpatient or inpatient hospital care, foster care, or special education programs) was accrued to the 130 participating children. Both the cost and benefit estimates were based upon the probability of abuse and service utilization as

identified by other researchers studying comparable populations which did not receive early intervention. The total program costs, estimated at $180,000, as well as the costs associated with program failure (i.e., those children who were maltreated despite early intervention) were subtracted from the total projected savings and benefits to arrive at the program's net savings and benefits.

Despite the positive program picture suggested by this analysis, Armstrong cautioned that such cost-effectiveness studies are limited to outcomes that can be quantified and must rely upon "estimates" or the experiences of non-matched samples for generating anticipated cost savings. In addition, the method still poses the type of interpretation difficulties cited by critics of benefit-cost analysis. For example, Armstrong assumed that time spent in foster care reduced a child's total number of "healthy years." Findings by Kent (1976), among others, however, suggest children in foster care may actually make greater progress in resolving various functioning problems than children remaining with their birth parents, particularly if reabuse occurs. Given this finding, time in foster care may actually enhance a child's well-being rather than indicate an unhealthy situation.

4. Although equal percentages of both the adolescent and children samples who were victimized by multiple forms of maltreatment were judged by staff to have experienced severe harm (18% of both groups), a greater percentage of the adolescents had experienced maltreatment for three or more years. Across all four types of maltreatment (i.e., emotional maltreatment, neglect, physical abuse, and sexual abuse), 38% to 53% of the adolescents studied were identified as having experienced abuse or neglect for three or more years, in contrast to only 16% to 27% of the children studied.

5. The APWA noted that 22% of the children in foster care at anyone time have been in the system less than six months; 32% for six months to two years; 30% for two years to five years; and 18% for over five years. For purposes of this calculation, the group was divided into two categories—those staying less than six months and those remaining at least six months to one year. The midpoints of these two categories (i.e., three months and nine months, respectively) were used to calculate average foster care costs during the initial year following the report of maltreatment.

6. Again, this is a rather conservative estimate, based upon the 1982 APWA data which found that the children in the foster care system had been there for an average of 2.8 years. Subtracting the initial year in the system (accounted for in the "immediate cost" category) and assuming 50% of the 133,020 children originally placed in foster care would have left during the initial year, the long-term foster care cost figure was derived by multiplying the annual maintenance payments ($5,400) by 1.8 years by 66,510 children.

7. Gershenson used two assumptions in calculating the approximate cost savings resulting from PL 92-272:

Assumption A estimates of the children in foster care were obtained by a linear projection from 1977 to 1982 based on the experience between 1972 and 1977. This assumes that whatever complex factors were affecting the increase during 1972 and 1977 were still operating for the 1977–1982 period.

Assumption B estimates of the children in foster care were based on the fact that the number of children in foster care is directly related to the number of children less than 18 years of age in the general population. In 1977, there were 77 children in foster care for every 10,000 children in the population. Estimates of the foster care population were derived by multiplying this rate by the estimated population of children for each of the years between 1978 and 1982.

The average maintenance costs utilized in the model were obtained from the FY 1981 and FY 1982 total state claims divided by the total average number of children in care. As this figure represented only the federal share of the costs (i.e., 53% of the total cost), an adjustment was made to include the state portion of these payments. The estimates for previous years were based on decreasing the total by $500 per year based on the actual difference between FY 1981 and FY 1982.

8. In assessing the effectiveness of California's permanency planning legislation (State Senate Bill 14), the state's Legislative Analyst's Office found that the increase in foster care intakes (27%) compared very favorably to the 35% increase in the rate of confirmed child abuse reports. The authors went on to note, however, that a reduction in placement rates is a positive outcome only if the child is not reabused (*Child Welfare Services*, 1985).

9. This calculation utilized a $13.18 average per-client cost of providing a single parenting education class recorded by the 19 clinical demonstration projects funded by the National Center on Child Abuse and Neglect between 1978 and 1982 and U.S. Census data which indicated 360,707 babies were born to women with household incomes under $5,000 in 1982. Total costs for providing 12 parenting education classes to this high-risk group were derived by multiplying $158 (i.e., 12 classes at $13.18 each) by 360,707.

10. Although child abuse is by no means restricted to families with lower incomes, many of the poor health care and stress factors most frequently identified with an increased propensity toward maltreatment are dominant characteristics of AFDC families. Stress associated with poverty, unemployment, large family size, social isolation, lack of adequate knowledge regarding child development, and single-parent households, as well as the lack of prenatal care and adequate nutrition and routine health examinations, have all been documented as increasing the likelihood that families experiencing these conditions, either alone or in combination with each other, will also experience physical neglect or abuse. To the extent that the general health prevention services funded under Medicaid expand the health services and health screening available to newborns and their parents, such efforts facilitate the early detection of a number of physical and developmental problems commonly associated with physical abuse and neglect. In addition, provision of these services has been found to reduce future health care costs. For a fuller discussion of these findings, see *Opportunities for Success; Cost-Effectiveness Programs for Children*, A Staff Report of the Select Committee on Children, Youth and Families 99th Congress (Washington DC: U.S. Government Printing Office), August 1985.

11. These costs generally exceeded those of the actual demonstration projects because the models assume an "ideal" service plan for each client. In reality, projects are often not able to achieve these service levels due either to a lack of sufficient resources or to client resistance.

12. Because service data in the most recent BPA evaluation was collected in terms

of individual family members rather than in terms of the family unit, certain logistical and methodological problems emerged in developing conditional probabilities for the service models outlined in Table 6.6. In addition, the strong influence on client outcomes of such nonservice-related variables as client characteristics, initial type of maltreatment, the severity of the maltreatment, and the client's willingness to participate in services further complicated attempts to generate reliable estimates of the impact of services on an "average" caseload.

13. This calculation utilized a $13.18 average per-client cost for a single parenting education class and a $14.48 average cost for a single parent-child supervision session recorded by the 19 clinical demonstration projects. These figures were each multipled by 104 weeks and by 469,682, the number of women ages 15 to 19 who gave birth in 1984.

Chapter 7

1. A recent comprehensive survey of states by the House Select Committee on Children, Youth and Families found that although variation in the rate at which reports are substantiated exists across states, the percentage of substantiated cases within a given state has generally remained stable over the past five years. Further, other emergency response systems, such as police and fire, have similarly high rates of unsubstantiated calls. For example, only about one-third of all calls to fire departments involve an actual fire and reviews of police time studies suggest beat patrol officers spend less than 25% of their time dealing with violent crimes.

2. Belief in the efficacy of this approach is a central component of the National Committee for Prevention of Child Abuse's goal to reduce child abuse 20% by 1990. Beginning in the fall of 1986, NCPCA's National Center on Child Abuse Prevention Research implemented a specific plan for assessing the organization's success in achieving this goal. Key features of this assessment strategy include:

   (1) Drawing upon comparative data generated by various national surveys to monitor child abuse rates, levels of family violence, risk factors associated with increased levels of child abuse, and attitudes toward child abuse prevention. These data bases include Richard Gelles and Murray Straus's 1980 and 1985 family violence incidence studies; annual summaries of national child abuse reporting statistics compiled by the American Association for Protecting Children (AAPC); comprehensive National Incidence Studies funded by the federal National Center on Child Abuse and Neglect (NCCAN); and the National Committee for Prevention of Child Abuse's (NCPCA's) public opinion polls.

   (2) Development and monitoring of a "Risk for Child Abuse" Index to assess the potential for child abuse within each of the 50 states as well as the nation as a whole.

   (3) Doing evaluative research throughout NCPCA's chapter network to assess the long-term effectiveness of innovative child abuse prevention strategies.

(4) Monitoring changes in a representative sample of counties throughout the country betwen 1986 and 1990 with respect to local service profiles, reported rates of child abuse, the number of serious injuries to young children reported by local hospitals, and the frequency of "red flag" events such as dramatic drops in employment levels, natural disasters, and highly visible child abuse or child kidnapping cases.

Bibliography

Aaron, H. *Politics and the Professors: The Great Society in Perspective.* Washington, DC: The Brookings Institute, 1978.

Abel, G., J. Beckcr, J. Cunningham-Rathner, J. Renlean, M. Kaplan and J. Reid *The Treatment of Child Molesters* (mimeo). New York: SBC-TM, 1984.

Abt Associates. *Impact Evaluation of Twenty Demonstration and Innovative Child Abuse and Neglect Treatment Projects.* Prepared for the National Center for Child Abuse and Neglect under Contract No. 105-77-1047. May 1981.

Addams, J. *The Second Twenty Years at Hull House.* New York: Macmillan, 1930.

Affholter, D., D. Connell, and M. Nauta. "Evaluation on the Child and Family Resource Program: Early Evidence of Parent-Child Interaction Effects." *Evaluation Review* 7:1 (1983) 65–79.

Alfaro, J. "Report on the Relationship Between Child Abuse and Neglect and Later Socially Deviant Behavior" in R. J. Runner and Y. E. Walker (eds.), *Exploring the Relationship Between Child Abuse and Delinquency*, Montclair, NJ: Allanheald, Osmun, 1981.

———. *Summary of Findings and Issues: Survey of Impediments to Mandated Reporting of Suspected Child Abuse and Neglect.* Report to the Mayor's Task Force on Child Abuse and Neglect, City of New York. May 1984.

Altemeier, W.A., S. O'Connor, P. Vietze, H. Sandler and K. Sherrod. "Antecedents of Child Abuse." *Journal of Pediatrics* 100:5 (May 1982) 823–829.

Alvy, K. "Preventing Child Abuse." *American Psychologist* 30 (September 1975) 921–928.

American Association for Protecting Children. *Highlights of Official Child Neglect and Abuse Reporting, 1983.* Denver, CO: American Humane Society, 1985.

———. *Highlights of Official Child Neglect and Abuse Reporting, 1984.* Denver, CO: American Humane Society, 1986.

American Humane Association. *National Analysis of Official Child Neglect and Abuse Reporting.* Prepared for the National Center on Child Abuse and Neglect under Grant 90-CA-862, 1981.

Anderson, L., and R. Settle. *Benefit-Cost Analysis: A Practical Guide.* Lexington, MA: Lexington Books, 1977.

Anderson, L., and G. Shafer. "The Character-Disordered Family: A Community Treatment Model for Family." *American Journal of Orthopsychiatry* 49 (July 1979) 436–445.

Andrews, S., J. Blumenthal, D. Johnson, A. Kahn, C. Ferguson, T. Laster, P. Malone, and D. Wallace "The Skills of Mothering: A Study of Parent Child Development Centers." *Monographs of the Society for Research in Child Development,* 47 No. 6, Serial No. 198 (1982).

Appelbaum, A. "Developmental Retardation in Infants as a Concomitant of Physical Child Abuse." *Journal of Abnormal Child Psychology* 5 (December 1977) 417–423.

Armstrong, K. "Economic Analysis of a Child Abuse and Neglect Treatment Program." *Child Welfare* 62 (January-February 1983) 3–13.

Badger, E. "Effects of a Parent Education Program on Teenage Mothers and Their Offspring," in K. G. Scott, T. Field, and E. Robertson (eds.), *Teenage Parents and Their Offspring,* New York: Grune & Stratton, 1981.

Baldwin, J., and J. Oliver. "Epidemiology of Family Characteristics of Severely Abused Children." *British Journal of Prevention and Social Medicine* 29 (December 1975) 205–221.

Bander, K., E. Fein, and G. Bishop. "Evaluation of Child Sexual Abuse Programs" in S. M. Sgroi (ed.), *Handbook of Clinical Intervention in Child Sexual Abuse.* Lexington, MA: Lexington Books, 1982.

Barnes, G., R. Chabon, and L. J. Hertzberg. "Team Treatment for Abusive Families." *Social Casework* 55 (December 1974) 600–611.

Barth, R., and B. Blythe. "The Contribution of Stress to Child Abuse." *Social Service Review* 57:3 (September 1983) 477–489.

Bartolome, F. "The Work Alibi," *Harvard Business Review* 61 (March-April 1983) 66–74.

Bean, S. "The Parents' Center Project: A Multi-Service Approach to the Prevention of Child Abuse." *Child Welfare* 50 (May 1971) 277–282.

Bedger, J. E., J. Buben, M. Hughes, S. Reed and T. Jones *Child Abuse and Neglect: An Exploratory Study of Factors Related to the Mistreatment of Children.* Chicago: Council for Community Services, 1976.

Beezley, P. "Sexual Mistreatment of Young Children: An Intervention Model." Paper presented at the Annual Conference of the National Center for the Prevention and Treatment of Child Abuse and Neglect. Denver, CO, 1977.

Berk, R., and P. Rossi. "Doing Good or Worse: Evaluation Research Politically Reexamined." *Social Problems* 26:3 (February 1976) 337–349.

Berkeley Planning Associates. *Child Abuse and Neglect Treatment Programs: Final Report and Summary of Findings from the Evaluation of the Joint OCD/SRS National Demonstration Program in Child Abuse and Neglect. 1974–1977.* Prepared for the National Center for Health Services Research under Contracts No. 106-74-120 and No. 230-75-0076. December 1977.

———. *National Evaluation of the Runaway Youth Program: Final Report and Summary of Findings.* Prepared for the Youth Development Bureau under Contract No. 105-77-2000. May 1979.

———. *Resource Allocation Study.* Evaluation of the Clinical Demonstration Projects on Child Abuse and Neglect. Prepared for the National Center on Child Abuse and Neglect under Contract No. 105-78-1108. September 1981.

———. *Child Neglect: Definition and Response.* Evaluation of the Clinical Demonstration Projects on Child Abuse and Neglect. Prepared for the National Center on Child Abuse and Neglect under Contract No. 105-78-1108. June 1982a.

———. *Therapeutic Child Care: Approaches to Remediating the Effects of Child Abuse and Neglect.* Evaluation of the Clinical Demonstration Projects on Child Abuse and Neglect. Prepared for the National Center on Child Abuse and Neglect under Contract No. 105-78-1108. February 1982b.

———. *The Exploration of Client Characteristics, Services, and Outcomes.* Evaluation of the Clinical Demonstration Projects on Child Abuse and Neglect. Prepared for the National Center on Child Abuse and Neglect under Contract No. 105-78-1108. June 1983.

Besharov, D. "State Intervention to Protect Children." *New York Law School Law Review* 16 (November 1981) 723–772.

———. *The Vulnerable Social Worker: Liability for Serving Children and Families.* Silver Springs, MD: National Association of Social Workers, 1985a.

———. "An Overdose of Concern: Child Abuse and the Overreporting Problem." *Regulation: AEI Journal on Government and Society* (November and December, 1985b) 25–28.

———. "Unfounded Allegations—A New Child Abuse Problem." *The Public Interest* 83 (Spring, 1986) 18–33.

Blizinsky, M. "Parents Anonymous and the Private Agency: Administrative Cooperation." *Child Welfare* 61:5 (May 1982) 305–311.

Blum, H. *Planning for Health: Development and Application of Social Change Theory.* New York: Human Sciences Press, 1974.

Blumberg, M. "Treatment of the Abused Child and the Child Abuser." *American Journal of Psychotherapy* 31 (April 1977) 204–215.

Boehm, B. "The Community and the Social Agency Define Neglect." *Child Welfare* 43 (1964) 453–463.

Boisvert, M. "The Battered Child Syndrome." *Social Casework* 53 (October 1972) 475–480.

Boleck, J. F., and A. Kilpatrick. "Abused Adolescents: Who's Responsible?" *Social Work Education* 4:2 (1982) 5–16.

Bolton, F. G., J. W. Reich and S. E. Gutierres "Delinquency Patterns in Maltreated Children and Siblings." *Victimology* 2 (1977) 349–357.

Borkin, J., and L. Frank. "Sexual Abuse Prevention for Preschoolers: A Pilot Program." *Child Welfare* 65:1 (January/February 1986).

Brace, C. *The Dangerous Classes of New York and Twenty Years' Work Among Them*. New York: Wynkoop and Hallenbeck, 1872.

Brant, R. T., and V. Tisza. "The Sexually Misused Child." *American Journal of Orthopsychiatry* 47 (January 1977) 80–90.

Bronfenbrenner, U. *The Ecology of Human Development*. Cambridge, MA: Harvard Press, 1979.

Burgess, R. L., E. Anderson, C. Schellenbach, and R. Conger "A Social Interactional Approach to the Study of Abusive Families" in J. P. Vincent (ed), *Advances in Family Intervention, Assessment and Theory: An Annual Compilation of Research (Vol. 2)*. Greenwich, CT: JAI Press, 1981.

Burland, J. A. R. G. Andrews, and S. J. Headsten. "Child Abuse: One Tree in the Forest." *Child Welfare* 52 (November 1973) 585–592.

Buxbaum, C. "Cost-benefit Analysis: The Mystique versus the Reality." *Social Service Review* 55 (September 1981) 453–471.

Caffey, J. "On the Theory and Practice of Shaking Infants: Its Potential Residual Effects on Permanent Brain Damage and Mental Retardation." *American Journal of Diseases of Children* 24 (1972) 161–169.

California Consortium of Child Abuse Councils. *Emphasis on Child Abuse Prevention in California*. Sacramento: CCCAC, 1984.

Cameron, J. R. "Parental Treatment, Children's Temperament, and the Risk of Childhood Behavioral Problems (1) Relationship Between Parental Characteristics and Changes in Children's Temperament over Time." *American Journal of Orthopsychiatry* 47:4 (October 1977) 568–576.

——. "Parental Treatment, Children's Temperament, and the Risk of Childhood Behavioral Problems (2) Initial Temperament, Parent Attitudes, and the Incidence and Form of Behavioral Problems." *American Journal of Orthopsychiatry* 48:1 (January 1978) 140–147.

Carr, A. "A Report to the Administration for Children, Youth and Families, National Center on Child Abuse and Neglect—Some Preliminary Findings on the Association Between Child Maltreatment and Juvenile Misconduct in Eight New York Counties." Unpublished report, University of Rhode Island (October 20, 1977).

Cherry, B. J., and A. M. Kirby. "Obstacles to the Delivery of Medical Care to Children of Neglecting Parents." *American Journal of Public Health* 61 (March 1971) 568–573.

Child Welfare League of America. *Too Young to Run: The Status of Child Abuse in America*. New York: The Child Welfare League of America, 1986.

Child Welfare Services: A Review of the Effects of the 1982 Reforms on Abused and Neglected Children and Their Families. Report prepared by the Legislative Analyst to the State of California General Assembly. May 1985.

Cicchetti, D., and R. Rizley. "Developmental Perspectives on the Etiology, Intergenerational Transmission, and Sequence of Child Maltreatment." *New Directions for Child Development* 11 (1981) 31–55.

Cohn, A. "Effective Treatment of Child Abuse and Neglect." *Social Work* 24: 6 (November 1979) 513–519.

———. *An Approach to Preventing Child Abuse.* Chicago: National Committee for Prevention of Child Abuse, 1983.

———, and Beverly DeGraaf. "Assessing Case Management in the Child Abuse Field." *Journal of Social Service Research* 5:1/2 (1982) 29–43.

Coleman, K. H. "Conjugal Violence: What 33 Men Report." *Journal of Marital and Family Therapy* 6:2 (1980) 207–213.

Collins, J. *Child Sexual Abuse Prevention Materials: Evaluation Report.* Report submitted to the U.S. Department of Health and Human Services, Office of Human Development Services, Administration of Children, Youth and Families, June 1986.

Commission on the Enforcement of Child Abuse Laws—Final Report. Submitted to the State of California Attorney General John K. Van de Kamp, April 1985.

Conte, J., C. Rosen, L. Saperstein, and R. Shermack. "An Evaluation of a Program to Prevent the Sexual Victimization of Young Children." *Child Abuse and Neglect* 9:3 (1985) 329–334.

Coolsen, P. "Relationship of Child Abuse to the Workplace: Employer-Based Strategies for Prevention." Working Paper No. 4. Chicago: National Committee for Prevention of Child Abuse, 1982.

Coughlin, B. *Church and State in Social Welfare.* New York: Columbia University Press, 1965.

Culp, R., J. Heide, M. T. Richardson "Maltreated Children's Developmental Scars: Treatment Versus Non-Treatment." *Child Abuse and Neglect* 11:1 (1987) 29–34.

Curry, B. "Incest Victims Seek Redress in Lawsuits." *Fort Worth, Texas Star Telegram* (May 26, 1982).

Daro, D., and L. Mitchel. *Deaths Due to Maltreatment Soar: The Results of the Eighth Semi-Annual Fifty State Survey.* Chicago: National Committee for Prevention of Child Abuse, 1987a.

———. *Public Attitudes and Actions Regarding Child Abuse and Its Prevention.* Chicago: National Committee for Prevention of Child Abuse, 1987b.

Dawson, P., J. Robinson, and C. Johnson. "Informal Social Support as an Intervention." *Zero to Three: Bulletin of the National Center for Clinical Infant Programs* 3:2 (1982) 1–5.

Dean, D., "Emotional Abuse of Children." *Children Today* 8 (July-August 1979) 18–20, 37.

DeFrancis, V. *Child Abuse Legislation in the 1970's.* Denver: American Humane Association, 1970. Revised 1974.

Delson, N., and M. Clark. "Group Therapy with Sexually Molested Children." *Child Welfare* 60 (1981) 175–182.

Delsordo, J. "Protective Casework for Abused Children." *Children* 1 (November-December 1963) 46–51.

DePanfilis, D. "Clients Who Refer Themselves to Child Protective Services." *Children Today* 11:2 (March-April 1982) 21–25.

Dickie, J., and S. Gerber. "Training In Social Competence: The Effects on Mothers, Fathers and Infants." *Child Development* 51 (1980) 1248–1251.

Downer, A. "Evaluation of Talking About Touching." Unpublished manuscript (Author, P.O. Box 15190, Seattle, WA 98115), 1984.

E. M. White & Co., Inc. *Analysis of Client Case Reports.* Evaluation of the Service Improvement Grants. Prepared for the National Center on Child Abuse and Neglect under Contract No. 105-78-1107. October 1981.

Egeland, B., A. Sraufe, and M. Erickson. "The Development of Consequences of Different Patterns of Maltreatment." *Child Abuse and Neglect* 7:4 (1983) 459–469.

Elmer, E. "Hazards in Determining Child Abuse." *Child Welfare* 45 (January 1966) 28–33.

———. "A Follow-Up of Traumatized Children." *Pediatrics* 59 (February 1977) 273–279.

———. *Fragile Families, Troubled Children: The Aftermath of Infant Trauma.* Pittsburgh: University of Pittsburgh Press, 1977.

Epstein, A., and D. Weikart. "The Ypsilanti-Carnegie Infant Education Project: Longitudinal Follow-Up." *Monographs of the High Scope Educational Research Foundation* 6 (1979).

Eron, L., R. Huesmann, P. Brice, P. Fischer, and R. Mermelstein. "Age Trends in the Development of Aggression, Sex Typing, and Related Television Habits." *Developmental Psychology,* 19:1 (1983) 71–77.

Evans, A. L. "An Eriksonian Measure of Personality Development in Child-Abusing Mothers." *Psychological Reports* 44 (June 1979) 963–966.

Faller, K., and M. Ziefert. "The Role of Social Workers in Multidisciplinary Collaboration." In K. Faller (ed.), *Social Work with Abused and Neglected Children: A Manual of Interdisciplinary Practice.* New York: Free Press, 1981.

Fanshel, D. "Parental Failure and Consequences for Children." *American Journal of Public Health* 65:6 (June 1975) 604–612.

Field, T., S. Widmayer, S. Stringer, and E. Ignatoff. "Teenage, Lower-Class, Black Mothers and Their Preterm Infants: An Intervention and Developmental Follow-Up." *Child Development* 5 (1980) 426–436.

Finkelhor, D. *Child Sexual Abuse: New Theory and Research.* New York: Free Press, 1984.

———. *Sexually Victimized Children.* New York: Free Press, 1979.

Folks, H. *The Care of Destitute, Neglected and Delinquent Children.* New York: Macmillan, 1902.

Fontana, V. "Further Reflections on Maltreatment of Children." *New York State Journal of Medicine* 68 (1968) 2214–2215.

Fritsche, N. "States Are Sued For Non-Compliance With Nation's Child Welfare Policies." *NAFFC Newsletter* (May 1986) 5.

Fritz, M. "Parents Anonymous: Helping Clients to Accept Professional Services, A Personal Opinion." *Child Abuse and Neglect* 10 (1986) 121–123.

Frost, N. "The Rights of Emotionally Abused Children (editorial)." *The Journal of Pediatrics* 101:2 (August 1982) 215–216.

Friedman, S. B., and C. W. Morse. "Child Abuse: A Five-Year Follow-up of Early

Case Findings in the Emergency Department. *Pediatrics* 54 (October 1974) 404–410.

Gabinet, L. "Prevention of Child Abuse and Neglect in an Inner-City Population: II. The Program and the Results." *Child Abuse and Neglect* 3:3/4 (1979) 809–817.

Gaines, R., A. Sangrund, A. Green, and E. Power. "Etiological Factors in Child Maltreatment: A Multivariate Study of Abusing and Neglecting and Normal Parents." *Journal of Abnormal Psychology* 87 (October 1978) 531–540.

Galleno, H., and W. Oppenheim "The Battered Child Syndrome Revisited." *Clinical Orthopaedics and Related Research* 162 (January-February 1982) 11–19.

Garbarino, J. "The Human Ecology of Child Maltreatment: A Conceptual Model for Research." *Journal of Marriage and the Family* 39 (November 1977) 721–735.

——. "What We Know About Child Maltreatment." *Children and Youth Services Review* 5:1 (1983) 3–6.

——, and A. Garbarino. *Emotional Maltreatment of Children.* Chicago: National Committee for Prevention of Child Abuse, 1986.

——, and N. Jacobson. "Youth Helping Youth in Cases of Maltreatment of Adolescents." *Child Welfare* 57:8 (September-October 1978) 505–510.

Gaylin, W., I. Glasser, S. Marcus and D. Rothman *Doing Good: The Limits of Benevolence.* New York: Pantheon Books, 1978.

Gebhard, P., J. Gagnon, W. Pomeroy, and C. Christenson. *Sex Offenders: An Analysis of Types.* New York: Harper & Row, 1965.

Gelles, R. "Child Abuse As Psychopathology: A Sociological Critique and Reformation." *American Journal of Orthopsychiatry* 43 (July, 1973) 611–621.

Gelles, R. *Family Violence: Sage Library of Social Research* Vol. 84. Beverly Hills, CA: Sage, 1979.

Germain, C. "Space: An Ecological Variable in Social Work Practice." *Social Casework* 59 (1978) 515–522.

Gershenson, C. "The Cost Saving Impact of Permanency Planning." *Child Welfare Research Notes* No. 6 Washington, DC: Department of Health and Human Services Administration for Children, Youth and Families. April, 1984.

Giarretto, H. "The Treatment of Father-Daughter Incest: A Psychological Approach." *Children Today* 5 (1976) 2–5, 34–35.

——. "Humanistic Treatment of Father-Daughter Incest." *Journal of Humanistic Psychology* 18 (Fall 1978) 59–76.

Gibson, T., and M. R. Lewis. "Sowing the Seeds of Trouble: An Historical Analysis of Compliance Structures in Child Welfare." *Journal of Sociology and Social Work* 7:5 (1980) 679–707.

Gil, D. *Violence Against Children.* Cambridge, MA: Harvard University Press, 1970.

——. "Violence Against Children." *Journal of Marriage and the Family* 33 (November 1971) 637–648.

——. "Unraveling Child Abuse." *American Journal of Orthopsychiatry* 45 (April 1975) 346–256.

———. "The United States versus Child Abuse" in L. Pelton (ed.), *Social Context of Child Abuse and Neglect*. New York: Human Services Press, 1981.

Gil, E. "The Child Abuse Reporting System: Dilemmas for Community-Based Treatment and Prevention Agencies." Paper presented at the first Public Policy Seminar sponsored by the Family Welfare Research Group, School of Social Welfare, University of California, Berkeley, May 20, 1985.

Gilbert, N. *Capitalism and the Welfare State*. New Haven: Yale University Press, 1983.

Giovannoni, J. M. "Parental Mistreatment: Perpetrators and Victims." *Journal of Marriage and the Family* 33 (November 1971) 649–657.

———. "Prevention of Child Abuse and Neglect: Research and Policy Issues." *Social Work Research and Abstracts* 18:3 (1982) 23–31.

———, and R. Becerra. *Defining Child Abuse*. New York: Free Press, 1979.

———, and A. Billingsley. "Child Neglect Among the Poor: A Study of Parental Adequacy in Families of Three Ethnic Groups." *Child Welfare* 49 (April 1970) 196–204.

Gladston, R. "Observations on Children Who Have Been Physically Abused and Their Parents." *American Journal of Psychiatry* 122 (April 1965) 440–443.

Goldson, E., R. Cadol, M. Fitch, and H. J. Umdauf, Jr. "Nonaccidental Trauma and Failure to Thrive." *American Journal of Diseases of Children* 130 (May 1976) 490–492.

Gray, D. R. "Physical Child Abuse: A Review of All Cases Seen at Sacramento Medical Center in 1975." *The Western Journal of Medicine* 129 (December 1978) 461–464.

Gray, E. *Final Report: Collaborative Research of Community and Minority Group Action to Prevent Child Abuse and Neglect, Vol. 1: Perinatal Interventions*. Chicago: National Committee for Prevention of Child Abuse, 1983.

———. *What Have We Learned About Preventing Child Abuse: An Overview of the "Community and Minority Group Action to Prevent Child Abuse and Neglect" Program*. Chicago: National Committee for Prevention of Child Abuse, 1983.

———, and J. DiLeonardi. *Evaluating Child Abuse Prevention Programs*. Chicago: National Committee for Prevention of Child Abuse, 1982.

Gray, J., C. A. Cutler, J. G. Dean, and C. H. Kempe. "Prediction and Prevention of Child Abuse and Neglect." *Journal of Social Issues* 35:2 (1979) 127–139.

Gray, S., and K. Ruttle. "The Family-Oriented Home Visiting Program: A Longitudinal Study." *Genetic Psychology Monographs* 102 (1980) 299–316.

Grazio, T. "New Perspectives on Child Abuse/Neglect Community Education." *Child Welfare* 60:5 (1981) 679–707.

Green, A. H. "A Psychodynamic Approach to the Study and Treatment of Child-Abusing Parents." *Journal of the American Academy of Child Psychology* 15 (Summer 1976) 414–442.

———. "Self-Destructive Behavior in Battered Children." *American Journal of Psychiatry* 135 (1978a) 579–582.

———. "Psychiatric Treatment of Abused Children." *Journal of the American Academy of Child Psychiatry* 17 (Spring 1978b) 356–371.

———, R. W. Gaines, and A. Sandgrund. "Child Abuse: Pathological Syndrome of Family Interaction." *American Journal of Psychiatry* 131 (August 1974) 882–886.

Green, F. "Child Abuse and Neglect: A Priority Problem for the Private Physician. Symposium on Childhood Trauma." *Pediatric Clinic of North America* 22 (1975) 329.

Green, M., and R. J. Haggerty. *Ambulatory Pediatrics.* Philadelphia: W. B. Saunders, 1968.

Greene, N. B. "A View of Family Pathology Involving Child Molest—From a Juvenile Probation Perspective." *Juvenile Justice* (February 1977) 29–34.

Gregg, G. S., and E. Elmer. "Infant Injuries: Accident or Abused?" *Pediatrics* 44 (1969) 434–439.

Groth, N. A. "Treatment of the Sexual Offender in a Correctional Institution" in J. Greer and I. Stuart (eds.), *The Sexual Aggressor: Current Perspectives on Treatment.* New York: Van Nostrand Reinhold, 1983.

Groth, N., and Burgess, A. "Sexual Trauma in the Life Histories of Rapists and Child Molesters." *Victimology: An International Journal* 4 (1979) 10–16.

Gutierres, S., and J. Reich. "A Developmental Perspective on Runaway Behavior: Its Relationship to Child Abuse." *Child Welfare* 60 (1981) 89–94.

Guevarra, L. "Abused Orphan, 7, Awarded $70,000." *San Francisco Examiner* (April 29, 1983).

Gullotta, T. P., and K. C. Donohue. "Corporate Families: Implications for Prevention Intervention." *Social Casework* 62:2 (1981) 109–114.

Gutelius, M., A. Kirsch, S. MacDonald, M. Brooks and T. McErlean. "Controlled Study of Child Health Supervision: Behavior Results." *Pediatrics* 60 (1977) 294–304.

Gutheil, T. G. "Multiple Overt Incest as Family Defense Against Loss." *Family Process* 16 (1975) 105–116.

Guyer, M. J. "Child Abuse and Neglect Statutes: Legal and Clinical Implications." *American Journal of Orthopsychiatry* 52:1 (January 1982) 73–81.

Haase, C., C. Magaz, M. Lazoritz, and J. Chiaro. "Clinical Experiences of the Therapeutic Group Program for Sexually Abused Preschool Children." Unpublished manuscript, Child Protection Team, Orlando Regional Medical Center, Orlando, FL. 1982.

Hall, M., A. DeLaCruz and P. Russell "Working with Neglecting Families." *Children Today* 11:2 (March-April 1982) 6–9, 36.

Halpren, R. "Lack of Effects for Home-Based Early Interventions? Some Possible Explanations." *American Journal of Orthopsychiatry* 54:1 (January 1984) 33–42.

———. "Home-Based Early Intervention: Dimension of Current Practice" *Child Welfare* 65:4 (August 1986) 387–398.

——— and M. Larner. "Lay Family Support During Pregnancy and Infancy: The Child Survival/Fair Start Initiative." *Infant Mental Health Journal* forthcoming.

Harling, P. R., and J. K. Haines. "Specialized Foster Homes for Severely Mistreated Children." *Children Today* 9:4 (1980) 16–18.

Haugaard, J., and B. Hokanson. *Measuring the Cost-Effectiveness of Family Based Services and Out-of-Home Care.* Prepared by the National Resource Center on Family-Based Services for the Maryland Department of Human Resources, Office of Children, Youth and Families, Department of Health and Human Resources under Grant 90-CW659/02. June 1983.

Helfer, R. E. "The Etiology of Child Abuse." *Pediatrics* 51 (April 1973) 777–779.

——. *The Diagnostic Process and Treatment Programs.* Washington, DC: U.S. Department of Health, Education and Welfare, 1975.

——. "A Review of the Literature on the Prevention of Child Abuse and Neglect." *Child Abuse and Neglect* 6 (1982) 251–261.

Herrenkohl, E. C., and R. C. Herrenkohl. "A Comparison of Abused Children and Their Nonabused Siblings." *Journal of the American Academy of Child Psychology* 18 (Spring 1979) 260–269.

Herrenkohl, R., E. Herrenkohl, B. Egolf and M. Seech "The Repetition of Child Abuse: How Frequently Does It Occur?" *Child Abuse and Neglect* 3:1 (1979) 67–72.

Hindman, M. "Child Abuse and Neglect: The Alcohol Connection." *Alcohol Health and Research World* 1:3 (1979) 67–72.

Hochstadt, N. J., and N. J. Harwicke, "How Effective Is the Multidisciplinary Approach: A Follow-up Study." *Child Abuse and Neglect* 9:3 (1985) 365–372.

Hornick, J. P., and Clarke, M. E. "A Cost-Effectiveness Evaluation of Lay Therapy Treatment for Child Abusing and High-Risk Parents," *Child Abuse and Neglect* 10 (1986) 309.

Hutchinson, J. *A Comparative Analysis of the Costs of Substitute Care and Family Based Services.* Prepared by the National Resource Center on Family Based Services for the U.S. Department of Health and Human Services, Office of Human Development, Administration for Children Youth and Families under Grant No. 90-CW659/01, July 1982.

Hunter, R. S. and N. Kilstrom. "Breaking the Cycle in Abusive Families." *American Journal of Psychiatry* 136 (1979) 1320–1322.

Jason, J. "Epidemiologic Differences Between Sexual and Physical Child Abuse." *Journal of the American Medical Association* 247:24 (June 25, 1982) 3344–3348.

——, N. Andereck, J. Marks, and C. Tyler "Child Abuse in Georgia: A Method to Evaluate Risk Factors and Reporting Bias." *American Journal of Public Health* 72:12 (1982) 1353–1358.

Johnson, D. L. and J. N. Breckenridge. "The Houston Parent-Child Development Center and the Primary Prevention of Behavior Problems in Young Children." *American Journal of Community Psychology* 10 (1982) 305–316.

Johnson, W., and J. L'Esperance. "Predicting the Recurrence of Child Abuse." *Social Work Research and Abstracts* 20:2 (Summer 1984) 21–26.

Jones, J. G. "Sexual Abuse of Children: Current Concepts." *American Journal of Diseases of Children* 136:2 (February 1982) 142–146.

Jones, M., S. Magura, and A. W. Shyne. "Effective Practice with Families in Protective and Preventive Services: What Works?" *Child Welfare* 60:2 (1981) 67–80.

Junewicz, W. J. "A Protective Posture Toward Emotional Neglect and Abuse." *Child Welfare* 62:3 (1983) 243–52.

Juvenile Protection Association. *The Bowen Center Project: A Report of a Demonstration in Child Protective Services, 1965–1971.* Chicago: Juvenile Protective Association, 1975.

Kadushin, A. *Child Welfare Services: Third Edition.* New York: Macmillan, 1980.

Katz, S. *When Parents Fail: The Law's Response to Family Breakdown.* Boston: Beacon Press, 1971.

—— L. Ambrosino, M. McGrath, and K. Sawitsky "Legal Research on Child Abuse and Neglect: Past and Future." *Family Law Quarterly* 11:2 (1977) 151–184.

Kempe, C. H. "Cross Cultural Perspectives in Child Abuse." *Pediatrics* 69:4 (April 1982) 497–498.

——, F. Silverman, B. Steele, W. Droegemueller, and H. Silver "The Battered Child Syndrome." *Journal of the American Medical Association* 181:17 (1962) 17–24.

Kempe, R. S., and C. H. Kempe. *Child Abuse.* Cambridge, MA: Harvard University Press, 1978.

Keniston, K. *All Our Children: The American Family Under Pressure.* New York: Harcourt Brace Jovanovich, 1977.

Kent, J. "A Follow-Up Study of Abused Children." *Journal of Pediatric Psychology* 1:2 (Spring 1976) 25–31.

——, H. Weisberg, B. Lamar, and T. Marx. "Understanding the Etiology of Child Abuse: A Preliminary Typology of Cases." *Children and Youth Services Review* 5:1 (1983) 7–29.

Kercher, G. *Responding to Child Sexual Abuse.* Huntsville, TX: Sam Houston State University, Criminal Justice Center, 1980.

Kinard, E. M. "Experiencing Child Abuse: Effects on Emotional Adjustment." *American Journal of Orthopsychiatry* 52:1 (January 1982) 82–91.

Kinney, J., B. Madsen, T. Fleming, and D. Haapala. "Homebuilders: Keeping Families Together." *Journal of Consulting and Clinical Psychology* 45:4 (1977) 667–673.

Klagsburn, M., and D. Davis. "Substance Abuse and Family Interaction." *Family Process* 16:2 (June 1977) 149–174.

Klein, M., and L. Stern. "Low Birth Weight and the Battered Child Syndrome." *American Journal of Diseases of Children* 122 (July 1971) 15–18.

Koel, B. "Failure to Thrive and Fatal Injury as a Continuum." *American Journal of Diseases of Children* 118 (1969) 565–567.

Koerin, B. "Child Abuse and Neglect: Changing Policies and Perspectives." *Child Welfare* 59:9 (1980) 542–550.

Konopka, G. "Requirements for Health Development of Adolescent Youth." *Adolescence* 8 (Fall 1973) 291–316.

Kratcoski, P. "Child Abuse and Violence Against the Family" *Child Welfare* 61:7 (1982) 435–44.

Laird, J., and A. Hartman (eds.). *Handbook of Child Welfare.* New York: Free Press, 1985.

Landsman, M. *Evaluation of Fourteen Child Placement Prevention Projects in Wisconsin.* Iowa City, IA: The National Resource Center on Family Based Services, University of Iowa. 1985.

Larson, C. "Efficacy of Prenatal and Postpartum Home Visits on Child Health and Development." *Pediatrics* 66 (1980) 191–197.

Laughlin, J., and M. Weiss. "An Outpatient Milieu Therapy Approach to Treatment of Child Abuse and Neglect Problems." *Social Casework* 62:2 (1981) 106–109.

Leeds, S. *Evaluation of Nebraska's Intensive Services Project.* Iowa City, IA: The National Resource Center on Family Based Services, University of Iowa, 1984.

Leiby, J. *A History of Social Welfare and Social Work in the United States.* New York: Columbia University Press, 1978.

Leishman, K. "Child Abuse: The Extent of the Harm." *Atlantic Monthly* 252:5 (November 1983) 22–32.

Levant, F., and G. Doyle. "An Evaluation of a Parent Education Program for Fathers of School-Aged Children." *Family Relations* 32 (January 1983) 29–37.

Levin, P. "Teachers' Perceptions, Attitudes and Reporting of Child Abuse/Neglect." *Child Welfare* 62 (January-February 1983) 15–20.

Lewis, D. O., S. Shanok, J. Pincus and G. Glaser. "Violent Juvenile Delinquents: Psychiatric, Neurological, Psychological and Abuse Factors." *Journal of the American Academy of Child Psychiatry* 18 (1979) 307–319.

Lewis, H. "Parental and Community Neglect: Twin Responsibilities of Protective Services." *Children* 16 (1969) 114–118.

Light, R. J. "Abused and Neglected Children in America: A Study of Alternative Policies." *Harvard Educational Review* 43 (November 1973) 556–598.

Lochman, J. E., and M. V. Brown. "Evaluation of Dropout Clients and of Perceived Usefulness of A Parent Education Program." *Journal of Community Psychology* 8 (1980) 132–139.

Lourie, I. "The Phenomenon of the Abused Adolescent: A Clinical Study." *Victimology* 2:2 (Summer 1977) 268–276.

——, and A. M. Cohan. "The Abuse and Neglect of Adolescents." *Child Abuse and Neglect Reports* 16 (February 1976) 6–8.

Love, J., M. Nauta, C. Coelen, K. Hewett, and R. Ruopp. *National Home Start Evaluation: Final Report, Findings and Implications.* Ypsilanti, MI: High Scope Educational Research Foundation, 1976.

Magura, S. "Are Services to Prevent Foster Care Effective?" *Children and Youth Services Review* 3 (1981) 193–212.

——, and B. Moses. *Outcome Measures for Child Welfare Services: Theory and Applications.* New York: Child Welfare League of America, 1986.

Martin, H. "The Child and His Development" in C. H. Kempe and R. E. Helfer (eds.), *Helping the Battered Child and His Family.* Philadelphia: J. B. Lippincott, 1972.

———, P. Beezley, E. Conway, and H. Kempe. "The Development of Abused Children." *Advances in Pediatrics* 21 (1974) 25–73.

McAnarney, E., K. Roghmann, B. Adams, R. Tatlebaum, C. Kash, M. Coulter, M. Plume, and E. Charney. "Obstetric, Neonatal, and Psychosocial Outcome of Pregnant Adolescents." *Pediatrics* 61:2 (February 1978).

McCarty, L. "Investigation of Incest: Opportunity to Motivate Families to Seek Help." *Child Welfare* 60:10 (1981) 679–689.

McCord, J., "A Forty-Year Perspective of the Effects of Child Abuse and Neglect," *Child Abuse and Neglect* 7 (1983) 265–270.

McGowan, B., and W. Meezen. *Child Welfare: Current Dilemmas and Future Directions.* Itasca, IL. F. E. Peacock, 1983.

McGuire, J., and B. Gottlieb. "Social Support Among New Parents: An Experimental Study in Primary Prevention." *Journal of Clinical Child Psychology* 8 (1979) 111–116.

McKeel, N. "Child Abuse Can Be Prevented." *American Journal of Nursing* 78 (September 1978) 1478–1482.

McNeese, M. "When to Suspect Child Abuse." *American Family Physician* 25:6 (June 1982) 190–197.

McNeil, J., and M. McBride. "Group Therapy with Abusive Parents." *Social Casework* 60 (January 1979) 36–42.

Meadow, R. "Munchausen syndrome by proxy." *Lancet* 2 (1979), 343.

Miller, D., and G. Challas. "Abused Children as Adult Parents: A Twenty-Five Year Longitudinal Study." Presented at the National Conference for Family Violence Researchers, Durham, New Hampshire, July 1981.

Miller, K. "Child Abuse and Neglect." *Journal of Family Practice* 14:3 (March 1982) 571–575.

Milner, J. *The Child Abuse Potential Inventory Manual.* Webster, NC: Psytec Corporation, 1980.

———, and R. Wimberly. "An Inventory for Identification of Child Abusers." *Journal of Clinical Psychology* 35 (January 1979) 95–100.

Moore, J. "Project Thrive: A Supportive Treatment Approach to Parents of Children with Nonorganic Failure to Thrive." *Child Welfare* 61:6 (June 1982) 389–398.

Moore, J. The Experience of Sponsoring a Parents Anonymous Group. *Social Casework: The Journal of Contemporary Social Work* (December, 1983) 585–592.

Moore, J. F., A. Galcius and K. Pettican. "Emotional Risk to Children Caught in Violent Marital Conflict: The Basildon Treatment Project." *Abstracts: Third International Congress Child Abuse and Neglect* 53 (April 1981) 33–34.

Morse, C. W., O. Sahler and S. Friedman "A Three-year Follow-Up Study of Abused and Neglected Children." *American Journal of Diseases of Children* 120 (1970) 439–446.

Mouzakitas, C. "An Inquiry into the Problems of Child Abuse and Juvenile Delinquency" in R. J. Hunner and Y. E. Walker (eds.), *Exploring the Relationship Between Child Abuse and Delinquency*. Montclair, NJ: Allanheld, Osmun, 1981.

Mulford, R., and M. Cohen. "Psychological Characteristics of Neglecting Parents—A Study of Psychosocial Characteristics." Monograph published by the American Humane Association, 1967.

Nakashima, I., and G. Zakus. "Incest: Review and Clinical Experience." *Pediatrics* 60 (1977) 696–701.

Nance, K. "Understanding and Overcoming Resistance to Primary Prevention." *Social Work Research and Abstracts* 18:3 (1982) 32–40.

National Center for Child Abuse and Neglect. *Innovative Treatment Approaches for Child Abuse and Neglect*. Report from a Symposium on Issues and Directions for Future Research. Washington, DC: U.S. Government Printing Office, June 1977.

Nelson, B. *Making an Issue of Child Abuse*. Chicago: The University of Chicago Press, 1984.

Nelson, D., S. Cameron, and D. Barrett. "Evaluation of the 'You're in Charge' Curriculum." Unpublished manuscript (Author, National Committee for Prevention of Child Abuse, Salt Lake City, UT 84105). 1986.

Newberger, C., and E. Newberger. "Prevention of Child Abuse: Theory, Myth, and Practice." *Journal of Prevention Psychiatry* 1:4 (1982) 443–451.

Newberger, E. *The Helping Hand Strikes Again*. Testimony given before the Subcommittee on Family and Human Services, Committee on Labor and Human Resources, U.S. Senate, April 11, 1983.

———, and J. Marx. *Ecologic Reformulation of Pediatric Social Illness: Final Report of the Family Development Study*. Prepared under grants from the Administration for Children, Youth, and Family (OCD-CD-CB-141) and the National Institute of Mental Health (5 TO1 MH155 7-03 CD). Undated.

———, C. Newberger, and R. Hampton. "Child Abuse: The Current Theory Base and Future Research Needs." *Journal of the American Academy of Child Psychiatry* 22:3 (1983) 262–268.

Nikelly, A. "Maternal Indulgence and Neglect and Maladjustment in Adolescents." *Journal of Clinical Psychology* 23 (April 1967) 148–150.

O'Connor, S., P. Vietze, K. Sherrod, H. Sandler, and W. Altemeier. "Reduced Incidence of Parenting Inadequacy Following Rooming-In." *Pediatrics* 66 (1980) 176–182.

Olds, D., R. Chamberlin, and R. Tatlebaum. "Preventing Child Abuse and Neglect: A Randomized Trial of Nurse Home Visitation." *Pediatrics* 78 (1986) 65–78.

Olson, R. "Index of Suspicion: Screening of Child Abusers." *American Journal of Nursing* 76 (January 1976) 108–110.

Oppenheimer, A. "Triumph Over Trauma in the Treatment of Child Abuse." *Social Casework* 59 (June 1978) 352–358.

Ory, M., and J. Earp. "Child Maltreatment: An Analysis of Familial and Institutional Predictors." *Journal of Family Issues* 1:3 (September 1980) 339–356.

Ozawa, M. "Public Interest in Children." Paper presented at the Seabury Lecture, School of Social Welfare, University of California, Berkeley, April 29, 1985.

Pagnozzi, A. "Raped Foster Girl Gets 225G." *New York Post* (May 17, 1982).

Paschal, J., and L. Schwahn. "Intensive Crisis Counseling in Florida." *Children Today* 15:6 (November-December 1986) 12–16.

Paulson, M., and P. Blake. "The Physically Abused Child: A Focus on Prevention." *Child Welfare* 48 (February 1969) 86–95.

Pelton, L. *Social Context of Child Abuse and Neglect.* New York: Human Services Press, 1981.

Phelan, P. "The Process of Incest: Biologic Father and Mother and Stepfather Families." *Child Abuse and Neglect* 10:4 (1986) 531–539.

Pirro, J. "Domestic Violence: The Criminal Court Response." *New York State Bar Journal* 54 (October 1982) 352–357.

Plummer, C. "Research Prevention: What School Programs Teach Children." Unpublished manuscript (Author, P.O. Box 421, Kalamazoo, MI 49005), 1984.

Polansky, N., M. Chalmers, E. Buttenweiser, and D. Williams *Child Neglect: State of Knowledge.* Final Report to the Social and Rehabilitation Service, Community Services Administration, U.S. Department of Health, Education and Welfare. July 1974.

———, and D. P. Williams. "Class Orientations to Child Neglect." *Social Work* (September 1978) 397–401.

———, M. Chalmers, E. Buttenweiser, and D. P. Williams. "The Absent Father in Child Neglect." *Social Services Review* 53 (June 1979a) 163–174.

———, M. Chalmers, E. Buttenweiser, and D. P. Williams. "Isolation of the Neglectful Family." *American Journal of Orthopsychiatry* 49 (January 1979b) 149–152.

Polit, D. "Routes to Self-Sufficiency: Teenage Mothers and Employment". *Children Today* (January-February 1987) 6–11.

Porter, F., L. Blick, and S. Sgroi. "Treatment of the Sexually Abused Child" in S. M. Sgroi (ed.), *Handbook of Clinical Intervention in Child Sexual Abuse.* Lexington, MA: Lexington Books, 1982.

Powell, D. "Parent Education and Support Programs" *Young Children* (March 1986) 47–53.

Powell, T. F. "Comparison Between Self-Help Groups and Professional Services." *Social Casework* 60 (November 1979) 561–565.

"Private Violence: Child Abuse, Wife Beating and Rape." *Time* 122:10 (September 5, 1983) 18–29.

Prochaska, J. M. "Intra-Agency Contracting: High Quality Comprehensive Service Delivery at Lowered Cost." *Child Welfare* 63:6 (1984) 533–539.

Provence S., and A. Naylor. *Working With Disadvantaged Parents and Children: Scientific Issues and Practice.* New Haven, CT: Yale University Press, 1983.

———, A. Naylor, and J. Patterson. *The Challenge of Daycare*. New Haven, CT: Yale University Press, 1977.

Riggot, A. "Evaluation of the 'Touch' Program." Unpublished manuscript (Author, Illusion Theater, 528 Hennepin Ave. #704, Minneapolis, MN 55401), August 1985.

Rosen, B. "Self-Concept Disturbance Among Mothers Who Abuse Their Children." *Psychological Reports* 43 (August 1978) 323–326.

Rosen, H. "How Workers Use Cues to Determine Child Abuse." *Social Work Research and Abstracts* 17 (1981) 27–33.

Rosenbaum, A., and K. O'Leary. "Children: The Unintended Victims of Marital Violence" *American Journal of Orthopsychiatry* 54:4 (1981) 692–699.

Roskin, M. "Integration of Primary Prevention into Social Work Practice." *Social Work* 25:3 (1980) 192–196.

Russell, D. *Sexual Exploitation: Rape, Child Sexual Abuse, and Sexual Harassment*. Beverly Hills, CA: Sage, 1984.

Scheffler, R., and L. Paringer. "A Review of the Economic Evidence on Prevention." *Medical Care* 18 (May 1980) 473–484.

Schilling, R. F., S. P. Schinke, B. Blythe and R. Barth. "Child Maltreatment and Mentally Retarded Parents: Is There a Relationship?" *Mental Retardation* 20:5 (October 1982) 201–209.

Schmitt, B. "Battered Child Syndrome" in C. H. Kempe, H. Silver, and D. O'Brien (eds.), *Current Pediatric Diagnosis and Treatment*. Fifth edition. Los Altos, CA: Lange, 1978.

———, and P. Beezley. "The Long-Term Management of the Child and Family in Child Abuse and Neglect." *Child Abuse and Neglect Pediatric Annals* (March 1976) 60–78.

———, and C. H. Kempe. "The Battered Child Syndrome" in R. Gellis and J. Kagen (eds.), *Current Pediatric Therapy*. Sixth edition. Philadelphia: W. Saunders, 1974.

Schultz, L. "The Child Sex Victim: Social, Psychological and Legal Perspectives." *Child Welfare* 52:3 (March 1973) 147–157.

———, and P. Jones, Jr. "Sexual Abuse of Children: Issues for Social and Health Professionals." *Child Welfare* 52:2 (1983) 99–108.

Scott, J., and T. Birch. *Summary of Children's Trust Funds*, Working Paper No. 20. Chicago, IL: National Committee for Prevention of Child Abuse, 1986.

Seagull, E. "Social Support and Child Maltreatment: A Review of the Evidence." *Child Abuse and Neglect* 11 (1987) 41–52.

Seigel, E., K. Bauman, E. Schaefer, M. Saunders, and D. Ingram. "Hospital and Home Support During Infancy: Impact of Maternal Attachment, Child Abuse and Neglect, and Health Care Utilization." *Pediatrics* 66 (1980) 183–190.

Seitz, V., L. Rosenbaum, and N. Apfel. "Effects of Family Support Intervention: A Ten-Year Follow-Up." *Child Development* 56 (1985) 376–391.

Sen, A. "Rational Fools: A Critique of the Behavioral Foundations of Economic Theory." *Philosophy and Public Affairs* 6:4 (Summer 1977) 317–344.

Sever, J. and C. Janzen "Contradictions to Reconstitution of Sexually Abusive Families." *Child Welfare* 61:5 (May 1982) 279–288.

Sgroi, S. *Handbook of Clinical Intervention on Child Sexual Abuse.* Lexington, MA: D. C. Heath, 1982.

Shapiro, D. *Parents and Protectors: A Study of Child Abuse and Neglect.* New York: Child Welfare League of America, 1979.

Silver, L., C. C. Dublin and R. S. Lourie "Does Violence Breed Violence? Contribution from a Study of the Child-Abuse Syndrome." *American Journal of Psychiatry* 126 (September 1969) 404–407.

———, C. C. Dublin, and R. Lourie. "Agency Action and Interaction in Cases of Child Abuse." *Social Casework* 52 (March 1971) 164–171.

Smith, S. *Child Welfare in the States: Fifty State Survey Report.* Denver, CO: National Conference of State Legislatures, 1986.

Spinetta, J. "Parental Personality Factors in Child Abuse." *Journal of Consulting and Clinical Psychology* 46 (December 1978) 1409–1414.

———, and D. Rigler. "The Child Abusing Parent: A Psychological Review." *Psychologist Bulletin* 77 (1972) 296–304.

"Specter Takes Up Physical and Sexual Abuse as Issue in Juvenile Delinquency." *Child Protection Report* 9:21 (October 21, 1983) 5.

Steele, B., and C. Pollack. "The Battered Child's Parents" in A. S. Skolnick and J. H. Skolnick (eds.), *Family in Transition.* Boston: Little, Brown, 1971.

Stein, T. *Social Work Practice and Child Welfare.* Englewood Cliffs, NJ: Prentice-Hall, 1981.

Steinberg, L., R. Catalano and D. Dooley "Economic Antecedents of Child Abuse and Neglect." *Child Development* 52:3 (September 1981) 975–985.

Steiner, P. "The Public Sector and the Public Interest" in R. H. Haveman and J. Margolis (eds.), *Expeditures and Policy Analysis.* Chicago: Rand McNally College Publishing, 1970.

Stokey, E., and R. Zeckhauser. *A Primer for Policy Analysis.* New York: W. W. Norton, 1978.

Straus, M., and R. Gelles. "Societal Change and Change in Family Violence from 1975–1985 as Revealed by Two National Surveys" *Journal of Marriage and the Family* 48 (August 1986) 465–479.

———, R. Gelles, and S. Steinmetz. *Behind Closed Doors: Violence in the American Family.* Garden City, NY: Anchor Press/Doubleday, 1980.

Sudia, C. "Preventing Out-of-Home Placement of Children: The First Steps to Permanency Planning." *Children Today* 15:6 (November-December 1986) 4–5.

Summit, R. "The Child Sexual Abuse Accommodation Syndrome," *Child Abuse and Neglect* 7 (1983) 177–193.

———, and J. Kryso. "Sexual Abuse of Children: A Clinical Spectrum." *American Journal of Orthopsychiatry* 48 (April 1978) 237–251.

Swan, H., A. Press, and S. Briggs. "Child Sexual Abuse Prevention: Does It Work?" *Child Welfare* 64:4 (July-August 1985) 395–405.

Sze, W., and S. Lamar. "Causes of Child Abuse: A Reexamination." *Health and Social Work* 6:4 (November 1981) 19–25.

Taitz, L. "Follow-up of Children 'At Risk' of Child Abuse: Effects of Support on Emotional and Intellectual Development." *Child Abuse and Neglect* 5:3 (1981) 231–239.

Teitz, M. "Evaluating Program Evaluations." *Journal of the American Institute of Planners.* 55:3 (April 1978) 214–218.

Thomas, J. "Yes, You Can Help a Sexually Abused Child." *RN Magazine* (August 1980) 23–29.

Tracy, J., C. Ballard, and E. Clark. "Child Abuse Project: A Follow-Up." *Social Work* 20 (September 1975) 388–399.

Travers, J., M. Nauta, and N. Irwin. *The Effects of a Social Program: Final Report of the Child and Family Resource Program's Infant and Toddler Component.* Cambridge, MA: ABT Associates, 1982.

URSA Institute. San Francisco, CA *Proposed Research Strategies on the Link Between Child Abuse and Juvenile Delinquency.* Paper presented at the Wingspread Conference, Child Abuse: Prelude to Delinquency, conducted by the National Committee for Prevention of Child Abuse for the Office of Juvenile Justice and Delinquency Prevention, U.S. Department of Justice, April 8–10, 1984.

U.S. Comptroller General. *Report to the Congress: Increased Federal Efforts Needed to Better Identify, Treat and Prevent Child Abuse and Neglect.* Washington, DC: U.S. Government Printing Office, 1980.

U.S. Department of Health, Education and Welfare (DHEW). *Report of the Department to the President and Congress on the Implementation of PL 93-247, the Child Abuse Prevention and Treatment Act.* Washington, DC: U.S. Government Printing Office, 1975.

Virkkunen, M. "Incest Offenses and Alcoholism." *Medicine, Science and the Law* 14 (April 1974) 124–128.

Wald, M. "State Intervention of Behalf of 'Neglected Children': Standards for Removal of Children from Their Homes, Monitoring the Status of Children in Foster Care and Termination of Parental Rights." *Stanford Law Review* 28 (1976) 623–706.

Wandersman, A., L. Wandersman, and S. Kahn. "Stress and Social Support in the Transition to Parenthood." *Journal of Community Psychology* 8 (1980) 332–342.

Warner, S. "Understanding the Effects of Child Abuse." *Radiologic Technology* 49 (July-August 1977) 29–38.

Watts, C., M. Jackson, and J. P. LoGerfo "Cost Effectiveness Analysis: Some Problems of Implementation," *Medical Care* 17 (April 1979) 430–434.

Westat and Development Associates. *National Study of the Incidence and Severity of Child Abuse and Neglect.* Prepared for the National Center on Child Abuse and Neglect under Contract No. 105-76-1137, September 1981.

Westra, B., and H.P. Martin. "Children of Battered Women." *Maternal Child Nursing Journal* 10 (1981) 41–54.

Whitworth, J., M. Lanier, R. Skinner, Jr. and N. Lund "A Multidisciplinary Hospital-Based Team for Child Abuse Cases." *Child Welfare* 60:4 (1981) 233–243.

Withey, V., R. Anderson, and M. Lauderdale. "Volunteers as Mentors for Abusing Parents: A Natural Helping Relationship." *Child Welfare* 59:10 (1980) 637–644.

Wolock, I. "Community Characteristics and Staff Judgments on Child Abuse and Neglect Cases." *Social Work Research and Abstracts* 18:2 (1982) 9–15.

———, and B. Horowitz. "Child Maltreatment and Material Deprivation Among AFDC-Recipient Families." *Social Service Review* 53 (June 1979) 175–194.

Woods, S., and K. Dean. *Community-Based Options for Maltreatment Prevention: Augmenting Self-Sufficiency. Final Report.* Prepared for the National Center on Child Abuse and Neglect under Contract 90-CA-1001. July 1986.

Woollcott, P., Jr., and T. Aceto, Jr., C. Rutt, M. Bloom and R. Glick. "Doctor Shopping with the Child as Proxy Patient: A Varient of Child Abuse." *The Journal of Pediatrics* 101:2 (August 1982) 297–301.

Young, L. *Wednesday's Children.* New York: McGraw-Hill, 1964.

Zigler, E. "Controlling Child Abuse in America: An Effort Doomed to Failure?" Paper presented at the First National Conference on Child Abuse and Neglect, Atlanta, Georgia, January 1976.

Index